Subject Without Nation

POST-CONTEMPORARY INTERVENTIONS

Series Editors: Stanley Fish & Fredric Jameson

Subject Without Nation

ROBERT MUSIL AND

THE HISTORY OF

MODERN IDENTITY

STEFAN JONSSON

DUKE UNIVERSITY PRESS

Durham & London   2000

© 2000 Duke University Press

All rights reserved   Printed in the United States of America on acid-free paper ∞

Designed by C. H. Westmoreland   Typeset in Times Roman with Futura display

by Tseng Information Systems, Inc.   Library of Congress Cataloging-in-Publica-

tion Data appear on the last printed page of this book.

for Sara

Contents

1   EXPRESSIVITY

Chapter 1. Topographies of Inwardness

The End of Man? / Georg Lukács's History of Subjectivity / Nature and Culture: Interior Sources of Individual and Collective Identity / Femininity as an Image of Harmony / Aesthetic Education and the *Bildungsroman* / The Retreat into the *Intérieur* / *Jugendstil* and the Shattering of the *Intérieur* / Expressionism as the End of Expressive Subjectivity

Chapter 2. The Architecture of Modern Identity

New Buildings, New Bodies / Subjectivity and Interior Space / Beyond Reification / The Double as an Image of the Subject's Otherness / The Collapse of the Expressivist Paradigm / Modernist Mysticism

Chapter 3. A Story with Many Ends

Expressive Realism and Beyond / The Impossible Art of Reporting the Weather / On the Difference between an Accident and an Incident / The

Preface

In his Nobel Lecture of 1992 Derek Walcott evoked a city inhabited by transcultural citizens. "It would be so racially various that the cultures of the world—the Asiatic, the Mediterranean, the European, the African—would be represented in it, its human variety more exciting than Joyce's Dublin. Its citizens would intermarry as they chose, from instinct, not tradition, until their children find it increasingly futile to trace their genealogy." Persons in such places will learn, Walcott continued, to cross cultural boundaries, to reassemble the broken pieces of history and redefine the world.

Walcott's lecture epitomizes a notion of human subjectivity that has emerged in late-twentieth-century art, literature, music, architecture, cinema, and cultural theory. By and large, the concept of a transcultural subject is conditioned by contradictory global processes that have produced mobile, transnational patterns of cultural affiliation, at the same time reinforcing political and economic barriers between north and south, rich and poor, white and colored. The effects are seen everywhere around the globe, especially along geopolitical faultlines such as the Caribbean world, the scarred archipelago that Walcott remaps in his work. In literature from such regions, nearly everything is political; its political dimensions are typically made manifest as interrogations of identity and community.

This book is a study of the works of the Austrian writer Robert Musil (1880–1942), who lived in a historical situation similarly intersected by cultural, social, and economic contradictions, and who also envisioned a human being who would trespass cultural limits. Musil's Austria was the first postimperial culture in modern Europe. Although the Austro-Hungarian Empire had no overseas colonies, it ruled over a vast array of nationalities, and in terms of *cultural* diversity and conflict it is therefore comparable to the major colonial powers. The rapid modernization of the empire and its eventual collapse in 1918 triggered an intense intellectual activity commonly discussed under rubrics such as "fin-de-siècle Vienna" or *modernité viennoise.* Behind these labels, I would like to suggest, we find a historical experience that is structurally akin to a phenomenon that was to affect other European states only later, the experience of postcoloniality. Indeed, Austria's postimperial culture was characterized not only by explosive conflicts between a residual feudal system and an emerging capitalist society, but also by the struggle between a crumbling imperial regime and various movements of what we today would call identity politics: Zionism and anti-Semitism; women's movements and antifeminism; nationalism, racism, and fascism. These conflicts compelled Musil and other intellectuals of his time, such as Sigmund Freud, Georg Lukács, Hermann Broch, Elias Canetti, Karl Kraus, Otto Bauer, Franz Kafka, and Joseph Roth, to examine the force of collective identities of ethnicity, nationhood, or masculine authority. Today's intellectuals address similar issues, mapping a world of postcolonial migration, globalization, and intercultural conflicts.

Robert Musil's works projected a "new human being," one who would resist assimilation into imperialist, nationalist, or fascist communities. I would like this study to honor that intention and to convey a sense of its theoretical and political urgency. The parallels between our time and Musil's are so striking that it is no longer possible *not* to read his writings historically and politically. My aim in writing this book is to explore these parallels. I will use Musil's work to shed light on our current interrogations of identity, and I will use contemporary theory to elucidate Musil's work, in an effort to grasp both as belonging to one and the same historical process. Such a dialectical approach will deepen the understanding of the postimperial situation in Austria and

Germany between the two world wars; conversely, it will expose the historical legacies resonating in contemporary discourses on nationalism, ethnicity, Eurocentrism, universalism, and multiculturalism.

My discussion of Musil's work is thus intertwined with an inquiry into the *history* of human subjectivity and identity. Consequently, this book is situated at the intersection of literary criticism, intellectual history, and cultural theory.

First, as a study of early-twentieth-century Austrian and German literature and culture, it discusses Musil's monumental novel *The Man Without Qualities* (*Der Mann ohne Eigenschaften*) and presents a new interpretation of its theoretical content, aesthetic specificity, and historical significance.

Second, as a historical account of theories of human subjectivity, *Subject Without Nation* delineates a sequence of ideological paradigms, from 1789 to the present, which have served to define "human nature"; this book may therefore be read as a history of modern identity.

Third, as an intervention into contemporary debates, my study provides a critical perspective on the disputes between universalists and particularists, Eurocentrists and multiculturalists, protectors of universal human values and defenders of cultural rights.

What unites these objectives is the old Kantian question "What is man?" Is there a universal human element? If so, how should it be described? Musil's intriguing answer is that the universal element consists of "a big, vacuous, round O," or "a vacuum through which all the feelings glow like blue neon tubes" (*MWQ* 432, 444 / *MoE* 398, 409). In short, what human beings have in common is emptiness and lack. That the human is distinguished by lack implies that it is characterized by need. In Musil's view, however, human lack is irremediable; the subject's need for psychic unity and recognition cannot be satisfied. No matter what role, group, profession, model, or ideal the subject may identify with, it still will never be but "an emergency substitute for something that [is] missing" (*MWQ* 416 / *MoE* 384).

Such a view of the human being directly contests the one prevailing in Musil's culture, which held that a person possesses a particular essence that is expressed in—and hence determines—his or her race, culture, gender, and social rank. It is also directly opposed to the liberal conception, according to which the human being has a universal essence that makes the person independent of social identities, sex, and cultural origin. Therefore it also challenges both of the major alternatives that are regularly repeated in contemporary discussions about identity politics and universalism. These discussions are generally framed by the assumption that we have to choose one of the alternatives above, either the rooted order of the "tribe" or the disembodied liberty of the individual. The paradigm of human subjectivity articulated in Musil's work, and later elaborated in poststructural, psychoanalytic, and postcolonial theories, suggests a radical alternative. In this view, the human being is at once particular, due to a constitutive need to assert an identity that guarantees social recognition and communal belonging, and universal, due to an ineffable capacity to exceed the identities that condition this belonging.

Robert Musil lived and worked in a historical moment when cultural identities had become so fixed that they appeared to predetermine the destiny of every citizen and to reduce men and women to their status of belonging. At the height of scientific racism, Musil responded to such fascist tendencies by stating, scandalously, that there was no difference between a German and an African. Even more important, he wrote a novel, *The Man Without Qualities,* that depicts a person who, being without identity, was able to assume any identity and to disclose the illusory nature of each. Encountering monolithic ideologies at every turn, Musil reacted by multiplying difference and by stressing that the human being always differs from his or her cultured self. The universal human element, Musil's novel asserts, resides in this inexpressible ability to differ, in this "inclination toward the negative," which, according to the novel's narrator, leads a person "to abolish reality" and to change the world.

In present-day intellectual discussions, Musil's reply to the question of "human nature" retains its progressive force. That Musil conceptualized such an idea as a response to the authoritarian ideologies in postimperial Austria and Germany is crucial, because it reveals the historical depth and genealogical beginnings of our own discourse, and it indicates the cultural values and political positions that are at stake.

This book is indebted to the intellectual energy and orientation of the Program in Literature at Duke University in Durham, North Carolina. I wish to express my gratitude to all the members of this collective for generating and sustaining a unique blend of critical commitment and intellectual brilliance. Fredric Jameson gave the initial inspiration for this project. He provided me with innovative conceptual frameworks, gave detailed criticism of every chapter, and, always, demonstrated the excitement and relevance of serious scholarship. Julia Hell scrutinized my various drafts and strengthened my argument considerably; and she not only pointed out enigmas in Musil's novel that otherwise would have been overlooked (Agathe!) but also suggested where to look for solutions. I am also profoundly grateful to V. Y. Mudimbe, for teaching me how to understand identities and explore borderlines; to Toril Moi, for sharpening my views of subjectivity, femininity, and psychoanalysis; and to James Rolleston, for sharing his extensive knowledge of German literature and intellectual history.

The manuscript was revised during the first months of my tenure as a fellow at the Getty Research Institute in Los Angeles, California, the economic and intellectual support of which I acknowledge with gratitude. I thank Michael Roth and the staff of the Scholars and Seminars Program for providing me with ideal working conditions; Allison Millions Gorrie for her help as I was preparing the manuscript for publication; Zaia Alexander for assisting with important translations; and Ulrich Bach for giving a hand at the end.

For critical comments and suggestions on various parts of the manuscript I am indebted to Jonathan Beller, Page duBois, Martha Feldman, Andreas Huyssen, Kristen Kramer, Reinhart Meyer-Kalkus, Torsten Pettersson, Dorothea von Schweitzer, and Salvatore Settis. I have been able to explore my ideas at seminars in Copenhagen, Gothenburg, and Durham, and I thank Aris Fioretos, Peter Madsen, Kai Evers, Lily Phillips, Jennifer Doyle, and Sven-Eric Liedman for letting me present my work on these occasions. I have benefited from discussions with

Anne Longuet Marx and Peter Nielsen. Karl Corino generously lended me material from his collection of Musiliana.

Anders Stephanson was always available when personal encouragement and academic savoir faire was needed; other brilliant friends— Rebecca Karl, Neferti Tadiar, Catherine Benamou, Michael Speaks, Richard Dienst, and Zhang Xudong—inspired me as the book was taking shape.

I have profited from the services of Perkins and Lilly Libraries at Duke University, the Research Library of the Getty Research Institute, and the manuscript collections of the Österreichische Nationalbibliothek in Vienna. I also want to thank the editors and staff at Duke University Press, Reynolds Smith, Sharon P. Torian, and Pam Morrison, among others, for the meticulous attention and editorial skills they devoted to my manuscript when preparing it for publication. My research has been generously supported by grants from the Fulbright Commission, the Scandinavian-American Foundation, the Knut and Alice Wallenberg Foundation, and the Lars Hierta's Memorial Fund.

Sara Danius, my wife and colleague, is the one to whom I am most obliged. From the first word to the last, and from drafts to galleys, she has read everything, with care and precision, delivering constructive criticism and suggesting innumerable improvements. Whenever I have been in need of fresh ideas, new visions, critical comments, and personal support—she has been the provider. My entire work is forever indebted to her, and *Subject Without Nation* more so than anything else.

An earlier version of chapter 2 was published in *New German Critique,* no. 66 (1996). Sections of chapter 5 appeared in Danish translation in *Ny Poetik: Tidskrift for Literaturvidenskab,* no. 8 (1998); and parts of chapter 6 were published, in Swedish translation, in *Ord & Bild,* no. 6 (1997).

Abbreviations

GW 2   Robert Musil. *Gesammelte Werke.* Vol. 2, Prosa und Stücke, Kleine Prosa, Aphorismen, Autobiographisches, Essays und Reden, Kritik. Edited by Adolf Frisé. Reinbek bei Hamburg: Rowohlt, 1978.

MoE   Robert Musil. *Der Mann ohne Eigenschaften.* Vol. 1 of *Gesammelte Werke.* Edited by Adolf Frisé. Reinbek bei Hamburg: Rowohlt, 1978.

MWQ   Robert Musil. *The Man Without Qualities.* Translated by Sophie Wilkins and Burton Pike. New York: Knopf, 1995.

PS   Robert Musil, *Precision and Soul: Essays and Addresses.* Edited and translated by Burton Pike and David S. Luft. Chicago: University of Chicago Press, 1990.

PP   *Posthumous Papers of a Living Author.* Translation of *Nachlass zu Lebzeiten* by Peter Wortsman. Hygiene, Colo.: Eridanos Press, 1987.

T   Robert Musil. *Tagebücher.* 2 vols. Edited by Adolf Frisé. Reinbek bei Hamburg: Rowohlt, 1976.

Quotations of Robert Musil's works are given in the main text, first to the translation, if there is one for the quoted passage, then to the standard German edition. Primary and secondary sources in French and German are quoted in English translations, where such are available, with references to the originals following directly after. Translations without reference are my own. References followed by an asterisk (*) indicate that the translation is modified.

Introduction

Hier wird heute abend ein Mensch wie ein Auto ummontiert

Ohne dass er irgend dabei verliert. —Bertolt Brecht

A writer who wants to change the world is bound to be discouraged. Robert Musil was no exception. "Some writers, Thomas Mann and the like, address people who are out there; I write for people who are not there!" he confessed in his journal in late 1936 (*T* 1:880). A few years earlier, in 1930 and 1933, Musil had published the first two volumes of *The Man Without Qualities,* and he was disappointed in the reception of his novel.

If the prospect of oblivion was more frightening to Musil than to most writers, it is because few have been so dedicated to posterity as he was. Attempting to understand a European society in which racial and national identities were being converted into icons, Musil did in a sense write for future generations. He pictured a human being who would not repeat the atrocities he had experienced but instead institute a utopian world of solidarity. "An attempt to find another human being" ("Versuche, einen anderen Menschen zu finden") was the title of a collection of essays he planned to publish. Like so many other audacious projects of this writer, the book was never completed.

Musil's fear of oblivion has proved unfounded. Half a century after his death, *The Man Without Qualities* counts among the canonical European novels, and the secondary literature on his oeuvre is vast. Still, the central concern of his work remains to be brought out and examined in detail: the question of identity. As I shall argue, *The Man Without Qualities* is an unequaled and presageful exploration of the ways in which collective identities — of culture, gender, class, nationality, social character, and the like — are ascribed to human beings. It is well known that the plot of the novel turns around the so-called Parallel Campaign, an ideological project that the political and intellectual elite of Vienna launches in 1913, with an aim to restore popular support for the imperial regime. It is equally well known that the novel's protagonist, Ulrich, suffers from a peculiar personality disorder that makes him resistant to all kinds of "qualities." What has gone unnoticed, however, is the nexus between these dimensions of Musil's narrative. The novel's depiction of the Austro-Hungarian Empire's quest for its cultural essence and its account of Ulrich's discovery that he lacks personal essence have to be considered in tandem. For it is precisely through its trenchant critique of the prevailing conception of personal identity, or the self, that Musil's novel manages to rebut all claims made in the name of collective or cultural identities. The novel thus reveals the ways in which dominant ideologies of patriarchy, nationalism, and racism reduce the human subject to its cultural origin or sexual disposition by imposing on it an allegedly natural, and hence inescapable, essence, coded in terms of ethnicity, gender, and class. More sharply than any other intellectual of his era, Musil comprehended the intrinsic link between the "I" and the "we," between the constitution of the singular human being and that of the community.

As I will discuss shortly, *The Man Without Qualities* has typically been read as a story about an "alienated individual" searching for his "true self." Ulrich, it has been argued, tries — and fails — to adjust to society and to synthesize the various parts of his fragmented existence. Such an approach assimilates Musil's work to a nineteenth-century idea of human nature, in accord with which every person possesses an intrinsic essence, expressed through behavior, character, and profession, from which the person may be estranged, but to which he or she will always strive to return. Because the adventures of Musil's protagonist have commonly been framed by this essentialist ideal of personal cultivation, *The Man Without Qualities* has been handed down to us as a story about a character who is existentially disturbed, lacking a personal center and a sense of belonging.

This is all the more ironic since, as I shall maintain, Musil mustered all his intellectual powers to challenge such a belief in personal essences and cultural roots. This, then, is the first principal argument of this book. In fact, not only does Musil dismiss the idea that the identities of persons and communities are expressions of inborn dispositions, he also introduces a paradigm founded on the assumption that the human subject is historically constituted by the ways in which it is named, gendered, educated, and shaped by social institutions and cultural conventions.

Second, I shall propose that this paradigm can be usefully related to notions of human subjectivity that have emerged in late-twentieth-century philosophy and cultural theory. I am not arguing that these theories be applied as methodological grids to determine the specificity of Musil's thought; it would be reductive to interpret his work through any contemporary theory of subjectivity. My claim is a more radical one: I want to suggest that the representation of subjectivity in *The Man Without Qualities* establishes fundamental components of the discourse on "the subject" that characterizes recent cultural theory and continental philosophy, whether this discourse be called postmodern, poststructural, postcolonial, or other. To be sure, this does not mean that Musil's novel is the origin or cause of this discourse. Nor does it imply that *The Man Without Qualities* is the only place to look for its beginnings; the following pages will indicate how they also may be traced in other modernist writers, such as Franz Kafka, Hermann Broch, and Alfred Döblin. I do argue, however, that Musil's novel presents us with an early instance of the historical paradigm within which current discussions of subjectivity and identity are articulated, and, further, that the novel actualizes this paradigm in such uniquely variegated ways that present-day theory has only recently caught up with it. I even maintain that Musil's typically modernist text explains the political rationality of certain typically poststructural reconceptualizations of human subjectivity and identity.

My third and perhaps most important argument is that there is a specific historical reason for Musil's radical insights into the contingencies of identity. The reason, I submit, is that *The Man Without Qualities* was conceived in a postimperial space, Austria's first republic, which was pervaded by ideologies of nationality, race, and patriarchal authority.

This book, then, offers the first systematic attempt to investigate the representations of cultural identity in *The Man Without Qualities*. In addition, it is the first attempt to integrate a feminist reading with a comprehensive analysis of the novel. In this way, my study opens a new window onto the intellectual and aesthetic core of Musil's work, addressing issues that, moreover, characterized the cultural situation in postimperial Germany and Austria in general.

A truly encyclopedic novel, *The Man Without Qualities* intended to summarize the cultural and political situation in Europe between the wars. The novel veers from war to mysticism, from a madman's perversities to popular uprisings in the streets; it mocks the gatherings of Vienna's bourgeoisie and celebrates incestuous love between brother and sister; it laces together scathing portraits of the gurus of the cultural elite, dry accounts of scientific problems, and a lyric prose stretching toward the moon. For all the heterogeneity that marks this exemplary modernist experiment, the present study nevertheless attempts to distinguish the pattern that organizes it, the narrative logic that integrates the novel's journey into the labyrinth of the self, its dizzying modernist style, its spiritual charge, and its inventory of the ideological conflicts in early-twentieth-century Europe. As we shall see, my approach affords an assessment of the historical tenor and theoretical cogency of Musil's text, in a way that does justice to its radical critique of modern European culture, its German varieties in particular. By establishing the proximity of Musil's interrogation of identity to current theories of the human subject, finally, this study also enables a historical comprehension of the disputes on nationalism and ethnicity that characterize our contemporary culture.

Robert Musil started work on *The Man Without Qualities* shortly after World War I. A first part, entitled "Seinesgleichen geschieht," trans-

1 Robert Musil
(1880–1942). Bildarchiv,
Österreichische
Nationalbibliothek.

lated as "Pseudoreality Prevails," was published in 1930. In 1933, a second volume followed, containing the first thirty-eight chapters of the final part, called "Into the Millennium (The Criminals)." Musil never finished the novel. At the time of his death in 1942 he had been living in exile in Switzerland for almost four years, and he left behind approximately five thousand manuscript pages of finished or half-finished chapters, many of them in different versions, without a definite plan on how to order them, in addition to cryptic drafts and outlines for the end of the novel.[1]

The novel is set in Vienna in 1913 and 1914. Ulrich, an exceedingly talented thirty-two-year-old man, no longer knows what to do with his talents. Summoned by his father, he agrees to become secretary for the Parallel Campaign, the purpose of which is to unify all the peoples and nations of "Kakania" — Musil's nickname for the Habsburg empire — in a celebration of the seventieth anniversary of Emperor Franz Joseph's rule. Ulrich fulfills his secretarial duties absentmindedly, being much more fascinated by the case of Moosbrugger, a psychotic sex murderer. Halfway into the novel, at the transition from part 1 to part 2, the protagonist is notified about his father's death. He returns to his childhood home to attend the funeral. On his arrival, he meets his long-forgotten sister, Agathe. The siblings become attracted to each other and decide to flee to a world of their own. The story then develops in two directions, one lyrical and spiritual, rendering Ulrich and Agathe's conversations in their secluded Viennese garden and their journey "to the brink of the possible," the other satirical and historical, representing political developments in Vienna. According to Musil's plans, both narrative lines were then to converge in the outbreak of World War I, which indeed unifies all Kakanian citizens in a disastrous celebration.

A vast canvas depicting imperial Austria after the turn of the century, *The Man Without Qualities* records how the process of modernization gradually transforms society and culture, offering rich digressions on scientific problems, politics, mythology, sociology, aesthetics, and the future of civilization. The novel succeeds in establishing this longitudinal view of modernity because it focuses on one integral aspect of it: the gradual disappearance of the early-modern conviction that personal and cultural identities are grounded in intrinsic dispositions and how it is imperceptibly replaced by the idea that the social or symbolic order constitutes and consolidates the identity of the human subject. This historical shift is the organizing principle of Musil's work as a whole.

An entry from Musil's journal illustrates this break. In July 1905, Musil states that a person must preserve, maintain, or defend [*wahren*] his innermost individuality [*innerste Eigenart*] and the originary source of personal life [*das Ursprüngliche des persönlichen Lebens*] (*T* 1:155). A few days later he writes, "Each soul ought to perfect its own possibilities into reality" (*T* 1:161). In 1918 or 1919, when Musil began working on his novel, he went over these notes and commented on his old reflections: "False definition!"; "Is there really such a thing [as an innermost individuality]?" In places where the twenty-five-year-old Musil had confessed his belief in soul and human nature, the mature Musil states, in red ink: "Youthful stupidity!" [*Jugenddummheit*].

Musil's 1905 entries show that he at that time supported what I will call an *expressivist* notion of the human subject. According to this view, the identity of a person is grounded in an intrinsic disposition. A person's statements, behavior, and social position are seen as *expressions* of his or her identity, the essence of which is taken to be an internal personal kernel. In 1919, by contrast, Musil believed that the expressivist view of the human subject was a "false definition."

What triggers this change is a series of historical events: not only the patriotic fanaticism at the outbreak of World War I and the destruction of the Habsburg empire, but also the continuing dominance of nationalism and racism in Europe after the war. Until 1918 the identity of Austria and its peoples were forged to a greater or lesser extent by the ideological narrative of the Habsburg empire. After the war, the empire was divided into separate nation-states, and Austria had to make do with the territory that remained after all the nationalities of the former empire had claimed their shares. "The rest is Austria!" the French minister Georges Clemenceau is reported to have exclaimed at the peace negotiations in Saint-Germain, which spelled the end of the Habsburg story. Now that the material and institutional support of the imperial apparatus had vanished, the values and traditions that had anchored every Austrian subject in the imperial order were revealed in all their contingency. Cultural identities that had been honored as necessary and natural expressions of the order of the world evaporated and left emptiness behind. It is no coincidence that it was in this period that Musil became critical of the expressivist paradigm, which held that personal and collective identities were manifestations of permanent essences, and instead began exploring the notion that human identity is founded upon nothingness and lack. In his essays from the early 1920s, Musil thus stated that the war led to the refutation of the idea that human beings are inherently rational or good, which did not imply, however, that they are inherently irrational or evil. In turning the caring father into a murderer, the war exposed that the human subject has no intrinsic disposition at all but can move between extremes of monstrous evil and angelic goodness. Neither good nor bad, the human subject is shapeless in itself, shaped only by situations and events, just as capable of writing *The Cri-*

tique of Pure Reason as of becoming a cannibal.[2] Identities of cultures and persons, Musil concluded, "come from the outside, not the inside" (*PS* 164 / *GW* 2:1368).

But although Musil argued that the Great War made people recognize that identity was a fiction, he also maintained that the war had revealed a great demand for that fiction. In order to be what they were, human beings had to construe a reason for being what they were; hence their belief that their identities expressed their origin, community, sexuality, nationality, race, or some other allegedly natural essence. In his major essay "The German as Symptom" (1923; "Der deutsche Mensch als Symptom"), Musil admitted that the modernization of society had eroded the traditions that once ensured the propagation of this belief. Yet this only magnified the general need to secure a firm cultural belonging. Linking the individual to society in an almost physical way, the patriotic enthusiasm of August 1914, as well as the nationalist and racist movements of the 1920s, compensated for the social bonds that were dissolved in modern society. According to Musil, the war was a symptom of a yearning for belief, a "Glaubenssehnsucht," that drove millions of people to stake their lives on the destiny of their nation.

The political and economic development in postwar Germany and Austria served only to strengthen this yearning for belief in stable identities, not least among intellectuals. In his essays, Musil dismissed the efforts of such intellectuals to reinforce collective identities of masculinity, femininity, nation, race, and ethnicity. In his view, the discovery of the illusory nature of all identities, and the consequent refutation of the expressivist paradigm, offered an opportunity to work out new ideas of the human being, better adapted to the condition of modernity. In trying to solve this task, Musil's novel presents an innovative notion of human subjectivity—the Musilian subject, as I will call it. This subject cannot be defined in terms of an intrinsic disposition. Rather, Musil conceptualizes subjectivity as a processual phenomenon, moving toward subject positions, or identities, that it must assume because these positions promise unity and recognition, and which it must then reject because they never fulfill that promise. Subjectivity *is* this process, a process best understood in terms of *negativity*. It cannot be grasped in pure form except as lack, a lack that generates a need, which, in turn, drives the human agent toward the identities offered to it by the social milieu, and then away from them. Exceeding all identities, this mode of subjectivity transforms itself reactively through its resistance to the laws of culture, which work to affix it in one stable position.

"A vast experimental station for trying out the best ways of being a human being and discovering new ones" — this is how Musil's protagonist imagines his ideal society (*MWQ* 160* / *MoE* 152). Evidently, Musil's historical situation compelled him to conceptualize the possibility of a human subject who would not be captivated by homogenizing ideologies. If Musil's conception of subjectivity corresponds to concerns that have dominated recent philosophy and cultural theory, this is because later theorists, seizing the same possibility, are working within the paradigm that Musil was among the first to explore — and in this regard it may be instructive to compare his achievement with that of Freud. Contemporary thinkers have reached widely divergent conclusions, to be sure. Yet most of them share Musil's assumption that the human subject is a site of lack and negativity. To mention a few examples that I will refer to later, Julia Kristeva's "subject in process," Paul Ricoeur's notion of ipseity, Theodor W. Adorno's stress on the particular as an agent of negativity, Jean-Paul Sartre's view of an "ecstatic" consciousness, Louis Althusser's idea of the subject of ideological interpellation, Giorgio Agamben's concept of singularity, Gilles Deleuze and Félix Guattari's idea of deterritorialized subjectivity, Gayatri Spivak's theorization of the subject as being "superadequate" to its identities, not to mention notions of hybridity and transculturation introduced by postcolonial theory — although each of these theories has its own proper conceptual structure and complexity, they are all actualizations of the paradigm of negativity that Musil, in both his novel and his essays, articulates in earlier form. Jacques Rancière describes the subject as "an *in-between*, . . . between several names, statuses, and identities, between humanity and inhumanity, citizenship and its denial." [3] This is also an adequate account of the Musilian subject. Rejecting cultural roots and social roles, the Musilian subject liberates itself from all conditions of belonging. It is a subject without nation.

Of course, Musil's conception of the subject is nowhere in the novel accessible as a proper philosophical argument. It is worked out in the course of the narrative, always in tension with the cultural and historical raw material that he used when constructing his narrative picture of the world. Since this material is largely constituted by various manifestations of the expressivist paradigm, I devote my first chapter to a historical explanation of the dominating presence of this paradigm in nineteenth- and early-twentieth-century German culture. The subsequent chapters are then organized so as to demonstrate, step by step, how and why Musil abandons this paradigm and begins to explore a paradigm of negativity.

In chapter 2 I analyze how *The Man Without Qualities* actualizes a range of expressivist figurations of identity, only to dissolve them. "Human nature" is revealed to be a social fabrication, while the "soul," that apparently inviolable foundation of German idealism, is "a black hole." Instead of staging the human subject as an interiority expressing itself externally and recognizing the world as a manifestation of its own activity, Musil's novel depicts the subject as a surface shaped by the pressures of urban life.

Chapter 3 analyzes how the exhaustion of the expressivist view affects the narratological mechanisms of *The Man Without Qualities.* Through its shifting points of view, its blurred temporality, and multiplicity of narrative lines, the novel implicates a human subject so heterogeneous and polycentric that it explodes the conventions of character depiction of the realist novel, which rested on the idea that the individual realized his inner self as an unfolding story. As these chapters will make clear, to trace the dynamics of the Musilian subject is to produce a new reading of the novel. Indeed, to circumscribe the Musilian subject as a subject of negativity is at once to identify the narrative logic that drives this immense novelistic machinery, the principle that makes all its seemingly disparate elements cohere.

Chapter 4 contains the theoretical core of my argument. It exposes the Musilian subject as a subject of negativity, visible only in its passing between different ideologically imputed identities. Hence the novel's predilection for characters without qualities or identities, who trans-

gress social boundaries and violate sacred taboos—figures embodying
the principle of negativity. Central among these scandalous acts, the incestuous love of Ulrich and Agathe symbolically destroys the social and
cultural order. What emerges from the ashes is a subject who has violated all ideas of humanness. "I may be a monster," Ulrich concludes
(*MWQ* 313 / *MoE* 290).

As I explain in chapter 5, these figures of monstrosity are conjured
up by an imagination afflicted by historical trauma, that is, a historical moment when ideological appellations malfunction and the normative point of identification on which the citizens normally rely recedes. Well-established categorizations of gender, class, and ethnicity
are then subjected to debate, and the fabric of the community disinte-
grates. World War I and its aftermath, I argue, constituted a crisis of this
kind in Austrian culture. It is in relation to this crisis that *The Man Without Qualities* attains its ultimate meaning. My sixth chapter will support
this radical claim: the novel's meaning is infinitely enriched if it is seen
as a response to, or even a negation of, the politics of imperial, national,
and racial identity that Musil experienced during and after World War I.

The trajectory of this book thus moves from Musil's theoretical configurations of the human being to their determinations in politics and
history. On another level, my discussion departs from the expressivist
paradigm and enters a paradigm of negativity—a progression that allows this book to be read as a history of modern conceptions of identity,
from the early nineteenth century to the present.

Most interpretations of *The Man Without Qualities* have moved in the
opposite direction, quickly deserting the historical coordinates of the
text so as to address the challenging philosophical and aesthetic problems that the novel sets up. If the historical and political aspects of the
novel are discussed at all in Musil scholarship, they are typically treated
as external to the discursive complexity of the work itself and hence
relegated to the status of biography and historical background or accounted for as the novel's setting and plot.[4] The result is that there are
a great number of sophisticated accounts of Musil's ethical program,
philosophical inquiry, and aesthetic innovations. This body of work also
includes admirable studies on the intellectual sources of Musil's work.[5]

There are also, to be sure, many examinations of the novel's representation of subjectivity, yet none of these has explored how this topic relates to its discussion of community and collective identities. In fact, analyses of the representation of nation and culture in *The Man Without Qualities* are absent from Musil scholarship.[6] Nor has there been much written on Musil's explicit views on nationalism, racism, and Nazism.[7] The lack of analyses of this topic is conspicuous. Again, Musil's novel turns around an axis—the Parallel Campaign—that consists almost entirely of a discourse on empire and nationhood; and Musil's greatest essays, written while he laid the novel's foundation, are predominantly concerned with questions of national identity. Christian Rogowski's conclusion, in his survey of Musil scholarship, is in this regard justified: "Over the decades, Musil criticism has shown signs of petrification and fatigue."[8]

One reason for such lacunae is, as already indicated, that studies discussing Musil's representation of subjectivity have been guided by the expressivist paradigm.[9] Since this paradigm presupposes and valorizes an expressive connection between subject and society, and since the Musilian subject negates such a connection, this subject will be described, almost by default, as being estranged from an authentic sense of selfhood. In contrast to my approach, which brings Musil closer to our present by reading his novel as a first instance of the current paradigm of subjectivity, previous scholarship has generally taken Musil back in time, recontaining him in the expressivist paradigm that his novel explodes.[10] These analyses have therefore failed to grasp the meaning of Musil's project: by turning the lack of expressive links between collective ideologies and the subject into a virtue, *The Man Without Qualities* enacts a refusal of any membership based on culture or gender.

Since the early 1980s, Musil scholarship has begun to move out of the expressivist paradigm: Pierre Zima, Anne Longuet Marx, Peter Henninger, Roger Willemsen, Dieter Heyd, and others have situated the Musilian subject in relation to contemporary poststructuralist or psychoanalytic theory.[11] Parts of their analyses intersect with mine, and I will return to them in the following chapters. However, these works are almost exclusively interested in the linguistic, aesthetic, narrative, or psychological mechanisms of textual production. It is not that they deny the historical influences on Musil's writing. It is rather that they are so intent on its theoretical and formal intricacies that they refrain from digressing into historical dimensions that seem marginal to their interests. As I will show, however, it is precisely these allegedly external factors that explain the intrinsic aesthetic and ethical matter of *The Man Without Qualities*. Musil's historical context cannot be separated from his text; even those features of the novel that are foregrounded as most universal and timeless—its treatises on emotions, hymns of mysticism, scientific analyses, and discourse on ethics—are mediated by the historical and political background that the narrator constantly refers to.

Two of the most innovative interpretations of *The Man Without Qualities,* by Hartmut Böhme and Alexander Honold, are informed by a historical approach of this kind. Böhme has stressed the importance of the change in Musil's conception of subjectivity, from his expressivist affirmation of a substantial self at the beginning of the century to his condemnation of the same position after World War I; the result is the most interesting historical analysis to date of Musil's view of subjectivity.[12] Honold's work usefully demonstrates that *The Man Without Qualities* is the outcome of the writer's shocking encounters with urban life and technological warfare.[13] Still, like other scholars, Böhme and Honold ignore the fact that in Musil's novel the experience of modernity and the consequent transformation of human subjectivity are overdetermined by ideological projects aiming to glue a selection of approved identities of gender, class, and ethnicity to the subjects of Kakania.

A final reason for the conspicuous lack of attention to this fundamental feature of the novel may be what Claudio Magris has called the Habsburg myth.[14] In accordance with this myth, *The Man Without Qualities,* along with much other Austrian literature, readily appears as a story about the disintegration of old Vienna and Central Europe, the apocalypse of a world of cultural marvels predestined to founder in the clash between the rural harmony of the old *Gemeinschaft* and the mechanized *Gesellschaft* of modernity. Myths tend to simplify history. Being no exception to this rule, the Habsburg myth has marginalized more adequate historical accounts of the decline of the Austro-Hungarian Empire and the outbreak of World War I.[15] More important, it offers a stereotypical picture of the *postimperial* culture in Austria. According to Magris, it was during this period that the Habsburg myth was reinvented by writers like Joseph Roth, Franz Werfel, Hugo von Hofmannsthal, Stefan Zweig, Hermann Broch, and Robert Musil, in their allegedly nostalgic escape from the misery following the war.[16] As regards Musil, Magris's analysis thus echoes Broch's contention, that *The Man Without Qualities* chronicles "the wearing out and the almost mystical disintegration of a culture"; and this analysis has seemed so compelling that scholars and critics have rarely bothered to take a second look at Musil's representation of imperialism and nationalism.[17]

As we shall see, the representation of old Habsburg in Musil's novel is not a backward-looking myth but a forward-oriented transfiguration of Musil's historical experiences during the 1920s and 1930s. Being convinced that the postimperial crisis necessitated a society that would not reduce its subjects to their particular positions in the social hierarchy, Musil projected his exploration of this possibility into the immediate past, using the fallen empire as a field of experiments for trying out new notions of humanity and society. The empire that preceded the war was thus transformed into a past future, an open historical horizon that included the utopian possibility of a supranational and transcultural space, in which the human subject cherished the absence of homogenizing ideologies of nation or culture and recognized the heterogeneity of all identities — an idea that we may associate, not entirely anachronistically, with postcolonial theories of hybridity and *métissage,* and which therefore, finally, takes us back to the more implicit theme of this book: the ways in which Musil's postimperial novel sheds light on political and cultural issues in the present.

On what principles should a new, postimperial society be based? Between 1918 and 1933 the intellectual world of Austria and Germany struggled, ominously, with this issue. To the extent that today's intellectuals are preoccupied by related attempts to weigh definitions of universal human values, national interests, and ethnic rights against one another, this is surely because Western society is undergoing a transformation of the same order, though not, perhaps, of the same magnitude. Global economic and technological changes work to undermine, among other things, the ideology of universal progress and solidarity that was based on the class identity of the labor movement. The same forces erode the ideology of the homogeneous nation-state, according to which all conationals partake in a single community, share the same history, and move toward a common destiny.[18] As the integrative capacity of both class and national identity dwindles, the labor movement and the nation-state are transformed into mere containers of diverging political projects, much in the same way as the Austro-Hungarian Empire in Musil's time became a field of opposing forces, a predicament that, in turn, betokened the structures of conflict that appeared in the wake of Europe's colonial empires.

Today, as in Musil's time, these conflicts reappear on the cultural and ideological level as a struggle concerning "identity." Deconstructed and disputed by theorists, only to be reconstructed or forcibly imputed by intellectuals and politicians, "identity" has emerged as a pseudoconcept, which rephrases the questions we ask about the world, and hence conditions the answers we produce. "Identity" is pervasive, affecting everything from popular jokes and news items to cultural theory and international relations.[19] In the humanities and the social sciences, new discursive fields, as yet without firm designations, are materializing before our eyes, summoned by the need to analyze this transformation, as is seen in the contradictory debates on "cultural studies," "postcoloniality," and "globalization," as well as in the conservative backlash against these phenomena. These discourses reflect how social, cultural, and economic relations are increasingly polarized between a tendency to accept or affirm cultural identities as the fundamental building blocks of society and a tendency to deny the importance of cultural origins. Numerous politicians and activists, especially in Europe, and in Austria more than elsewhere, are preoccupied with cultivating their ethnic and national particularity. As in Musil's time, such attempts are often justified by allusions to roots and homelands, but more often by pretensions to save the national economy from transnational corporations and refugees. At the other end we find those who deny the relevance of identities, homes, and stable communities altogether. They celebrate a universal cosmopolitanism, traveling cultures of persons with multiple identities, or the allegedly liberating potential of free trade and finance capital.

It is impossible to choose either of these alternatives. Although they seem to present a genuine existential and political choice, they in fact only complement each other as two ideological reflections of our cultural predicament—a situation in which identity has become a fetish, reified and elevated to the status of some autonomous agency that can then be either espoused or disavowed. There are other alternatives, of course, offered both on a theoretical level, by philosophers and intellectuals, and in social praxis, by a wide range of new social and political movements. Yet they have been without tangible impact on a world locked in a struggle between the deterritorializing momentum of liberal capitalism and the reterritorializing efforts of various "fundamentalisms." [20]

As the following pages will show, *The Man Without Qualities* demonstrates the historical necessity and political rationality of those alternatives. Against ideological regimes that sought to exclude every sign of social, cultural, and ethnic difference, *The Man Without Qualities* reacted by augmenting negativity and intensifying difference. Evidently, the exigencies affecting Musil's writings were so great that he was impelled to formulate possibilities that retain their validity beyond their moment of enunciation. We are therefore invited to read *The Man Without Qualities* in the same way as Musil pictured the fallen empire, as a past future, a horizon of possibilities that should not just be shelved in our archives, but judged in their own right, as future possibilities indicating a way to get around our stalled debates on identity politics, multiculturalism, and universalism.

What Musil's novel shows, in brief, is that "identity" is always to be understood as an effect, not as a cause. If identity is an effect, it follows that it cannot be understood as a cause or explanation of social and cultural events. Like all ideological phenomena, identities are invented, reinforced, and unmade in accord with the psychic and material needs of a certain population, whose individuals depend on collective identities to recognize themselves and others as members of *their* group, nation, state, or culture. Such collective identities cannot be analyzed in terms of substance, for they have none, but only in terms of function. An identity may be defined, then, to cite Marx, as "an ensemble of social relations," and its function is to stabilize these relations. Just as identities cannot be abstracted and judged apart from the communities that they hold together, so they can also not be freely chosen or "performed" at will. As a consequence, there is only one way to grasp "identity": by inquiring into its historical origins and social functions, so as to explain how and why it emerges in its current forms.

This book is therefore also called a "history of identity." In the following pages, "identity" refers to a crossroad where the psyche is imbricated with the social, a site of negotiation between human subjectivity and society. "Subjectivity," on the other hand, refers to an ineffable agency that precedes language, culture, and ideology, and hence also the identities that both enable and constrain the human's articulation of its being. Human subjectivity will necessarily aspire to socially recognized identities. Just as necessarily, it will negate these identities. Identity is obviously a phenomenon that no human being can do without, and which, at the same time, no human being can fully tolerate. Those who disclaim the need for identity and those who claim it as a foundation of being are therefore equally wrong. "Identity" must be neither denied nor accepted. It must, on the contrary, be historicized.

PART 1

EXPRESSIVITY

Aber das menschliche Wesen ist kein

dem einzelnen Individuum innewohnendes Abstraktum.

—Karl Marx

Topographies of Inwardness

The Expressivist Paradigm of Subjectivity

In 1932, the year Robert Musil completed the second volume of *The Man Without Qualities,* Ludwig Bauer observed, "The air smells of dullness and stupidity." Bauer had no doubts regarding the main symptom of the cultural decay. "A strangely frightening spectacle: The I is disappearing." [1]

Karl Jaspers had made a similar diagnosis the year before. Charting the "spiritual situation of the age," he suggested that the "basic problem of our time is whether an independent human being in his self-comprehended destiny is still possible." [2]

In the spring of 1940 Martin Heidegger lectured on Nietzsche and European nihilism at Freiburg University in the Third Reich. He confirmed, triumphantly, that the individual "I" was vanishing. He also prophesied about an age that would bring forth a new kind of human subject.

The modern age, Heidegger states in these lectures, "is defined by the fact that man becomes the measure and the center of being." [3] This era began when Descartes posited the cogito, the disengaged subject of rational knowledge, as the foundation of being. Yet it is not until the arrival of Nietzsche's doctrine, Heidegger argues, that this philosophy reaches its finale. It is only in "the doctrine of the Overman, the doctrine of man's absolute preeminence among beings" that "modern

metaphysics comes to the full and final determination of its essence." [4]
The true embodiment of the Western subject of knowledge is the Nietzschean subject of power, *der Übermensch.*

What is striking is not only Heidegger's bold relativization of the
Cartesian conception of subjectivity but the political overtones of his
argument. We cannot avoid asking what resonance such lines had in
1940, a year when Hitler's armies of "Aryan" supermen triumphed on
battlefields throughout Europe, and Western history appeared to enter a
new era.[5] Heidegger's statements demonstrate how a certain historical
conjuncture inevitably invests an argument about the relation of subjectivity and Western history with pressing political content, and this
even if the argument as such pertains only to the realm of philosophy.

In *The Man Without Qualities* Robert Musil sometimes describes the
links between history and subjectivity in terms that recall those of
Bauer, Jaspers, and Heidegger: "Probably the dissolution of the anthropocentric point of view, which for such a long time considered man
to be at the center of the universe but which has been fading away for
centuries, has finally arrived at the 'I' itself" (*MWQ* 159 / *MoE* 150).
Musil, too, linked a particular conception of subjectivity to a specific
historical epoch. He held that the European situation between the wars
entailed the decomposition of the individual "I" and the emergence of
new forms of subjectivity. Musil's idea of a future human society was,
to be sure, antagonistic to Heidegger's. Still, both shared a historical
and theoretical problem, which forced both to invent the human subject anew.

The End of Man?

Why this urgency to project a new human being? And why did these
thinkers believe that the era of anthropocentrism was coming to an end?
They certainly were not alone. What we call the ego, the modern subject, and liberal individualism had many adversaries in this period—
from Freud's psychoanalysis to feminist theories of patriarchy, from
Oswald Spengler's account of the decline of Western civilization to

Marxist objections to bourgeois individualism, from Ernst Mach's materialist demolition of the psyche to Martin Buber's mysticist notion of the expanded self, and from the language theories of Ferdinand de Saussure and Ludwig Wittgenstein to anthropologists and ethnographers such as Melville Herskovits, Michel Leiris, Jan Vansina, and Claude Lévi-Strauss, who argued that rationality comes in several different cultural forms and hence that the Western subject of knowledge owns no pregiven epistemological privilege.[6] These theories challenged the idea of the rational subject as the source and center of power and knowledge, some by discarding it as an illusion, others by unmasking the interests that lurked behind the subject's apparently disinterested representation of the world.

The critique was usually motivated by the sense that there was a price to be paid, socially and culturally, for the gifts of modern civilization, and by the conviction that the purveyor of these mixed blessings could be identified with Enlightenment reason, capitalist individualism, Western utilitarianism, or some other manifestation of the so-called subject of modernity. Modernity, it must be remembered, arrived relatively late in Germany and Austria. Once the development of industrialization and urbanization had gained momentum, however, the transformations that followed were felt to be all the more dramatic. Many were alarmed by the prospect of a future society in which economic quantification, scientific abstraction, and professional specialization would make it impossible for the individual to relate "naturally" to the world and to fellow beings. A preview of this future can be glimpsed at the beginning of *The Man Without Qualities:* a "super-American city where everyone rushes about, or stands still, with a stopwatch in hand. . . . Questions and answers synchronize like meshing gears; everyone has only certain fixed tasks to do; professions are located in special areas and organized by group; meals are taken on the run. Other parts of the city are centers of entertainment, while still others contain the towers where one finds wife, family, phonograph, and soul" (*MWQ* 27 / *MoE* 31).

To this fear of a Taylorized future, organized in accord with the principles of scientific management, should be added the impact of the First World War. It drew a "great red balance line under the bourgeois era,"

Ernst Jünger said in 1931. Less a fight between nations than a struggle that "two epochs conducted against each other," the war attained immense symbolic dimensions for the defeated German and Austrian intelligentsia.[7] As the historian Erich Marcks remarked, it entailed "a monstrous fall from the brightest height to the darkest depth."[8]

The sequence of upheavals culminating between 1914 and 1918 generated a steady flow of conservative reactions.[9] Fearing that the intellectual spirit of modernity was too rationalistic and that the emergent social forms were too individualistic, or, even worse, too democratic, German and Austrian intellectuals sought to redress the powers of instrumental reason by asserting the spiritual powers of German culture, and to hedge the leveling impact of the masses by propagating the ideal of personal *Bildung.* The work that best codified this response to modernity and also exerted the greatest influence on later generations was no doubt Ferdinand Tönnies's *Gemeinschaft und Gesellschaft* (1887, *Community and Society*). Tönnies distilled the essence of a wide range of ideas about the human condition, presented by German writers since Goethe and Schiller, and he synthesized these ideas into a theoretical system so compelling that it came to crystallize the worldview of the intelligentsia up until the 1930s. Tönnies, often called the father of German sociology, is therefore a good place to begin our investigation of the prevailing cultural patterns that Robert Musil reacted against.

It is well known that Tönnies distinguished between *Gemeinschaft,* a rural or small-town community regulated by the customs of tradition, and *Gesellschaft,* an urban society geared toward the maximizing of individual happiness.[10] It is less often noted that this sociological distinction was based on a theory of the human subject that distinguished between the subject of "natural will" (*Wesenwille*) and the subject of "rational will" (*Kürwille*). Tönnies argued that the human being is most fundamentally defined by the natural will. "Natural will is the psychological equivalent of the human body," he explained.[11] Just as the individual's physical existence is constituted by his or her body, so is the individual's psychic existence constituted by his or her inborn natural will. As the term (*Wesenwille*) makes clear, natural will is thus an expression of the nature or essence (*Wesen*) of the subject. What the human being feels, does, or thinks is a manifestation of this nature.

Of all the manifestations of the natural will that appear in the evolution of humanity Tönnies focused particularly on the capacity of abstract thinking. With this capacity is born what he called rational will, or Kürwille, which designates a person's ability to deliberately opt or choose (*küren*) the object of his or her will. The person's volition is thereby turned into an instrument, subordinated to the power of reason, and calculated to realize rationally determined ends. Henceforth, what a person feels, does, or thinks is no longer an expression of the person's natural essence but an effect of his or her mental deliberation.[12] "Rational will" is thus Tönnies's term for the rational subject. He underlines that this rational mode of being is secondary to the natural will, out of which it develops. As soon as the rational will becomes the dominant motive of human action, however, social life is transformed accordingly—the Gemeinschaft becomes a Gesellschaft. For what characterizes the latter is precisely that it is regulated by rational will; people pursue their own happiness and treat their fellow beings as means to their individualistic ends. In the Gemeinschaft, by contrast, rational will has no such autonomy. Individuals are not yet individualists, not even proper individuals. The social order "rests on harmony and is developed and ennobled by folkways, mores, and religion."[13] All persons and activities remain expressions of one communal essence.

In formulating his concepts of Gemeinschaft and natural will, Tönnies gave the most coherent account of what I throughout this book will call the expressivist paradigm. I regard this paradigm as the dominant cultural superstructure in Germany and Austria between 1800 and 1930. What unites the ideas belonging to this paradigm is the view that personality, identity, morality, culture, art, politics, and ultimately the historical world as a whole are *expressions* or *objectivations* of an intrinsic disposition that resides in all beings and unites them in an organic totality. If Tönnies called this principle the natural will, others spoke of *Geist,* soul, life, subjectivity, personality, or individuality.

Many of these terms were used vaguely. Those who articulated the expressivist paradigm at the beginning of the twentieth century often drew freely upon the archive of German idealism—from old masters like Goethe, Fichte, Humboldt, and Hegel, to later thinkers like Nietzsche and Tönnies, including the Stefan George circle and the so-called *Lebensphilosophie* of Wilhelm Dilthey, Wilhelm Windelband, Georg Simmel, and Max Scheler.[14] Furthermore, the expressivist paradigm was reflected not only in books and ideas but also in buildings, objects, and bodies; indeed, as I will discuss in this chapter, it constituted a virtual topography that encompassed the cultural world as a whole.

To be sure, there are crucial historical and theoretical differences between the various systems and ideas that I fold into the expressivist paradigm. Despite these differences, however, these ideas all share one principal notion: that the identity of the individual subject and of the collective is grounded in an intrinsic essence, which conditions those manifestations, utterances, and ways of behavior through which this identity is externalized or expressed. It is precisely this notion of expressivity that allows us to grasp the significance of Musil's reconceptualization of subjectivity, for he argued that the human being is defined, on the contrary, by its lack of any interior essence.

Tönnies made no normative judgments regarding the historical transformation from community to society, from "living organism," as he called it, to the "mechanical and artificial aggregate" of modernity. Since he held this process to be irreversible, he thought it was futile to lament the passing of the old order. Most of his contemporaries and followers saw the same process as a decline. They wanted to put the train of progress in reverse and return to the authentic and harmonious Gemeinschaft.[15] This is why, as the intellectual historian Fritz Ringer explains, "Tönnies's concept of community was converted into a popular slogan" during the First World War. By the 1920s, Ringer adds, "no German professor doubted that a profound 'crisis of culture' was at hand."[16]

Most scholars and intellectuals attempted to contain the "crisis" by supporting an educational, cultural, and political program aimed at resurrecting the cultivated personality and reviving the organic national community. In 1925, Ulrich Peters, editor of the *Zeitschrift für Deutsche Bildung,* suggested that the "German soul" must return to itself; William Stern and Eduard Spranger argued that the integral "I" and the "soul" should be reinstituted as foundational psychological and philosophical concepts, while the educator Aloys Fischer asserted that these concepts should serve to "create the irrational bases and forces of communal life." [17] Though these statements are torn out of their contexts, they are typical of a dominant discourse in the 1920s. It was upheld by intellectuals who assumed the task of developing a cultural synthesis and of reeducating people so as to make them believe in an interior truth or communal essence, which in the view of these cultural leaders had to be realized, both individually and socially, in order to save society from imminent decline. If Peters, Stern, Spranger, and Fischer dismissed most things modern—its scientific methodology of abstraction, its social logic of specialization, and its political ideals of democracy and equality—it was because they believed such phenomena distanced the individual from this internal truth, preventing him or her from expressing the sources of national vitality.

Musil had little patience with the jargon of soul, personality, culture, and community. He fervently attacked the expressivist paradigm, along with the entire idealistic notion that there is a hidden cultural essence. "People believe there is a degeneration they must cure," he wrote in his 1923 essay, "The German as Symptom":

> The literature of our time . . . has poured out an ocean of complaints about our soullessness, about our mechanization, our calculatedness, our irreligion; and the accomplishments of science as well as art are regarded as excesses of these conditions. All the individual does now is calculate, and even his supposedly great scientific achievements are said to be nothing but excesses of this drive to calculate. Except for socialism, the remedy is nearly always sought regressively in turning away from the present. For the liberated man the old bonds are recommended: faith, prescientific thinking, simplicity, humanity, altruism, national solidarity, subordination of the citizen to the state: the abandonment of capitalist individualism and its frame of mind. (PS 176 / GW 2:1381f.)

As I shall argue in the first part of this study, The Man Without Qualities represents the exhaustion of the expressivist paradigm in literature and intellectual discourse. In the second part I will explore in detail how this exhaustion compelled Musil to radically reconceptualize human subjectivity, and I will clarify this shift by relating it to the moment of historical danger and cultural crisis to which he devoted all his intellectual powers. In order to assess the importance of Musil's anti-expressivist turn, however, we must first understand why the expressivist paradigm emerged as a dominant cultural matrix during the nineteenth century and why, after the first decades of the twentieth century, it lost its normative function.

Musil's work, however, offers only an oblique analysis of the historical constitution of the expressivist paradigm.[18] But there is another work of this period that addresses the historicity of human subjectivity directly, namely Georg Lukács's *History and Class Consciousness* of 1923. Lukács belonged to the same generation as Musil; both were subjects of the same imperial dominion, educated in similar institutions, and they experienced the same political events.[19] Although Lukács and Musil did not believe in the same solutions to the problems characterizing Central-European culture around 1920, they were both keenly aware that the idealist and expressivist ideas that appealed so strongly to intellectual Germans and Austrians of the period represented an intellectual irrationalism, or even "a destruction of reason," as Lukács later stated.[20] Most importantly, both staged their respective analysis of modern mass society as a drama about the fate of the self.

Unlike his contemporaries, Lukács did not ask how to prevent modern civilization from deforming the self. Turning this question on its head, he instead analyzed how this self came into being in the first place. In *History and Class Consciousness* he thus asks if the idea of a timeless human nature, commonly believed to be endangered by modern society, had not.in fact been produced, at an earlier stage, by the very same society. Exploring this problem, Lukács developed a critical history of the modern subject.

Georg Lukács's History of Subjectivity

Lukács's history of subjectivity bridges what look like opposites. Starting with a critique of Kantian *Aufklärung,* it ends with an analysis of the Taylorization of industrial labor.[21] In objecting to Kant's philosophy of rationalism, Lukács follows mainstream German philosophy. He argues that Kant's pure reason, by subsuming a world of particularity and change under the abstractions of the concept, locks all phenomena into permanent identities, thus repeating the procedure of the Cartesian cogito. In Lukács's view, this rationalist method is fraught with contradictions. Reason wants to establish the formal similarities and conceptual identities of its object. Yet, since reason can grasp only those aspects of reality that fit the pregiven categories that it projects onto the world, it ends up rejecting as irrational and unknowable—as a *Ding an sich*—all those aspects and elements that fail to correspond to its principles.[22] The limit of irrationality is reproduced by the very act whereby reason attempts to erase it.

It is precisely those aspects of reality that fall through the grid of Kantian epistemology—particularity, individuality, nature, morality, cultural difference, intuition, emotion—that are elaborated and valorized by nineteenth-century German philosophy. The result is a tension that, in Lukács's view, is constitutive of post-Enlightenment German thought and its Kantian legacy: on the one hand, the subject is disengaged and free to use a reason that recognizes no restrictions; on the other hand it is part of a nature governed by natural laws of uncompromising necessity.

Kant's successors attempted to bypass this frozen dualism of a rational subject confronting a world of inert objects, and they did so by construing a position anterior to this opposition. Hence Fichte's claim that the passive gaze of reason must be replaced by the category of the deed, by an active subject creating the world of objects. By virtue of its own creative activity, the subject can claim comprehensive knowledge of the world, because the totality of the world is nothing but the expression of its own subjectivity.[23] Hegel developed this idea further in his notion of the *Geist,* or Absolute Spirit.

Fichte and Hegel's resolutions of Kant's antinomies were correct, Lukács argues—but correct only in a theoretical sense. They posited the subject as capable of shaping its self and the world according to a superior moral law, or *Sittlichkeit,* in an act that is also the full realization of its freedom. As soon as one transposes this act of free self-formation to the empirical world, however, it becomes clear that it can be realized only in imagination, in a purely contemplative state, because in the real world the subject cannot choose *not* to adapt to the laws of nature and society. Hence Lukács's conclusion that the "freedom and the autonomy that is supposed to result from the discovery of the ethical world are reduced to a mere *point of view from which to judge* internal events." [24]

The tension thus reappears, only this time internalized in the subject. The subject is split into an *outward* tendency, which has to adapt to the laws of necessity prevailing in the external world, and an *inward* movement, in which the subject preserves the liberty to imagine itself and society being transformed according to moral standards. In relation to the world, however, such standards remain powerless. Moral freedom is thus limited to interior life, Lukács states: "The attitude of the subject then becomes purely contemplative in the philosophical sense." [25]

In his earlier works, *Die Seele und die Formen* (1910–1911; *Soul and Form*) and *Theorie des Romans* (1916; *Theory of the Novel*), Lukács resigned before these antinomies. Like so many of his colleagues, he lamented how modern society—its cultural habits, scientific rationality, and economic constraints—blocked "soul" from expressing itself. By the beginning of the 1920s he had developed a different response. In *History and Class Consciousness* he returned to the issues of quantification and depersonalization formulated most sharply by Tönnies and Simmel, but he now analyzed them in historical and materialist terms.[26] Previously, most if not all German thought had posited the oppositions between subjective creation and external reality, morality and rationality, inner soul and outward form as a genuine dilemma that determined the tragic destiny of modern culture. Lukács recast the issue, refusing to see it as an exclusively philosophical problem but rather as a local difficulty deriving from what he called "the antinomies of bourgeois thought." He proceeded to identify a number of analogous antinomies in other sectors of life. The discourses of political economy, bureaucracy, jurisprudence, science, and other intellectual and professional fields were all organized according to the same "structure of consciousness" as the one prevailing in philosophy. Lukács then boldly proposed that this structure of consciousness is "the structural analogue to the behavior of the worker *vis-à-vis* the machine he serves and observes, and whose functions he controls while he contemplates it." [27]

In Lukács's view, this new structure of consciousness is the result of reification. Reification involves the disconnection of individuals and social functions from the traditions in which they previously were embedded; they are reduced to isolated parts and reorganized in accordance with rational principles.[28] The most obvious cases of this process are the Taylorization of industrial production and the bureaucratization of social governance. But, Lukács insists, it also makes itself felt in the areas of philosophical inquiry and the production of knowledge. In these areas reason is first separated from mythological providence, and a new model of reality is then constructed based on formal laws of rationality.[29] Grasping cosmos as a set of rational mechanisms, reason effects a demystification, what Max Weber called a "disenchantment of the world." [30] The result is a system of binding laws of causality, in the face of which the individual—like the factory worker—can merely assume a contemplative stance and sacrifice his autonomy and freedom. He becomes like Hugenau, the protagonist in Hermann Broch's novel *The Sleepwalkers* (1932), who sits for hours before his printing press, affectionately watching its revolving reels.

These processes of reification thus imply a new structure of consciousness, or a new form of subjectivity. Lukács's account of the constitution of modern subjectivity contains three principal moments, which, taken together, help to explain the emergence of the expressivist paradigm. The first moment is the appearance of what is variously referred to as "the individual," or the autonomous, centered, atomized, or monadic subject.[31] With industrialization, the vanishing of feudal and theological hierarchies, and the advent of liberalism and civil rights, the individual is constituted as free and equal with his fellow human beings.[32] This moment in the history of the subject is also the moment of "individualism," a word that emerged after the French Revolution.[33] Balzac, writing in 1839, could still refer to this new idea as "the most horrible of all the evils." Like many other writers of the period, notably Edmund Burke, Balzac held that individualism destroyed the bonds of loyalty and duty that once unified different social groups into a harmonious social whole.[34] A product of modern bourgeois society, the concepts of individualism and the individual underwrote the soon-hegemonic liberalism of the middle classes, and they were hence coded in masculine terms. Its hero was someone who did not need society, or else was able to build it with his own hands.[35] Robinson Crusoe typifies this hero. Rousseau and Marx, for example, regarded Defoe's Robinson as the incarnation of the "individual" in his primordial and nonalienated stage. Interestingly, Defoe's novel (1719–1722) is compulsory reading for Rousseau's pupil in *Emile; ou, De l'éducation* (1762). If Emile were to digest Robinson's example, Rousseau argues, he will forever have internalized that *natural* standard against which he will always be able to judge his social self.[36]

The emergence of individualism is the first phase in Lukács's analysis of reification. His most crucial suggestion, however, and one that has not been properly recognized, is his account of the second moment of reification. What he argues here is, in effect, that *the theoretical and ideological constitution of the centered subject, or the individual, simultaneously entails the actual constitution of the divided subject.* Moreover, he holds that the notion of the centered subject is an ideological idea functioning to alleviate the social and experiential tensions resulting from this division of the subject. Lukács thus detects a contradiction between the way in which the subject is materially constituted (as a divided being) and the way in which it is ideologically perceived (as self-centered and autonomous). The cause of this contradiction is the process of reification and the division of labor. In order to realize himself as free and independent, the individual must objectify his qualities. The bourgeois, for instance, must assume a certain profession, a role that has no internal relation to the rest of his being. The worker, for his part, must sell to the capitalist the only thing he possesses, his labor power, and is forced to expend the substantial part of his existence as a commodity being circulated and reproduced by a machinery of production over which he exercises no control. Whether bourgeois or proletarian, this objectification of the individual's social activity leads to a corresponding objectification of his private existence, which is constituted as a separate realm, often in explicit opposition to the external world. If social existence is deprived of meaning, "private" existence must now be warded as a reservoir of emotions and noninstrumental behavior. A new form of inwardness emerges. The separation between inside and outside, between private and public, becomes the determining feature of the modern subject. As Anthony Cascardi puts it, the subject is divided against itself: "Outwardly, its actions must comply with a set of formally instituted rules, while inwardly its mind remains at liberty, in secret free." [37]

The third moment in Lukács's analysis discusses how the reified structure of the divided subject promotes a strictly contemplative attitude. The external world of commodity exchange appears to consciousness as second nature, to which the individual must adjust in order to survive. Unable to exert an influence on the social world, he assumes an attitude of reflection and contemplation. As regards the desires cultivated in his interior, here, too, he must accept an attitude of contemplation, because the world does not allow these desires to be realized. "The field of his activity thus becomes wholly internalised," Lukács concludes.[38]

Lukács's account thus sheds light on the ambiguity inherent in the concept of the subject. According to the Cartesian, rationalist, and liberalist interpretation of this concept, the human subject is posited as *subiectum,* or *hypokeimenon,* that is, as the foundation of knowledge and power. Yet this idea of the subject is only apparently true. For as Lukács brings out, the theoretical and ideological constitution of the subject as the foundation of the world is enabled by a historical transformation that actually realizes the concept of the subject as *subjectus:* the individual is subjected, reduced to being subject to a power that rules him.[39]

The ideological figure of the self-constituting subject is thus, as Herbert Marcuse once wrote, "the *frozen* manifestation of the general repression of mankind," the product of a society in which the subject is de facto objectified and depleted of its agency.[40] In a rare moment of crude materialism, Musil's narrator hints at a similar conclusion, declaring, albeit ironically, that we may explain "the celebrated moral freedom of the personality as a . . . mental appendix of free trade" (*MWQ* 328* / *MoE* 303).

Nature and Culture:
Interior Sources of Individual and Collective Identity

What, then, does the individual contemplate as he directs his attention inward, toward his private self? He contemplates "nature," an apparently authentic and organic essence representing all the qualitative values that are exiled from a world ruled by numbers. Lukács argues that the concept of nature underwent a series of transformations from the seventeenth to the nineteenth century. "Nature" first referred to the physical and biological world as described by rational schemas of classifications and laws of causality. But "nature" was also abstracted and transformed into a value concept. It came to denote an allegedly "natural" order of things, and in this sense it became part of the revolutionary worldview of the bourgeoisie, which mobilized this idea to reveal the artificiality and preciosity of the aristocracy. Through yet another transmutation, first articulated by Rousseau, nature became "the repository of all these inner tendencies opposing the growth of mechanisation, dehumanisation and reification." [41] Nature was now identified with an authentic self; or as Diderot said, "one is one's self by nature," ("on est soi de nature").[42]

Rousseau's idea became a foundational concept in German culture around 1800.[43] In Schiller's letters *On the Aesthetic Education of Man* (1795), nature is explicitly defined as the intrinsic essence of the human being. As society is rationalized and compartmentalized, this essence is prevented from realizing itself, and the individual is molded by external pressures: "Everlastingly chained to a single little fragment of the Whole, man develops into nothing but a fragment; everlastingly in his ear the monotonous sound of the wheel that he turns, he never develops the harmony of his being, and instead of putting the stamp of humanity upon his own nature, he becomes nothing more than the imprint of his occupation or of his specialized knowledge."[44] An explicit response to the French Revolution, Schiller's program for an aesthetic education intended to mend the broken relationship between individual and society. This became the primary aim of German speculative philosophy in general from Herder and Hegel onward. They all recognized the political urgency of the task. They hoped to save humanity, and German culture in particular, from the ideas of 1789 that, in their view, made manifest all the dangers of a liberal and individualistic understanding of the human condition. In England and France, they argued, the emphasis on the autonomous subject of rationality had fostered a utilitarian mentality, a civilization valorizing external appearance, abstract legality, and material achievement at the cost of the organic growth and personal cultivation that alone could secure a true *Kultur.* Reacting against this individualistic paradigm of subjectivity, these thinkers reinserted the subject into an organic order of things. They did so by imagining an "expressive" relationship between individual consciousness and the world. Herder's name for this relationship is *Einfühlung,* a word that captures the subject's power to "feel itself into" things and creatures. In conjuring up this power of "feeling into," the human subject discovers and realizes its authentic nature; and since the subject is an organic part of the world, this path toward self-realization also leads to the discovery of an inner voice of nature that shares in the nature of everything else. Self-expression is thus at once a realization of one's own essence and a realization of the essence of universal being.

In the holistic configurations elaborated by German romanticism, the identities of all manifest particulars are thus derived from one underlying essence.[45] In this philosophical system, therefore, the distinction between subjectivity and identity has no meaning. Both terms denote the same concept: an essence that is natural and intrinsic to the human being. Crucially, this concept also erases the line between the identity of the individual and that of the collective. In expressing his own essence, the individual is also, and necessarily, expressing the essence of his nation and his people.

Herder thus exalted the notion of *das Volk*—"as much a plant of nature as a family"—by defining it as an expressive totality in which all individuals branch out from the nourishing identity of the collective.[46] Fichte went on to install the notion of an expressive community as the core of German nationalism. His *Reden an die deutsche Nation* (1808; *Addresses to the German Nation*) gave metaphysical sanction to the idea of the people as an indestructible spiritual unit. Only the national destiny, Fichte maintained, can arrange the random events of everyday individual life as meaningful episodes in a story beginning in primeval times and continuing into the future. Fichte strung together all particulars into the totality of the national community, the thread connecting them being no less than a "divine law," which, moreover, bars entry to strangers: "The noble-minded man's belief in the eternal duration of his activity," Fichte stated, "is thus founded on the hope of the eternal duration of the people from which he has developed, and of the characteristics of that people as indicated in that hidden law, without admixture of, or corruption by, any alien element." [47]

Musil's critique of the expressivist paradigm is a response to later elaborations of such conceptions of the nation and the people. Musil even subjects Fichte's *Addresses* to a devastating irony in *The Man Without Qualities*. In his notebooks of the 1930s he discusses the legacy of Herder and Fichte, stating that German and Austrian nationalism and racism are founded upon the romanticist notion of an "I" that taps its essence from the people. The nation consequently becomes a mythological unit, for which the individual must sacrifice himself, Musil writes.[48]

It needs to be stressed that both Fichte and Herder, different as they are, locate the identity of the individual and the collective, which in the end are one and the same, in the *interiority* of the subject.[49] Internal nature is the wellspring of the world, an invisible inside gradually disclosed and realized by a visible outside. Returning once again to Fichte's stipulation of a subject that creates the objective world through the expressions by which it externalizes itself, we have come full circle. This time, however, Fichte's idea stands revealed as an ideology responding to the contradictions of modernity. Such is the ultimate lesson of Lukács's analysis of subjectivity: the expressive relationship between subject and object is an imaginary ideal of a home beyond the disenchanted world of modern civilization.[50]

Lukács's analysis of the constitution of expressivist subjectivity is supported by a number of more recent inquiries. Charles Taylor, for instance, argues that the expressivist subject is a typically modern construct, one which, furthermore, is not as far removed from our day as it might seem. He even contends that the notion of "expressive individuation" is "one of the cornerstones of modern culture." [51] What I have argued so far is that the constitution of a subjectivity divided between inward and outward tendencies is *structurally determined* by the historical predicament of modernity. The conflict between the subject's inwardness and outwardness must thus be placed among these immense cultural complexes that cannot be resolved by the intellectuals of the period in question, because this conflict constitutes the very horizon of their era, a historical paradigm that permeates all other issues, not only disputes about subjectivity, but also, as we shall see, ideas of femininity, the novel, art, architecture, and culture in general. The problem as to how a person living in capitalist society may establish an expressive relationship to himself, his products, and his fellow beings is, consequently, one to which there can be no solution; or, stated differently, it is a problem worked through by history itself. For just as modernity is a distinct period, so is the expressivist idea of subjectivity a historically limited mode of self-interpretation, one that, as Taylor states, had "a beginning in time and space and may have an end." [52]

In the case of the expressivist paradigm, however, this "working through" has entailed unthinkable human suffering, because it is precisely the belief in an expressive link between the individual and the community that has been used to legitimize most of the horrors of the twentieth century. In 1943 a new edition of Fichte's *Addresses to the German Nation* was published in Germany. In his foreword, Eduard Spranger quoted a previous laudation of Fichte by Heinrich von

Treitschke, once the official historiographer of Prussia. Spranger stated that Treitschke's words are true "still today, yes, especially in our days." Which were those words that seemed to ring so true when Nazi power reached its zenith? Treitschke had written that we "will be most faithful to Fichte's spirit" if we "contribute to the cultivation and ripening among our citizens of that 'warrior character,' who knows to sacrifice himself for the state." [53]

Femininity as an Image of Harmony

For almost a century and a half, from Goethe's *junge Werther* of 1774 to Musil's *Zögling Törless* of 1906, the expressivist idea of subjectivity structured aesthetic and intellectual activity in Europe, notably in Germany and Austria. Along with the notion of an expressive subject-formation there evolved a vast number of specific yet intertwined discursive and symbolic forms. For if the development of bourgeois society entailed the constitution of a subject split between inwardness and outward activity, it also produced a field of compensatory ideas, a topography of symbols allowing the subject to imagine an expressive relationship to the world by which the division could be healed. I have already discussed one conspicuous site in this topography, the nation as an expressive totality allowing the members of the community to mirror their identities in a shared essence. I will now introduce some others, all of which we will then revisit in Musil's fictional landscape, where they remain as ruins.

One striking feature of the expressivist paradigm is the pseudoconcept of femininity. Before the modern era, gender identities were commonly derived from a social and economic hierarchy, which defined the woman as her master's servant. With the emergence of the expressivist paradigm, these identities were redefined in terms of natural, quasi-biological essences, which, significantly, were deposited in the interior of each individual.[54] Just as peoples, races, and nations were taken to be expressions of intrinsic essences, so were the ideas of masculinity and femininity seen as innate and inescapable. This transformation runs parallel to the diversification of labor in bourgeois society and the re-drawing of the limit between private and public space. Formerly social units of production, home and family were now reconverted into a private realm of reproduction. For instance, when Rousseau posited the state of nature as a norm, this nature was embodied not only by *le bon sauvage* but also by the natural woman. Rousseau feared that exposure of women to public life and politics would spoil their inborn capacity to nourish and comfort, thus disturbing the delicate balance of private and public, home and market, which was the basis of a healthy society. As Jean Bethke Elshtain explains: "Without women to guard, nurture, and renew the private sphere, Rousseau's public world cannot exist." [55]

In the expressivist paradigm, femininity is made accessible as a symbol of everything that is supposedly unaffected by public life. For the male subject, home, family, and woman are codified as images of harmony and wholeness, all according to the rationale that, as Tönnies postulated, "woman's activity is more inward than outward." [56] Tracing this image of the feminine through three centuries of European culture, Silvia Bovenschen evokes the male perception of this topos: "There, where the man dreams, fantasizes, imagines, poetizes, the feminine becomes the medium for his idea of a happier world set against his coercive everyday bourgeois routines—Werther's Lotte, surrounded by playing children, an image of peace and happiness!" [57] This constitution of the feminine as something naive and next to nature meant that women were seen as naturally inferior to men in matters of art and culture. At the same time woman's essentialized status as an embodiment of harmony turned her into an object to which art and culture always appealed, an image that artists strove to conjure up and possess. In Goethe's *Faust* (1832), the most magnificent example of the expressive individualism of the romantic era, the theme of femininity fuses with the telos of history itself: "Woman, eternally, / shows us the way" ("Das Ewig-Weibliche / Zieht uns hinan").[58] While imagined woman, "das Ewig-Weibliche," became prized as an immediate yet evasive source of meaning, real women were seen as incapable of producing cultural meaning. According to Bovenschen, this explains the strange fact that while real women are nearly absent from the culture of modernity, images of the feminine abound. As we will see, this is true of Musil's work as well.

Aesthetic Education and the *Bildungsroman*

Nature, community, and femininity are thus situated in an imaginary topography that entices the alienated male subject. While art came to evoke and represent this realm, the discourse of aesthetics undertook to chart and systematize it, thereby aiming to harmonize the two sides of subjectivity: the public self, subject to the laws of the world as it *is*, and the inner self, scouting for the world as it *ought to be*.[59]

As M. H. Abrams has demonstrated in his classic study *The Mirror and the Lamp* (1953), the expressivist notion of subjectivity is at one with the emergence of the modern idea of art and literature. Toward the end of the eighteenth century, Abrams explains, the idea of literature as *mimesis* of ideal nature is replaced by the idea of literature as *expression*: "The paramount cause of poetry is not, as in Aristotle, a formal cause, determined primarily by the human actions and qualities imitated; nor, as in neoclassic criticism, a final cause, the effect intended upon the audience; but instead an efficient cause—the impulse within the poet of feelings and desires seeking expression, or the compulsion of the 'creative' imagination which, like God the creator, has its internal source of motion." [60] The subject of literary creation thus becomes structured as an interiority filled with emotions urging to be expressed, while art is reconceived as that which expresses the hidden interconnectedness of being.

Since art was endowed with the capacity to transcend the experiential contradictions inherent in the subject of modernity, on the one hand, and since it was assigned to an apparently autonomous and strictly limited field of activity on the other hand, it fulfilled an indispensable function in bourgeois society. This function was at once utopian and ideological. From the perspective of the individual, art and aesthetics could funnel the release of individual desires for coherence and community, which were otherwise contained in the political unconscious.

From the perspective of the social machinery as a whole, however, art and aesthetics funneled such desires into a field isolated from the rest of society. For even though aesthetic activity was codified as the fulfillment of one's innermost being, actual social conditions recontained this activity to a narrow sector of human life: aesthetic experience remained a private and contemplative affair.[61] Excluded from public life, the aesthetic experience assumed the character of what Robert Musil called a "holiday mood" (*PS* 196 / *GW* 2: 1140; cf. *MWQ* 833 / *MoE* 767). This autonomization and marginalization of aesthetic activity is vividly evoked in Horkheimer and Adorno's analysis of the *Odyssey*. In their telescopic view of history, Odysseus comes before us as the first bourgeois individual. Tying himself to the mast of his ship, he saves himself from the tempting song of the Sirens, keeping to his duties and at the same time putting their song into his service as a source of enjoyment. The otherworldly call of the Sirens is neutralized, turned into an object of contemplation, into art.[62]

Both Musil and Lukács emphasized the intimate relationship between this notion of the bourgeois subject and the literary genre of the bildungsroman, the novel of apprenticeship.[63] As exemplified by Goethe's *Wilhelm Meisters Lehrjahre* (1795–1796; *Wilhelm Meister's Apprenticeship*)—but also by its great precedent, Rousseau's *Émile*—this genre provides a mimetic illustration of the expressive individuation implicated by the romanticist idea of an aesthetic education of man.[64] This is why Friedrich Schlegel, one of the ideologues of the romanticist notion of expressivity, rated *Wilhelm Meister* highest among modern epics.[65] The bildungsroman introduces its reader to a role model who represents an imaginary solution of the contradictions of modernity. On the one hand, the modern individual is constituted as an autonomous male agent expected to pursue his happiness; on the other hand, he is forced by the social dynamic to objectify himself, splitting himself in an outward moment, whereby he assumes the position assigned to him by society, and an inward moment, whereby he cultivates what he takes to be his human nature. Such is the contradiction that the bildungsroman manages to transcend.[66] According to Lukács's analysis, Goethe's *Wilhelm Meister* shows how a person learns to realize his natural will, his *Bildungstrieb*, by participating in the affairs of the world: "A reconciliation between interiority and reality, although problematic, is nevertheless possible." [67] In this way the bildungsroman offers, as Franco Moretti maintains, "one of the most harmonious solutions ever offered to a dilemma conterminous with modern bourgeois civilization: the conflict between the ideal of *self-determination* and the equally imperious demands of *socialization*." [68] In this genre one's formation as an autonomous individual coincides with one's integration into the communal whole. The bildungsroman thus persuades the reader that he or she, like the hero, can feel at home in society and become, as Moretti puts it, "the well-cut prism in which all the countless nuances of the social context blend together in a harmonious 'personality.' " Analyzing a later stage of the same narrative tradition, Russell Berman observes that the genre's chief social function was to turn the reader into a realist, an agent of action, perception, and judgment, who shared the dominant outlook of mid-nineteenth-century bourgeois society. Berman argues that this outlook involved a certain logic, similar to the expressivist principles of idealist philosophy, where the particular appearance is treated as the expression of a general essence.[69]

The figure of subjectivity that was realized in this narrative form was a powerful construct, which confirmed the ideological boundaries as well as the utopian longings of the middle classes. Yet its base in reality was weak. The task of producing a story that presented both a truthful account of social reality *and* a truthful view of the expressive individuation of the hero was a difficult one indeed. For one thing, it presupposed a division of labor between the sexes. The hero's homecoming after his hazardous travels and hard-won victories could be rendered as a moment of self-fulfillment only on condition that his wife or betrothed had stayed behind to ensure that he had a place to return to. Due to her female "nature," she had to remain in a state of naïveté, while the hero had to pass several stages of alienation before returning, but now at a higher level of consciousness, to her state of immanence. Moreover, the bildungsroman presupposed a division of labor between the classes. In order to allow the hero to enjoy the fruits of his aesthetic education, the narrative had to exclude the world of labor. Odysseus is permitted the pleasure of the song of the Sirens only as long as his oarsmen keep the vessel of progress moving; they must therefore be prohibited the enjoyment of art. Had the narrator of the bildungsroman taken into account the smoke-belching factories and textile mills, market competition, laborers, the bureaucratic apparatus, unemployment, or any other of the institutions on which bourgeois culture also depended, it would have proved more difficult to give a realistic representation of how the hero manages to establish a harmonious relationship to the world.[70]

The fate of the bildungsroman therefore duplicates that of aesthetic education, which in turn is tied to the idea of aesthetics as such. As rationalization increases, and the social totality escapes beyond the horizon of ordinary men and women, a representation of an individual's self-realization through harmonious participation in social life loses its credibility as a realistic view of society. Just as capitalist society can no longer accommodate the aesthetic education of man, the aesthetic education of man can no longer tolerate capitalist society. Consequently, the bildungsroman, where the realization of the social totality translates directly into the self-realization of the individual, loses its rationale.

This transformation does not mean that literature relinquishes the idea of an aesthetic education. It means, however, that this idea is marginalized. If the aesthetic had once been able to harmonize conflicting aspects of existence, let alone that the reconciliation only applied in the imaginary, it now merely offers an imaginary escape from an existence irrevocably fragmented by conflicts. What remains of the imaginative potential instituted by aesthetics is "the great refusal" enacted by modernist art and critical theory, that is, the emergency exit leading to another dimension of being, radically opposed to existing society, be this alternative dimension mystic, communist, fascist, or a Barthesian realm of linguistic pleasure. The modernist novel testifies to the disintegration of expressive individuation. At the same time, and for the same reason, it registers the emergence of new forms of subjectivity that are not shaped by the mutual adjustment of individual and world, but rather—and this is important—through their mutual rejection.

A brief look at *The Man Without Qualities* is in order here. Musil's narrator actualizes and explores the project of an aesthetic education, only to refute it when finding that it fails to conform to the conditions of early-twentieth-century society. Ostensibly, Ulrich, the novel's hero, is the perfect subject of the bildungsroman. His decision to take a year's leave from life in order to seek an appropriate use of his abilities sets the story in motion, and it is as though he wants to discover his right place in society. Seen in this light, Ulrich's move belongs to the plot of the bildungsroman, inviting an interpretation informed by an expressivist conception of subjectivity and making us expect a gradual outgrowth of personal qualities germinating in the hero from the outset. On closer consideration, however, Ulrich's decision to go on holiday from life signifies a resolution to step outside the destiny laid out for him by society. Ulrich discovers that there is no place for him in society, or, indeed, that his "right" place is outside society. He will never become the mature character who adapts to the world and who, in the last pages, can look back on his life concluding that the interventions of fate always were for the best. As Musil himself pointed out: "The story of this novel amounts to this, that the story that ought to be told in it is not told" (*MWQ* 1760 / *MoE* 1937). Ulrich's subjectivity mismatches social processes. No expressive individuation is to be had. In this way, Musil's narrative negates the expressive relation between inwardness and outside world at the heart of the bildungsroman. As Jean-François Peyret has proposed, *The Man Without Qualities* "murders the novel of apprenticeship and signs its crime. Better still: it attempts to build itself on its corpse." [71]

Musil's satire is never more crushing than when the novel targets those characters who evade the real contradictions of modernity by upholding the hollow idea of "personal cultivation," as the conservative aristocrat Leinsdorf does, or by attempting to harmonize the qualities of art with the quantities of industrial wealth, as in the case of the German businessman Arnheim.[72] "Art" is a denial of "life," Musil emphasizes in one of his essays: "Softly quote a poem to yourself on the floor of a stock exchange, and the stock exchange will become for a moment just as meaningless as the poem is in it" (*PS* 197 / *GW* 2:1141f.). It is hard to invent a more pertinent image of the incompatibility between the rules of the world and the domain of art. This particular essay, "Ansätze zu neuer Ästhetik" (1925; "Toward a New Aesthetic"), is significant, because it contains one of Musil's germinal attempts to define his idea of art. Aesthetics, in his view, reveals an alternative state of being, an other condition, which he posits as a negation of the world. In Musil's realm of the aesthetic, "man" can be made whole again, but, paradoxically, only by splitting himself in two, so that he may step out of his social identity.

Such a conception of the aesthetic is the terminal station on a long route. In romanticism, the aesthetic signals the attempt to make the external world an expression of internal reality. Modernist appropriations of this idea are on the contrary informed by the attempt to protect internal reality from the pressures exerted on it by the external world. As the subject finds that its wishes for an expressive relationship to the social totality are being thwarted, it thus withdraws into a more marginal, inward sphere where, under the banners of aestheticism, *l'art pour l'art,* or other emergent modernisms, it can imagine new communities, capable of realizing the subjective human capacities that from now on are opposed to society and often sealed inside the invisible *intérieur* of human existence.[73]

The Retreat into the *Intérieur*

Friedrich Nietzsche and Søren Kierkegaard gave two opposing assessments of the reification of subjectivity. Of the two, Nietzsche is the more conventional, voicing a pessimism that was a stock commodity in German culture from Schiller to Oswald Spengler. What is absent in modern man, Nietzsche contends in *Vom Nutzen und Nachteil der Historie für das Leben* (1874; *History in the Service and Disservice of Life*), is the expressive relationship between what he calls substance and form, or inwardness and visible outside, or what he refers to by yet other dualisms. The reason is that the minds of modern individuals are clogged up by facts and information that have no purpose in their lives. "In the end modern man carries around with him an enormous load of these indigestible stones of knowledge, which then at every opportunity, as the fairy tale has it, rattle loudly inside his stomach. This rattling reveals modern man's most characteristic trait, the strange contradiction between an interior that has no corresponding exterior, and an exterior that has no corresponding interior, a contradiction unknown to the ancient world." [74] Nietzsche's ideal is a correspondence between inner and outer life. Indeed, such a correspondence is his definition of true culture: "A people to whom we attribute a culture must in every aspect of reality be a vital unity, and not so wretchedly fragmented into inward and outward, content and form." [75] But culture in this sense becomes increasingly rare, Nietzsche argues. The organic unity of the healthy personality and community is replaced by a disorganized mass society of weaklings.

Obviously, Nietzsche's diagnosis deals with the divided subject. On the one hand, there is a spiritual and intellectual interior, formerly a source of energy for great deeds but now so confused that it can no longer be expressed, much less exert any influence on the world. On the other hand, there is the public sphere, previously an emanation of the substance of the people but now transformed into hollow conventions. Confronting this reified reality with the ideal of an expressive unity attributed to organic culture and the strong personality, Nietzsche fabricated not only a critique of modernity, as incisive as it is insidious, but also that fantastic proposal for a new kind of subject, *der Übermensch,* who would reject the fallen world of bourgeois civilization and resurrect authentic, expressive subjectivity. Indeed, who but a superman would have the muscles to respond to Nietzsche's exhortation: "This gulf between inward and outward must, under the hammer blows of necessity, once again disappear"? [76] As I have already mentioned, scores of German and Austrian intellectuals at the beginning of the twentieth century rose to Nietzsche's challenge, one of the most prominent being Ludwig Klages, whom, incidentally, Musil ridiculed in his portrait of Meingast— "this eagle, who had floated down from Zarathustra's mountains," and who at one point is standing, "like a totempole," in the meadow outside the house of Walter and Clarisse, preaching his "doctrine of the will" (*MWQ* 1586, 1589 / *MoE* 1514, 1517).

By contrast, Kierkegaard's reaction to reification does not attempt to rescue the expressive unity of individual and society. Against the fallen nature of the social world the Danish philosopher postulated his slogan "Subjektiviteten er Sandheden" (Subjectivity is Truth). In his study of Kierkegaard, Adorno casts light on this gesture by which the Kierkegaardian subject constitutes itself as pure interiority: the "I" is thrown back onto itself by "the overwhelming power of Otherness"; therefore "free active subjectivity is for Kierkegaard the bearer of all reality." [77] What is other in relation to subjectivity—be it world, nature, people, society, or church—is posited as epiphenomenal appearance by Kierkegaard. In order to realize its existential and ontological truth, the subject must set itself apart from such worldly matters and conjure up truth and meaning from within itself. Adorno demonstrates how Kierkegaard's notion of subjectivity therefore runs the risk of disappearing into the black hole of an otherworldly silence. Only one alternative is consistent with Kierkegaard's own premises, Adorno argues, and this alternative is aesthetics.

Kierkegaard's notion of the aesthetic, however, does not imply the romanticist idea of an aesthetic education. In fact, it negates this idea. Denying the possibility of an expressive individuation where self-realization is at one with socialization, Kierkegaard instead construes the aesthetic as one of several existential stages in life. The aesthetic comes to denote the way in which pure subjectivity manifests itself in an internal dialogue with God. In order to convey truth, this manifestation of subjectivity must be stripped of everything historically specific, because aesthetic expressions are true only to the extent that they are nonhistorical, that is, they must match the pure ideas that subjectivity derives from its own perennial inwardness. These ideas, then, constitute the medium that enables Kierkegaard's subject to articulate itself and, hence, to save itself from the nothingness that otherwise threatens to engulf it.

According to Adorno, however, the viability of this alternative depends entirely on Kierkegaard's premise that aesthetic expressions correspond to universal ideas, cleansed of historical content. Refuting such an epistemological realism, Adorno argues that aesthetic expressions necessarily carry the imprints of history. Hence it follows that they, like all words and images, draw the outside world with them, rush into the secluded sphere of inwardness, and flood it with the very history that Kierkegaard's subject tried to escape.

This is why Adorno posits the image of the *intérieur* of the nineteenth-century bourgeois home as the center of gravity of Kierkegaard's thought. The interior is the protective shield behind which nineteenth-century man can escape the reification he must endure in public life. Outside he is a bourgeois citizen; in the intérieur he can be his true self. The intérieur affords the individual an expressive relationship with his authentic being, which he cultivates by externalizing and expressing it through the agreeable objects and routines satiating a life at once spiritual and domestic. In the model of existence materialized by the intérieur, history is replaced by eternity, objective reification by subjective truth. "In the *intérieur* things do not remain alien. It draws meaning out of them. Foreignness transforms itself from alienated things into expression; mute things speak as 'symbols.' " [78] Contrary to the commodities of the outside world, the objects gathered in the intérieur enter into intrinsic relationships with subjectivity and become expressions of natural essences determining the human condition. Yet, as Adorno demonstrates, these interior objects are mirror images of the reification of social life. Just as Kierkegaard's philosophy of the aesthetic led him back to the world, the image of the intérieur, too, testifies to the presence of the world of high capitalism, because without this world there would be neither inwardness, nor any symbolic objects with which to furnish it. "The image of the *intérieur,*" Adorno concludes, "draws all of Kierkegaard's philosophy into its perspective, because in this image the doctrine's elements of ancient and unchanging nature present themselves directly as the elements of the historical constellation that governs the image." [79]

Better still, the image of the intérieur draws the entire topography of expressivity into perspective. Indeed, to contemplate the history of this image is to contemplate the history of modern subjectivity. An even more striking illumination is provided by a piece on the interior written by Walter Benjamin, who influenced Adorno's study of Kierkegaard. It is one of six sections of "Paris—the Capital of the Nineteenth Century," an exposé in which Benjamin outlines his Arcades Project.[80] The dialectical caption of this section reads "Louis-Philippe or the Interior." The true subject of the piece, however, is the private citizen (in French, *le particulier;* in German, *der Privatmann*), who, under Louis-Philippe, enters "upon the historical scene."

The private citizen is shaped by the dual world of reification and mediates its contradictions. On the one hand there is Louis-Philippe, the monarch who supervised the rapid industrialization of France, encouraged the expansion of capitalist institutions, and consolidated the political victories of the bourgeoisie. On the other hand there are "the phantasmagorias of the interior," making up for the private citizen's efforts to adjust to a public life that is rapidly transformed by capitalism: "The interior was not only the private citizen's universe, it was also his casing. After Louis-Philippe we encounter in bourgeois man this tendency to compensate himself for the absence of all traces of private life in the big cities. He attempts to find this compensation between the four walls of his apartment." [81]

The intérieur is thus a compensatory realm, where "man," estranged from the world of commodities which he has produced, and which now begin to produce him, can preserve an authentic relationship to the world. Inside the home, things are still use-values, and personal qualities that are rendered superfluous by the instrumental logic of capitalism can still contribute to the completion of one's well-rounded humanity. Inside the house, sheltered from a social world that annihilates the past so as to facilitate the exchange of commodities and individuals, personal history is retained and memories preserved through a number of devices whose sole function is to enable the registering of the traces left by objects and persons. Every object has its own casing to protect its uniqueness, while frames, albums, and boxes preserve traces of bygone years. Even the fabrics of the interior, velvet and plush, are chosen for their ability to preserve marks left by hands and feet.[82] In short, the intérieur is the padded case of the self. Therefore it is not surprising that Benjamin also regards the intérieur as the shrine of art. Its typical inhabitant is the collector, who manages to purify the objects from their commodity-character, thereby establishing an expressive relationship to them.[83]

But Benjamin is mistaken when appointing the collector as chief guardian of this domus. Balzac, also portraying the era of Louis-Philippe, is more to the point as he lets his narrator fall into a reverie about the following "scene of Parisian life":

> You will be able to comprehend love as a principle which only develops in all its grace on carpets of the Savonnerie, beneath the opal light of an alabaster lamp, between guarded and discreet walls hung with silk, before a gilded hearth in a chamber deafened to the sounds of the neighbors, street and everything by shades, by shutters, by billowy curtains. You will require mirrors in which to show the play of form, and in which may be repeated infinitely the woman whom we would multiply, and whom love often multiplies; then very low divans; then a bed which, like a secret, is divined without being shown; then, in this coquettish chamber are furlined slippers for naked feet, wax candles under glass with muslin draperies, by which to read at all hours of the night, and flowers, not those oppressive to the head, and linen, the fineness of which might have satisfied Anne of Austria.[84]

Balzac's description lists all the crucial elements of the intérieur. The noisy world is shut out by curtains and blinds. The body is sheltered, warm, and comfortable. It walks on the soft carpets, leans on the cushioned divans, or rests by the fireplace. Yet the intérieur also contains eternal nature (the flowers). It is the place of culture (candles shaded so that one can stay up reading all night). Most of all, it is the place of love and the beloved woman, or rather the image of the ideal woman, multiplied a thousandfold in the mirrors of the intérieur. For, not surprisingly, the paradigm of expressivist subjectivity also implies that the home and the intérieur are the places in which the feminine, as Georg Simmel claimed, attains the status of "objective spirit."[85] It is into this intimate sphere of femininity that Balzac's hero must reach in order to realize his heart's desire for wholeness, and to enjoy the integrity and authenticity offered by its hostess, Mme Jules Desmarets. As the structural opposite of the home and Mme Jules, Balzac sets the crowded urban space populated by people like the "ugly" working-class woman Ida, *la grisette*. Like society and subjectivity, the image of femininity is now divided. Noble women like Mme Jules symbolize a positive, inward reality. They must be sheltered from the external reality symbolized by Balzac's grisette, or Baudelaire's prostitute.[86]

Yet if the distance between interiority and exteriority continues to increase, this only signifies that the interior, even in its presumed autonomy, continues to be mediated by the exteriority of modern society, against which it reacts and claims to protect. Benjamin evokes this dialectical tension in a piece from 1928, where we encounter the entire city of Paris lingering in the intérieur: "The Goddess of the capital of France, in her boudoir, resting wistfully. A marble fireplace, cornices, bulging upholstery, animal furs on divan and flooring. And knickknacks, everywhere knickknacks. Models of Pont des Arts and the Eiffel Tower."[87] Street, city, and world are here folded together inside the private apartment. The division between external world and interior is thus undone as soon as it becomes clear how even the tiniest cell of private life is submerged in metropolitan life. Yet, even in this image the intérieur retains some of its power to domesticate the forces of modernity, subordinating them to the sacred authority of the goddess. As we approach Musil's time and location, it becomes increasingly difficult to sustain the idea of the intérieur as a sheltered place, invulnerable to the shocks of modern life. Consider a poem written in 1892 by Felix Dörmann, translator of *Les Fleurs du mal* and a representative of the Viennese decadence. Entitled "Intérieur," the poem follows a standard pattern, or so it appears. First we get the setting with decorations:

An interior of luminous scarlet silk,
An intimate abode warmed through and through.
A rosy warm stream of light trembling down
From slender-shaped floor lamps
Muted by multicolored *abat-jour*s.

The inhabitant is then introduced:

2 Bourgeois interior, 1890s. A safe refuge in which nineteenth-century man could uphold an expressive relationship to his self. Museum of the City of New York, Byron Collection.

> A slender woman lost in reverie,
> Her lips half-parted,
> Reclining on a lush polar-bear fur,
> Her weary eyes faintly circled in blue.

At this point, where earlier depictions of the intérieur typically went on to clarify the relationship between the dwelling and its resident, Dörmann freezes the image, suspending further action in order to inhale an atmosphere of passivity and reverie, exposing how the resting woman

> . . . dreams and dreams of rapturous joy,
> Of unbridled lust and drunken frenzy,

. . .
Of one last never-known delight
Of a bliss called the ultimate
And yet not love—and dreams and dreams.[88]

Dörmann's intérieur may still promise the male subject pleasure and
fulfillment. Yet the image is ambiguous, for it also conveys the sense
that the woman's dreams of delight will never come true, that they will
forever remain mere dreams. The intérieur in this poem is no longer
self-sufficient but only a transit hall between the social world and that
Dionysiac world of plenitude and presence soon to be explored in ex-
pressionist art. Whereas Balzac saw the boudoir as a place where desires were gratified, a site of fulfillment, Dörmann's intérieur is a place
of insatiable desire—a site of lack. The room has been evacuated, its
sacred contents dissolved in a distant transcendence, and it is henceforth populated only by the specter of the pleasure and comfort it once
offered. No longer the source of the subject's identity, the intérieur is
only a station of rest in an endless search for identity. This is to say that
the intérieur gradually loses its credibility as guarantor of the subject's
capacity to uphold an expressive relationship to its existence, just as the
bildungsroman lost its legitimacy some decades earlier.

Jugendstil and the Shattering of the Intérieur

Aesthetic education, Volksgeist, bildungsroman, imagined femininity,
nature, intérieur: these phenomena arrange themselves around one and
the same historical moment, which knits them together in one and the
same experiential and ideological constellation, the paradigm of expressivist subjectivity. According to this paradigm, the subject entertains an
expressive relationship to its life-world, as its individual self-realization
is compatible with socialization.

Yet this equilibrium between inwardness and outwardness is not a
permanent historical settlement; it is, rather, a brief, transitional stage,
where the power of tradition declines but is still strong enough to moderate the force of modernization, and where the force of modernization

expands but not yet to the extent that it can liquidate tradition. Such is the situation that generates those at once ideological and utopian symbols that attempt to manage the crisis springing from modernity's destruction of tradition. Generally speaking, the bildungsroman and the realist novel can be seen as such crisis-managing devices. The notion of a national character, tying the individual to the community, fulfills a similar function, as does the idea of an aesthetic education, in addition to femininity and the intérieur. The comfort they offer is the stillness prevailing in the eye of the hurricane called capitalist modernization. There comes a moment, however, when this force reaches right into the interior space of aesthetics, art, and private experience and rearranges if not destroys this space. As we shall see, few novels depict this moment with such cogency and vivacity as *The Man Without Qualities*.

According to Benjamin's periodization, the shattering of the intérieur is brought to completion at the turn of the century in art nouveau, or *Jugendstil*. Of course, this was not the conscious aim of art nouveau. On the contrary, it attempted to perfect the interior, which it considered to be tantamount to the perfecting of the individual. "The transfiguration of the lone soul was its apparent aim. Individualism was its theory. With Van de Velde, there appeared the house as expression of the personality." [89] The real significance of art nouveau, however, was that it represented "the last attempt of art to break out of the ivory tower in which it had been imprisoned by technology." And to this end, as Benjamin stresses, it "mobilized *all the reserve forces of interiority.*" [90]

The House of the Secession, built in 1898 in Musil's capital Vienna, is emblematic of this aesthetic mobilization. According to the architect Josef Olbrich, the exhibition hall of the Secessionists, the Austrian flank of the Jugend movement, was intended as "a temple of art which would offer the art-lover a quiet, elegant place of refuge." [91] Significantly, it also sought "the purposive development of an *Innenraum.*" [92] Art nouveau explored new forms of expressivity that would enhance the space of art and inwardness. To this end it endowed modern building materials, such as iron and concrete, with a new degree of organic plasticity. The influences of modernization and technology were domesticated by shaping commodities and construction elements into expressive imitations of nature's forms.

The idea of expressivity celebrated in art nouveau was summarized in the notion of the ornament. The great significance that this period attributed to this notion may be gauged by the fact that writers as different as Oswald Spengler and Hermann Broch saw the ornament as the essence of culture. In their view, the ornament expressed the totality of the social and artistic situation. The absence of expressive ornamentation should, consequently, be taken as a sign of confusion and disorientation, a cultural situation too chaotic to be captured and expressed in visual or material form. Both Spengler and Broch interpreted the crisis of ornamentation at the beginning of the century as a sign of cultural decline.[93]

Part aesthetic concept, part artistic practice, the ornament provided the mediatory link between each particular artifact produced by tools or machines and the primordial essence that it supposedly made manifest. Revealing a deep-lying *élan vital,* the ornament was invested with the power to connect all particular objects into a plastic expression of a common cultural essence.[94] As I have mentioned, another symbolization of this natural essence was the notion of femininity. This explains why images of femininity frequently fused with ornamentalism, as the designers of art nouveau often deployed female bodies and body parts to mark the crude functionality and industrial origin of the objects of the life world. The curved forms of the woman's body were sculpted and added onto household objects, furniture, and buildings, as though to furnish the male subject with a protective padding, as he crashed into the sharp-edged world of machine-made commodities. Later architects and designers such as Adolf Loos were to ridicule this penchant for hiding the use-value of the object behind superfluous ornaments derived from a feminized nature: "Do you want a mirror? Here: a naked woman holds it. Do you want an inkstand? Here: naiads bathe between two jagged reefs, ink in one and blotting sand in the other. Do you want an ashtray? Here: a serpentine dancer lays spread before you and you can use the tip of her nose to flick the ashes from your cigar." [95]

In corresponding ways, then, the intérieur, ornamentalism, and the myth of femininity reveal the crisis of the expressivist paradigm of subjectivity. All testify to the attempt to find a foundation for the identity of the individual and the community in an era when such foundations are destabilized. The example of ornamentalism is instructive, moreover, because it vividly manifests the material causes of this destabilization of the expressivist paradigm. In the production and uses of the ornament, and in the debate concerning its raison d'être, factors such as new techniques of production, new divisions of labor, and the conflicts between aristocracy, bourgeoisie, and proletariat are palpably present. When Loos attacked the ornament in his 1908 article "Ornament and Crime" he did so not primarily on aesthetic grounds, or because he thought the ornament was functionally useless, but rather by referring to the national economy. The fabrication of decorative interiors and façades, Loos argued, was simply a waste of scarce resources of finance, labor, and raw material.[96]

The success of Jugendstil turned out a Pyrrhic victory. When the new methods of construction enabled by iron and concrete were introduced, they soon proved superior and replaced the older organic forms on which the idea of the ornament and the bourgeois intérieur depended. After the transient moment of Jugendstil, when aesthetics still sought to domesticate technology, and feeling still gained the upper hand against engineering, the productive forces of iron, concrete, and new technology were unleashed from the fetters of tradition, and suddenly burst out into the emergent architectural modernisms which, culminating in International Style, would liquidate the bourgeois dwelling and transform the entire physical and sensuous environment.[97] Less than two decades after its inauguration, Olbrich's House of the Secession, that secluded interior cordoned off from worldly matters, was turned into a military hospital for soldiers wounded in the Great War.

Expressionism as the End of Expressive Subjectivity

Charles Taylor, as we have seen, maintains that the paradigm of expressive subjectivity had both a beginning and an end in time. We have followed almost the whole cycle of this paradigm, from the bildungs-roman to the ornamented intérieur. We have moved from an ideology of expressive harmony and totality, where socialization and individuation are aspects of the same process, to the rejection of society in the name of authentic individuality, and finally to the obsession with the inner-most substance of the self as the last source of personal identity and reality. The final stage in the cycle is represented by Musil's contempo-raries, the expressionists, who speak for the inviolable "I" as the bearer of all truth. Beneath the lifeless conventions of a society that they de-spised, artists and intellectuals such as Georg Trakl, Oskar Kokoschka, Gottfried Benn, Egon Schiele, and Georg Heym sought to unearth a naked human essence, an unimpaired resource of vitality and passion—instincts so repressed by the prevailing culture that they could only be liberated by doing violence to social and cultural authorities. In 1911, Arnold Schoenberg evokes this spirit in a letter to Wassily Kandinsky: "One must express *oneself*! Express oneself *directly*! Not one's taste, or one's upbringing, or one's intelligence, knowledge or skill. Not all these *acquired* characteristics, but that which is *inborn, instinctive.*" A few days later Kandinsky replies: "Fundamentally, I agree with you. That is, when one is actually at work, then there should be no thought, but the 'inner voice' alone should speak and control." [98]

But at the height of expressionism there was also a gnawing suspicion that the subject whose expressions were to be recorded perhaps did not exist. In the words of Thomas Harrison, "one discovers that even this 'self in itself' is nothing. It is nothing whatsoever outside its objective relations." [99] Absolute subjectivity thus passes over into absolute ob-jectivity. Lofty words such as "soul," "individuality," "subjectivity," and "self" lose their meaning, or are taken apart and shown to consist of impersonal processes of historical or physiological provenance. The most concise statement on this matter we owe to Adorno:

Only the subject is an adequate instrument of expression however much, though it imagines itself to be unmediated, it is itself mediated. However much the expressed resembles the subject, however much the impulses are those of the subject, they are at the same time apersonal, participat-

ing in the integrative power of the ego without ever being absorbed by
it. The expression of artworks is the nonsubjective in the subject, not
so much the subject's expression as its impression. ["Der Ausdruck der
Kunstwerke ist das nicht Subjektive am Subjekt, dessen eigener Ausdruck weniger als sein Abdruck"].[100]

Expression is really impression. Thus, while Freud taught that the
formative elements of the human psyche have been placed there by
the external world throughout the subject's socialization, Ernst Mach
argued that the "I" is just a complex of sense impressions, changing
its form and content in accordance with the individual's environment.
The self that previously appeared as the bedrock of truth and identity,
and was pictured as a sacred intérieur, is now vacated and transformed
into Freud's *Wunderblock* where the external world inscribes its mes-
sages, or into an empty "waiting room for sensations," which was Otto
Weininger's name for Mach's conception of the subject.[101] Meanwhile,
the Viennese critic Hermann Bahr popularized this ego beyond rescue
under the banner of "das unrettbare Ich." [102]

These, then, are some of the processes—economic, social, ideological, and cultural—that conditioned Robert Musil's observation, quoted
at the beginning of this chapter, that the dissolution of the anthropocentric attitude, which for so long had placed the human being at the
center of the universe, "has finally arrived at the 'I' itself." Expressionism pursues the ideal of the self-constituting subject, introduced
by Descartes, reinterpreted in German romanticism, and necessitated
by, among other things, bourgeois economy, politics, and culture, to its
point of collapse.[103] In art and literature, expressionism marks the end
of the paradigm of subjectivity that I have discussed in this chapter. In
the same way, Nietzsche and Heidegger represent the end of it in the
realm of philosophy, just as does Jugendstil in the areas of architecture
and design.

Musil's novel, however, stands not so much at an end as at a new
beginning. Contrary to the expressionists, and contrary also to Nietzsche's last attempt to inflate subjectivity with superhuman powers, not
to speak of Heidegger's repetition of the Fichtean and Hegelian ma-

neuver (his recovery of *Dasein* as a foundation anterior to the split between subject and object), Musil's novel conceives of the end of expressivist subjectivity as a possibility for a radically different idea of
the human subject.[104] In this sense, too, his path crosses that of Lukács,
who analyzed the constitution of modern subjectivity in order to assess
the possibilities for a new historical subject called the proletariat. To be
sure, many of the characters in *The Man Without Qualities* attempt to vie
with the inexorable forces of modernization, trying to revive the symbolic forms, from Bildung to expressionism, which I have discussed.
But these attitudes are actualized only to be negated, because Ulrich,
the narrator's mouthpiece, valorizes the past and the present only to the
extent that it may be converted into future possibilities.

An appropriate coda to this chapter, which has relied much on spatial
and architectural metaphors to explain the history of expressivist subjectivity, is offered by Strindberg's famous celebration of the demolition
of old and oppressive bourgeois apartment buildings — "Tear down, let
flood with air and light!" — which clears the ground for those new forms
of subjectivity that would emerge in modern urban space.[105] We are then
placed in the shoes of Rainer Maria Rilke's Malte Laurids Brigge, standing in a Paris street, looking at the partly demolished houses nearby,
and experiencing the insecurity of the modern individual who must live
without the protective identity of the intérieur: "The stubborn life of
these rooms had not let itself be trampled out. It was still there; it clung
to the nails that had been left, it stood on the remaining handsbreadth of
flooring, it crouched under the corner joints where there was still a little
bit of interior. . . . [T]he breath of these lives stood out — the clammy,
sluggish, musty breath which no wind had scattered." [106]

There was a time, Ulrich admits in *The Man Without Qualities*, when
people expressed their innermost identity through their actions and professions. There was a time when one's house and external environment
could be molded into plastic expressions of one's self. But in the world
of modernity, Ulrich tells his sister Agathe, social and personal relations
are not sufficiently firm to be contained by houses. A formless life is the
only form that corresponds to the variety of purposes and possibilities
life is filled with (*MWQ* 971 / *MoE* 895).

2

The Architecture of Modern Identity

Subjectivity and Urban Space

Robert Musil once wrote a short essay about doors. He presented a rather eccentric thesis: "Doors are a thing of the past, even if back doors are still said to crop up at architectural competitions." [1] Indulging in the quasi-scientific jargon that is typical of his satirical idiom, Musil defines the door as "a rectangular wooden frame set in the wall, on which a moveable board is fastened" (*PP* 57 / *GW* 2:504).

The point, according to Musil, is that this piece of wood loses its function in modernity. It belongs to an earlier stage of social development. Or at least this is what he is able to maintain, since he refrains from considering the basic, arguably timeless functions of doors, like shutting out the cold or keeping strangers away. In explaining why doors have lost their importance, he instead presents a bizarre literary motif as his supporting argument: the door used to enable a person to eavesdrop, "and what secrets you could sometimes hear! The count had disowned his stepdaughter, and the hero, who was supposed to marry her, heard just in time that they planned to poison him" (*PP* 57 / *GW* 2:504).

The door is here described as an instrument of knowledge. It allows for espionage, enabling clandestine operations in the household. Musil's essay evokes a historical panorama of everyday life, where certain things are secret and others public, where some people can afford privacy and others are shut out, and where the ones who are shut out may still, through boldness and cunning, pry into the affairs of the privileged. The motif returns in *The Man Without Qualities,* when the servants, Rachel and Soliman, post themselves, ear against the wood and eye at the keyhole, behind the closed door to the salon in which the social elite deliberates the Parallel Campaign, that is, the project of unifying all the peoples of the Habsburg empire in a commemoration of the seventieth anniversary of the reign of the emperor Franz Joseph. It is the servants, compiling their own fragmentary impressions, who first notify the reader about where, in fact, the campaign—as well as the story itself—is headed: "At the keyhole, 'Rachelle' reported: 'Now they're talking about war!' " (*MWQ* 192 / *MoE* 180).

Yet nothing can last forever, not even doors. If we still hang on to them, Musil assures the reader of his essay, it is only for sentimental reasons. New methods of construction make it pointless to eavesdrop behind doors. When walls no longer are thicker or more sound-absorbing than doors, anyone may stand anywhere and still hear what is said everywhere else in the house.

Musil's brief text shifts perplexingly among architectural history, social criticism, and sheer mockery. Precisely because of its outlandish claims, however, the argument resounds more clearly: new ways of building produce new bodies, new modes of perception, and new ways of relating to others. What becomes obsolete in modernity is not primarily the door as an instrument of intelligence but the widespread idea that, as the Philippine writer José Rizal observed in 1886, "men are like turtles; they are classified and valued according to their shells." [2] Or as Musil states: "The man of former times, whether lord of the manor or citydweller, lived in his house; his station in life manifested itself therein, had accumulated there. . . . Back then your house served the purpose of maintaining appearances for which there is always money at hand; today, however, there are other objects that satisfy this same purpose: travel, cars, sports, winter vacations, suites in luxury hotels" (*PP* 57 / *GW* 2:505).

Musil here sketches his own history of the shift from the organic Gemeinschaft to the modern Gesellschaft. He suggests that there is a qualitative difference between a society in which building was individualized craftmanship and one in which it is a standardized assembling of prefabricated modules. It is the latter mode of construction, the age of *Eisenbeton,* of reinforced concrete, that throws doors and doorframes into one and the same dustbin with drawbridges and half-timbered houses already discarded by history. Simultaneously, ways of being are dropped that were functional only in a society where human subjectivity could be arranged into what is inside and outside, private and public, personal secret and *lieu commun.*

But if we abandon this way of understanding the self, in what ways are human identities reorganized by the architecture of a later era? In a famous short story by Musil, "The Blackbird" ("Die Amsel"), also included in *Nachlass zu Lebzeiten,* one of the characters evokes a functionalist utopia worthy of a Le Corbusier or any advocate of high International Style:

> The kitchens and bedrooms . . . lie close together like love and digestion in the human anatomy. Floor upon floor, the conjugal beds are stacked up one on top of the other; since all the bedrooms occupy the same space in each building — window wall, bathroom wall, and closet wall prescribe the placement of each bed almost down to the half yard. The dining-rooms are likewise piled up floor on floor, as are the white-tiled baths and the balconies with their red awnings. Love, sleep, birth, digestion, unexpected reunions, troubled and restful nights are all vertically aligned in these buildings like the columns of sandwiches at an automat. In middle-class apartments like these your destiny is already waiting for you the moment you move in. (*PP* 130 / *GW* 2:550)

In this environment Le Corbusier's idea of the house as a "dwelling machine" (*machine à habiter*) is already realized.[3] In the first half of the twentieth century a number of thinkers with differing political and philosophical loyalties used to portray the modern, urban landscape in similar ways, the first of them being Georg Simmel with his essay "The Metropolis and Mental Life" (1903; "Die Grossstädte und das Geistesleben"). Few of them shared Le Corbusier's belief in its liberating potential. For Adorno, the modern cityscape with its "living cases" served to exemplify how the links between the individual and society had been severed. He stated that "dwelling, in the proper sense, is now impossible." Heidegger also lamented the metaphysical homelessness of the time. According to Joseph Roth, modern people were shut up, like animals in a zoo, in cages made of "glass and stupidity and chromed metal," while Gaston Bachelard, some years later, searched through Paris for the organic qualities that endow buildings with "roots" and "cosmicity" — a search that was in vain because, as Bachelard asserted, in Paris there are no houses, and the inhabitants live in "superimposed boxes." [4]

These thinkers shared a view of the modern city as a realm of alienation. For many of them, urban modernity epitomized the process by which individual identities are erased by the rapid standardization of the life world. A similar attitude is frequently ascribed to Musil, by commentators who presuppose an expressivist notion of subjectivity. As I argued in the previous chapter, this notion defines the subject in terms of an inwardness that supposedly finds organic expression in acts, speech, thoughts, and, indeed, the built environment. The truth and meaning of the external products of human individuals are conditioned by the internal nature of the subject. This intrinsic nature is seen as a site of authenticity, an invisible inside that is gradually made manifest by a visible outside. Moreover, this understanding assumes a phenomenological conception, as opposed to a historical or structural one, where the subject's interiority is seen as a source of meaning or intentionality that conditions the subject's bodily experience of space. This experience, in turn, functions as a "natural" norm against which the sociophysical space of the modern city may be mapped and evaluated.[5] In this view, the subject's incapability of investing urban space with meaning signifies that the relation between the self and its environment is disturbed. The conclusion thus follows neatly from the premises: assuming that an authentic identity is one that the subject can recognize as an expression of its inner self, and finding that Musil's hero is deprived of this recognition, we are led to conclude that the hero is estranged from an authentic mode of being.

As I will argue, Musil presents a different scenario. The representation of subjectivity and urban space in *The Man Without Qualities* subverts the expressivist notion of the subject.[6] Already the assertion that doors lose their function in modernity suggests that Musil's narrator reconfigures the spatial coordinates of subjectivity in some as yet unspecified way.

New Buildings, New Bodies

Musil's novel is saturated by images that link the structure of the subject to the modern city.[7] Modern urban space functions as a virtual laboratory in which values, bodies, and social processes are combined in ever new figurations. Old models of the self are juxtaposed with new ones and then tested on their adaptability to a new world of mobility and change. The problems with the expressivist approach appear the moment we observe that, in Musil's view, the city of modernity, as it emerged at the beginning of the twentieth century, constitutes a "post-individual" space.

The nineteenth-century liberal ideal of the good society situated the individual at the center of the social world. A healthy environment was seen as a result of an organic equilibrium between individuals pursuing their own interests, be they egoistic or altruistic. Just as in the bildungs-roman, the individual's self-realization, on the one hand, and the constitution of the social, on the other, were seen as related expressions of a shared Gemeinschaft. In this traditional milieu, it was the everyday of labor and leisure that shaped the structure of the city. Modern urban planning, by contrast, had as its goal to let the structure of the city shape everyday life, and a better life at that. The appeal to the morality of the individual as a means of reforming society, as in liberal philanthropy, was replaced by more efficient measures where the results from statistical surveys were put into practice through large-scale planning and the technocratic procedures of the nascent welfare state. The environment in which Musil wrote *The Man Without Qualities,* Vienna of the 1920s, is in fact one of the most successful instances of such strategies, which partly explains the novel's fascination with urban planning and architecture. Between 1919 and 1934, the social democrats who governed

3   The reality of metropolitan life. Kärntnerstrasse in central Vienna, late
1920s. A few blocks away, in Rasumofskygasse, Robert Musil wrote *The Man
Without Qualities.* Direktion der Museen der Stadt Wien.

Vienna executed a program of urban renewal that was remarkable not
only in its architectural quality but also in its bold scope, as it drasti-
cally improved the conditions of living for hundreds of thousands of
persons from the lower classes.[8]

According to Paul Rabinow, the planned city of modernity presupposes a new epistemology, in which the fundamental concept of human
reality is no longer the *individual,* but *society,* which refers to something very different from a community of individuals.[9] Rabinow also
argues that the line between a democratic and an authoritarian incep-
tion of urban planning was always a thin one. He points to the French
officer and colonialist Hubert Lyautey, who envisioned an urban organization that would encourage everybody to search for "a common ideal,

a common reason to live," without abdicating any of their individual conceptions.[10] But the opposite tendency also made itself felt. A case in point is the project of socialist reformer Henri Sellier, whose idea of a *plan de ville* soon turned into a *plan de vie*. Drawing on a distinction made by Georges Canguilhem, Rabinow characterizes this tendency as "a shift from utilitarianism—utility for man—to instrumentalism, i.e., man as a means of utility." [11]

The image of the modern city, then, represents either a flow of possibilities for adventure or a homogenizing grid. These two poles are present in Musil's depiction of urban life as well. Like the architects of "Red Vienna," Ulrich believes in rational planning as a means for enabling spontaneity, creativity, and emotional intensity. This is what the narrator's various blueprints for a better society, his "utopia of exact living" and his proposition for a "General Secretariat for Precision and Soul" are all about. At the same time, these proposals remain just blueprints. They cannot alleviate or transform the condition of modernity, which Musil's narrator often renders as a condition of disorder and monotonous repetition.

Discussing representations of the city in German literature, Klaus Scherpe points to a large group of works that stage a "traumatic opposition" between a rural utopia and an urban nightmare. The modern city here symbolizes the ways in which "an earlier, allegedly peaceful subjective identity is threatened by advancing industrial civilization." [12] Early-twentieth-century Austrian culture is even more marked by this tension than the German literature that Scherpe discusses, the reason being that the Habsburg empire remained dominated by rural and semifeudal institutions up until its destruction in 1918.[13] Yet, as Scherpe argues, this mode of representing urban life gradually gave way to two others, both of which are signs of the diminishing force of the expressivist paradigm as a model for coding the subject's encounter with the metropolis. First, the opposition between country and city is pushed aside by class conflict. The opposition between the individual and the masses is dramatized, and the urban crowds are represented as an object of both terror and fascination. In the 1920s, yet another way of representing urban experience becomes dominant, its prototypical manifestation being Alfred Döblin's *Berlin Alexanderplatz:*

> In an atmosphere of urban overload and loss of subjective identity through a surplus of communication, commodity exchange, and productivity so particularized as to defy comprehension, a type of aesthetic representation of the city is introduced that takes pure functionality, the pure abstraction of metropolitan complexity, as its non-objective object. . . . The oppositions between country/nature and the city, between the individual and the masses, are leveled, even annihilated. The "city" is newly constructed as a "second nature" in terms of the dynamic flow of its commodities and human movements, which appear to take place according to self-sufficient and complementary patterns in space and time.[14]

If we now apply Scherpe's typology to *The Man Without Qualities,* we find that all three modes of registering the city are superimposed in the novel. This surely demonstrates the singular complexity of the narrative form, which I will analyze in the next chapter. It suggests, moreover, that in the novel the metropolis is approached from several perspectives or lived by several modes of subjectivity at once. The opposition of country and city is represented by characters of an older generation, notably Count Leinsdorf and Ulrich's father, whose ideal society is a tight and hierarchic Gemeinschaft. In addition, *The Man Without Qualities* thematizes the opposition between the individual and the masses, as can be seen in the opening pages where Ulrich is looking out through the window of his palace, contemplating the crowds in the street, and also at the end of the novel's first part, where Ulrich, again from an elevated window, observes how the masses are raging against the Parallel Campaign. The opposition between the individual and the collective also appear in the portrayals of the fanatic nationalist Hans Sepp and the young socialist Schmeisser. Confronted by these mass movements, a constitutive element in the modern city, Ulrich seeks to protect a vulnerable sense of authenticity.[15]

Yet the most magnificent representations of the city in *The Man Without Qualities* are the ones that thematize the pure functionality and abstraction of the metropolis. Musil's city is a space where each and everyone are transformed into functions of an incomprehensible whole. Identities therefore lose their meaning as denominations of particular substances, and they become mere designations of variable systemic operations. Hence the narrator's awkward way of welcoming his reader to Vienna: "So let us not place any particular value on the city's name. Like all big cities it was made up by irregularity, change, forward spurts, failures to keep step, collisions of objects and interests" (*MWQ* 4 / *MoE* 10). This, then, is not really a story about a place; it is about any place. Vienna is just an image. It is an image of the modern city, to be sure, but also of a less tangible phenomenon: the abstract life-world of modernity as such. Musil's representation of the modern metropolis thus approximates that of Döblin, or, better, presents the narrative equivalent of the compressed urban scenes glimpsed in the films of Fritz Lang, the images of Georg Grosz, and the photomontages of László Moholy-Nagy (fig. 4). In chapter 8, the metropolitan scenario is enlarged and presented as the possible destiny of mankind:

> Air and earth form an anthill traversed, level upon level, by roads live with traffic. Air trains, ground trains, underground trains, people mailed through tubes special-delivery, and chains of cars race along horizontally, while express elevators pump masses of people vertically from one traffic level to another; at the junctions, people leap from one vehicle to the next, instantly sucked in and snatched away by the rhythm of it, which makes a syncope, a pause, a little gap of twenty seconds during which a word might be hastily exchanged with someone else. Questions and answers synchronize like meshing gears; everyone has only certain fixed tasks to do; professions are located in special areas and organized by group; meals are taken on the run. Other parts of the city are centers of entertainment, while still others contain the towers where one finds wife, family, phonograph, and soul. Tension and relaxation, activity and love, are precisely timed and weighed on the basis of exhaustive laboratory studies. (*MWQ* 27 / *MoE* 31)

Society as machine, the ultimate Taylorization of life: the powers whereby humankind once asserted its freedom from nature's constraints have developed into powers that abolish freedom altogether. Musil's narrator renders these powers as a force exerted by city space on the human body and mind. But this force is not seen exclusively as an aspect of modernization. Unlike most interpretations of modernization, Musil's narrative does not regard tradition and modernization as a priori contradictory phenomena. They are both seen as different, though related, causes of the reification of social space. Tradition refers to the habits and institutions accumulated throughout history, subsequently frozen into a second nature that limits the subject positions of each human being. Yet, although modernization entails the destruction of traditional habits and institutions and thereby opens up new opportunities, it has the same effect as tradition in the sense that it produces a social environment where the individual must move from one predetermined slot to the another. As one irresistible force, tradition and modernization constitute the realm of necessity, a petrified world of objects conditioning the shape of the subject, determining its choices, desires, possibilities, and experiences. Endowing each subject with a function that guarantees the reproduction of the system, this force thus preserves a status quo that Musil's narrator captures with the untranslatable word *Seinesgleichen,* which denotes a reality that repeats itself eternally.[16]

Consider, for example, the episode when Ulrich, strolling through Vienna, is captivated by the sight of a cathedral. The narrator here locates the modern city at the point of convergence where the density of both tradition and modernization reach maximum. Before the authority of these two, or of *das Seinesgleichen,* the tiny human being must bow down, much in the same way as the subject of the past came to worship its mythic masters in the church:

> It was only seconds that Ulrich stood outside the church, but they rooted in him and compressed his heart with all the resistance of primal instinct against this world petrified into millions of tons of stone, against this frozen moonscape of feeling where, involuntarily, he had been set down. . . . The houses beside it, the firmament above, the indescribable harmony of all the lines and spaces that caught and guided the eye,

4 The imaginary of metropolitan life. László Moholy-Nagy, "Stage Design for *Der Kaufmann von Berlin*" (1929). Gelatin silver, 8.3 × 16.7 cm. The J. Paul Getty Museum, Los Angeles.

the look and expression of the people passing below, their books, their morals, the trees along the street . . . it all seems at times as stiff as folding screens, as hard as a printer's die stamp, complete—there is no other way of putting it—so complete and finished that one is mere superfluous mist beside it, a small, exhaled breath God has no time for anymore. At this moment he wished he were a man without qualities. (*MWQ* 136 / *MoE* 130)

In this passage, Ulrich is first positioned in front of a cathedral, embodying the weight of tradition. Then the narrator has him reflect on city space. A series of metaphors likens urban space to the density and solidity of a rock, to the lifelessness of a moonscape, to the firmness of "folding screens," and to the sharpness and durability of a printer's stamp. The human subject, on the other hand, is a feebly pulsating heart, a thin haze, or an invisible exhalation of life. A man without qualities: it is here, in this state of mobility and weightlessness, that Ulrich wishes to remain. Were he to acquire "qualities," he would be fixed in a role, immobilized.

When Ulrich interrupts his promenade again, he finds himself in front of a complex of modern buildings. Now the reference to architecture is explicit: "He came to a halt again, this time in a square where he recognized some of the houses and remembered the public controversies and intellectual ferment that had accompanied their construction" (*MWQ* 138 / *MoE* 132). A few years earlier the young generation, including Ulrich, had fought over the plans determining the future transformation of urban space. These people were "the rebels" who wanted to change the world. To be sure, they did defeat their opponents; the new buildings were constructed. But to what good? The once controversial buildings soon merged with tradition, and now "these houses stood in the late, already fading afternoon light, like kindly aunts in outmoded hats, quite proper and irrelevant and anything but exciting" (*MWQ* 138 / *MoE* 132). The revolutionary energy intended to clear the ground for a better future ends up thickening the already stifling atmosphere of the present.

In such passages, the modern city, where space is a depository of layers of sedimented time, emerges as a sublime object, compared to which the individual human body is reduced to insignificance. Musil offers his own version of the dialectic of enlightenment. Now ironic, now tragic, this is a story about how the world created by collective efforts arises in front of the individual as an implacable force determining even the slightest details of his or her everyday life. History becomes fate rather than project: "The course of history was therefore not that of a billiard ball—which, once it is hit, takes a definite line—but resembles the movement of clouds, or the path of a man sauntering through the streets, turned aside by a shadow here, a crowd there, an unusual architectural outcrop, until at last he arrives at a place he never knew or meant to go to. Inherent in the course of history is a certain going off course [*ein gewisses Sich-Verlaufen*]" (*MWQ* 392 / *MoE* 361).

This *Sich-Verlaufen*—which is the way of life in das Seinesgleichen—is the terminal stage in the reification of the social aspects of subjectivity as presented in Musil's novel. Judging from other elements in this picture, however, we see that this predicament lacks the agreeable air of going astray in a city. *The Man Without Qualities* represents the social universe as at once too chaotic and too rigidly structured, and both these features spring from the same fundamental tendency. Requiring rigid order in each specialized sphere, the process of modernization leads to a disconnection of all spheres from one another and hence to the disorder of the whole. When Musil's narrator tries to evoke this dynamic, two images regularly present themselves. The first is that of the beehive state or the anthill. It corresponds to the functionalist idea of society. Each individual is reduced, as in sociological behaviorism, to an apparatus reacting with a limited set of adequate responses to an equally limited set of external stimuli. If anything like a seriality of such apparatuses is conceivable, it would be functionally indistinguishable from the beehive or the anthill—or Musil's metropolis. Immediately following the glimpse of the futuristic city quoted above, for instance, the narrator adds: "Besides, zoology teaches that a number of flawed individuals can often add up to a brilliant whole" (*MWQ* 27* / *MoE* 32). The theme suggests itself to Ulrich over and over.[17] If will and agency are suspended, the social totality may well be improved as a whole. An organism reacting instinctively, without consciousness or moral will, would somehow be better adapted to life under modernity.

True, Ulrich is thrilled by such scenarios, and he thirsts for the organizing principle found wanting in both individual and social life. He explores the possibilities for a social and spiritual reorganization promised by the scientific methods to which he has devoted his professional life. But when taking the negative effects of rationalization into account, he reaches the point where he does not dare to spell out the grim consequences. For these consequences include the risk of a partial or total demise of individuality under an instrumental reason that transforms all particulars into mere means for the maintenance of the irrational whole.

Yet the truly terrifying scope of this theme is only revealed by the second image of this extreme form of reification. If the first image is the beehive or the anthill, this second one entails the destruction of organic life as such: "Just imagine a total universal order embracing all mankind—in short, the perfect civilian state of order: that, I say, is death by freezing, it's rigor mortis, a moonscape, a geometric plague!" It is left to the only military person among the characters, General Stumm von Bordwehr, to pronounce the ultimate lesson of unbridled modernization: "Somehow or other, order, once it reaches a certain stage, calls for bloodshed" (*MWQ* 505 / *MoE* 464f.). Musil's exploration of the social reification of subjectivity thus reaches a point from which there is neither continuation nor return, because at this point, reification equals the physical annihilation of the human organism.

The harmonious adjustment of individuation to socialization once codified by the expressive paradigm and the narrative of the bildungsroman has reached its opposite pole in *The Man Without Qualities.* Urban space appears to preclude the possibility of intentional, phenomenological meaning. The incompatibility between individual and society, or inwardness and externality, is accentuated by a figural language which naturalizes this opposition. Subjectivity is rendered through a series of metaphors organized on a scale stretching from what is mobile, flexible, soft, warm, organic, and glowing with life to what is petrified, frozen, hard, inorganic, and dead.

The experience of this opposition constitutes a kind of *Grundstim-*

mung that colors Musil's life and work as a whole. In his notebooks, in which he wrote down ideas and drafted stories and essays, the tension between vulnerable forms of organic life and a dead, unyielding environment returns in ever new figurations. In what is perhaps Musil's first literary attempt, "Blätter an dem Nachtbuche des monsieur le vivisecteur" ("Leaves from the night book of monsieur le vivisecteur"), written at the age of twenty, the narrator is a man living isolated in the arctic night, "as if underneath a 100 m deep layer of ice." The first thought of "monsieur le vivisecteur" concerns his memory of once having seen a mosquito inside the clear mass of a rock crystal (*T* 1:1). The most grandiose metaphors of Musil's novel result from an analysis of the mismatch between life and the forms that imprison it; for example, what separates a person from his psychic inwardness is at one point described as "a wall of diamonds growing daily more encrusted" (*MWQ* 425 / *MoE* 392). Musil is here a true spokesman for the *Lebensphilosophie,* or vitalism, of his era. The same oppositions are everywhere in Viennese culture. Hugo von Hofmannsthal despairs over a literary culture in which individuality is silenced rather than encouraged to express itself. Karl Kraus loathes petrified customs and journalistic babble that preclude thought altogether. Adolf Loos crusades against the exaggerated attention to surface and ornament that stifles the creative energies of everyday life. The explosions of dissonance in the works of expressionists like Arnold Schoenberg and Oskar Kokoschka defy the dead forms of bourgeois culture. Meanwhile, as we have seen, the young Lukács establishes an insurmountable disjunction between soul and form.

Similarly, for Musil, the ideal is a subjectivity that remains like a mere lifegiving breath, *ein Atemzug.* The nightmare is a subjectivity fixed by qualities, by an imputed character, or by a disciplinary social machinery that reduces it to a docile body, which, obediently assuming its place and renouncing its desires, becomes a lifeless rock in Musil's lunar landscape of tradition—an image, by the way, that recalls paintings and photographs of the cratered, barren landscape of the Western front.[18]

This disclosure of modernization's darkest tendencies also links Musil's novel to two other major categories of modernist narrative. The scenario where the individual is captured, dispossessed of everything personal, and finally put to death by an immense social machinery is precisely the condition that Kafka evokes in all its brutality.[19] As Deleuze and Guattari have argued, Kafka's characters can escape being victimized only by becoming animals and monsters.[20] Another variation of this horrid tale of modernity is Döblin's *Berlin Alexanderplatz* (1929), which draws a direct parallel between the fate of the calves, steers, and hogs that are led into the slaughterhouses along Eldenaer Strasse and the fate awaiting poor Franz Biberkopf: "As the beast dies, so Man dies too" — "scalded, gutted, then hacked up; this is done step by step" — "strangled, killed, extinguished — such is life." [21]

Yet this same state of affairs is triumphantly affirmed in the essays and novels Ernst Jünger wrote before World War II. The common precondition of these two diametrically opposed accounts of modernity are revealed with astonishing lucidity in Musil's narrative. Jünger's ideal, as developed in his essay *The Worker* (*Der Arbeiter,* 1932), is the human-turned-machine, who happily lets himself be chained to his fragment of the whole.[22] In Ulrich's view, society inexorably moves in this direction. The novel's exploration of the reification of the outward aspects of subjectivity must thus end with a wholesale rejection of social reality. Again, the prospect of a liquidation of individuality is here formulated in terms of urban space: "Evening had come; buildings as if broken out of pure space, asphalt, steel rails, formed the cooling shell that was the city. The mother shell, full of childlike, joyful, angry human movement. Where every drop begins as a droplet sprayed or squirted; a tiny explosion caught by the walls, cooling, calming, and slowing down, hanging quietly, tenderly, on the slope of the mother shell, hardening at last into a little grain on its wall" (*MWQ* 161 / *MoE* 152f.).

If this is the thesis, the narrator immediately supplies Ulrich's antithesis, his rejection of the modern urban condition: "Within the frozen, petrified body of the city he felt his heart beating in its innermost depths. There was something in him that had never wanted to remain anywhere, had groped its way along the walls of the world, thinking: There are still millions of other walls; it was this slowly cooling, absurd drop 'I' that refused to give up its fire, its tiny glowing core" (*MWQ* 162/ *MoE* 153).

Heat and cold, mobility and rigidity — the opposition of subject and world seems absolute. Operative in most art forms in the nineteenth century, the expressivist ideal provides a utopian and ideological remedy for this structurally determined split between inwardness and outside. But in Musil's twentieth-century universe, this ideal stands powerless in the face of the massive weight of urban reality. Although the paradigm of expressivist subjectivity is rendered powerless, however, the figurative model on which this paradigm is based remains in place even in Musil. The subject is still described in terms of an inside that supposedly should radiate meaning outward. The difference is that Musil's narrator reverses the process, stating that the walls along the streets radiate ideologies (*MWQ* 1759 / *MoE* 1932). The city is rendered as a cold, unyielding container in which subjectivity is caged, forced to turn in ever more narrow circles until it is finally compressed into a tiny atom of heat and life. Only the continued operation of this matrix, the expressivist notion that inside and outside should reflect each other, can explain that muffled yet clearly perceptible cry of despair in the passage above. Not only does the city of modernity disconnect the subject's inwardness from its social being: it then compresses interiority until it is crushed.

Apart from the narrative strategies of Jünger, Kafka, and the writers already mentioned, this predicament generates also a number of other significant symbolic responses, detectable in the literature of the period. One is the symbolic unification of the subject through the transgression of the opposition between the individual and the collective. This reso lution is sought by Lukács and Benjamin in the theoretical realm, while Brecht, Döblin, Tucholsky, and others envision it in their literary works. Another solution is the revival of the country as an alternative to the alienating city. Many of Musil's contemporaries sought to escape from the conditions of urban modernity, pursuing a place where the division between inwardness and world could be healed, and at the end of the journey they were likely to end up either in the rural community of the old or in the stylized nature of Jugendstil.

Musil does not belong in any of these groups. His brilliant satire targets the regressive yearning for *Heimaterde,* as well as art nouveau's strained effort to reinvest urban architecture with organic natural forms.²³ Nor is the collective ever posed as a solution in Musil's narrative. Like urban space itself, the uniformity of the masses is a container that immobilizes the subject. This is especially true of the fascist and nationalist collective, whose hierarchic discipline, in Musil's view, is second only to death: "The popular spirit [*Volksgeist*] of the true-born people is like that of a beehive state" (*T* 1:958).

Since Musil's narrator rejects these possibilities, the representation of the reification of the subject's exterior being gradually transforms *The Man Without Qualities* into a drama about self-preservation. Indeed, what is at stake in Ulrich's decision to take a year off from life is nothing short of rescuing his individuality (*die Rettung der Eigenheit*) (*MWQ* 44 / *MoE* 47). Describing this attempt to salvage autonomy and authenticity, the narrator falls back on the model that constitutes subjectivity in terms of inside and outside. And since the outside is hopelessly reified, the nucleus of authentic subjectivity is constituted as an inwardness that, strange as it may sound, can have no corresponding outside. It cannot even be embodied, because the body, formerly the organic link between inside and outside, behaves according to a logic all its own. Ulrich is not at home inside his own skin; the "surface and depths of his person [are] not one and the same" (*MWQ* 309 / *MoE* 286).

What kind of sensitive substance lies concealed in Ulrich's interior depths? The first time the novel addresses this problem, the narrator again stages the problem in terms of architectural space. Thus the narrator tells us why Ulrich so extravagantly chose a palace instead of leasing a more modest dwelling. In explaining this choice, the novel's vocabulary lacks its usual playfulness. Obviously, the narrator finds it necessary to underscore this: Ulrich quite simply detests, even loathes [*verabscheut*], normal apartments. Why is the Musilian self unable to fit in normal apartments? Ulrich's intérieur is a peculiar one, indeed.

Subjectivity and Interior Space

The same fate that the Musilian subject encounters as it explores urban space, searching in vain for the social and spatial forms that would answer its call for meaning, befalls the subject as it searches for this meaning inside. Each time it attempts to express its innermost being, it stumbles on clichés, stereotypes, inherited or prefabricated conventions for speaking about psychic essences, and finally loses itself in an interior landscape of petrified mental objects: "das Seinesgleichen," the molds of earlier generations, ready-made languages to speak with, but also for sensations and emotions (*MWQ* 135 / *MoE* 129). "We no longer have any inner voices," one character complains (*MWQ* 112 / *MoE* 109). This situation is further clarified in a conversation between Ulrich and General Stumm von Bordwehr:

> For when is a feeling really natural and simple? When it can be automatically expected to manifest itself in everybody, given the same circumstances . . . , and if you escape from this drab of repetitiveness into the darkest recesses of your being, where the uncontrolled impulses live, those sticky animal depths that save us from evaporating under the glare of reason, what do you find? Stimuli and strings of reflexes, entrenched habits and skills, reiteration, fixation, imprints, series, monotony! (*MWQ* 410 / *MoE* 378)

In other words, there is no substance, no identity, behind what we call the "I," the self, the ego, the individual, or the subject. There is just a flow of general, impersonal elements. Not only the external world but also the processes of the mind come across as coincidental combinations of foreign elements. What happens inside a person, the narrator enlightens us, is just a collision of "something impersonal" (*MWQ* 116 / *MoE* 112). This idea is related to the philosophy of Ernst Mach, on which Musil wrote his doctoral dissertation in philosophy in 1908.[24] Mach replaced the idea of causality by an idea of functionalism. The "I," he argued, is not dependent on a causal relationship between a substance, or a set of permanent dispositions, and its effects or manifestations. Rather, it is a force field where several nonpersonal elements (earlier positivists would have said "sensations") are temporarily co-ordinated and crystallized, and then once again dissolved. Mach's "I" thus becomes what Otto Weininger ironically called a waiting room for sensations.[25] The idea that the subject-ego is a substance is replaced by the idea that the subject is a changing series of functional responses to its environment. Indeed, Musil's satire always targets characters who, trying to bypass such scientific findings, affirm the substantial reality of soul and authentic feeling. Those are the followers of the fanatic romantic attitude that Kant once termed *Schwärmerei* and that had a strong revival in Musil's period.

The most sorry of these figures is Walter. He and Ulrich were inseparable in their youth, their thoughts and ambitions identical. In the story's present, however, they have developed into opposites. While Ulrich, the mathematician, defends the intellect that pursues order, Walter, the artist, believes in the artistic vocation and places his future in the hands of inspiration. But once Walter finally has cleared his life from everyday worries and can devote himself to his inner voice, this voice is no longer there: "Now that there was no longer anything left to be overcome, the unexpected happened: the works promised for so long by the greatness of his mind failed to materialize. Walter seemed no longer able to work" (*MWQ* 49 / *MoE* 52). Pure inspiration ends up being an illusion; still, the lack of inspiration paralyzes Walter and only aggravates his longing for strong expressions. He therefore refuels his self with the spiritual intensities of Wagner, whose music he previously had dismissed as "the epitome of a philistine, bombastic, degenerate era," but with which he now willingly intoxicates himself (*MWQ* 50 / *MoE* 52). In the portrait of Walter, Musil dismisses aesthetic strategies from Jugendstil and Lebensphilosophie to expressionism. The example of Walter demonstrates how the celebrated inwardness of young Vienna degenerates into a storehouse for the same stock of cultural commodities that are consumed by masses of people who thereby believe themselves to be expressing their "personality." Interiority is thus also a realm of reification. It, too, leads to a dissolution of individuality. If the representation of Walter's condition is a satire of this predicament, the representation of Ulrich deals with the same predicament in an analytical register. We find the most striking instances of this in the episodes when Ulrich is pondering the intérieur of his palace.

Dispersed throughout *The Man Without Qualities* are miniature essays dealing not only with architecture but also with interior decoration.[26]

The interior of Ulrich's father's house is described as an expression of an enlightened reaction against the heavy decorations and superfluous ornaments of the baroque (*MWQ* 779f. / *MoE* 717f.). The exuberant rococo façade and elegantly furnished rooms of Count Leinsdorf's residence are easily interpreted as allegorical images of an aristocracy whose cultural refinement enable it to retain its position at the center of the political arena (*MWQ* 91f. / *MoE* 90f.). Bearing traits of the seventeenth, eighteenth, and nineteenth centuries, the features of Ulrich's small château are more difficult to pinpoint: "the whole had something blurred about it, like a double-exposed photograph" (*MWQ* 6 / *MoE* 12). The interior, once completed, is equally bewildering: "All these circular lines, intersecting lines, straight lines, curves and wreaths of which a domestic interior is composed and that had piled up around him were neither nature nor inner necessity but bristled, to the last detail, with baroque overabundance" (*MWQ* 134 / *MoE* 128). In the older generation, the expressive correspondence between the house and its owner is still taken for granted. "The man who had lived here," Ulrich reflects about the home of his dead father, "had formed the egg of his life from the shell of [his forebears]" (*MWQ* 746 / *MoE* 687). In the case of Ulrich, however, there is no such relation between the self and its dwelling. "I've arranged everything so carelessly and wrong that it doesn't have anything at all to do with me," he tells Agathe upon her first visit to his home in Vienna (*MWQ* 970* / *MoE* 893).

When Ulrich first moved into this house he was still resolved to furnish it so as to make it appear as an "extension of his personality" (*MWQ* 15 / *MoE* 20). But although he spent hours of introspection, he found no personal substance whatsoever to assist him in the selection of wallpapers. Trying to find the right way of manifesting his self in his rooms, he encounters endless possibilities generating new prospects in an ever expanding play of ideas spreading out in all directions. A space corresponding to this oscillating psyche would have to be furnished with "revolving rooms, kaleidoscopic interiors, adjustable scenery for the soul." As the narrator fills in, "his ideas grew steadily more devoid of content" (*MWQ* 15 / *MoE* 20). Finally, Ulrich lets his servants and professional interior decorators decide for him.

5 Modernist interior, 1930s. A space constructed for the shapeless human being of the twentieth century. Living room with adjacent gym designed by Walter Gropius, 1930. Bauhaus-Archiv, Berlin.

I have already quoted Ulrich's contention on these matters: social and personal relations are no longer firm enough for houses (*MWQ* 971 / *MoE* 895). Echoing Musil's essay on doors, the protagonist goes on to state that people once used to show who they were by the number of their rooms, servants, and guests. But nowadays, he asserts, young people "either prefer stark simplicity, which is like a bare stage, or else they dream of wardrobe trunks and bobsled championships, tennis cups and luxury hotels along great highways, with golf course scenery and music on tap in every room" (*MWQ* 971f. / *MoE* 895).

Apparently, the modern zeitgeist can only be expressed through formlessness; yet a life without forms, whether architectural, linguistic, or artistic, is of course inconceivable. The remaining option for Ulrich is that of mixtures and assemblages—a world made up by a collection of fragments, the sheer heterogeneity of which would be the only external manifestation corresponding to internal formlessness. None of these forms, taken separately, would have an expressive relation to the self, but together they would represent a psyche in accordance with Mach's model, a changing nexus of impersonal elements. Yet these forms would still be meaningful. After all, the people hired to furnish Ulrich's home do not go about their task blindfolded. Their work is carefully calculated to fit Ulrich's taste, lifestyle, and social position. Previously, the individual could supposedly decide matters of interior decoration by introspection, letting his home grow from the inside out. If the substance of the subject now is replaced by a functional combination of sensations, the expressive relationship between inside and outside must, accordingly, be replaced by laws of probability that establish different dispositions of taste as functions of differing social and economic parameters. Professional decorators know the average taste and the margin of error governing purchases of carpets and tables. In order to find out how to furnish Ulrich's home properly, they just need to determine Ulrich's position on the social ladder and then apply a preestablished formula. This implies that the meaning of objects and space no longer has its source in the depths of the human psyche, but rather in a statistical average. It also applies to human life in general: "What we still refer to as a personal destiny is being displaced by processes that are grasped collectively and finally also statistically," Ulrich asserts (*MWQ* 785* / *MoE* 722).

   In all these instances we are witnessing the literal and figurative collapse of the protective walls that allowed the subject to maintain at least the illusion of an authentic expressive attitude toward its existence. The intérieur in which it laboriously constructed the image of its own inviolable identity can no longer withstand the forces of the outside. Consequently, subjective inwardness cannot be sustained as a sphere of existence qualitatively different from the social. Internal and external dimensions of reality finally demonstrate the same fundamental mark of reification.

Beyond Reification

But as the process of reification subverts psychic inwardness and shatters the secluded sphere of the intérieur, reification appears to lose its utility as a concept describing the relation between subjectivity and social processes. Most theories of reification presuppose that there is a stable point of reference, a subject with an enduring identity, which can be used to measure reification. If this identity, too, is set in motion and drawn into the contingent flux of modernity, where then is the norm or yardstick that enables us to register the stages in the process of reification? In the final analysis, it seems as though any theory of reification that is inferred from a theory of human experience itself presupposes an expressivist conception of subjectivity. It cannot function if it is not able to envision a nonreified experience, unaffected by instrumental reason, exchange value, and commodification, which allows the subject to recognize the external world and its identity as authentic expressions of its own desire and activity.[27] When Musil analyzes the dissolution of the personal into the impersonal, he suggests that the sphere of experiential inwardness is undermined and consumed by rationalization. The alienation of subject and object, which in our context translates into the fundamental contradiction between individuality and social totality, or between inwardness and exteriority, finally becomes so strained that the contradiction breaks down and gives way to some as yet unknown relationship between subjectivity and being, which cannot be represented within the expressivist paradigm.[28] If this, then, is the point at which the Musilian subject negates the expressivist paradigm, it is also the point at which it oversteps the conceptual limits of Lukács's theory of reification, which I used in the previous chapter to sketch out the historical determinants of that paradigm.[29]

The Double as an Image of the Subject's Otherness

Where does this leave Musil's narrator, having rejected all false attempts to rescue a centered self living in expressive unity with the world? Moosbrugger, the insane murderer posted at the obscure center of this novel, hints at an answer. As a character, Moosbrugger embodies those alterations in the structure of subjectivity that the narrative entrusts Ulrich to analyze and respond to. Indeed, Moosbrugger signals the end of character, an extreme example of a person who is no longer one, the opposite of order, stability, unity, coherence, and reliability. He incarnates all the impulses that society believes it must control and suppress. At the same time Moosbrugger is first and foremost a product of the same society: "If mankind could dream as a whole, that dream would be Moosbrugger" (*MWQ* 77 / *MoE* 76).

In the case of Moosbrugger, the absence of relations between self and its manifestations has reached a pathological level. He is unable to establish any identity, because, among other things, he is incapable of arranging his experiences in temporal sequence. Furthermore, agency is in his case transferred from the self to the outside world. Moosbrugger is literally a function of impersonal forces, which causes an endless debate in the judiciary corps as to whether he can be held accountable for his crimes. A hasty diagnosis of his condition is likely to indicate that he suffers from psychosis. Though this mental disorder cannot be discussed here, it should be emphasized that the psychotic individual is what R. D. Laing has named a "divided self." An internal world of fantasies and hallucinations has replaced his or her sense of reality.[30]

Moosbrugger is incapable of distinguishing between mind and external reality: "It is not at all important whether something is inside or outside; in his condition, it was like clear water on both sides of a transparent sheet of glass" (*MWQ* 258 / *MoE* 239). The psychotic person hallucinates, perceiving the signifiers of his mind as though they were things in the external world. Moosbrugger suffers from fits of hearing "voices or music or a wind, or a blowing and humming, a whizzing and rattling, or shots, thunder, laughing, shouts, speaking, or whispering. It came at him from every direction; the sounds were in the walls, in the air, in his clothes, in his body" (*MWQ* 257 / *MoE* 239).

The connection between Moosbrugger and Ulrich is underlined especially in the novel's first part. In both characters, the distinction between inside and outside is questioned. Little wonder, then, that Moosbrugger, as an incarnation of evil, irresistibly attracts Ulrich's attention. "Moosbrugger seized him like an obscure poem in which everything is slightly distorted and displaced, and reveals a drifting meaning fragmented in the depths of the mind" (*MWQ* 126 / *MoE* 121). These words testify to a strange affinity. In fact, they signify a final exhaustion of the phenomenological notion of the embodied "I" as the source of meaning. For in this case, the "drifting meaning" in the depths of Ulrich's mind quite literally emanates from another subject, Moosbrugger. The totalizing process of individuation thus gives way to an opposite mode of identity construction. The most obvious literary expression of this mode is of course the story about the double.[31] Adalbert von Chamisso and H. C. Andersen, the authors who first contemplated such a character, attempted to solve the dilemma of the divided subject in novellas about a hero strangely haunted by his shadow. But while their characters still remain intact and potentially unitary (if nothing else, the man who has sold his shadow can always buy it back), Robert Louis Stevenson, Hermann Hesse, and others manage the dilemma, now aggravated, through a character who, curiously, is two. The daytime "I" adjusts to rigid bourgeois life. After twilight, Hesse's Steppenwolf resurfaces in the city and lives out all the possibilities that the daytime subject must repress. With Brecht's *Die sieben Todsünden der Kleinbürger* (1933; *The Seven Deadly Sins*) this doubling of the subject is complete. The halves of the schizoid person here materialize in two sisters bearing the same name, Anna and Anna; since the narcissistic projection is as real as the projecting subject, it is impossible to distinguish who is the double of the other. Instead of inviting a psychological reading of the double, Brecht's text suggests the economic determinants of the split subject. As in Lukács's analysis, Brecht's divided subject is caused by an economic dynamic in which the individual can survive only if he or she ensures that emotions never interfere with instrumental reason. In order to gain a living, Anna must split herself in two, and she introduces her two personas as "one heart and one cheque book" (*ein Herz und ein Sparkassenbuch*).[32] As Musil's narrator remarks, "Every man is two people" (*MWQ* 466 / *MoE* 429).

This generic background clarifies the enigmatic position of Moosbrugger in *The Man Without Qualities*. He is one of Ulrich's two principal alter egos, whose presence enables a transient resolution of the dilemma of the modern subject. The attraction Moosbrugger exerts on Ulrich—who, the narrator states, always felt like a visitor among reasonable people—prevents the latter from becoming fixed in das Seinesgleichen[33] (*MoE* 1751). At the same time, however, this attraction constantly threatens to project the narrative into a supernatural or melodramatic realm where doubles actually exist and paranormal events upset everyday life. Since such a narrative development would bring the novel's historical and political references to nothing, the theme of the double must be checked by the narrator's reality principle: " 'Thrill-seeking!' [Ulrich] pulled himself up short. To be fascinated with the gruesome or the taboo, in the admissible form of dreams and neuroses, seemed quite in character for the people of the bourgeois age. 'Either/ or!' he thought. 'Either I like you [i.e., Moosbrugger] or I don't. Either I defend you, freakishness and all, or I ought to punch myself in the jaw for playing around with this monstrosity' " (*MWQ* 126 / *MoE* 121). Thinking that Moosbrugger is too crazy and dangerous to identify with, Ulrich must accept that the criminal is locked up, sentenced, and finally executed.

It is not until the emergence of his other alter ego, Agathe, that the theme of the double assumes its right proportions and turns the whole story around while indicating a radical reconceptualization of subjectivity. Agathe, to be sure, retains traits of the feminized image of the expressive totality that awaits the male hero at the end of his successful individuation. Still, as I will argue in chapter 5, her function exceeds this limited role. Neither the organic nature awaiting the male hero weary of an alienating civilization nor a reliable source of recognition for the male gaze, Agathe is rather a principle of what I will call negativity, which implies a process in which subjectivity is constituted not as in the expressivist paradigm, through the maturation of an identity, but, on the contrary, through the negation of all identities.

The Collapse of the Expressivist Paradigm

According to the expressivist paradigm, social roles develop as natural externalizations of qualities slumbering inside the self, which are realized under the surveillance of a benevolent environment. In this view, the formation of a stable identity is the result of a dialectic where interiority and exteriority confirm and legitimize each other. As I have shown, in Ulrich's case there is no inside that can be expressed by the outside, and there is no outside that manifests the inside. Toward the end of the novel, Ulrich concludes that the issue as to "what in an emotion is internal and what is external, and what in it is 'I' and what in it is the world, practically loses its meaning" (*MWQ* 1264* / *MoE* 1161). But apart from the suggested thematics of the double, there is no model that can replace the expressivist one either, and the latter hence continues to reinscribe subjectivity as though it consisted of an inwardness realizing itself in the external world. In the culminating events of chapter 120 in the middle of the novel, at the transition between its two parts, this spatial framework collapses. The insufficiency of the spatial metaphors of inwardness and outwardness as regards the representation and containment of the subject of modernity is exposed in a moment of hallucinatory clarity. Ulrich is standing by a window, looking at the demonstrators marching in the street outside Count Leinsdorf's house, and what he experiences is so remarkable that it deserves to be quoted at some length:

> With his eyes still moving from the threatening open-mouthed faces to the high-spirited ones farther back, and his mind refusing to absorb any more of this spectacle, he was undergoing a strange transformation. "I can't go on with this life, and I can't keep rebelling against it any longer, either!" was what he felt; but he also felt, behind him, the room with the large paintings on the wall, the long Empire desk, the stiff perpendicular lines of draperies and bell ropes. And this now seemed like a small stage, with him standing up front on the apron, outside of which the events of the larger stage were passing by, and both these stages had their own

peculiar way of fusing into one without regard for the fact that he was standing between them. Then his sense of the room, which he knew he had behind his back, contracted and turned inside out, flowing through him or around him like something that was very soft. "A strange spatial inversion!" Ulrich thought. The people passed by behind him, he had gone through them and beyond them and reached a Nothingness; perhaps they passed by both before him and behind him, and he would be washed over by them like a rock is washed over by the same but everchanging ripples of a stream. It was an experience half beyond understanding, and what struck Ulrich in particular was the glassiness, emptiness and tranquility of the state in which he found himself. "Is it possible, then, to get out of one's space and into a second, hidden one?" he thought, because he was feeling just as though chance had led him through a secret connecting door. (*MWQ* 688f.* / *MoE* 631f.)

The references to interior and exterior here first appear to be of the usual kind.[34] Ulrich stands in an apartment looking out on the world through a window. Yet, as it turns out, interiority and exteriority are dislocated. The space of the subject is no longer an inwardness from which it observes or acts in outward directions. Rather, subjectivity situates itself outside. But outside of what? The world literally invades the stage where Ulrich's consciousness used to perform in splendid solitude. The crowd takes control of the position from which the subject exerted its mastery. Attempting to account for Ulrich's experience in the spatial terms of an inside manifesting itself in an outside, the narrative ends up virtually deconstructing itself. In the quoted passage, the expressivist paradigm is still active on the surface level of the narrative discourse. It is present in the inherited ideas about the human subject that saturate the linguistic material that Musil cannot not use. At the same time, this paradigm no longer conforms to the experience of urban modernity that the discourse and the linguistic material in question are supposed to convey. Evidently, Ulrich's experience does not fit the model of the intérieur vis-à-vis the social sphere. Having no alternative model at his disposal, however, the narrator must, as it were, compensate for this lack by introducing a swarm of metaphors, thus attempting to represent a mode of subjectivity that resists all available conventions of representation. In this respect, Musil's novel induces the same effect as Fredric Jameson attributes to Edvard Munch's painting *The Scream:* "It disconnects its own aesthetic of expression, all the while remaining imprisoned within it." [35]

What is finally left of the subject is just this empty, spatial marker: the door, a secret passage supposedly leading to some new kind of subjectivity. Where to? It cannot lead to the outside. That would take the subject back to the alienating city or away to a regressive rural arcadia. Nor can it lead inward to an authentic self. In Musil's novel, there is no such substance as the self.

Indeed, we have seen that this spatial model is linked to an expressivist paradigm that cannot account for Ulrich's subjectivity in other than negative terms. But we have also seen that this paradigm nonetheless is indispensable if the narrator is to be able to discuss subjectivity in the first place. Musil's response can only be to represent subjectivity through a negation of this paradigm which nevertheless remains part of that very same paradigm. There is neither inside nor outside any longer. There is just, well, a door, that is, an in-between. No longer a *Dasein,* subjectivity becomes a mere *Dazwischen.* But isn't this solution exactly the one that was ruled out from the very beginning? Or are doors after all not as outdated as Musil made us think? Some years before Musil begun his novel, Lukács stated that every novel leads to a great door — through which there is no passage.[36]

Modernist Mysticism

In the second part of *The Man Without Qualities,* entitled "Into the Millennium," the position of a subject that is located dazwischen, in between, is projected into a new, utopian reality. I am referring to the phenomenon that Musil termed *der andere Zustand,* "the other condition." Throughout Ulrich and Agathe's intricate discussions at the beginning of the second part of the novel they approach an existential experiment guided by the promise of "the Millennium" in which this "other condition" would be realized. Musil's narrator frequently conjures up this state of being as an Arcadia of presence and love. The other condition has commonly been interpreted as a dialectical sublation of Ulrich's alienation, elevating him toward a state of being where an intensified experience of wholeness replaces reification.[37] In such a view, this condition appears as the last and most exclusive idea in a series of projects—the utopia of exact living, the utopia of essayism, the General Secretariat for Precision and Soul—through which Ulrich imagines an "ideology" that would reinstate the subject in a harmonious relationship with the universe. The other condition apparently promises the subject an expressive relationship to the world. The essence of the individual would again correspond to external reality.

Yet such a conception cannot explain why Musil's narrator never describes the other condition in terms of the individual's expressive relation to reality. On the contrary, the other condition is characterized by the dilution or even dissolution of the subject's identity. If we attend to the spatial metaphors used by the narrator to describe the experience of the other condition, it is evident that this is a state of being where the subject relinquishes its essence, its individuality, in order to become a tiny nucleus of consciousness and energy in a field of social and historical forces. For just as in the passage quoted above, the subject experiencing the other condition possesses neither exteriority nor interiority. The subject does not stand outside the object of its perception; but it is also not positioned inside the world that it perceives. Like Ulrich's experience of the urban scene with the crowd, the other condition is without exception rendered as a liminal condition; the subject embraces a reality by which it is simultaneously embraced.

Ulrich at one point reflects upon the fact that there are two kinds of concepts and experiences—"one based on a sense of being enveloped by the content of one's experiences, the other on one's enveloping them." Since this opposition between two experiential attitudes occurs in such a variety of conceptual forms and linguistic tropes—"a 'being on the inside' and 'looking at something from the outside', a feeling of 'concavity' and 'convexity', a 'being of spatiality' as well as a 'being of corporeality', an 'introspection' [*Einsicht*] and an 'observation' [*Anschauung*]" — Ulrich concludes that "one might assume a primal dual form of human consciousness behind it all" (*MWQ* 747f.' / *MoE* 688). The other condition can be defined as that attitude which strikes a balance between these two opposite ways of relating to the world. Agathe's experience of this harmony is described as "that miraculous feeling of the lifting of all bounds, the boundlessness of the outer and inner that love and mysticism have in common" (*MWQ* 830 / *MoE* 765).

If, then, the other condition can be described in terms of expressivity, we must add a proviso: what is at issue is a preindividualistic notion of expressivity. In the other condition, the human subject, the surrounding world, and the categories of time and space themselves appear as emanations or expressions of a boundless cosmic reality, or they are indeed dedeveloped, folded back into that originary stage preceding the creation of the world when earth and sky, animals and humans, men and women, did not yet exist as separate beings. In order to identify this hidden reality, Musil commonly falls back upon more time-honored designations, such as love and mysticism, both of which are characterized by "this vague trembling of the borderline" (*MWQ* 831 / *MoE* 765). Musil's narrator and hero thus evolve nothing less than a cosmogony, a story about the creation of the world and the originary condition of the human species, according to which modern men and women are led astray from their true, ontological homeland. This homeland, the other condition, is sometimes rendered as a state of mysticism. Furthermore, Musil asserts its proximity to religious or aesthetic experience. It is also described with reference to the Platonic myth of a hermaphroditic stage in which the sexes were not yet separated into opposing genders, and where man and woman thus were but two equally possible incarnations of the hidden "dual sexuality of the soul" (*MWQ* 983 / *MoE* 906). This fantasy of a nonalienated origin is then associated with childhood as well, for in one's early years, Ulrich admits, "there was hardly any separation between inside and outside" (*MWQ* 979 / *MoE* 902). In this way Musil uses religion, mythology, and childhood memories to elucidate the other condition: the state of being in between different identities, rather than inside or outside them, the feeling of how the self is dispersed into the world and the ego emptied of agency. Such is the *Urphantasie* constantly actualized by Ulrich and Agathe as they attempt to transform it into a permanent condition of living.

My suggestion that the Musilian subject represents a subjectivity of "in-betweenness" removes some false problems that have prevented readers from understanding this intensely debated topic in Musil's novel. The other condition should be seen as a projection of Musil's wish to formulate an alternative definition of subjectivity, one that is able to come to terms with a historical predicament in which the expressivist paradigm of the subject has lost its raison d'être. In order to justify his new notion of subjectivity, and in order to ground it philosophically, Musil situates it in the timeless sphere of myth, religion, and mysticism, seeing it as a link to the authentic origins of mankind.[38] My analysis of the tension between the Musilian subject and urban space points in a different direction, however. For whenever Musil's narrator ventures to actually represent, rather than simply justify or judge, the experience of this blessed existential state, what is represented is always the experience of modernity as such.[39] In fact, when Ulrich and Agathe discuss the other condition, the primary example they keep repeating is Ulrich's experience of the city. However unexpected and paradoxical it may seem, the *Urerlebnis* of the Musilian subject, its originary experience of the mystery of life, is firmly anchored in a historically specific experience of urban space. Consider, for instance, the following passage from the beginning of the second part of the novel. Having been notified about his father's death, Ulrich has left Vienna and has just arrived in his childhood town B., where he will soon meet Agathe. The experience rendered by the passage contains the very model of the other condition, as it is then repeated throughout the novel:

> For whenever his travels took him to cities to which he was not connected
> by business of any kind, he particularly enjoyed the feeling of solitude
> this gave him, and he had rarely felt this so keenly as he did now. He
> noticed the colors of the streetcars, the automobiles, shop windows, and
> archways, the shapes of church towers, the faces and the façades. . . . Such

aimless, purposeless strolling through a town vitally absorbed in itself, the keenness of perception increasing in proportion as the strangeness of the surroundings intensifies, heightened still further by the connection that it is not oneself that matters but only this mass of faces, these movements wrenched loose from the body to become armies of arms, legs, or teeth, to all of which the future belongs—all this can evoke the feeling that being a whole and inviolate strolling human being is positively antisocial and criminal. But if one lets oneself go even further in this fashion, this feeling may also unexpectedly produce a physical well-being and irresponsibility amounting to folly, as if the body were no longer part of a world where the sensual self is enclosed in strands of nerves and blood vessels but belongs to a world bathed in somnolent sweetness. These were the words that Ulrich used to describe to his sister what might perhaps have been the result of a state of mind without goal or ambition, or the result of a diminished ability to maintain an illusory individuality, or perhaps nothing more than that "primal myth of the gods," that "double face of nature," that "giving" and "taking vision," which he was after all pursuing like a hunter. (*MWQ* 785f. / *MoE* 723)

In this passage, the startling yet sweet experience of a city is reduced to "nothing more" than an illustration of the "primal myth of the gods." But if my analysis of the ideology and topology of Musilian subjectivity is relevant, we must now shift the priorities of the argument. The primal myth of the gods, painstakingly explicated by both Musil and his commentators, would then come across as "nothing more" than an illustration of a specific experience of the emerging space of the modern metropolis, of its peculiar rhythms of life, its shocks and sensations, its multiple social roles and identities, of crowds and traffic, of an otherness constantly overflowing the ego. Instead of regarding Musil's analysis of the subject as a search for the primal essence of humanity, we should see it as a product of that specific experience of modernity which was first formulated by Baudelaire: "The pleasure of being in a crowd is a mysterious expression of sensual joy in the multiplication of number." [40] The French poet established that affinity between religious exaltation and modern experience that we have observed in Musil's work: "Religious intoxication of great cities. Pantheism. I am all things. All things are myself. Whirlwind." [41]

Musil registers a similar pantheism: "The style of the big city is lyric —it alludes only in order to let disappear again into the unknown, like many excellent stylists" (*T* 1:76). Crucially, the metropolitan style that Musil evokes here in his journal is what literary historians call Viennese impressionism, thus referring to the style cultivated by Peter Altenberg and Arthur Schnitzler, for example. As early as 1904, the perceptive Viennese critic Hermann Bahr linked this style to Ernst Mach's theory, calling the latter a "philosophy of impressionism." [42] Just as impressionist writing posited the truth of life in the flux of sensations generated by the big city, so did Mach's philosophy dissolve the "I" into an ever-changing stream of sense data and emotions. One reason why Musil and his contemporaries were drawn to Mach's psychology and to its prospect of emptying the self into a quasi-mystical totality, was that Mach confirmed an experience to which they were already habituated and which they already performed in stories and feuilletons: the religious intoxication of the metropolis. Explaining the social conditions of impressionism, Arnold Hauser observes that it is an urban style, which "describes the changeability, the nervous rhythm, the sudden, sharp but always ephemeral impressions of city life." Precisely because of this, Hauser adds, impressionism entails "an enormous expansion of sensual perception, a new sharpening of sensibility, a new irritability." [43]

What this implicates, then, is that we must relocate the source of the utopian energies that in Musil's view promised a transfiguration of human society. Contrary to what most commentators have taken for granted, this source is not situated in some dim prehistory of humankind, nor in the models codified by religion and mysticism. Rather, *The Man Without Qualities* places this utopian source in the as yet unrealized possibilities of the present moment of modernity. Indeed, as I will argue in chapter 6, the experience of the other condition is enabled not only by the exhilarating pulse and sensory shocks of the metropolis, but above all by the collective intoxication and pseudoreligious frenzy that took place at the outbreak of World War I, that ultimate event which is the absent center of the novel. *The Man Without Qualities* is characterized by incompletion and indeterminacy, to be sure. But there is one conviction that is never questioned: in order to actualize the utopian potentialities of humanity, one must examine *all* aspects of modernity, from the extremes of violent regression to the opposite extremes of art and science, so as to identify the progressive elements that can serve, like reinforced concrete, in the construction of a new society.

A Story with Many Ends

Narratological Observations

Musil's hero enacts an existential attitude and an ethical program. In the previous chapter I analyzed Ulrich in this role. I treated him as a human-like figure and explained how he responds to the rationalized life world of urban modernity. But Ulrich is also a lens, a perspective, and a point of view. He is not only part of the subject matter but also the cognitive and narrative instrument through which the reader accesses the world of the story. That Ulrich is such a dodging figure is because he occupies a dual position, both the human-like character and the frame within which the other characters are portrayed.

The Musilian subject must consequently be interpreted on several levels. In order to find out what the novel says, we must learn how it works. In this chapter I will examine how the narrative form generates a temporal and spatial experience, from which we may deduce a certain structure of subjectivity. In brief, I want to analyze the subject as an effect of narrative production. My focus will be on the first nineteen chapters of the novel, which constitute the section called "A Sort of Introduction," because it is here that Musil's narrator establishes the laws of time and space that govern the novelistic representation as a whole.

Expressive Realism and Beyond

Every reader senses that *The Man Without Qualities* does not conform to the mimetic representations that can be found in, for instance, nineteenth-century realist novels. Also, it deviates from Musil's early prose, the novel *Die Verwirrungen des Zöglings Törless* (1906; *The Confusions of Young Törless*) and the two novellas *Die Vollendung der Liebe* (*The Completion of Love*) and *Die Versuchung der stillen Veronika* (*The Temptation of Quiet Veronica*) that he published in 1911 under the title *Vereinigungen* (*Unions*), in which a mimetic rendering of the external world is punctuated by astounding sections of psychological narration. Nothing in *The Man Without Qualities* can be trusted as true or real. The novel speaks in several voices, each contesting the others. The text operates with satire, irony, and self-irony. Undermining every reliable arrangement of events, it shakes the foundations of reality. Indeed, there is no privileged viewpoint from which to discern the causes of the subtle displacements that gradually transform the political and social sphere of Vienna, a sphere populated by people living among illusions and motivated by illusions, who move forward with the same slow sureness as Hermann Broch's sleepwalkers, until they stumble on the threshold of war.

A passage at the beginning of the novel describes this state of affairs: "Time was on the move. . . . But nobody knew where time was headed. And it was not always clear what was up or down, what was going forward or backward" (*MWQ* 7 / *MoE* 13). This passage is meant to capture a specific zeitgeist. It is a preliminary diagnosis of that "mysterious malady of the times," evoked a few chapters later, which lies at the core of the complications rendered by the plot. Yet, the passage also draws attention to a formal feature of the representation: this is a narrative that relativizes categories like *up* and *down, forward* and *backward, truth* and *falsity, good* and *bad.* The meaning of these categories comes to depend on what perspective the reader assumes.

True, the narrative structure of every novel integrates a multiplicity of perspectives, often linked to different characters, who serve as mouthpieces of different worldviews. Although these perspectives may be contradictory, they are in general balanced by the narrative structure as such, for they are all organized by a central voice and vision. In Catherine Belsey's words, there is a "hierarchy of discourses." The privileged discourse is normally that of the narrator, who has the power to arrange and evaluate the other discourses incorporated into the novel, typically by presenting them as thoughts or statements coming from the characters.[1] This structure, moreover, is modeled on a certain conception of reality and human character to which both the narrator and the reader must adhere if the mimetic illusion is to hold. As long as the narrator does not violate his poetic license, making sure he does not transgress the limits of an established conception of reality, his status as the omniscient, implicit author manipulating his fictitious figures is concealed behind the mimetic illusion itself, which now assumes a lifelike quality, and its characters start to address the reader as human beings of flesh and blood.[2]

The narrative form resulting from this ordering of various discourses and characters may be called "classical realism." According to Philippe Hamon, the realist text is characterized by a double tendency, driving the text in two directions at once.[3] First, the novel charts a social world with its specific topography, habits, conflicts, and symbolic systems. This is the horizontal tendency of the text, through which it establishes an inventory of a particular social sector. This tendency is strongly felt in *The Man Without Qualities*, which presents a broad panorama of Viennese life and thought.[4] But a novel cannot just keep adding material, characters, and events, or else it would become a formless encyclopedia. This is why there must also be a vertical tendency at work, one that organizes and interprets the surface of society, stabilizing its various manifestations by leading them back to a deeper law or structure. In order to realize this tendency, the narrative usually turns an object or a character into a representative of the social body as a whole. In this way, the object and character in the realist novel fulfill two functions. On the one hand, they are knots in a web of numberless other elements that make up the extensive totality of the world. On the other hand, they are signs indicating those deeper social structures, historical processes, or psychological laws that constitute the meaning of the represented totality.

The successful coordination of the two tendencies results, in Hamon's view, in a realist narrative. In such a narrative, each object and character is independent and self-sufficient, and at the same time an expression of a hidden totality, a symptom of a concealed infrastructure that gives meaning and stability to the ephemeral present moment of the story. Hamon's definition of realism confirms what I said about the bildungsroman in the first chapter. The bildungsroman demonstrates a convergence between the horizontal axis—the detailed account of the complicated and multifarious social world through which the characters move—and the vertical axis—which ascribes a historical and symbolic meaning, a specific "typicality," to certain characters and events. The realist novel turns the two axes into mirrors of one another. Joining forces, they construct a mimetic illusion that is as convincing as reality itself, and which, moreover, shows that this reality is meaningful.

What happens if the formal innovations of *The Man Without Qualities* are analyzed against the background of this model of realist expressivity? As we shall see, the novel does not coordinate the horizontal and the vertical tendencies. On the contrary, it brings them into contradiction. The process by which the realist novel turns the individual and the social into expressions of one other is inverted in *The Man Without Qualities;* indeed, subject and society negate each other.

The Impossible Art of Reporting the Weather

Musil's novel establishes a perplexing ambiguity already from the beginning. Although the first chapter has the title "From which, remarkably enough, nothing develops," it makes at least two things clear. First, it introduces us, in some awkward way, to the setting: Vienna, 1913. Second, and more important, it institutes a discrepancy between an authoritative representation purporting to convey objective knowledge and a narrative mode accounting for the perspective of the particular individual.[5] In the opening paragraph, there is first an extensive account of the meteorological situation over Europe: "A barometric low hung over the Atlantic. It moved eastward toward a high-pressure area over Russia without as yet showing any inclination to bypass this high in a northerly direction." Saturated by a terminology intelligible only to the specialist, this description expands over almost half a page. Suddenly, it is translated into ordinary language: "It was a fine day in August 1913" (*MWQ* 3 / *MoE* 9). The first register is scientific and seemingly objective; the other anthropocentric and invested with human emotion and intentionality, as indicated by the adjective "fine" (*schön*).

When the narrator juxtaposes the individual's ordinary experience of the weather with an enumeration of the countless climatological factors that make this experience possible, the result is, of course, a demonstration of the insufficient precision of the former. This feature is then amplified in the following chapter. A fairly precise description of the architectural style of Ulrich's palace is juxtaposed with the individual reaction to the same building ("Ah!"), thus highlighting the sheer banality of a subjective experience that cannot communicate the richness of reality.

As the first chapter unfolds, these two discursive registers generate two narrative modes running side by side. One is fixed to an impersonal perspective, scanning reality from above. The other accommodates the perspective of the individual character. The textual fabric constituted by these two narrative modes may easily be untied. By erasing the sentences generated by the opposite mode, we may transcribe chapter 1 in two versions. The first would look like this:

> A barometric low hung over the Atlantic. It moved eastward toward a high-pressure area over Russia without as yet showing any inclination to bypass this high in a northerly direction. . . . Automobiles shot out of deep, narrow streets into the shallows of bright squares. . . . Hundreds of noises wove themselves into a wiry texture of sound. . . . Like all big cities it was made up of irregularity, change, forward spurts, failures to keep step, collisions of objects and interests, punctuated by unfathomable silences; made up of pathways and untrodden ways, of one great rhythmic beat as well as the chronic discord and mutual displacement

of all its contending rhythms. . . . Something had spun around, falling sideways, and come to a skidding halt—a heavy truck, as it turned out, which had braked so sharply that it was now stranded with one wheel on the curb. . . . Now the siren of an approaching ambulance could be heard. . . . The victim was lifted onto a stretcher and both together were then slid into the ambulance. . . . People dispersed, almost with the justified impression that they had just witnessed something entirely lawful and orderly. (*MWQ* 3ff.* / *MoE* 9ff.)

If this is the view of an eye observing things from a great distance, a more pedestrian experience of the same reality generates a different story:

It was a fine day in August 1913 . . . in the Imperial and Royal City of Vienna. . . . The two people who were walking up one of its wide, bustling avenues . . . belonged to a privileged social class, which could be seen on their distinguished bearing, style of dress, and way of conversing with each other. . . . Their names might have been Ermelinda Tuzzi and Arnheim. . . . The pair now came to a sudden stop when they saw a rapidly gathering crowd in front of them. . . . The lady and her companion had also come close enough to see something of the victim over the heads and bowed backs. . . . "According to American statistics," the gentleman said, "one hundred ninety thousand people are killed every year by cars and four hundred fifty thousand are injured." "Do you think he's dead?" his companion asked, having still the unjustified feeling that she had experienced something unusual. (*MWQ* 3ff.* / *MoE* 9ff.)

The impersonal tone of the first version makes it sound like a news report communicating facts. The second conforms to the codes of the narrative discourse of the classical novel. The narrator could of course have constructed a narrative in which the two registers were inseparable, letting the whole give meaning to the part, and using the description of the part to enhance the understanding of the whole. But in *The Man Without Qualities* there is no such gradual rapprochement. The novel evinces the fractures between the two narrative modes. Passing from the panoramic survey of the city to the perspective of an individual within that city, the narrator makes a point of indicating all other similar and equally possible passages between general and particular. Thus we are told that it is a beautiful day in August 1913. Juxtaposed with the meteorological account, however, this piece of information also transmits the opposite message: it could have been any year. We are told that the city in question is Vienna. But the narrator states that the city's name is unimportant, for it could have been any city. And as soon as the pedestrians seem to have been identified ("Let us assume," the narrator suggests, "that they are called Arnheim and Ermelinda Tuzzi"), this identification is ruled out as an impossibility—"because in August Frau Tuzzi was still in Bad Aussee with her husband and Dr. Arnheim was still in Constantinople" (*MWQ* 4 / *MoE* 10). Therefore, the narrator continues, we are "left to wonder who they were." But of course, the names of these persons are enigmatic only insofar as they could be anybody. The point is that their names do not matter. They are ants in an anthill. What counts in this case study of street life is not any particular identity or personality but the description of a position that could belong to any person with any identity. The particular—be it a place, an individual, or an object—becomes an accidental instance of a general totality which is independent of its parts. Consequently, a narrative representation focalized through these parts conveys no knowledge about the whole which nonetheless determines them.

If this applies to the individual, the place, and the object, it also applies to the status of the event within the depicted social world. Just as the specific identities of the pedestrians add nothing to the whole, the accident they witness does not have any significance in itself. It is merely an example of normal life in the era of crowds and traffic—"something entirely lawful and orderly." Reducing the injured man to a statistical fact, the gentleman witnessing the accident is the mouthpiece of the objective and authoritative voice organizing most of the chapter. However, the lady accompanying him makes a contrary assessment of the same event, "having still the unjustified feeling that she had experienced something unusual." The narrator now steps in to evaluate these opposing ways of judging the event. To see it from the standpoint of the general, as "entirely lawful and orderly," is said to be justified (*berechtigt*). The feeling of having witnessed something unique, a feeling attributed to the woman, is, on the other hand, an "unjustified feeling." Comparing the experiential "feeling" (*Gefühl*) with the impersonal "impression" (*Eindruck*) of the same event, the narrative suggests that an adequate account of it rules out individual experience, which is rendered as a bizarre deviation or a too personal view.

Yet, in order to invalidate individual experience by proving its insignificance within a broader view of society, this experience must all the same be evoked as a narrative event in its own right. Thus, through the perspective of the woman, individual experience is at least momentarily affirmed. The tension inherent in the dual narrative mode organizing the text is thereby preserved. The two representations of that beautiful day in August 1913 remain disjunctive. Scientific objectivity and subjective experience are displayed as two incommensurable approaches to the world.

The conflict between *objective knowledge* and *experiential knowing* is a key theme in Musil's work. According to Musil, the natural sciences were ahead of other realms of thought, which did not operate with the same precision. However, Musil did not see the difference between the two as a distinction between rationality and irrationality. Rather, the difference was constituted by the fact that objective science, linking fact to fact and argument to argument, circumvents the self and excludes subjective factors. Objectivity is therefore necessarily abstract, Musil states in his essay "Helpless Europe" (1922). It sacrifices the inner aspects of objects: "*We exclude our ego, our self, from our thoughts and actions. Therein lies, of course, the essence of our objectivity; it connects things one with the other, and even where it sets us in relation to them, or, as in psychology, takes us as its very object, it does so in a way that excludes the personality*" (*PS* 131 / *GW* 2:1092).

The epistemological conflict in the first two chapters is thus not merely a collision between belief and knowledge, or delusion and reality. It is a confrontation between subjectivity and objectivity, as Musil defines it in the passage above. In the novel, the function of each of these epistemologies is to bring the opposing one into crisis by contradicting it. In his discussion of so-called *narrative moods,* Gérard Genette has indicated how conflicts of values and knowledge are articulated in literary texts. Just as verbs have grammatical moods, Genette argues, so is each narrative governed by a certain *mood,* which determines the "point of view from which the life or the action is looked at." [6] In contradistinction to the more general *mode,* a narrative mood thus designates a specific narratological device, which always entails a *perspective.* The tension we have observed in Musil's novel can hence be described as a result of a narrative that shifts between two narrative moods, each corresponding to a particular perspective on the world, one invested with feeling and interest, the other without such qualities.

Crucially, this entails another opposition, also at play in Musil's text. For the same abstraction that is carried out with respect to the perceiving subject can also be executed with regard to the object perceived. An object or an event can be seen either as a unique phenomenon characterized by its own irreducible essence, or as a relationally determined effect of the whole. On this level, the conflict between objective knowledge and experiential knowing becomes a conflict between perceiving an event or a person as a structurally determined fact or as an expression of essence.

In a narrative text, moreover, the issue of perceiving is of course transformed into a question of representing, or narrating. In fact, the first paragraphs of the novel constitute a subtle attempt to write a narrative of facticity, a story purged of experiential aspects. This narrative mood is juxtaposed with a subjective and perceptual mood according to which the world is vibrating with human intentions. The two narrative moods can be characterized by literally distinguishing the two perspectives involved. The first is a story told from the point of view of a cloud. The second is a story told from the point of view of a person experiencing the weather. The first evokes the countless circumstances contributing to a particular meteorological situation and suggests that the addition of new factors would have created a different situation, thus conveying an idea of other possible situations, which could just as well have been realized. The second tells how the subject responds to a situation that he or she must accept as a necessary reality.

Already in the first chapter, then, the narrative's horizontal tendency, enumerating the factors that affect a particular situation, is brought into conflict with its vertical tendency, accounting for the meaning of this situation. We no longer have two perspectives complementing each other and expressing a totality that encompasses both of them; we have two perspectives that are mutually exclusive.

On the Difference between an Accident and an Incident

The first two chapters of *The Man Without Qualities* suggest the presence of a solar eye looking down on the world. Having observed the meteorological situation over Europe, the narrator's perspective narrows. It settles over Vienna, fixes a particular street, and follows two persons walking toward the crowd gathered around the man who has been hit by a lorry. In chapter 2, the narrative trajectory moves further along the same street until it finally stops in front of "a sort of little château with short wings, a hunting lodge or rococo love nest of times past" (*MWQ* 6 / *MoE* 12). Scanning the exterior of this building, the ocular imagery of the narrative directs the reader toward a certain window of the house. Standing in the window, and now introduced for the first time, is the man without qualities.

It would seem as if the divine machinery, having launched the narrative and targeted the window, is dismantled as soon as the man in the window, Ulrich, appears and begins to act on his own. Strangely, however, Ulrich continues the same visual operation, as though the narrator had only cut to a new camera angle in his protocinematographic spectacle.[7] Like the solar eye observing Europe from above, Ulrich scientifically examines the vehicles and pedestrians in the street below, reflecting on the "antlike" character of the crowd. What catches his attention is the enormous amount of energy expended on trivial acts such as crossing the street or rushing to catch the trolley. Ulrich's interest is arrested not by any individual phenomenon but by the process as a whole. He perceives the world as a scientist collecting data. Imagining himself as part of the machinery, he then makes a discouraging summation: " 'No matter what you do,' the man without qualities thought with a shrug, 'within this mare's nest of forces at work, it doesn't make the slightest difference!' " (*MWQ* 7 / *MoE* 13). Here, too, as in chapter 1, individual agency is negligible when seen from the perspective of the observer who reduces individuality and particularity to statistical facts.

Yet, this conclusion, too, is challenged as the narrative switches to another mood or perspective. A few pages later it so happens that Ulrich is victimized by the same street life he previously surveyed with the cool gaze of the scientist. One night on his way home, he is knocked unconscious and robbed by three hooligans. This assault, which leaves Ulrich injured on the sidewalk, echoes the accident in chapter 1. The assault brings out the contradictory nature of Ulrich's attitude. In his role as a detached observer in chapter 2, he formulated a maxim: "No matter what you do, it doesn't make the slightest difference." Still, as soon as he walks out into the street, he must violate his own maxim, thus reasserting the importance of agency and individual experience. His actions are no longer indifferent. He must react on the actions of others, and he must, indeed, react in the "right" way, or else he may not get home without being robbed of his wallet. There are no intermediary stages between these attitudes in Musil's novel. In fact, the narrator emphasizes the discontinuity between them and implies that this generates two different stories. In chapter 1, a serious accident is reduced to a mere incident. In chapter 7, an incident—Ulrich's fight with the hooligans—is presented as a matter of life and death.

Meanwhile, we notice that the tension is transposed from form to content as the narrative moves from chapter 1 to the episodes involving Ulrich in chapters 2 and 7. In the first chapter, the tension occurs at the level of cognition and narrative modality. The event is represented as both negligible and exceptional, depending on whether the narrator uses the detached account of the scientist or the omniscient vision of the narrator of the classical novel. In chapters 2 and 7 the same tension reappears as Ulrich's ambivalent attitude toward his involvement in social affairs, or even as a choice between two ethical programs: stoic resignation or committed vocation. Thus what previously presented itself as two cognitive, perceptual, and narrative moods is now recorded as two ethical or even ontological moods, that is, as a conflict between two ways of *acting* and *being*. Crucially, Ulrich cannot be situated on either side of this tension. He embodies the struggle, is the container of opposing attitudes toward the world.

The presence of two conflicting narrative moods is hence linked to the presence of two conflicting ethical standards. On the one hand, the subject can be seen as the origin and source of meaning, knowledge, action, and history. In this view, social formations are constituted by free subjects expressing themselves and associating with others, gradually realizing an essence inherent in their human nature. On the other hand, the subject can be seen as a product of already existing social and cultural formations, as bound by tradition, habits and history. In this view, the subject becomes a replicable unit. My analysis in the previous chapter showed that Ulrich was left in suspension between these two notions of subjectivity. The expressivist notion that regards the subject as the inner source of meaning was just as unacceptable as the functionalist notion that defines it as a product of external pressures.

The Narration of Events

Some chapters later, Ulrich visits his old friends Walter and Clarisse, who are now introduced to the reader. Ulrich and Clarisse go for a stroll in the garden. They have barely begun talking when the scene suddenly is interrupted by a long retrospective section providing information about Walter's life. Serving as a summary of the past, this analepsis covers some three pages. It ends as abruptly as it started, and the reader awakens anew to the present moment of the story, realizing that the conversation between Ulrich and Clarisse still goes on; the narrator's swift move to another temporal level was just an interruption. In this way, a scene with a duration of no more than a few minutes envelops a narrative sequence representing many years.

As the chapter ends, the conversation seems concluded. In the following chapter, the narrator abandons Ulrich and Clarisse as well as the mimetic mode of representation, reflecting instead on the "cultural revolution" at the turn of the century. Then comes a chapter containing a similar reflection, now presented from Ulrich's point of view. The conversation between Ulrich and Clarisse seems firmly anchored in the story's past. But in the next chapter the reader is oddly enough transported back to the same evening. Again, we must conclude that everything told since we last saw Ulrich and Clarisse was an intermission in the story. Two chapters have passed, decades have elapsed, the cultural situation has been thoroughly analyzed, yet Ulrich and Clarisse still remain, exchanging thoughts, in the same corner of the garden. The present moment expands to enclose decades of action. To be sure, this is a general strategy of modernist narrative, masterly developed by Proust and Woolf, and perhaps most congenially expressed in Joyce's *Ulysses,* where twenty-four hours equal eternity.

Had the narrator adhered to the codes of the classical novel, he would perhaps have used the mimetic scene depicting Ulrich and Clarisse's dialogue as a narrative device to communicate the information that is now conveyed by his own voice. In Musil's novel, however, scenes of mimetic representations are rare. They mostly function as narrative relays leading from one discursive and diegetic section to another. But they also constitute brief periods of rest as they bring the narrative back to the story's present: they provide temporal and spatial coordinates that build the narrative's syntagmatic axis. Thus they help the reader retain the impression of a narrative progression and regain his or her orientation in the fictional universe.

The mimetic representation of dialogue is only one of a number of comparable narrative devices developed in the realist novel that *The Man Without Qualities* reappropriates for new purposes. The nineteen chapters in the introductory part rely on the entire tool kit of the old storyteller. Ancient and approved narrative conventions—codes designed to begin a story, to present a character, a scene, a setting, or an event—are picked up and rehearsed, only to be dropped, much in the same way as happens in chapter 14, where that otherwise privileged form of novelistic narration, the dialogue, in this case of Ulrich and Clarisse, is abandoned as soon as it is put to use.

We have already seen how a standard opening clause—"It was a fine day in August 1913"—is held up to ridicule when confronted with the narrator's amassing of meteorological data. The same fate befalls conventional phrases of similar kinds, presented only to be undermined: "The man without qualities whose story is being told here" (*MWQ* 13 / *MoE* 18); "When he set about putting his house in order, as the Bible has it" (*MWQ* 14 / *MoE* 19); "At the age when one still attaches great importance to everything connected with tailors and barbers" (*MWQ* 26 / *MoE* 31); "It turned out that Bonadea, too, yearned for great ideas" (*MWQ* 38 / *MoE* 41); "The Moosbrugger case was currently much in the news" (*MWQ* 67 / *MoE* 67); "So the time passed" (*MWQ* 77 / *MoE* 77). The satirical effects of Musil's narrative are to a large extent produced by the witty insertion of older narrative idioms, the obsoleteness of which is revealed when confronted with the realities of modern life.[8] *The Man Without Qualities* exhausts batallions of received ideas and literary paradigms that once gave meaning to human existence. Its use of conventional narrative codes to wrap a content or an argument for which these conventions are insufficient creates comic effects that produce a state of indeterminacy, in which various discursive registers collide and are undone.

The point is that the narrator can neither make do with these codes, nor do without them. They are inadequate for representing modern experience, and yet indispensable because they are the only ones at hand. One crucial aspect of their indispensability has already been mentioned. These codes constitute the text as a recognizable aesthetic artifact, continually checking and confirming the contract between reader and narrator. But they also establish a certain measure of internal coherence, without which the text would become a mosaic of fragments.

There are, to be sure, strong tendencies of fragmentation in *The Man Without Qualities*. In the first part of the novel there is no unfolding through time and no plot, but a constellation of narrative segments— biographical material, psychological analyses, political overviews, historical expositions, scenes from bourgeois life, a report of a criminal case, and a letter to Ulrich from his father—which all contribute their shares to the story. These pieces do not form an integrated whole. Yet together they construct something like a hero, a subject. It would be wrong to call this construction a montage, however. In modernist textual montages, plot disappears or goes underground. What is left on the manifest level is the other material of the narrative—segments of dialogue, disconnected pieces of traditional narrative paradigms, mimetic scenes where characters act and speak, ideas picked from the storehouses of cultural history—which the reader must recombine in conformity with a subtext that he or she must invent.[9]

In *The Man Without Qualities,* traditional plot is also disrupted. But this does not produce a plotless representation. The fragmented character of Musil's novel derives not from the fact that the story is hidden underground but from the fact that the story is continuously interrupted. Ernest Hemingway once said that his stories only showed the tip of an iceberg, nine-tenths of the action being situated under the surface. In Musil's novel, these nine-tenths erupt to the surface. What in the realist novel used to be a finite sequence of long mimetic scenes is in Musil transformed into a series of disconnected frames through which the narrator breaks in as he wishes, in order to supply an ongoing interpretation of characters, scenes, and events. It is not without reason that most critics have observed how *The Man Without Qualities* sways uneasily between a comedy of manners and a philosophical treatise, while the author himself admitted that he was not interested in specific facts and events. "What interests me is the culturally typical!" (*GW* 2:939). The narrated moments that construct the story are thus reduced to a subordinate role. They seem to emerge from a discursive magma consisting of an infinite narratorial commentary that constructs its own temporality and assumes any perspective.

This is how the repeated interruption of the conversation between Ulrich and Clarisse finally should be understood. Their conversation constitutes a segment of an unfolding story. But this story is just a grid, the squares of which are filled in by the narrator's commentary. In most novels, mimetic scenes constitute the greater part of the text. Individual and society are stitched together by a story that represents their continual interaction. In Musil, the real action takes place when interaction is postponed, during the intermissions, when the narrator is left to himself.

As we saw in the previous chapter, social reality in Musil's novel

equals the dull and repetitive realm of das Seinesgleichen. The point
of the narrator's constant interruptions of the story is precisely to defa-
miliarize this realm. The representation of society, which was the main
object of the realist novel, hence becomes Musil's pretext for entering
an underlying space of possibilities that are suppressed by das Seinesgleichen. It is in order to articulate these possibilities that the Musilian
narrator exposes the vacuity of the narrative frames that make the story
of the realist novel cohere.[10] This is the reason for his continuous negation and ironic subversion of cultural codes, discourses, ideas, and
habits. This cultural debris must be cleared away, for it hides more than
it reveals.

The Narration of Time

The reader of *The Man Without Qualities* may get the impression that
the story, just like any other novel, unfolds through time. First, the hero,
Ulrich, is introduced. Second, the hero is characterized: he is a man
without qualities who has already begun several careers without liking
any of them and who has now chosen to take a year's leave from life in
order to reach a decision about his future. Third, the hero is sent out on
a mission: he receives a letter from his father urging him to make ap-
pointments with influential persons. On closer consideration, the reader
realizes that temporal coordinates dissolve.

In the order of events there is, apart from the supposed ending of the
story, August 1914, only one fixed point of reference, August 1913. This
date is mentioned on the first page. Chapter 3 states that Ulrich has recently returned to Vienna and relates how he furnishes his new home.
The novel states that he had rented his château, as he "some time ago"
(*vor einiger Zeit*) had returned from abroad (*MWQ* 8* / *MoE* 13). One
might thus divide the events of Ulrich's life as happening either before
or after this return to Vienna. Given that August 1913 is the present moment of the story, Ulrich's return can then be located earlier in 1913.
This is a plausible interpretation of "some time ago."

In chapter 13, the narrative again apparently refers to this event in

Ulrich's life, revealing his resolution "to take a year's leave of absence from his life" (*MWQ* 44 / *MoE* 47). This decision is made "in another city and street from where he was now, but only a few weeks ago" (*aber erst vor wenigen Wochen*) (*MWQ* 43 / *MoE* 46). Obviously, then, this resolution is made a few weeks before the present of the story time, August 1913, and also before Ulrich moves to his château. However, the narrator has already informed the reader that Ulrich moved to his château "some time ago," and according to a common phenomenological presumption—that the measurement of a period of time becomes less precise the longer that period is—"some time ago" designates a longer period of time than "only a few weeks ago." In order to make sense of Ulrich's past, we must, however, assume the opposite, that "only a few weeks" is more time than "some time" (*einiger Zeit*). Otherwise, Ulrich's decision to return to Vienna would, paradoxically, take place after he had already carried out that decision.

Of course, we can assume that "only a few weeks" signifies more time than "some time." But such a claim is neither reasonable nor practical. Given other instances where the chronology is notoriously vague, it seems plausible to regard this ambiguity as a deliberately fabricated temporal enigma serving to destabilize Ulrich's personality. This impression is magnified by all the chapters where the historical "now"— August 1913—and the temporality of the story are simply abandoned, chapter 4 being the first case in point. There are places in Musil's narrative—Genette would call them instances of *achronic* time—where linear chronology is simply irrelevant. Political and biographic histories implode into one great atemporal event.

With regard to tense and duration, the nineteen chapters in the first section can be divided into three categories: (1) summaries of past events, that is, events taking place before August 1913; (2) mimetic or diegetic representations of events taking place in the present of the story time, that is, in or after August 1913; and (3) "achronic" discourses without any specific temporal relation to the story.

The chapters containing summaries of the past together form a story in which Ulrich emerges as the hero. There is a brief biography of Ulrich's father, fragments of Ulrich's past, particularly of his consecutive careers as officer, engineer, and mathematician. Finally there are the reminiscences of his friendship with Walter at the turn of the century. These pieces of information may readily be organized into one extended, chronologically unfolding narrative following Ulrich from cradle to the age of thirty-two. This is precisely how the life of Ulrich's father is narrated in chapter 3, as an evolutionary history of a person advancing toward maturity and social eminence, as though life were a fulfillment of fate. The difference between this and the representation of Ulrich's life is conspicuous, and this is of course the point. Compare the ease with which the father adjusted to society with the smoothly flowing biographical narrative of chapter 3. Ulrich's father could well be a hero of a bildungsroman or a classical realist novel. By contrast, the labyrinthine character of Ulrich's life, advancing by way of sidetracks and detours, corresponds to the constantly interrupted narrative through which his past is related. As we have seen, the narrative provides different versions of his past, and the order in which this past is narrated is different from the order in which it was lived. Above all, there are no connections demonstrating how one stage in life led to the next, which makes it appear as if the link were gratuitous, decided by chance rather than will, and certainly not by any intrinsic essence expressing itself as personal destiny. Pierre Zima observes that the consecutive accounts of Ulrich's "three attempts to become a great man" should be read as three beginnings, or three variations on the same theme: "that of the bourgeois career." [11] Yet the final product of the story is three equally possible variations of the bourgeois subject—the once unitary individual divided in three. Incidentally, this conforms to the self-understanding of the hero himself. Looking back at his past, "thinking over his time up to that point today, Ulrich might shake his head in wonder, as if someone were to tell him about his previous incarnations" (*MWQ* 35 / *MoE* 38).

This absence of connections and temporal indications also characterizes the chapters dealing with the present of the story time, the second category above. The setting of the first two chapters is the August day in 1913. Then follows a series of chapters describing Ulrich's mistresses, Leona and Bonadea. Finally, chapters 14 through 17 relate Ulrich's visit to Walter and Clarisse, which I have already discussed. Each of these sequences has its own internal chronology, but there is no chronology that establishes the order among them. Does Ulrich's visit to his friends occur before or after that beautiful day in August? Does this take place before or after meeting Bonadea? It is impossible to know. The narrative discourse neglects, even distorts, the temporality of the narrated story. As a result, the narrative logic yields a temporality of its own, independent of historical causality.

This temporal discrepancy is visible not only in the arrangement of the chapters, however. It is even more striking at the microlevel of the text, where the reader finds numerous temporal data but never the overall temporal structure that would allow for a reconstruction of the "real" order of events. Consider the following sentences. "Two weeks later Bonadea had been his mistress for fourteen days" (*MWQ* 26 / *MoE* 30). "The next morning Ulrich got out of bed on his left foot and fished halfheartedly for his slipper with his right" (*MWQ* 43 / *MoE* 46). "Since his return, Ulrich has already been a few times to see his friends Walter and Clarisse, for these two had not left town, although it was summer, and he had not seen them for a number of years" (*MWQ* 45 / *MoE* 47). Such phrases abound in most novels. In order to make sense, however, they must be related to a general chronological table. This table is conspicuously absent from Musil's novel, which makes such seemingly precise chronological data enigmatic, if not absurd. Typically, the reader turns back a few pages, searching in vain for the piece of missing chronological information, only to conclude that Musil's narrator refuses to establish a consistent temporal order.[12]

Events assumed to happen in temporal sequences are thus reshaped by a strong tendency to expand the present to the point where it swallows the past, transforming the latter into raw material for retrospections and interpretations through which the present, in turn, is abolished as a discrete and chronologically identifiable moment. Thereby, the order of das Seinesgleichen is again dissolved, and another level of experience is gradually uncovered. What is left after this derealization is a narrative that does not correspond to familiar models of reality: an event in the near past is located in two different temporal dimensions; a biography is cut in pieces, and the pieces are presented as if they belonged to different protagonists; the present of the story has no progression, constituting instead an achronic space where decades elapse in the course of a conversation. Turning now to the novel's representation of character, I will discuss that particular human subject who may experience time in this peculiar way.

The Narration of Character

Let us return to Ulrich and Clarisse and their conversation in the garden on the outskirts of Vienna. Beginning as a dialogue, the scene is interrupted by the narrator, who makes a lengthy digression, only to return suddenly to the same scene, finding Ulrich and Clarisse where he left them some pages earlier. Their dialogue continues, or so it would seem. Yet no words are pronounced. What appears to be said is merely thought, and what is thought, moreover, has the same transparency and intelligibility as anything spoken. But then again, Ulrich and Clarisse are silent, just observing each other while smoking:

> "How much does Ulrich know about this?" Clarisse wondered on her hummock. "Anyway, what could he possibly know about such struggles?" She remembered how Walter's face fell apart with pain, almost to extinction, when the agonies of music and lust beset him and her resistance left him no way out; no, she decided, Ulrich knew nothing of this monstrous love-game on the Himalayas of love, contempt, fear, and the obligations of the heights. She had no great opinion of mathematics and had never considered Ulrich to be as talented as Walter. He was clever, he was logical, he knew a lot; but was that any better than barbarism? She had to admit that his tennis used to be incomparably better than Walter's, and she could remember sometimes watching his ruthless drives with a passionate feeling of he'll get what he wants, such as she had never felt about Walter's painting, music, or ideas. And she thought: "What if he knows all about us and just isn't saying anything?" Only a moment ago he had, after all, distinctly alluded to her heroism. The silence between them had now become strangely exciting.

But Ulrich was thinking: "How nice Clarisse was ten years ago—half a child, blazing with faith in the future of the three of us." She had been actually unpleasant to him only once, when she and Walter had just got married and she had displayed that unattractive selfishness-for-two that so often makes young women who are ambitiously in love with their husbands so insufferable to other men. "That's got a lot better since," he thought. (*MWQ* 51f.* / *MoE* 53f.)

From which perspective is this language produced? Obviously, the sentences in quotation marks are thoughts registered by a narrator with complete access to both minds. In addition, there are pieces of what Dorrit Cohn has termed narrated monologue: "He knew a lot; but was that any better than barbarism?" But such instances are difficult to distinguish from passages where the narrator's reflections intervene, examples of what Cohn would call psychonarration.[13] Most likely, it is the narrator who supplies the information about how Clarisse felt when watching Ulrich defeating Walter on the tennis court. This would be the only explanation of the sudden insertion of a different mood, "she could remember" (*sie konnte sich erinnern*), signaling that Clarisse does not actually recall this as she sits there smoking a cigarette, but that the episode still is a good way of capturing her relationship to these men, whence the narrator can take the liberty of inserting it. But who is responsible for the peculiar analogy comparing the love play of Walter and Clarisse to the peaks of Himalaya? Is it really Clarisse who likens it thus? Is it the narrator's interpretation of her feelings? And who feels that the silence between them is "strangely exciting"? Clarisse? The narrator? Ulrich? Indeed, it is impossible to tell, for the narrative moves imperceptibly between these three points of focalization. We are dealing with yet another textual space marked by indeterminacy.

Confronted with cases like this, narratological typologies of character depiction and point of view run up against their limits, revealed as the abstractions they always were. If only negatively, however, in revealing their own insufficiency, such categories remain useful. Without them, it would be impossible to register the deviations in the Musilian narrative. Discussing the novella *Die Vollendung der Liebe* (1911; "The

Completion of Love"), Cohn points out that Musil's ways of rendering thoughts and feelings make the narrating consciousness fuse with the mind of the heroine. The line separating them is blurred.[14] We can never tell with certainty whether an association originates in the mind of the narrator or in that of the protagonist. Musil's friend Franz Blei was so bewildered by the floating perspective in the novella that he asked the author who the narrator really was. A very interesting question, Musil replied. "The point de vue is not in the author and not in the constituted person, there is in fact no point de vue at all, the stories have no central point of perspective" (*T* 2:943).[15]

Taken as a whole, the first nineteen chapters of *The Man Without Qualities* are marked by the same confounding feature. After chapter 14, from which I have just quoted, there follows a chapter in which the narrative appears to be unfocalized. The narrator steps back to depict the cultural atmosphere at the turn of the century, the formative years of Walter and Ulrich. As this chapter ends and a new one begins, a barely perceivable shift in perspective turns the depiction upside down. This is the transition between the chapters:

> Something went through the thicket of beliefs in those days like a single wind bending many trees—a spirit of heresy and reform, the blessed sense of an arising and going forth, a mini-renaissance and -reformation, such as only the best of times experience; whoever entered the world then felt, at the first corner, the breath of this spirit on his cheek.

16

A Mysterious Malady of the Times

> So they had actually been two young men, not so long ago—Ulrich thought when he was alone again—who, oddly enough, not only had the most profound insights before anyone else did, but even had them simultaneously. (*MWQ* 54 / *MoE* 56)

The text explains the intellectual intimacy between two young men captured by the zeitgeist. The most interesting element in the passage is, however, the first, inexplicable word in the new chapter: "So" (*also*).

This chapter is entirely focalized through Ulrich; what is said is attributed only to him, including the word "so." But this word refers back to
the end of the previous chapter, which, however, is entirely rendered
by the narrator. This is to say that a character here steps in to bring out
the conclusion of the narrator's account. An odd inversion of romantic irony: it is no longer the narrator informing the reader about things
unknown to figures in the story; it is a figure in the story entering the
scene behind the back of the narrator to rectify his information, which
implies that Ulrich somehow must have been listening to what the narrator stated in chapter 15. Or perhaps chapter 15 never was anything but
the narrated monologue of Ulrich himself, but in that case the narrator
forgot to indicate that this was so, thus making us mistake a diegesis rendered through Ulrich's perspective for the unfocalized discourse of the
narrator. The point is, again, that we cannot tell. The narrative attributes
the same discourse to two sources at once, much as it earlier situated
one discrete event at two separate moments in time.

An even more peculiar instance of this follows shortly afterward.
Ulrich, pondering his past, argues with himself. But what perspective
governs this passage?

> It seemed to Ulrich that with the beginning of his adult life a general
> lull had set in, a gradual running down, in spite of occasional eddies of
> energy that came and went, to an ever more listless, erratic rhythm. It was
> very hard to say what this change consisted of. Were there suddenly fewer
> great men? Far from it! . . . Had life in general reached a standstill? No, it
> had become more powerful! Were there more paralyzing contradictions
> than before? There could hardly be more! Had the past not known any
> absurdities? Heaps! *Just between ourselves:* people threw their support
> to the weak and ignored the strong. (*MWQ* 55 / *MoE* 57; my emphasis).

The reversal revealing that the narrator's commentary could have
been part of Ulrich's reflection is now reversed in turn, this time disclosing that Ulrich's monologue may be ascribed to the narrator. What else
is the import of the conspicuous apostrophe "Just between ourselves"
(*Unter uns gesagt*)? To whom is it addressed? By whom is it enunci-

ated? Is it Ulrich addressing himself, thus splitting himself in two? Is it Ulrich calling on an imaginary listener, perhaps the reader, thus usurping the role of the narrator? Is it Ulrich addressing the narrator, or the narrator addressing Ulrich? Or perhaps it is the narrator who, disguised as Ulrich, addresses the reader from Ulrich's position, only forgetting to unmask himself before speaking?

In his discussion of Proust's *A la recherche du temps perdu,* Genette concludes that the novel works in three modes of focalization at once, "passing at will from the consciousness of his hero to that of his narrator, and inhabiting by turns that of his most diverse characters." [16] This is something quite different from the simple omniscience of the narrator of the classical novel, Genette continues, although he does not develop the distinction. Also, since this focalization transgresses a "law of the mind," being inside and outside consciousness at the same time, it defies realistic illusionism. Genette's description is valid also for Musil's narrative, but only in part. It is true that Musil's narrator moves into and out of the minds of the characters, situating them in a wider, intersubjective narrative space. But while the Proustian narrator unifies this space, creating an experiential totality, the discourses and idioms that invade Musil's novel cannot be integrated into any totality, since they offer contradictory representations of time, space, and subjectivity. The narrator keeps adding these perspectives, but they fail to add up to a unity, as they do when Marcel stumbles on the pavement, recaptures the past, and starts to record it in narrative form.

Genette calls Proust's modernistic mood of narration "polymodality" of focalization.[17] This is also a valid designation of the narrative strategy in *The Man Without Qualities,* provided the qualification that the various modes never merge but are merely superimposed or juxtaposed. They do not supplement or replenish one another, nor are they unified in a more comprehensive order of consciousness. They just expose the limits of one another. As regards the question of how to represent human experience, then, Musil's narrator demonstrates that each system of inscription, perspective, and order is partial and arbitrary.

Musil's novel reverses the process by which the realist novel integrates individual and society into a meaningful totality. In Hamon's view of the realist text, as well as in Lukács's and Moretti's respective accounts of the bildungsroman, the social events on the narrative surface are given meaning by the life story of the individual, while the individual is socialized through his exposure to these events. In *The Man Without Qualities,* there is no reciprocity between society and subject. The truth of Musil's characters is not disclosed by representing them in situations of social interaction. They are not sufficiently autonomous to express themselves as free agents. Each encounter with the social world empties them, so as to show that outside the social systems and discourses that each character articulates, he or she is unintelligible. As J. P. Stern points out, "the very indeterminacy of the hero's personality makes it difficult to say where that personality ends and the social ambience begins." A planned indeterminacy, Stern adds, is the author's first intention.[18]

So even if Musil's protagonist has no trouble making his way through the social world, in a deeper sense he has no place there. As a social being Ulrich is portrayed as exchangeable and one-dimensional, consisting only of the discourses that he articulates. Prefiguring the poststructuralist idea that the subject is an effect of discourse, Musil played with the idea of putting together a human being entirely from citations.[19] The only way to represent such a character truthfully is to peel away layer after layer of the social material of which he is made. Hence these extended pauses where the narrator interrupts mimetically represented scenes and derealizes the situation. Hence the irony that undercuts every assertion. Hence the satirical destruction of the illusions of the realist novel. The narrator appears to unlock a passage to unexplored territories of human reality. The urge to represent these landscapes engenders the achronic time, the polymodal focalization, and the floating psychonarration, which are characteristic of the Musilian narrative.

In his essay on the position of the narrator in the modernistic novel, Adorno approaches this narrative process in more general terms: "The world is imperceptibly drawn into this interior space—the technique has been given the name 'interior monologue'—and anything that takes place in the external world is presented . . . as a piece of the interior world, a moment in the stream of consciousness, protected against refu-

tation by the objective order of time and space." [20] The real is reconstructed inside a psychic universe. The result is what Adorno calls an
"Innenraum," an interior space, which forces external reality to disappear beyond the narrative horizon and sets itself in its place as a
new, internal reality. Yet Adorno's remark neglects one crucial feature.
Musil's narrative shows that the psychic space described by Adorno
cannot be ascribed to any particular psyche. Strictly speaking, this psychic space cannot be an "Innenraum," for such a notion presupposes a
subject with a defined interiority. In the case of Musil, authentic subjectivity has neither interiority nor exteriority; it floats unanchored between the social roles and discursive matrices that it must use to articulate its being, but without ever finding any single role or idiom that can
capture its desire for meaning and identity.

My discussion in chapter 2 of the subject's relationship to social and
urban space is thus supported by this investigation of the narrative form:
the Musilian subject must be conceptualized not as intrinsic substance
nor as a socially imputed function, but rather as a barely tangible Zwischenraum that cannot be reduced to or explained by either of these.

I will conclude this analysis of Musil's narrative discourse with a brief
discussion of chapter 18, in which Moosbrugger is introduced to the
reader. Apparently, this episode relates how Ulrich runs into Moosbrugger in the street. This encounter then turns out to be a fake, another
instance of the narrator's mocking treatment of narrative codes:

> When Ulrich first laid eyes on that face with its signs of being a child of
> God above handcuffs, he quickly turned around, slipped a few cigarettes
> to the sentry at the nearby court building, and asked him about the con-
> voy that had apparently just left the gates; he was told . . . Well, anyway,
> this is how something of the sort must have happened in earlier times,
> since it is often reported this way, and Ulrich almost believed it himself;
> but the contemporary truth was that he had merely read all about it in
> the newspaper. It was to be a long time before he met Moosbrugger in
> person, and before that happened he caught sight of him only once dur-
> ing the trial. The probability of experiencing something unusual through
> the newspapers is much greater than that of experiencing it in person; in

other words, the more important things take place today in the abstract, and the more trivial ones in real life.

What Ulrich learned of Moosbrugger's story in this fashion was more or less the following. . . . (*MWQ* 68f. / *MoE* 69)

The narrator here limits Ulrich's field of knowledge and experience. The experience offered him is abstract; it is what he happens to read in the newspaper.[21] His personal investment in reality is thereby ruled out. The narrator then promises to deliver this kind of abstract experience ("[it] was more or less the following"). What follows, however, is not a compilation of news reports, not even a montage of clippings of the kind that other modernists of the period experimented with, notably Döblin in *Berlin Alexanderplatz* and John Dos Passos in his *U.S.A.* trilogy. What follows in Musil, on the contrary, is in fact a passage that is focalized through Moosbrugger himself. If this is what Ulrich experienced through the news, it must be remarkable news, for it amounts to an account of what it is like to be Moosbrugger, having his memories, feeling his feelings, perceiving with his senses, executing his actions, even killing his victim:

Then he felt something hard, in her pocket or his. He tugged it out. He couldn't say whether it was a scissors or a knife; he stabbed her with it. He had claimed it was only a pair of scissors, but it was his own knife. She fell with her head inside the booth. He dragged her partway outside, onto the soft ground, and kept on stabbing her until he had completely separated her from himself. Then he stood there beside her for maybe another quarter of an hour, looking down at her, while the night grew calmer again and wonderfully smooth. (*MWQ* 74 / *MoE* 74)

This is surely not what Ulrich experienced by reading the newspaper but a narrative of Moosbrugger's murder focalized through the murderer himself. Yet, the narrator explicitly states that this is what Ulrich "experienced" in the newspaper. What we see in this chapter on Moosbrugger, then, is a mode of narration that would seem to affirm the gap between experience and journalism. But as soon as this difference is established, the narrator offers an account that cancels it.

Looking at the chapter as a whole, we see how its perspective shifts among the narrator, Ulrich, Moosbrugger, and the judges. The impact of this polymodal focalization is amplified by a constantly changing distance and a voice sometimes sympathetic, sometimes sharply ironic —all of which contribute to the coming into being of an ambiguous space, at once social and psychic, in which several discourses collide and in which the representation of reality must be patched together from contradictory perspectives. As Anne Longuet Marx has argued, this is a primary trait of Musil's narrative. It does not follow an itinerary, much less an intrigue; it is regulated by a disposition, or a mood, which sutures discursive registers that are absolutely heterogenous.[22] In this way, the narrative process dissolves every authoritative account of reality, contrasting it with a set of alternative but conflicting perspectives. Meanwhile, the character is emptied of its traditional contents, liberated from any firm identity, and instead affirmed as an agency suspended in a state of mobility and possibility.

The Narrative Process of *The Man Without Qualities*

The Man Without Qualities is narrated by a disembodied and placeless voice whose irony cuts in all directions. I have argued that the narration refuses to give any authoritative account of events, objects, and characters. An event signifies different things, depending on the perspective from which it is seen. The meaning of an object varies with the discourse used to describe it. A character can obey contradictory principles, depending on the situation, and he or she is also equipped with alternative pasts. Furthermore, nothing in this novel acts or functions on its own accord but only in relation to the systems in which it is inserted. No epistemological paradigm is privileged. No particular narrative mood governs unchallenged over the representation. The laws of causality are suspended. The temporal structure is blurred. The absence of a superordinate narrative and temporal order creates the impression that everything happens more or less simultaneously: the narrative creates an achronic space. The absence of a central perspective and a predominating epistemology allows several perspectives and symbolic systems to coexist: the narrative generates a heterologic and polycentric space. Importantly, Musil's novel evokes this achronicity, heterology, and polycentricity in and by the *movement* of narration.

The narrator's swift changes of perspective, his instantaneous passage from one focus to another, serve to demonstrate that the choice of a particular focus, character, event, object, narrative code, or discursive register is arbitrary. The result is a textual practice demonstrating the seams and joints in the narrative surface, thus indicating that the frame within which a certain representation is fabricated is but one among an infinite number of other no less interesting frames. This creates what Genette would call "an iterative narrative" (*un récit itératif*): various possible narrative beginnings and developments are tested but they cannot be arranged along a unitary narrative line.[23] Stated in more technical terms, the syntagmatic axis, on which the narrative events are ordered in succession so as to drive the story forward, is eclipsed by the paradigmatic axis of combination.[24] Themes, scenes, and events no longer succeed one another in time but are evoked as various, sometimes contradictory possibilities of the same paradigm, and as a set of possible but mutually exclusive continuations of the story. Along each narrative thread actually chosen in the weaving of the story, the narrator thus pulls a bundle of others, the vibrations of which create strange resonances. It is not surprising that Jean François Lyotard, in his book on the postmodern condition, enlists *The Man Without Qualities* to support his account of "the decomposition of the great narratives." [25]

This narrative modality is central to Musil's conception of subjectivity, which can partly be seen as an effect of the narrative logic that I have examined here. The narrative structure of Musil's novel and the structure of subjectivity presented in the novel refuse the firm frames of existing reality. And they do so in order to preserve the possibility of different realities.[26]

My account of how Musil's narrative generates a polyvalent *Zwischenraum* thus merges with the conclusion reached in the previous chapter. As we saw there, the novel responds to social reification by postulating the possibility of another mode of experience, the other condition, which transcends the conflict between intellect and feeling, rationality and nonrationality. In the most beautiful passages of the novel, this mode of being is made concrete as an ethical and existential posture in which Ulrich momentarily recaptures a sense of meaning and presence, the barriers separating his self and the world suddenly falling away.

It should be added that Musil also linked the other condition to the possibility of reorganizing human life as a whole. Consequently, this condition suggested a path to social improvement. Art had an important pedagogic function in this project, for it provided the medium through which the articulations of the other condition could be explored. In his essays, especially "The German as Symptom" (1923), Musil attempted to substantiate this idea, tying the ethical and aesthetic qualities of the other condition to related ideas in human history, drawing on research in experimental psychology as well as the tradition of mysticism: "We have a great many accounts of this other condition. What seems to be common to all of them is that the border between self and nonself is less sharp than usual, and that there is a certain inversion of relationships. . . . Whereas ordinarily the self masters the world, in the other condition the world flows into the self, or mingles with it or bears it, and the like" (*PS* 186 / *GW* 2:1393).

This is an articulation, within the existential and ethical register, of Musil's imaginary solution of the historical dilemma of modernity. It is described as a state of being characterized by a transgression and reversal of boundaries. The same dilemma, then, is inscribed in the form of the Musilian narrative. The transgression of temporal order and the ironic subversion of discursive matrices contribute to the generation of a space of indeterminacy and potentiality that dissolves the mimetic representation of a lifelike character moving through a solid external reality.

The ethics of the other condition and the functioning of the Musilian narrative can thus be seen as two articulations of the same *mood*. If

Musil's narrative mood were projected onto the level of the narrative content and turned into an existential strategy, the result would be similar to what Musil describes as the other condition. Correspondingly, if the other condition could be converted into a narrative attitude, the result would be the kind of representation of time, space, and character that we find in Musil's novel: an achronic, polycentric, and heterologic Zwischenraum, in which subjectivity, no longer determined by social identities, floats in an experiential flux.

Interestingly, the same modality of a subject without identity emerges in even purer form in Hermann Broch's last novel, *The Death of Virgil* (1945). A boundless subject governs two of the main sections in this lyric novel. This subject is comparable only to the writing process itself, in the ways in which it rejuvenates itself with each additional letter and steps outside itself with each new phrase. Like Musil's subject in the other condition, Broch's subject floats "beyond the expressible as well as the inexpressible"; it penetrates the world and is simultaneously penetrated by it; it is a "no thing," a mere borderline of energy, which nonetheless fills up the empty consciousness and floods the universe.[27] As we shall see, the similarities between Broch's and Musil's renderings of this *ecstatic* mode of subjectivity indicate their common origin in Austria's postimperial culture.

Still, the difference between the narratological and the existential-philosophical articulations of this mood cannot be erased. On the one hand, there is the representation of Ulrich—or in Broch's case the dying Virgil—who ascend to this state of mind in transient epiphanies, or in the moment of death. Musil's Ulrich also turns it into the basis of an existential program that is necessitated by modern society and yet cannot be realized in this society; this gesture of aesthetic refusal is typical of modernist literature, as we saw in the first chapter. On the other hand, there is the narratological Zwischenraum that emerges through a continuous narrative production and an irony that derealizes language and identities.

On the level of content, then, the other condition is an ideological closure. On the level of form, by contrast, the narrative mood articulating the other condition can never constitute any closure, for it is the very generating force of the narrative—a process, not a fixed existential structure. It is important to distinguish these two levels of the problem. If we narrowly focus the content, we arrive at an ideological solution from which we may learn no more, and no less, than from any treatise on mysticism. If we compare this to what goes on on the level of narrative production, we see that the closure is constantly unmade, that the narrator must resist the solutions which he cannot but keep fabricating and project onto the world. Ulrich, as a character, is precisely a projection of that kind. As such, he is marked by the restrictions of his era and his society.

The Musilian narrative elaborates preestablished models of character representations in a number of conspicuous ways, in order to arrive at an atemporal and polymodal representation of human subjectivity. Yet the tension between this representation and the expressivist and realist convention that it negates remains in place. In order to make Ulrich play his role as a literary character, Musil was dependent on the categories and models that conditioned a novelistic representation of subjectivity at his historical moment. Hence, his novel cannot avoid articulating the expressivist paradigm of subjectivity, which, in Musil's time, determined the range of possible answers to the questions of identity and human nature. The point, however, is that Musil was unsatisfied with all available answers to this question, and he therefore tried to imagine new ones. In doing this, he used Ulrich as the vehicle for his new answers, thus projecting the hero beyond the narrative, psychological, and philosophical categories that in his period circumscribed the notion of the human.

Ernst Fischer once stated that Musil wrote "in the twilight of an era suspended between dying and becoming." [28] Indeed, seen from the point of view of the expressivist paradigm, the novel depicts what Broch summed up as "the almost mystical disintegration of a culture." [29] Ulrich consequently exemplifies the disappearance of established codes of "normal" behavior. Seen from the perspective of as yet unrealized possibilities, on the other hand, the novel inaugurates a time to come.

Ulrich then becomes an example of a human subject fit to meet the demands of a truly modernized world. The latter aspect alone accounts for Musil's unique aesthetic and philosophical innovations. An interpretation that applies this perspective therefore affords a richer and more complex view of the novel. Burton Pike has suggested, rightly, that while "Thomas Mann stands at the end of an old tradition, there is reason to believe that Musil stands at the beginning of a new one." [30]

PART 2

NEGATIVITY

Exterritorialität des geistigen

Menschen, *ist der richtige Term in dieser*

Blut-, Boden-, Rasse-, Masse-, Führer- und Heimatzeit.

—Robert Musil, 1938

4

Subjectivity Degree Zero

Toward a Theory of the Musilian Subject

On all levels of representation, *The Man Without Qualities* rejects the
idea that the subject is the wellspring of the world. Each chapter demonstrates that "man" is no longer master of society, culture, or even
his own being. The autonomous and expressivist subject, the novel suggests, is just one social inscription of the human being among others,
none of which can lay claim to truth.

This is the first part of the story, the one I have discussed in previous chapters. In Musil's work, however, the dethroning of the sovereign subject is not a problem that is simply noted down and lamented.
It presents a task to be solved. What forms of subjectivity and identity
can emerge beyond the old paradigms? This is the question posed by
Musil's novel, and it is to this question that I now turn in the second
part of this book.

The Man Without Qualities is least of all concerned with finding just
an alternative way of inscribing the subject. Rather, the novel seeks to
clarify how the social constitution of subjectivity functions and, equally
important, how it might be erased. The theory of subjectivity that is
present in the novel answers not so much the question of what the subject is, but of how it is produced by discursive and ideological formations. In this sense, Musil prepares for a conceptualization of subjectivity and identity that was not philosophically codified in his period

but that has become a focus of interest in more recent cultural theory and philosophy. In order to demonstrate that this is indeed the case I will in this chapter confront Musil's representation of subjectivity and identity with some theories of subjectivity that have been formulated in the late- or postmodern period. My choice of thinkers as different as, for example, Julia Kristeva and Paul Ricoeur is deliberate. I want to make clear that I am not interested in subsuming Musil's exploration of subjectivity under any specific contemporary "theory of the subject." My only aim is to establish a general but nonetheless profound affinity, arguing that Musil's novel in fact introduces a way of thinking about subjectivity and identity that was consistently theorized only later. In general terms, Musil is the first writer to systematically examine how the identity of the subject is constituted by an irreducible lack and otherness, which results in a structure of subjectivity characterized by internal difference and negativity.

Musil's representation of subjectivity, then, does not anticipate any specific antiexpressivist theory, and hence it cannot be explained or clarified by any single of these theories; such an approach would be reductionist.[1] It is, rather, the other way round: Musil's representation of subjectivity can be used to explain the emergence of later theories of the subject, because, as we shall see in chapters 5 and 6, Musil's novel articulates the historical conditions that enabled those antiexpressivist notions of subjectivity that have then been theorized, in different ways, by contemporary thinkers.

Narration and Identity

The previous chapter showed that the question of the subject is related to the question of narration. The Musilian subject is inseparable from the novel's eminently modernist narrative structure. This confirms a proposition that is often made in contemporary hermeneutics, where narration is commonly defined as the mediatory instance between the human subject and its cultural environment. In order to say something about a person's life or a career, the argument generally goes, we must arrange the various phases and events of this life in some kind of order. This order is necessarily temporal, for it must show how one event follows the other. It is also causal, for it must demonstrate that earlier moments in life determine later ones, or that some moments are teleologically determined by a person's ambitions and desires, or, again, that some events in a person's life are determined by his or her social habitus. If, then, a person's life can be rendered only by means of a temporal and causal order, it follows that it can be rendered only by means of *narrative* order. Identity, that is, the idea of a spatiotemporal constancy and continuity that allows a person to see himself or herself as the same person he or she was a few years ago, is thus always represented in narrative form.[2]

One might object that identity is often declared in a number of non-narrative ways, by mentioning, for instance, a name (Ulrich), a profession (mathematician), or a place of origin (the town of B. in Moravia). But such attributions are in fact indexes of narratives that have been flattened out, thus concealing their temporal dimension. What they tell about the identity of a person is actually a tale about that person: "I am the one who was given the name Ulrich; I am the one who became a mathematician; I am the one who was born in B. in Moravia." In these protonarrative statements the subject of speech, the "I," declares itself to be the *same* person as the person who was given the name Ulrich, trained as a mathematician, or born in the town of B. Differences are thus bridged and connections established across temporal distances through a *narrative act of identification.*

This view of identity also conforms to the notion of subjectivity presented in *The Man Without Qualities.* The novel affirms only one way of representing the human being, namely the identity that is gradually constructed through narrative production. The problematic and interesting feature of the Musilian subject, however, is that it cannot be represented in this way either. The implied author and the hero, as well as Musil himself, argue that the subject can never be captured by any code, narrative, symbolic, or other. On the one hand, then, Musilian subjectivity necessitates narration. On the other hand, it resists narrative mediation, something that is repeatedly brought out in the portrait of Ulrich. Remarkably enough, the hero is unable to claim his past as his *own* past, as part of his identity. Looking back upon the years gone by and the careers he has thrown himself into and then abandoned, Ulrich shakes his head in disbelief, as if someone had told him about his previous incarnations (*MWQ* 35 / *MoE* 38). If it were true that all human beings are storytelling animals, as Alasdair MacIntyre has said, Ulrich seems to belong to a different species.

The Loss of Narrative Order

At the end of the first part of the novel, "Pseudoreality Prevails," Ulrich is on his way home through Vienna at night. He has just witnessed the demonstrations against the Parallel Campaign, a key episode that I discussed in chapter 2. The German businessman Arnheim has asked Ulrich to become his personal secretary in his industrial empire. Such a position would not only bring wealth and power to Ulrich but also a structure to his ambitions, a destiny to his life, and an identity to his self. But he turns down the offer, and now, as he is strolling along the empty streets, he starts to doubt his ability to lead a meaningful life. He is unable to organize his life into a finite totality, the way painters would frame their motifs, or the way storytellers would organize their stories, so as to create the feeling "that we are masters of our own house" (*MWQ* 708* / *MoE* 649). Indeed, the "law" of life that Ulrich has lost is none other than the law of narrative order, a law that converts even the most chaotic circumstances into destiny: "Lucky the man who can say 'when,' 'before,' and 'after'! Terrible things may have happened to him, he may have writhed in pain, but as soon as he can tell what happened in chronological order, he feels as contented as if the sun were warming his belly. This is the trick the novel artificially turns to account" (*MWQ* 709 / *MoE* 650).

   Ulrich observes that public life has become nonnarrative; it "no longer follows a thread, but instead spreads out as an infinitely interwoven surface" (*MWQ* 709 / *MoE* 650). This signals a critical moment in the history of subjectivity and, as the passage indicates, also in that of the novel. To be sure, this theme is characteristic of modernist fiction at large. The art of storytelling is coming to an end, Walter Benjamin stated at the beginning of the 1930s.[3] "Narrating has become impossible," Alain Robbe-Grillet wrote in his manifesto for *le nouveau roman*.[4] The condition of modernity, it appears, is inimical to narration. As the narrative paradigm that stabilizes subjectivity is relinquished, the links between life's events are severed, as are the ones between the agent and the agent's acts, and this incongruity precludes the establishment of a stable identity.

As if to prove Ulrich's conclusion that he has lost his place in the story and, by extension, his identity, the novel stages a random encounter in the night. A number of characters, fantasies, and subplots are suddenly condensed into a single narrative event. Ulrich is approached by a young woman, a prostitute, as it turns out— "Come along, baby!" she invites (*MWQ* 710 / *MoE* 651). At first, Ulrich is disturbed, then perplexed, but soon enough he is swept away by fantasies. He considers accepting her offer: "If he showed himself willing, she would slip her arm in his" (*MWQ* 710 / *MoE* 651). He then revels in a fantasy of the two of them sleeping together. In reality, however, he just gives the woman some money and continues his walk. But the scene immediately ignites another fantasy: he imagines how the woman now rejoins her colleagues, who are whispering in the nearby alley, and shows them the money. This vision is in turn replaced by a projection that is even stranger. Ulrich pictures himself in the role of Moosbrugger, the serial killer:

Moosbrugger, the pathological comedian, the pursuer and nemesis of prostitutes, who had been out walking on that other, unlucky night just as Ulrich was this evening. . . . For an instant, Ulrich thought he could feel it himself. . . . His heart contracted, but his imaginings became confused and overran all bounds, until they dissolved in an almost enervating voluptuousness. He made an effort to calm down. He had apparently been living so long without any central purpose that he was actually envying a psychopath his obsessions and his faith in the part he was playing! (*MWQ* 711 / *MoE* 652)

Ulrich shakes off his obsessions and returns, momentarily, to his senses. Just as soon another daydream flares up, as he experiences what it would be like to liberate the incarcerated Moosbrugger. Picturing this as an authentic deed that would forever override all wimpish hesitations, Ulrich inflates his fantasy until it becomes a virtual ecstasy, "in which the movement of reaching out in some extreme state of excitement and that of being moved by it fused into an ineffable communion, in which desire was indistinguishable from compulsion, meaning from necessity" (*MWQ* 711 / *MoE* 652f.).

In the space of a few sentences, then, at least five different fantasies take shape and explode before fading away and disappearing as if they never existed. The storyline—walking home, encountering a prostitute, arriving home—is no more than an axis transmitting the psychic energy that fuels a novelistic machinery of representation in which every effect becomes a new cause, thus turning every finished event, real or imagined, into a new beginning for a series of alternative and often mutually exclusive actions and subplots. The same expansion affects the protagonist, as the agent is drained of his agency and semiconsciously dragged along by a train of uncanny projections. The passage demonstrates how resilient Ulrich's self has become—a man without qualities, a character without fixed boundaries, susceptible to a vast register of imaginary projections and identifications. In the previous chapter, we saw how a floating, polycentric, and achronological space of subjectivity emerges in the novel, a space that cannot be ascribed to any single character, nor, for that matter, to the narrator. The diffusion of the linear and mimetic narration led to the confusion of the boundaries of character. Here we witness the same process, but from the opposite end. The diffusion of the character confounds the linear movement of narration. The sudden turns of Ulrich's reflections and identifications spin and split the narrative line until it is expanded "as an infinitely interwoven surface."

All this being said, the proposition that identity can be established only by means of narration may still signify a number of different things. It may mean that narration offers the only adequate or possible way to *represent* the human subject. In a more radical sense, it may mean that narration is what *constitutes* this subject in the first place. According to the first alternative, the subject precedes the narrative act that represents it. Behind the stories we tell there is a substantial self, a foundational ego or cogito remaining permanent while it uses language and narration to express itself. But if this were the case, the transcendental subject would make a secret return, setting itself up as a metaphysical foundation in the true sense of the word *subiectum,* or *hypokeimenon* which, throughout a long tradition of Western thought, has become the dominant designation of the essence of human beings. In previous chapters, we have encountered this idea of the subject under the name of "expressivist subjectivity," and we have traced it through *The Man Without Qualities,* all the way to its imminent collapse.

For Musil, then, the only remaining possibility is the second of the above-mentioned alternatives. If there is no substantial psychic entity behind the expressions of the subject, no center securing its identity, narration would seem to be the only way to produce an identity for the subject. In this case, too, however, the link between narration and subjectivity may be understood in two ways. In its strong form, this relationship implies that subjectivity and narrativity are inseparable, the subject always being conditioned by narrative. To ask for a subject or an experience that precedes narration is pointless. This is the sense in which Anthony P. Kerby states that life is inherently of a narrative structure.[5] He quotes Barbara Hardy: "We dream in narrative, day-dream in narrative, remember, anticipate, hope, despair, believe, doubt, plan, revise, criticize, construct, gossip, learn, hate, and love by narrative."[6]

According to another approach to how narration relates to subjectivity, the two do not presuppose each other. Lived human experience is essentially nonnarrative, having neither beginning nor end, nor any prefigured emplotment. Although narration enables a comprehension of experience, it will always be introduced after the fact. Hence Louis Mink's counterargument that we "do not dream or remember in narrative." Our stories are secondary phenomena, forms that we impose on experience to "weave together the separate images of recollection."[7] Michel Foucault, a strong advocate of this view, argued that experience and history should be liberated from false notions of continuity. Our most fundamental experience should be conceived as "the pure experience of order and of its modes of being." [8] If we want to represent this primary level of experience truthfully, it must be approached as a group of neutral elements: "the material with which one is dealing is, in its raw, neutral state, a population of events in the space of discourse in general." [9]

That life is without any prefigured narrative form is a view repeatedly stated by Musil's narrator and hero. The world consists of an immense surface of discrete objects and discontinuous energies. Broken down into its molecular components, life is "irregularity, change, forward spurts, failures to keep step, collisions of objects and interests" (*MWQ* 4 / *MoE* 10). As regards individual psychic experience, it is enough to recall Ulrich's remark to General Stumm von Bordwehr: In "the darkest recesses of your being," there are only "stimuli and strings of reflexes, entrenched habits and skills, reiteration, fixation, imprints, series, monotony!" (*MWQ* 410 / *MoE* 378).

At the bottom of human experience there is neither substance nor structure, merely coincidental condensations of emotions, drives, desires, and impressions. This account can be related to Nietzsche's philosophy and Mach's positivist critique of late-nineteenth-century ideas of the ego. Musil appropriated parts of Mach's theory and explored its social implications. As a result, he developed his own "Theorem of Shapelessness" (*Theorem der Gestaltlosigkeit*), in his major but unfinished 1923 essay "The German as Symptom." Musil here argues that "the substratum" of the human being remains the same throughout history, regardless of social and cultural forms (*PS* 164 / *GW* 2:1368). This substratum, however, is formless; it is human in no more than a biological sense. Before this "material" has been shaped socially, there is no reason to talk about a human identity: "A person exists only in forms given to him from the outside. 'He polishes himself on the world' is much too mild an image; it ought to read: He pours himself into its mold. It is social organization which through its forms gives the individual the possibility of expressing himself at all, and it is only through expression that he becomes a human being" (*PS* 165 / *GW* 2:1370).

What Musil describes is apparently the process that institutes subjectivity as such. The social order provides the forms that enable an individual to *be,* in the most elementary sense of the word. These forms determine the nature and meaning of all human expressions. Only by using and thus realizing these forms can the human being emerge as a subject for itself and in itself.

Subject of Possibilities

A being that is determined by nothing, which is "gestaltlos" and "eigen-schaftslos," without either shape or qualities, is logically also a being capable of everything, as Hartmut Böhme has suggested.[10] Because Musil supports the idea of human shapelessness, he also recognizes the idea of the infinite possibilities of existence, and this triggers a narrative that explores all the other possible narratives that would remain unrealized, had the narrator followed only one linear narrative movement.

Ulrich's nocturnal encounter with the prostitute is thus no more than the beginning of a series of subsequent situations lined up as so many narrative projections in their own right. The linear narrative progression is thrown out of balance and splintered into a multiplicity of possible stories without closure. This technique was to be refined a decade or two later by Georges Pérec, Raymond Queneau, and the novelists linked to the nouveau roman. Transforming the storytelling function into a virtually endless recombination of a limited kit of characters and events, they created an impossible art of narrating that was masterly explored by Italo Calvino in *If on a Winter's Night a Traveler* (1979), and even more radically in *The Castle of Crossed Destinies* (1973) where the seventy-eight cards of the tarot deck are laid out as so many narrative segments that are endlessly combined into ever new sequences of stories.

Michael André Bernstein has called this narrative strategy "side-shadowing." It is "a gesturing to the side, to a present dense with multiple, and mutually exclusive, possibilities for what is to come." [11] Bernstein opposes this narrative method to the kind of narration that depicts the past as necessarily leading to—or "foreshadowing"—the present, and that sees the present as the necessary effect of the past. Against foreshadowing, sideshadowing rejects the conviction that there exists a hidden code or pattern beneath the heterogeneity of human existence. Sideshadowing instead affirms the unrealized possibilities of the past and disrupts every triumphalist and unidirectional view of history.

Bernstein uses Musil's novel as a showcase for the principle of sideshadowing, and there is much to support such an analysis. As we have seen throughout the previous chapters, Musil's narrator and hero are keener on possibilities than on realities. At the same time, however, *The Man Without Qualities* is, as a whole, also structured as one extended foreshadowing of a singular, catastrophic event.[12] The novel is a virtual time bomb, inexorably ticking away toward the war. Therefore sideshadowing cannot be defended as a mere alternative to foreshadowing, as Bernstein holds, just as the fragmentation of linear narration into countless possible subnarratives could never replace narration as such.[13] The principle of sideshadowing cannot be universalized, because this would necessarily stage the past as a depository of numberless future scenarios, all of which are equally possible, and all waiting, like cards in a deck, to reveal their face. It is just as questionable to universalize the idea of foreshadowing, as do a majority of Musil's commentators, because this could only stage the society depicted in the novel as a world waiting for an inevitable apocalypse. While the former interpretation implies that anything could happen, the latter suggests that everything had to happen the way it did.[14]

We must instead chart the dialectic between these two modes of comprehension and narration. The plot in Musil's novel begins in the summer of 1913. It was meant to end a year later, with the outbreak of war. All the energy released by the story's action is eventually absorbed by the decisive and all-encompassing event of the war. Indeed, the story has a temporal frame that is as unyielding as history itself. On this level of temporality, the narrator works according to what Bernstein designates as "backshadowing." A later historical stage casts a shadow on an earlier and more innocent era, inviting us to straighten out the cultural predicament of 1913–1914 retrospectively. On this level, then, the narrative chronicles a sequence: from peace to war. It also asks a question—*Why* war?—which it then tries to answer: *because* of the situation of 1913–1914. *The Man Without Qualities* thus offers no less than a novelistic explanation of World War I.

Onto this first temporal level we must now superimpose a second one, which generates a different modality of time. Here events are not recorded in linear manner through the methods of backshadowing and foreshadowing, nor is society framed so as to demonstrate why it had to be wrecked. Instead, the narrative freezes the present moment so as to examine it from different angles and uncover layers of meanings that have no place in, and cannot be incorporated into, the chain of historical causality imitated by the story. These layers of meanings are the repositories of a past present that would allow for different interpretations of history, and it is precisely this hidden resource of historical signification that the narrator draws on in order to envision alternative lives, a new human subject, and a whole new society. On this level, the narrative does not depict a sequence, nor does it present any personal or social destiny. Rather, it confronts us with an incomplete syllogism, of which Ulrich must find the supporting premises, so as to confirm a hypothetical argument: *if* the situation of 1913, *then* Utopia.

In a classical essay on Musil's work, Albrecht Schöne has argued that this tension between one narrative tendency foreshadowing the war and another dissolving reality into a wide spectrum of possibilities should be defined as a tension between the indicative mood and the subjunctive. As I mentioned in chapter 3, the mood of the verb is not only a matter of grammar; it indicates the standpoint of the speaker toward the action of which he or she speaks, the attitude he or she assumes when interpreting the world. Different moods thus register different forms of understanding history. A striking feature of Musil's narrative, Schöne maintains, is that the indicative narrative, the slowly progressing chain of temporal and causal links, is transformed into raw material for the narrator's construction of possibilities and possible realities.[15]

Musil's narrative thus contains a unique form of double articulation. All the situations anchored in the time and space of the story by means of indicative clauses will function within two registers at once. In the indicative universe of the story, they are inserted as links in a chain inevitably ending in war. But the same events and acts also provide material for an imagination working in the subjunctive mood, or what Schöne designates as *conjunctivus potentialis,* which subordinates the factual and referential world rendered in the indicative mood.[16] This is why Musil's novel tends to privilege reflection over action. This is also why it gives mimetic sections a subordinated position in relation to diegetic ones. "The indicative mood of the novel's action shrivels into a mere clue around which the tissue of the subjunctive is wrapped," Schöne summarizes.[17]

The narrator of *The Man Without Qualities* thus constructs his world on the principle that it could also be constructed in many different ways. This narrator acts like the divinity that Ulrich conjures up at the beginning of the novel, a God who "probably preferred to speak of His world in the subjunctive of possibility (*hix dixerit quispiam*— 'here someone might object that . . .'), for God creates the world and thinks while He is at it that it could just as well be done differently" (*MWQ* 14 / *MoE* 19). Ulrich, too, practices this heretical idea throughout the novel. He is entrusted with the magical gift of understanding reality in the mood of conjunctivus potentialis. Having little respect for the world as it is, he is more keen on its concealed possibilities. In a word, he has "a sense of possibility" (*Möglichkeitssinn*):

> Whoever has [a sense of possibility] does not say, for instance: Here this or that has happened, will happen, must happen; but he invents: Here this or that might, could, or ought to happen. If he is told that something is the way it is, he will think: Well, it could probably just as well be otherwise. So the sense of possibility could be defined outright as the ability to conceive of everything there might be just as well, and to attach no more importance to what is than to what is not. The consequences of so creative a disposition can be remarkable, and may, regrettably, often make what people admire seem wrong, and what is taboo permissible, or, also, make both a matter of indifference. (*MWQ* 11 / *MoE* 16)

But this talent usually operates undercover, disguised as aristocratic cynicism, intellectual irony, or the empiricist passion of the natural scientist. These three attitudes are frequently demonstrated in Ulrich's behavior, and they all emanate from his devotion to potentiality. Ulrich disregards the surrounding world in order to focus closely on a small part of it. Or else he rejects all current descriptions of the world in order to analyze it anew and find a more adequate description. In the final analysis, only the scrutinizing gaze of the scientist makes it possible to identify the latent possibilities present in reality. The aim of scientific precision is thus not to affirm facts or to establish what is already given, but to dissolve facts into their basic components and to subsequently reorganize these components so as to realize a different world, even a superior one. Precision, then, is not the enemy of fantasy but its assistant, forever allied with the mood of understanding of conjunctivus potentialis. A person equipped with such mentalities treats reality not as a fact but as a hypothesis.

> He suspects that the given order of things is not as solid as it pretends to be; no thing, no self, no form, no principle, is safe, everything is undergoing an invisible but ceaseless transformation, the unsettled holds more of the future than the settled, and the present is nothing but a hypothesis that has not yet been surmounted. What better can he do than hold himself apart from the world, in the good sense exemplified by the scientist's guarded attitude toward facts that might be tempting him to premature conclusions? (*MWQ* 269 / *MoE* 250)

The subjunctive passion of this novelist thus springs from the experimental instinct of the natural scientist and the constructive fantasy of the mathematician. The result is a work where each sentence and each chapter, as well as the hero, are directed by conjunctivus potentialis.[18] But the gift of *Möglichkeitssinn* also involves a responsibility. The task of the hero is to reroute history and force human evolution in a new direction. Reality hence becomes a laboratory for experiments with a view to invent Utopia. Because what is Utopia, if not a possibility which is as yet unrealized?

> Utopias are much the same as possibilities; that a possibility is not a reality means nothing more than that the circumstances in which it is for the moment entangled prevent it from being realized—otherwise it

would be only an impossibility. If this possibility is disentangled from its restraints and allowed to develop, a utopia arises. It is like what happens when a scientist observes the change of an element within a compound and draws his conclusions. Utopia is the experiment in which the possible change of an element may be observed, along with the effects of such a change on the compound phenomenon we call life. (*MWQ* 265f. / *MoE* 246)

The sense of possibility, the subjunctive mood, the experimental attitude of the scientist, and Utopia thus belong to the same project: a denunciation of existing reality and a prefiguration, in the realm of ideas, of a revolution leading to a new social order.

How can the novel accommodate this utopian impulse within a story relating how Austria-Hungary is ineluctably sliding into the abyss of war? Indicative narration and subjunctive imagination appear to block each other's way. In fact, these two registers constantly threaten to cancel each other out. In some of the unfinished sections of the final part of the novel, where Ulrich and his sister Agathe experience the bliss of "the other condition," the utopian tendency gains such momentum that it almost eclipses the representation of the Parallel Campaign.

This also indicates a more general narratological difficulty. How is it possible, if at all, to translate the subjunctive mood into a *narrative* structure, which must necessarily be dominated by an indicative register? If each narrative representation is a hypothesis that must be transcended by a subjunctive imagination looking for new possibilities, if we are forbidden "to believe in any completion," and if we always confront the present state of affairs with an "it could just as well be otherwise," then how is it possible to give an account of reality or history at all? Furthermore, how is it possible to represent a character, if we acknowledge that this character is not one but many, that, in fact, he or she accommodates his or her opposite and is subject to instantaneous change?

The same question reappears if we approach the problem from the other end: how is it possible to represent a better society, or Utopia, if we know that this society is just another hypothesis waiting to be undone by the simple statement: it might as well be done differently? Raising such questions in infinite variations, Musil's discourse provokes a dizzying anxiety that calls the reality of the real into question. Apparently, the confrontations between reality and possibility, between actuality and potentiality, between indicative and subjunctive, or between history and Utopia, mark out an antinomy without synthesis.

As many commentators have pointed out, Musil's novel had to remain incomplete.[19] Generally speaking, there might have been two ways of concluding it. The first ending would have amounted to a rejection of Ulrich and Agathe's utopian project; the second would have represented its realization.[20] In both cases, however, the indicative would have prevailed at the cost of the subjunctive, the order of reality established by sacrificing the possible. In the former case, the utopian project would have collapsed back into the developments of the Parallel Campaign and hence been absorbed by the temporality and mood that dominate the story—a story, as we know, leading toward war. In the second case, the utopian project would have succeeded, replacing the reality of Vienna and the Parallel Campaign and setting itself up as a reality in its own right. The reference of the narrative, that is, the story, would thus shift to another level. But since this level would no longer be evoked as a possibility, but rather instituted as a new reality, the reign of the indicative would return, and the novel would dissolve in the blessed state of "the Millennium" where time is arrested and all change suspended, the narrative movement slowly fading away like Dante's faint image of Paradise.

For Utopia is a place where clocks must stop and history end. It must be a self-enclosed realm of actuality and immanence, where potentiality is exhausted and all efforts toward transcendence interdicted. The reason poets were banned from Plato's republic, Kafka once said, was that they would teach the citizens to think differently and to use their imagination to dream up alternative worlds, ultimately subverting what Plato believed to be the perfect state. Yet Kafka's statement points to yet another paradox, which pertains to Musil's narrative. What Plato says is that no poets would be allowed to live in Utopia, were it realized. But if there were no poets in Utopia, there would be no poems about Utopia, and no stories or narratives either, and perhaps no representations of it at all. Consequently, there would be no way of knowing what utopian life was like. If, on the other hand, there were indeed representations of Utopia, if we had ways to find out what life is like there, this would imply that it could not be a true Utopia, but only a projection marked by our present cultural and literary conventions.

Musil attempted to approach Utopia in the chapter he was working on the day of his death in April 1942, "Breaths of a summer day": "Time stood still, a thousand years weighed as lightly as the opening and closing of an eye; she [Agathe] had attained the Millennium: perhaps God was even allowing his presence to be felt" (*MWQ* 1328 / *MoE* 1233). Yet, as the narration here runs up against its absolute limit, the utopian representation is disavowed in the very act of representation. The narrator asks himself how it is that he, if time indeed "stood still," can state that Agathe felt "things one *after* the other?" If spatial categories of distance and nearness no longer apply in Utopia, how can he even write that her brother "was *beside* her" (*MWQ* 1328 / *MoE* 1233)? Such phrases reintroduce the divisions of time and space that supposedly were abolished.[21]

Trying to picture Utopia is thus comparable to the impossible art of thinking pure difference and otherness. As soon as we believe that we can think otherness, we can be sure that we are wrong, because the very act of thinking otherness implicates an assimilation of "the other" into "the same," into our own conceptual paradigms and ideological fantasies; hence what we think of as otherness cannot be the real thing. This was the problem that confronted Musil. He was seeking a narrative gestalt that could incorporate both the indicative and the subjunctive mood, attempting to write a novel that would not only explain why history happened the way it did but also why it did not need to happen that way.[22]

Discussing the riddles of utopian imagination, Fredric Jameson suggests how to get out of the trap in which one is caught when trying to picture a future society of freedom, or attempting to answer questions such as the one— "the question of the right way to live" (*MWQ* 275 / *MoE* 255)—that haunts Ulrich. When we fantasize about a better society, there is always the risk, Jameson contends, of projecting our present modes of living and being onto the horizon of the future, thus letting the field of tomorrow's possibilities be restricted by the limitations of our own constrained habits.[23] If we already can say what our "longed-for exercise in a not-yet-existent freedom looks like," how can we be sure, Jameson asks, that this is an authentic expression of freedom and not just a repetition of our current mindset? All authentic Utopias and utopian narratives have had to confront this figural difficulty and structural contradiction. Some of these utopian narratives have even found a solution to it:

> However their various authors, like Fourier himself, longed to give us a picture of what they thought life really ought to be like . . . , they have for the most part rigorously restricted their textual production to a very different kind of operation, namely the construction of material mechanisms that would alone enable freedom to come into existence all around them. The mechanism itself has nothing to do with freedom, except to release it; it exists to neutralize what blocks freedom, such as matter, labor, and the requirements of their accompanying social machinery (such as power, training and discipline, enforcement, habits of obedience, respect, and so forth).[24]

Musil's novel excels in utopian thinking, notably in the chapters exploring "the utopia of exact living" and "the utopia of essayism"; these utopian projects are then partly realized in the second half of the novel as Ulrich and Agathe attempt to reach "the Millennium." But only partly realized, for what is depicted here is *not* a full-blown image of utopian living. What we find is instead a working-out of its conditions of possibility, the principles or "material mechanisms," to use Jameson's phrase, "that would alone enable freedom to come into existence." What Musil represents is not freedom, but the utopian energy that would release freedom and neutralize everything that would block it.

If we formulate the problem in this way, we avoid the antinomy between the indicative sense of reality and the subjunctive sense of possibility. Because from this perspective, we see that conjunctivus potentialis functions precisely as such a "material mechanism" that has the power to remove the limitations and restrictions of reality, thus clearing the ground for experiments in utopian thinking and living.

What must be stressed at this point is that the bearer and embodiment of this subjunctive mood, the conjunctivus potentialis, is, precisely, the Musilian subject. Only a "being of possibility" is endowed with the senses needed to discover the right place to be zoned for the construction of a new world. On the other hand, a man with qualities such as indeterminacy, potentiality, and flexibility — which is to say a man without qualities — would of course be just as well adapted to heaven as to hell. An Alyosha and a Stavrogin, an angel and a beast under the same skin, Musil's hero may be a purveyor of utopian prospects. But if he is not to lose his unsettling ability, that highly prized sense of possibility, he must also renounce the decisiveness and resolve that at the same time are needed in order to bring forth even a vague blueprint of Utopia. This is why Musilian subjectivity can only be represented in relation to something else, something that it works against and tries to transform, just as the subjunctive has meaning only in relation to a factual situation that it pictures to change. Musilian subjectivity is thus no more, but also no less, than a guide showing the way to Utopia, and yet unable to settle there itself, because for it, always, even the enchanted empire "could just as well be otherwise."

Definition of the Musilian Subject

The utopian principle in Musil's work can thus be defined as subjectivity in its state of indeterminate possibilism. This state of possibilism consists in a continual denial or negation of the reality constructed by past events. We are then faced with a notion of subjectivity similar to Sartre's definition of "freedom": a state of being in which the subject negates its past and confronts a range of future possibilities that, in Sartre's view, must be turned into projects. "Freedom is the human being putting his past out of play by secreting his own nothingness." [25] The Musilian subject, separating itself from being, is not determined by anything, and hence it is determined by *nothing,* that is, by a nothingness that allows it to free itself from the determinations of the world.

Unlike Sartre's subject, however, Musil's subject refuses to choose any possible future as *its own* future. It remains in a state of what Sartre would call "anguish," lingering in a nothingness through which it recognizes its indeterminacy and freedom, endlessly stripping the world of its "reality" in order to preserve its possibilities. It is as if Musil construed his hero only to prove that human subjectivity is constituted precisely by its power to negate, deny, distantiate, and dissolve the weight of being. In this sense it is foreign to any Sartrean commitment, and it comes to realize an agency that, I want to suggest, approximates the principle of *negativity,* as this is defined in some contemporary theories of subjectivity.

According to Julia Kristeva, in her reading of Hegel's *Logic,* the concept of negativity (*Negativität*) is a principle that is anterior to conceptual thinking. Emerging from the presymbolic flux that exists prior to the intervention of the delimiting categories of reason, negativity is a force that "figures as the indissoluble relation between an 'ineffable' mobility and its 'particular determination.' "[26] Crucially, negativity is prior to the Hegelian triad of thesis, antithesis, and synthesis (or thesis, negation, and negation of negation), which is to say that it also precedes the division between subject and object, or self and other; it is the very *mobile law* which sets up these oppositions and then dissolves them in a never ending dialectics which at once affirms the division between subject and object and calls it into question, thus dissolving such abstractions into the process which created them in the first place. In accordance with this view, Slavoj Žižek writes that "negativity is in a way *prior to what is being negated.*" It is a movement that opens the place where every positive identity can be situated and that at the same time undermines this identity in order to situate it in a different place.[27]

When Hegel designated negativity as the "soul of dialectics," he implied that negativity functions as the regulating mechanism of the dialectical process in which the Spirit, or to use a more mundane term, subjectivity, moves toward self-presence and unity.[28] Unlike Hegel's *Geist,* however, neither Kristeva's nor Žižek's subject is ever able to master either the force that moves it (negativity) or the social and symbolic order that circumscribes it and freezes it in identities. Subjectivity, in their view, is always situated at a crossroad or intersection between negativity and the symbolic order.[29] Just as the subject will never be able to assimilate these moments with its own being, so will it also avoid ever being fully assimilated by them.

Kristeva's theory consequently defines the dialectic as the subject's movement toward an *impossible* unity with itself. It is a movement toward unity, or self-unification, because the subject seeks to establish for itself a position as a speaking "I," or cogito, with a recognizable identity; the movement of negativity is thus momentarily arrested; Kristeva calls this part of the process the "thetic moment" (*le thétique*). Yet, at the same time, this self-unification is impossible, because subjectivity will always exceed the identity constructed by the thetic position. Since the cogito or the "I" is a position sustained only by the order of language and logical rationality, it will never correspond to the full reality of the subject's being, because this reality is also enveloped by a nonrational and nonlinguistic realm, what Kristeva calls the semiotic order, and what Žižek associates with Jacques Lacan's concept of the Real. This is not the place to discuss these concepts in detail. It should be enough to point out that both, different as they are, designate a dimension of the psyche that is anterior to the formation of an ego-identity, and which gives the person a certain disposition toward language, culture, and society.[30] This disposition is then activated symbolically with the thetic rupture, which causes the human being to emerge as a subject within the symbolic order. The subject suppresses its primary desires, resigns before the symbolic law governing family and culture, thus assuming the place and accepting the identity, the name, offered to it by this law, and, ultimately, by the language that enables it to represent itself as a subject.[31]

The acquisition of language and identity entails that the human being's immediate relation to the world is disrupted. Instead of merely being a part of experience, the subject must represent experience with words, which entails a repression of its immediate "semiotic" relation to reality. Henceforth, the subject's relation to itself is thus mediated by the symbolic order. This mediation involves at least three aspects of subjectivity: a speaking subject, a subject of speech, and a spoken subject.[32] Expressing itself within the order of language, the *speaking subject*, an embodied human agent, externalizes itself by claiming the position as "I." This "I" is what the linguists call a *subject of speech*, a purely grammatical position, independent of the human agent employing this "I" as a vehicle for its enunciations. The *spoken subject*, finally, is the referent of the enunciations made by this "I." The relationship between these three positions is processual: in order to articulate its desire, the speaking subject must project it onto a *sign*—the subject of speech—which it must first substitute for itself, and with whose *referent*—the spoken subject—it must then identify itself. Since both sign and referent are external to the speaking subject, these three positions will never coincide. Yet, the subject can exist only insofar as it persists in its efforts to find itself by losing itself in language. This, then, is the sense in which subjectivity is a locus of negativity. In order to articulate its self-identity, the subject must paradoxically negate each of the positions that it sets up when attempting to attain self-identity.[33] The notion of negativity demands that we see subjectivity not as a unit, substance, or structure, but as a process. Lacking any central and organizing core, the subject exists only in the shifting identifications that lead from one position to the other.

This process of subjectivity can also be described in phenomenological terms. Before the linguistic turn in philosophy, Sartre analyzed an analogous process of negativity, stating that identity is constituted through moments of "ekstasis," meaning that the subject always "stands out from" or "stands outside of" what it perceives as its self. Hence subjectivity, or the "for-itself," can never converge with the identities through which it attempts to unify itself. Whether it attempts to reflect on itself, project itself into the future or into the past, or perceive itself through the look of others, it cannot capture itself in any other way than by, paradoxically, negating itself. In order to be itself, the subject must step out of itself. Eventually, it must recognize that every time it consciously wants to coincide with its identity, it will distance itself from this identity. Subjectivity is always in a position of ek-stasis.[34]

I want to argue that the notion of subjectivity conveyed by these contemporary theories is present in *The Man Without Qualities,* though in a different code. The following passage provides an example:

> When I remember as far back as I can, I'd say that there was hardly any separation between inside and outside. When I crawled toward something, it came on wings to meet me; when something important happened, the excitement was not just in us, but the things themselves came to a boil. I won't claim that we were happier then than we were later on. After all, we hadn't yet taken charge of ourselves. In fact, we didn't really yet exist; our personal condition was not yet separated from the world's. It sounds strange, but it's true: our feelings, our desires, our very selves, were not yet quite inside ourselves. What's even stranger is that I might as easily say: they were not yet quite taken away from us. If you should sometime happen to ask yourself today, when you think you're entirely in possession of yourself, who you really are, you will discover that you always see yourself from the outside, as an object. You'll notice that one time you get angry, another time you get sad, just as your coat will sometimes be wet and sometimes too warm. No matter how intensely you try to look at yourself, you may at most find out something about the outside, but you'll never get inside yourself. Whatever you do, you remain outside yourself, with the possible exception of those rare moments when a friend might say that you're beside yourself. It's true that as adults we've made up for this by being able to think at any time that "I am" — if you think that's fun. You see a car, and somehow in a shadowy way you also see: "I am seeing a car". You're in love, or sad, and see that it's you. But neither the car, nor your sadness, nor your love, nor even yourself, is quite fully there. Nothing is as completely there as it once was in childhood. (*MWQ* 979 / *MoE* 902)

This statement contains, first, an evocation of the Imaginary order of early childhood, where impressions and experiences are not yet mediated by language. Second, it is a virtual deconstruction of the expressivist paradigm and its spatial coordinates of interiority and exteriority. Turning these coordinates back upon themselves, so as to bring their theoretical incoherence in evidence, this passage rejects the idea of an inner self externalizing itself in expressions and acts. Finally, and most important, this passage contains a theory of subjectivity in its own right. Subjectivity, in this view, emerges through a moment of negativity, as the imaginary order is disrupted and the subject is forced to use symbols to represent its reality. Before this moment, there is no subject ("In fact, we didn't really yet exist"). After this moment, there is no subject either. ("[Not] even yourself is quite fully there.") So, where is the subject? It is present only in the process of mediation between the three moments discussed above. First, there is the speaking subject (someone seeing a car and expressing this sense datum); second, the subject of speech (the grammatical subject in the sentence "I see a car"); and, third, the subject that recognizes itself as the spoken subject or implied reference of this statement (the subject that identifies with this act of seeing and the act of enunciation describing it). This dialectic has neither inside nor outside. When Musil's narrator says that a person is "outside" himself, he does not mean that this person is alienated from his true being, but that he can never escape the fact that he always must mediate his being through the symbolic order, and that in these processes of mediation alone is he present as a subject for others and for himself. In short, the subject always "stands outside" its identities; it is, therefore, "ek-static."

Whether described in psycholinguistic or phenomenological terms, identity is thus to be grasped as the phantom effect of that never ending process in which subjectivity is articulated. "Identity" equals the more or less permanent stabilization of subjectivity caused by the subject's recognition of itself as "the spoken subject," that is, as the reference of its own self-reflections, of its own speech, or of the appellation of others. This recognition is not of its own making, however, but it is imposed upon the subject by the surrounding symbolic order. As Anthony P. Kerby remarks, the symbolic mediation of identity is never a neutral mirroring process.[35] Although there is, in principle, an infinite range of signifiers that the subject may use to signify itself or identify itself, the surrounding social and symbolic order dictates which positions it is allowed to speak from, which signifiers it may occupy so as to make itself—or its *self*—intelligible before others. As Anika Lemaire maintains, "The subject becomes set in his utterances and social roles, and their totality is gradually built up into an 'ego,' which is no more than an 'objectification' of the subject." [36]

The subject thus slips into the forms, roles, characters, and qualities that are supplied to it by the social order. This is what Musil, in his essay "The German as Symptom," calls "bonding" (*Bindung*), arguing that the principal bond in modernity is the profession. "Outside these bonds the individual cannot raise an arm or lift a finger. He collapses like a deflated balloon or, if inflated by an impulse, he deforms himself immediately in some single, random direction. He has (aside from this) no shaping or guiding ideas" (*PS* 159 / *GW* 2:1362).

The crucial point of Kristeva's and Žižek's respective arguments is that negativity, like Musil's sense of possibility, immediately destabilizes these bonds. A subject that is initially circumscribed by socially recognized identities is thus transformed into what Kristeva calls "a subject in process." [37]

This subjectivity rejects fixed identities. Yet it cannot exist without identity. The preceding analysis affords a conception of identity as something that must be affirmed *and* immediately called into question. It must be affirmed to the extent that it is an indispensable product of a temporal development in which a subject integrates the various subject positions that it has assumed during its life. A person's history thus becomes what Paul Smith describes as a "colligation of multifarious and multiform subject-positions." [38] The resulting construct—the identity of the subject—may conform to the ideological appellation of the subject. In this case, the identity of the individual is shaped by the symbolic order in conformity with the norms and ideologies that pertain in any given society. The result is a fantasy of a permanent self, integrated with society and serving the reproduction of that society.[39]

The portrait of Ulrich's father illustrates this fiction of a well-integrated self. In his case, life is a natural fulfillment of personal truth and social meaning. Individual and social life are expressions of the same fundamental principle. This attitude is typical of the expressivist subject that underwrites the narrative order of the bildungsroman. What Musil's narrator terms "sense of reality" (*Wirklichkeitssinn*) is the individual's belief in the social and symbolic order; Ulrich's father is described as its ideal exponent.[40] Socially, the various subject positions that the father has occupied during his life merge into one dominant position that upholds the social order and at the same time is upheld by it. Symbolically, these positions have crystallized into a single sign of truth and normative reason. A professor of law, this patriarch is hence the ideal incarnation of that position of authority which Lacanian psychoanalysis names the phallus and which regulates the circulation of meaning and goods in the world.

But the colligation of the different subject positions of a person may also result in different forms of identity construction. Paul Smith, like Kristeva and Žižek, suggests that these positions, rather than being integrated with the normative narrative of a particular social order, may be bound together as a dynamic entity of differences, multiplicity, and conflict. The "internalized" conflicts between varying subject positions may thus turn the subject into an agency of transformation, a principle of negativity, which transgresses each identity conferred upon the subject. Such is, in the final analysis, the Musilian subject, operating in the mood of conjunctivus potentialis, and its primary example is of course the novel's protagonist, Ulrich. Musil's narrator explicitly invests Ulrich with the power of negativity. Inclining "toward the negative," defending "the negative side of life," Ulrich is said to be "hypercritical" and to live "against himself" (*MWQ* 512, 160 / *MoE* 470, 152). He "detests everything with pretensions to permanence, all the great ideals and laws and their little fossilized imprint, the well-adjusted character. [He] regards nothing as fixed, no personality, no order of things" (*MWQ* 163 / *MoE* 154). Only ever half-integrated with itself, the Musilian subject exposes "the human being as a passionate patchwork" (*MWQ* 766* / *MoE* 705).

The Power of Negativity

Kristeva identifies this "subject in process" by scrutinizing how pre-conscious dimensions of the psyche affect the vocality and rhythmicity of literary works by Lautréamont, Mallarmé, Bataille, and Joyce. In *The Man Without Qualities,* however, the central instance of negativity does not primarily make itself felt in the voice and rhythm of the novel's language, although there are several passages of this kind in Musil's narrative as well, particularly in Agathe's wordplays and in Clarisse's schizoid discourse. Nor is Musilian negativity a matter of a rejection of the referential logic of symbolization, as is the case with the avant-garde poetry that Kristeva examines. It is rather indicated by more sophisticated and sublimated modalities of symbolization. In previous chapters we observed a destabilization of character and temporality that led to the emergence of a heterological and polycentric space of subjectivity, a *Zwischenraum.* In this space, different matrices of identity and forms of narrative inscription contradict and undo each other, thus throwing the character into a perplexing void, while also confusing the narrative perspective and the points of identifications that are made available to the reader. This space of indeterminacy and potentiality is a case of the Musilian modality of negativity, summarized by the notion of conjunctivus potentialis. The subjunctive principle of possibility overrules and negates the logic that sustains the belief in the indicative representation of reality.

At the junction between the first and the second part of the novel, this power of negativity takes the entire narrative on a new track. Social reality finally stands revealed as a realm of hollow appearance, and the novel starts moving in a utopian direction. The mechanism that releases and propels this movement is the dialectic of negativity, driving the subject away from the social and symbolic order, and away from the illusion of a stable identity, while making it acutely aware of its "shape-lessness." Deprived of a stable position with which to identify, the hero undergoes a series of transfigurations, in which everything can emerge as a point of identification for him. All objects, persons, and images become a potential signifier for his self. As soon as Ulrich's desire seizes upon such a signifier and experiences an elusive moment of recognition, the motion of negativity tears him away from this stasis and presents a new point of identification that mediates his desire. Ulrich remembers an old photograph of himself, but cannot recognize himself in the picture. He tries to picture Moosbrugger, and now, indeed, he recognizes himself, realizing that "the image of a murderer was no stranger to him than any other of the world's pictures" (*MWQ* 712 / *MoE* 653).

Throughout these chapters, which connect the first half, "Pseudoreality Prevails," to the second, "Into the Millennium," and which also link the story about the Parallel Campaign and Vienna to the story about Agathe and "the other condition," we find an accelerating movement where one misrecognition is replaced by the other, illustrating the metamorphosis of desire described by René Girard, who regards this as the most characteristic trait of the modern novel. The once unitary subject is "decomposed," Girard argues, because of the multiplication of the points of identification for the hero's desire.[41] Ulrich works his way through the chain of signifiers of the symbolic order without finding a stable point of fixation for his desire. Kristeva's designation—*le sujet en procès*—is particularly relevant here: it captures how Ulrich continues to abandon his identity, "dissolving the buffer of reality in a mobile discontinuity, leaving the shelter of the family, the state, or religion," and how he "destroys all constancy to produce another and then destroys that one as well."[42]

In a climactic moment at the beginning of the second part of the novel, Ulrich reaches the peak of the hierarchy of the symbolic order and finds himself standing before the very incarnation of the Law: the father. The subject in process is literally confronted with the source of order and reason. A man without qualities faces a man with qualities:

He looked his father in the face. What if everything he regarded as his own personality was no more than a reaction against that face, originating in some childish antagonism? He looked around for a mirror, but there was none, only this blank face to reflect the light. He scrutinized it for resemblances. Perhaps there were some. Perhaps it was all there: the

race, the bonds, the non-personal, the stream of heredity in which the
individual is only a ripple, the limitations, disillusionments, the eternal
repetition of a mind going in circles, which he hated with his deepest
will to life. (*MWQ* 753f.* / *MoE* 693f.)

Ulrich looks for a mirror, that is, an instrument capable of confirming
his identity. But he finds none, just as there is no ego-image to stabilize
his subjectivity. The face of the father, on the other hand, presents an
image of the entire system of culture, race, and tradition, of the stream
of hereditary relationships, of everything that binds a person to the
social order and fixes his identity. The pressure that the paternal face
exerts on Ulrich is almost physical. It recalls the force emanating from
the symbolic centerpiece in Joseph Roth's *Radetzky March* (1932), a
majestic portrait of the ancestor of the Trotta family, the great hero
of Solferino, whose eternal fame reminds sons and grandsons of their
duties and debts to their Fatherland. Ulrich's encounter with the paternal
image also recalls the episode of the baptismal bowl in Thomas Mann's
The Magic Mountain (1924), a silver dish that symbolizes a venerable
tradition of family values and before which the young Hans Castorp
stands at attention while his grandfather names each of his forefathers:
"His father's name was there, as was in fact his grandfather's, and his
great-grandfather's; and now that syllable came doubled, tripled, and
quadrupled from the storyteller's mouth . . . , and he would listen to
the great-great-great-great — that somber sound of the crypt and buried
time." [43] Clearly, the face of Ulrich's father is similarly an index of the
phallic order that links present to past and sustains the status quo. At
one stroke, Ulrich now rejects this normative narrative — the bonds, the
stream of heredity, the eternal repetition of the same. For this reason,
Musil's protagonist can be counted among all the other black sheep in
the literature of the period. *Die vaterlose Gesellschaft* ("The Fatherless
Society") was the title of a book by Paul Federn that appeared in Vienna
in 1919. Ulrich is a citizen of such a society, as is Mann's Castorp, along
with Schnitzler's playboys and Hofmannsthal's aesthetes, not to speak
of Roth's Carl Joseph Trotta, the last and useless heir of the hero of Sol-

ferino. They all distrust the ideas and symbols of their fathers. Almost all of them sign up for annihilation in the trenches of the Great War.

Indeed, in Musil's novel the patriarch is already dead. He lies in his coffin, waiting to be buried. Ulrich and Agathe's attitude toward their deceased father — their absent-minded reception of condolatory visitors and their half-hearted participation in the funeral ceremony; their haphazard way of partitioning the inheritance as well as their sacrilegious jokes about the old man (culminating when Agathe stuffs her underwear into the pocket of the dressed corpse); their blatant negligence of the father's wishes and finally Agathe's daring forgery of his will — all this amounts to a symbolic parricide where the children sacrifice the Law and celebrate the death of the Father. This carnivalesque funeral is the pivotal point at which the pseudoreality of das Seinesgleichen turns into the hovering image of *The Millennium*. As Massimo Cacciari has underscored, it occurs at the peak of the explosion of the subject's ego and beyond the limits of order.[44] The episode takes place in early 1914: it is as though Ulrich and Agathe conduct their own odd version of *Le Sacre du printemps*.

The sacrifice of the patriarchal order is also a sacrifice of the law of narrative order. By the same token, it implies an exhaustion of social identities. Shortly after his father's death, Ulrich is approached by a journalist gathering information for an obituary. As Ulrich tries to give him the highlights, he finds that his father's life fades away. Incapable of apprehending the meaning of his father's career, he is given a few clues by the journalist. "Only then, in the grip of the forceps of a professional curiosity trained to extract what was worth knowing, did the interview proceed, and Ulrich felt as if he were present at the Creation." Ulrich's vague replies are then molded into the stereotyped phrases of the newspaper obituary. "For every piece of information he had received, the reporter had had in readiness some six- or eight-cylinder phrase: distinguished scholar, wide sympathies, forward-looking but statesmanlike, mind of truly universal scope, and so on." Ulrich looks at the remnants of his father's life in disappointment, thinking that "he would have liked to add something worth saying about his father, but the chronicler had his facts and was putting his notebook away; what remained was like trying to pick up the contents of a glass of water without the glass" (*MWQ* 752f. / *MoE* 692f.).

To understand a life, Anthony Paul Kerby suggests, "is to trace its development upon a narrative thread, a thread that unifies otherwise disparate or unheeded happenings into the significance of a development, a directionality, a destiny." [45] Meditating on the life of his father, Ulrich finds no such thread onto which the projects of his parent may be strung into narrative form. His life appears to be contained, but there is no container. Between life and the form that retrospectively shapes life, there is utter incompatibility. Thus, at the moment when his father's life is concluded and the heir is expected to commemorate his father's achievements and secure a place for him in posterity, Ulrich responds with a silence that barely conceals his own sense of absurdity. What is negated by Ulrich's statement—or rather by his inability to make any statement at all—is the idea that identity is an expression of a timeless personal truth. Identity is, rather, a procession of masks, which in the case of his father hardened as the years went by. Ulrich recognizes merely the sediments of the eternal narrative of tradition, race, and culture—the stream of heredity—to which he responds with a hatred surging up from the depth of his being.

Negative Ethics

At the beginning of this chapter, I stated that *The Man Without Qualities* maintains that the human subject can be represented only by a narrative that gradually constructs and reconstructs its identity. Yet I also argued that the novel asserts that the subject can never be captured by any code, narrative, symbolic, or other. Musilian subjectivity would thus necessitate narration, at the same time resisting it. What looked like a contradiction can now be explained as a question of focus. The previous pages have shown that identity, for Musil, must be affirmed and called into question at once. It must be affirmed, because the subject can be constituted and constitute itself in no other way than by identifying with a position prepared for it by the symbolic order and the ideological narratives of society. This is the sense in which the novel affirms no other foundation for the subject than the identity constructed through narration. But we may also focus on the fact that this mediation is also a repression, since each inscription of subjectivity confines it to the position of a particular identity. Hence, the movement of Musilian negativity always returns to challenge every attempt to circumscribe the identity of the subject. The function of narrative is thus enabling and constraining at once.

This is why Musil's narrator defines ethics not in terms of obedience to norms and commandments but as a violation of them; in this sense, too, *The Man Without Qualities* prepares the ground for more recent notions of ethics and subjectivity. In accord with such notions, authentic ethics is governed by the principle of negativity; it can be realized only in acts of transgression. Ethics is therefore closely related to aesthetic production, Kristeva maintains: dissolving meaning and creating new meaning, unseating the subject and placing it in a different place, poetic and aesthetic activity is ethical because it liberates the subject from its ideological confinement.[46] Musil's notion of subjectivity entails a similar ethics of transgression; that is why Ulrich and Agathe's extended discussions on the nature of morality can only lead to a program that posits true morality beyond Good and Evil. "The good," Ulrich says to Agathe, "has become a cliché almost by its very nature, while evil remains criticism. The immoral achieves its divine right by being a drastic critique of the moral! It shows us that life has other possibilities. It shows us up for liars" (*MWQ* 1040 / *MoE* 959).

True ethics is immoral, revealing our fictions of identity as lies. The source of ethical practice can also be subsumed under the concept of negativity; or, to be more specific, it is an aspect of Musilian subjectivity that is set in the utopian mode of conjunctivus potentialis. In Musil's world, ethical practice disrupts the dominant ideological narratives of society, and it is therefore antagonistic to the establishment of narrative meaning. We are far from the premodern world of Walter Benjamin's storyteller, in which each tale told was at the same time advice on how to lead a good life, that is, a lesson in ethics. In Musil's modernistic universe, by contrast, ethical practice serves to dissolve the norms and identities that are supported by the symbolic and social orders, while narrative practice serves to construct and maintain such norms and identities. A final digression, this time taking us to Paul Ricoeur's and Giorgio Agamben's respective hermeneutics of subjectivity, will shed light on this contradiction. I want to explain why Musilian subjectivity is the common source of both narration and ethics, a source in which they are as yet unseparated and from which they are then projected as two antagonistic practices, the practice of narrative leading toward an assertion of identity, the practice of ethics leading to a rejection of identity.

Identity as Otherness

Paul Ricoeur distinguishes between two modalities of identity. The first, identity in the sense of sameness (*mêmeité* or *l'identité-idem*), is defined in terms of continuity, numerical and qualitative identity, and temporal permanence. It states the answer to the question, "What are you?" The second, identity in the sense of selfhood (*ipséité* or *l'identité-ipse*), answers the question, "Who are you?" The latter cannot be defined in terms of sameness or temporality, however, because "identity in the sense of *ipse* implies no assertion concerning some unchanging core of the personality." [47]

Numerous misunderstandings in the history of philosophy have arisen from the confusion of identity and ipseity, Giorgio Agamben states.[48] Like Ricoeur, he suggests that we distinguish between a subjectivity that *is* something by virtue of its belonging to a predicate, that is, by virtue of being defined by qualities, essences, or properties, and a subjectivity that, by contrast, is something by virtue of being anterior to all predication. The former case exhibits the subject as defined by an unchanging substantial identity, the latter case exposes subjectivity as *ipsum,* what Agamben calls "singularity." [49]

Normally, *idem*-identity is sedimented upon the self, or *ipse.* This process is conditioned by the ability to understand a course of events as a story, Ricoeur maintains. Narrative is an act of emplotment, linking a subject to certain experiences and events and hence giving this subject its *idem*-identity, the sameness and permanence that make it possible to recognize this subject as a certain character. This process is represented in almost all fictitious and historical narratives. The characters are explained by their reactions to the events of the story, and these events, conversely, are explained by the intentions of the characters.[50]

As stories reach a certain level of complexity, however, they may also start to problematize the characters themselves, and the characters start to problematize the story. With modernism, Ricoeur argues, we reach narratives that expand the emplotment of character to an extreme. The events of the story no longer add to the identities of its characters but pull them in contradictory directions and thus decompose them into impersonal parts, sometimes even reducing them to the point where little or nothing is left. Ricoeur's exemplary text is *The Man Without Qualities,* which, in his view, exposes the complete loss of identity, personality, character, and qualities.[51] What Ricoeur and Agamben teach us about the dissolution of identity in Musil's novel, however, is that "the nonsubject" (*le non-sujet*) in fact remains a form of subjectivity. The subject deprived of its identity still curiously remains "a figure of the subject, be it only in the negative mode." For even though the Musilian self is confronted by the hypothesis of its own nothingness, it would be mistaken, Ricoeur explains, to conclude that this nothingness (*néant*) equals nothing (*rien*):

> The sentence "I am nothing" must keep its paradoxical form: "nothing" would mean nothing at all if "nothing" were not in fact attributed to an "I." But who is *I* when the subject says that it is nothing? A self deprived of the help of sameness, I have repeatedly stated. So be it. In this regard, the hypothesis is not unsupported by existential verifications: it may well be that the most dramatic transformations of personal identity pass through the crucible of the nothingness of identity, a nothingness that would be the equivalent of the empty square in the transformations

so dear to Lévi-Strauss. . . . In these moments of extreme destitution, the empty response to the question "Who am I?" refers not to nullity but to the nakedness of the question itself.[52]

What appears when the subject is stripped of its idem-identity, the sameness of character, is thus the ipse interrogating its proper noth-ingness. Ricoeur's reference to Lévi-Strauss's analyses of mythologi-cal transformations (a man turning into an animal, turning into a tree, turning into a stream, turning into mist) is crucial, because it conveys the idea that, despite the stark differences between the various phases in this chain of transformations, something is sustained throughout the process, be it only an unknown emptiness; despite the discontinuities between these positions, there is a constancy that can be ascribed to a *subject in process* of transforming. This is what Ricoeur calls *l'ipséité*, a modality of subjectivity for which the idem-identity merely serves as a temporary dwelling or incarnation. Ipse is thus posited as an inter-section, a crossroad, or at an empty space (*la case vide*), between the stases in which subjectivity is fixed in an identity. The subject as ipse is a subject in process, motored by negativity, oscillating between in-determinacy ("Who am I?") and signification ("I am").

The subject-as-ipse must thus be thought of as neither existence nor essence but as a "singularity." Agamben suggests that this subject is thinkable only as "a manner of rising forth," as an event in language grasped before it has turned into signification. Before the thetic mo-ment, when subjectivity crystallizes into meaning, there is a transient moment of negativity in which the utterance remains just an indica-tion of the presence of a subject that precedes qualities, properties, and meanings.[53] Agamben argues that this subject can only be described as a "whatever" (*qualunque*); stated differently, this subject indicates that there is no essence, substance, disposition, vocation, or biological destiny that humans must enact or realize.[54] This does not mean that humans are consigned to nothingness, or that they can freely choose to adopt or not adopt this or that identity. "There is in effect something that humans are and have to be, but this something is not an essence nor properly a thing: *It is the simple fact of one's own existence as pos-*

sibility or potentiality." [55] Attempting to define an antiexpressivist view of the human subject, Agamben thus employs the idiom of possibility and negativity also formulated in *The Man Without Qualities.*

Like Žižek's negativity and Kristeva's *le sujet en procès,* Ricoeur's ipséité and Agamben's singularity provide us with a way of conceptualizing identity not as a beginning or foundation but as a product and construction. They all examine the subject at the moment of its emergence, the very same moment that Musil intended to capture: subjectivity degree zero. At this point, subjectivity is absorbed in a silence in which every utterance is unsaid and thus possible to enunciate. But it is a silence that must be broken, broken by an utterance which will immediately situate the subject in a position that it must then defend or transform through further acts of enunciation. Subjectivity is thus suspended between the mobility where everything is possible, and the point where it is connected to systems of signification that are always ideologically invested.

The constellation of Musil's modernist narrative and the postwar or postmodern theories of subjectivity that I have discussed above throws new light on modernist literature in general. Few modernist works explore subjectivity as richly as *The Man Without Qualities* does, to be sure. Yet Musil was not alone in depicting a subject who must gather strength from its own negativity. Döblin's Franz Biberkopf, Kafka's K., Rilke's Malte Laurids Brigge, Roth's Tarabas and Job, and Broch's "sleepwalkers" are all gradually deprived of the social and psychological support of an identity and reduced to a state of nothingness in which their only agency is voiced in the naked despair of the question "Who am I?"

As long as these tormented characters are interpreted through the expressivist paradigm, they can only be understood as figures searching for roots and homes, for community and identity, and often searching in vain. The secondary literature on modernist literature normally presents not only Musil but also Döblin, Kafka, Rilke, Roth, Broch, and others as depictions of a deplorable condition of alienation, whose examples invite us to think that every human being ought to have a solid self that expresses his or her belonging. Seen through a more contemporary paradigm, however, these modernist tales are the first probings for a truly modern and antiexpressivist view of the human condition. The wretched nothingness crying out in Kafka and Döblin, especially, would then reveal that the human subject is fundamentally constituted by an irreducible negativity, which prevents it from ever being fully assimilated by the identities offered it by the surrounding cultural order. In the homogenizing cultural environment in which these writers worked, and which in many ways are still with us, this negativity should not be seen as a sign of alienation, but rather as a sign of dissent, or even, as Döblin's Biberkopf demonstrates, as a traumatic psychic eclipse, a threshold of madness that one must cross in order to be born anew as a free agent.

There is thus continuity between the notion of subjectivity found in modernist literature and postmodern or poststructural theories of decentered subjectivity.[56] This is not to say that there is any simple causality between, for example, Musil's *The Man Without Qualities* and Agamben's *The Man Without Content*.[57] Yet Agamben's choice of title for the book in which he approaches his theory of negativity is of course no coincidence either. We are dealing with an instance of delayed historical causality: the emergence of a "postmodern" concept of subjectivity allows us to identify the genealogical beginnings of this concept in a modernist notion of subjectivity, and this retrospectively transforms our view of modernist literature in general. More specifically, I am suggesting that it is only the emergence of later theories of subjectivity that has brought the implications of Musil's representation of subjectivity to the surface, and, furthermore, that it is only through this discovery of Musil's novel as an encrypted beginning of an antiexpressivist notion of the subject that we become aware of the historical reasons for the emergence of contemporary theories of subjectivity. Kristeva's subject in process, Ricoeur's subject as ipséité, and Agamben's subject as singularity—all indicate that subjectivity is founded on lack, that identity is constituted not as an expression of essence but only in relation to an other, and that the human being is defined by a force of negativity that resists and questions every homogenous social and symbolic order. In this sense, these theories are elaborations of the Musilian subject of

"shapelessness," which, as we shall see, is conceived as a historical response to monolithic ideologies that dominated German and Austrian
culture in the 1920s and 1930s.

Agamben and Ricoeur both state that ipse names the ethical substance of the subject. For it is only by conceiving of the human being in
this naked state, as a subject without identity, that we are able to account
for the fact that the ethical relation between the self and the other or,
rather, *ipseity* and *alterity,* precedes and determines the subject's constitution of an identity (in the sense of idem). Prior to any identity, prior
to the permanence of character and personality, there is a dialectic between the subject as ipse and the alterity of that which surrounds this
subject.[58] One's relation to the other precedes one's relation to the self,
which is to say that one's self-identity is necessarily mediated by an
other; the other is thus ontologically primary, because it is this alterity,
and it alone, that calls the self into being. The ego can arrive at its self-
identity only by being reflected in another man, Žižek explains; R. D.
Laing similarly states that "the sense of identity requires the existence
of another by whom one is known." [59]

Before the arrival of another person, the subject as ipse is at once
negativity and possibility. The question "Who am I?" here corresponds
to the answer "I am nothing," which, as Ricoeur and Agamben observe,
may be translated as "I can become anything." Once the other is approaching, however, the subject will give a different answer. The voice
of the other will force the subject to break its silence and reveal its presence and locality. This is the spirit of those very first words that must
be uttered before anything else can take place: "I am here!" Before
the processes of signification and predication that limit the subject's
being to an identity, this being must first be asserted as a presence in
its own right, and this can be done only through an act of indication by
which the subject constitutes itself in a specific time and place. This
act of indication marks the subject's emergence and reappearance in
the world.

In fact, this is also the primal scene that is rehearsed again and again
in the dual figure of Ulrich and Agathe. The siblings talk to each other,
we are told at one point, like someone would talk who is still young and

innocent and thus finds it easy, when he or she, "moved by someone else, is exchanging views on the eternal questions of 'Who are you? This is who I am.' " Ulrich, the passage continues, "derived the assurance that his sister was able to follow him word for word not from having reflected on it but from her inner being" (*MWQ* 980* / *MoE* 903). The words exchanged between the siblings are no longer signifiers whose references slip away. These words are messengers from another world, ready to uncover the meaning of Being itself—and their voices, says the narrator, were intertwined as in a responsory (*MWQ* 763 / *MoE* 702). Agathe's voice finally offers Ulrich a sense of recognition, a point of identification calling him back to life and reality after years of anomie.

At the heart of Musil's subject, there is thus a presence of another subject. In fact, it is the other who constitutes the very inwardness of the subject. Agathe's externality gives Ulrich a sense of having an interiority. At this point, if not earlier, it is evident that the paradigm that governs Musil's representation of subjectivity is not that of expressivity but its opposite: a constructivist paradigm of subjectivity according to which the origin of identity is the presence of the other. The identity of the Musilian subject, then, is always external to itself; in a word, it is *ekstatic*. In his relation with Agathe, Ulrich realizes that "his own secret self [is] peering out at him from behind the curtains of a stranger's eyes" (*MWQ* 982 / *MoE* 905).

A Face of Possibilities

On their first reencounter, it strikes Ulrich that Agathe looks quite like himself. The sister confirms the impression: "I had no idea we were twins!" (*MWQ* 734 / *MoE* 676). This is their first exchange. It occurs at the turning point in the story, at the beginning of "Into the Millennium," the second half of the novel. Ulrich has left Vienna and gone to his native town B. in order to attend his father's funeral. When preparing to dine with his sister on the evening of his arrival, he puts on a lounging suit which, the narrator underscores, resembles a Pierrot costume. To his amazement, his sister greets him in the same kind of costume;

she is a tall, blond Pierrot who looks quite like himself. As the narrator closes in on her face, this similarity is pronounced:

> [Her face] did not seem very like his own, but perhaps he was mistaken; maybe it was like the same face done in pastels and in a woodcut, the difference in the medium obscuring the congruence of line and plane. There was something in this face he found disturbing. After a while, he realized that he simply could not read its expression; what was missing was whatever it is that enables one to draw the useful inferences about the person. It was a face that contained much, but nothing in it was emphasized, nothing combined in the way that normally suggests traits of character. (*MWQ* 735* / *MoE* 676f.)

Ulrich discovers that Agathe's facial text lacks "expressivity." The counterpoint to this description is the passage quoted above, where Ulrich looks at the face of his dead father, finding that it expresses the entire culture that he hates. But the passage also contains a polemic against a view of the human face that was even more common in Musil's time than it is in ours. Georg Simmel, in his 1901 essay "Die ästhetische Bedeutung des Gesichts" ("The Aesthetic Meaning of the Face"), argues that the human face is an aesthetic symbol of the innermost personality, asserting that painting and sculpture tend to privilege the face because the soul expresses itself most clearly ["die Seele sich am deutlichsten ausdrückt"] there.[60] Needless to say, Simmel's idea is intimately related to the expressivist conception of identity. The depiction of Agathe's countenance in Musil's novel negates this physiognomic idea. Lacking expressivity and character traits, Agathe's face is a face of possibilities.

The quoted episode is the first in a series of encounters in which the narrator presents Agathe as a copy of Ulrich, but one made from another material and hence both similar and different. This would explain why Agathe attracts Ulrich. Due to her likeness, she is the only other human being who is allowed to enter the closed world into which Ulrich has withdrawn in order to entertain a narcissistic but futile search for identity—a search leading him ever deeper into a void. Mirroring this lack of identity, Agathe's lack confirms his sense of nothingness.

Agathe exemplifies a human being in the stage of shapelessness. She is an instance of what we discussed above: the nothingness of subjectivity—its lack of idem-identity—does not equal "nothing"; it is, rather, an indeterminacy that implies an infinity of possibilities waiting to be awakened by the voice of the other. Performing as this other for Ulrich, Agathe becomes Ulrich's double, the mirror in which he senses a range of possible identities. To a certain extent, the process also works the other way. Ulrich becomes the desired other for Agathe. When you talk with me like that, she says, "it's as if I were seeing myself in a splintered mirror" (*MWQ* 808 / *MoE* 744). Brother and sister end up treating each other as machines of simulation, each letting the other one rehearse the drama of identity formation over and over.

Two aspects in the relation of Ulrich and Agathe deserve emphasis. First, the relation is founded on a narcissistic desire. To be sure, such a desire conditions any identity formation, but in this case it is precipitated by the actual similarity between brother and sister, by an identity of appearances which the narrator stresses by comparing their respective faces and bodies, by having them wear similar clothes, or by a frequent use of mirror motifs. All these instances are thetic moments of stasis in which the subjectivities of Ulrich and Agathe are fixed by the presence of an other with whom they identify. This process of identification is summed up, in symbolical terms, by the figure of the siblings, who soon grow together to become twins, even "Siamese twins," as the narrator underscores. The mutual identification of the siblings also accounts for the balance and symmetry in their relationship.

But the narcissistic desire is then blocked by a second aspect that entails the rejection of identification. While the novel stresses Ulrich and Agathe's fundamental similarity, it also underlines their difference, generally by simply stating that Agathe is a female, sometimes also by reminding us that Ulrich is a male. Sexual difference becomes a sign of negativity that breaks the spell of the other, tearing Ulrich and Agathe away from their narcissistic identifications and forcing upon them an experience of lack. Their respective identities thus dissolve, being replaced by a nauseating void. The novel marks such moments by describing how Ulrich and Agathe are overwhelmed either by depression or aggression, psychic states that, typically, emerge when the desired object is withdrawn, or by an erotic desire that, in the beginning, is not recognized as such. The void or lack thus only fuels their desire and the process from identification and stasis to difference and negativity begins anew. This second moment, that of negativity, then accounts for a certain asymmetry in the relation of Ulrich and Agathe. As we shall see, this imbalance is evident in Musil's inability, shared by all his contemporaries, to represent the difference between Ulrich and Agathe without repeating ideologically invested notions of femininity.

The relationship between Ulrich and Agathe thus faces in opposing directions. They are identified with each other and yet differentiated, which is why the narrator calls them "the unseparated and not united" (*die Ungetrennten und Nichtvereinten*). In order to capture this ambiguity, to literally flesh it out, the novel introduces a rich array of mythological and literary motifs, which are to convey the relation of brother and sister. We are confronted by mirrors, masks, and costumes, by a drama of identity-exchanges, a parade of *Doppelgänger* and hermaphrodites. Ulrich and Agathe are not only described as siblings, twins, or Siamese twins but also as halves of a broken whole, as aspects of the originary bisexuality of a unitary human soul, as the stock figures in commedia dell'arte, Harlequin and Pierrot, or as Isis and Osiris in early Egyptian mythology.

In Musil scholarship such mythological, philosophical, and cultural allusions are commonly treated as explanations of Ulrich and Agathe's relationship.[61] The siblings are seen as a variation of a general pattern, the allegedly timeless validity of which would seem to be once again confirmed by their example. Here again, I would hesitate to interpret Ulrich and Agathe's other condition as statements on human nature or on universal principles of ethics and love. The novel's tendency to situate the relationship of Ulrich and Agathe in a transhistorical realm must rather be read as a problem in its own right: what can we infer about Musil's historical period from the novel's effort to justify the siblings' relationship by allusions to the secrets of mystics, visionaries, and myths? Once the problem is put in such terms, the seemingly asocial experiment of Ulrich and Agathe is revealed as a social and political gesture.

Nor is it sufficient to discuss Ulrich and Agathe as though they were independent subjects meeting on neutral ground, like a pair of atoms acting and reacting in empty space. In a chapter called "Special Mission of a Garden Fence," Ulrich and Agathe hide under a tree in their garden, spying on the strangers in the street on the other side of a strong fence (*MWQ* 1526–1531 / *MoE* 1405–1411).[62] Evidently, their existential experiment is energized by their opposition to a social world that is always already present, and in this case evoked by traffic, crowds, and even a homeless tramp. If the brother acts as a force of negativity on the identity of the sister, and she as a force of negativity on his, the two of them are also joined as a force of negativity undermining the customs and beliefs of society as a whole. This means that we cannot fully understand the relationship of Ulrich and Agathe without understanding how their relationship relates to the social arena at large.

So far, I have largely postponed this problem, in order, first, to remove the disputable interpretation of the Musilian subject that has been established by a long tradition of reception and criticism, and, second, to analyze this subject and its functioning on the level of narration and theory. Now, finally, turning to a new chapter, we must examine the cultural context and political pressures that necessitated Musil's search for a new model of being human, or even a new human being.

5

Monsters in Love, Angels at War

The Madness of Central-European Modernity

History often resides in the details. When Agathe and Ulrich first meet after their father's death, they are dressed in Pierrot costumes.[1] They mirror each other like doubles. Two halves of a broken whole, they have finally found the missing part. Using this episode as a point of departure, I will in this chapter and the next one explore the historical and ideological situation to which Musil's novel responded.

Pierrot

The figure of Pierrot derives from commedia dell'arte, an Italian genre that was introduced on the French stage in the seventeenth century. Maria de' Medici and her son Louis XIII used to invite Italian theater companies to their court in Paris, and the Théâtre Italien soon became a permanent institution. The performances of this ensemble inspired Molière in his composition of *Don Juan; ou, Le Festin de Pierre* (1665), where Pierrot, modeled on a character called Pedrolino or anonymously presented as a *zanni* in commedia dell'arte, makes his first appearance in history. By the time of Antoine Watteau's famous painting *Pierrot, dit Gilles* (1718), Pierrot had become a cultural icon, and he continues to enchant to the present day.

Pierrot's mercurial character has enabled the figure to adjust to four centuries of social and cultural change.[2] What has attracted artists and writers to Pierrot is apparently the blend of melancholy and comedy that radiates from his character. Pierrot incarnates an existence of secret marvels, which, however, is superfluous and redundant in the human world, and for that reason profoundly tragic. In the disenchanted world of modernity, Pierrot assumes the identity of an angel or a monster who would bear witness to the mystery of existence, or reveal the very meaning of life, had he not been mute. For half of Pierrot's secret is his silence. He refuses the production of meaning, but precisely because of his nonmeaning he can be turned into any meaning. The other half of Pierrot's secret is his mask. It is a refusal of identity, which therefore easily passes over into a symbol of multiple identities.[3] Who is Pierrot, if not the subject as ipse? Oscillating between despairing melancholia ("I am nothing!") and the triumphant plasticity of the clown ("I can become anything!"), Pierrot is a symbol of subjectivity in a state of nothingness, but also a living proof that this nothingness is not the same as nothing. Subjectivity degree zero: no wonder, then, that Musil's narrator has Pierrot enter at the moment when Ulrich and Agathe have reached a state of utter experiential destitution when all identities are void.

According to Thomas Kellein, Pierrot's historical function is analogous to what the natural sciences call a tracer or trace element. Pierrot normally appears in cultural periods marked by ideological disorientation, in situations where collective identities of class, gender, and ethnicity are restructured.[4] In Molière's France we thus find Pierrot as an observer of the class struggle between aristocracy and bourgeoisie. After the bourgeois revolutions in mid-nineteenth-century France, Pierrot often appears as an aspiring proletarian. On the eve of revolution in Russia, Pierrot fuses with the doll Petruschka in an effort to create new forms of popular art. In the postmodern 1980s, Pierrot's ambiguous sexuality questions standardized identities of gender, as exemplified by the works of artists such as Andy Warhol, David Hockney, and Bruce Naumann, and the film director Anne Fontaine.

But the truly triumphant era of Pierrot coincides with modernism.[5]

Pierrot was painted by, for example, Pablo Picasso, Henri Rousseau, James Ensor, Juan Gris, Paul Klee, Paul Cézanne, and Emil Nolde. He was sculpted by Archipenko, photographed by Nadar, dramatized by Frank Wedekind and Alexander Blok, directed and enacted by Vsevolod Meyerhold, put into music by Igor Stravinsky, Arnold Schoenberg, and Eric Satie, choreographed by Michel Fokine and danced by Nijinsky in Diaghilev's Ballets Russes. He was turned into poetry by, most notably, Jules Laforgue and Albert Giraud, and also by Charles Baudelaire, Paul Verlaine, Guillaume Apollinaire, T. S. Eliot, and Wallace Stevens, among many others. Later still, Pierrot was filmed by Federico Fellini, Ingmar Bergman, and Jean-Luc Godard. He also became the hero of a remarkable novel by Raymond Queneau. In periods such as the modernist, when old ideologies disintegrate and new ones are not yet shaped, it appears that artists and writers readily identify with Pierrot's lack of identity.

Lulu: *A Myth of Femininity*

Because Pierrot was a common motif in Musil's time, it is difficult to know which model inspired him.[6] That Pierrot is first introduced along with Agathe, and almost as her disguise, suggests an affinity with one of the most unsettling figures in German literature: Lulu, the famous heroine in Frank Wedekind's plays *Erdgeist* (1895; *Earth Spirit*) and *Die Büchse der Pandora* (1904; *Pandora's Box*), who dresses up as Pierrot.

Massimo Cacciari has called Lulu an angel of possibility.[7] Her ancestry is unknown. Her name echoes both streetwise promiscuity and childish innocence, comparable, in a way, to Zola's *cocotte* Nana. In French literature and theater, which influenced Wedekind, "Lulu" is also charged with transsexuality.[8] As in Pierrot's case, Lulu's identity is held in suspense. Accordingly, each of her suitors names her differently: Nelli, Mignon, Eva, Pierrot, Lulu. When the artist Schwarz attempts to draw Lulu's portrait, he realizes that her being exceeds all pictorial conventions. This is why he conceals her character behind the sad smile of Pierrot.[9] One mystery is thus superimposed on another. Lulu's nature is conveyed by an appearance that is just as likely to hide a goddess as a beast.

"God and animal lie closer together in woman," the cultural theorist Karl Scheffler asserted in his book *Die Frau und die Kunst* (1908; "Woman and Art"). According to Silvia Bovenschen, Scheffler's work illustrates the central theme of Wedekind's play. An angel of possibility, Lulu arouses the desire of all the men around her—directors, actors, spectators alike. She becomes a target for their projections of various myths of femininity.[10] Still, as she moves from one persona to another, sampling images of femininity, the males also demand that she stop playing roles. As the prologue declares, Lulu must offer them the essence of true femininity: "Thou hast no right to spoil with meows and lying / the archetypal woman [*die Urgestalt des Weibes*] which you are hiding. . . . You should—this I now emphasize carefully— / be speaking naturally and not unnaturally."[11] Such is Lulu's impossible task: she must conform to the cultural images of femininity, but she must also act naturally, unspoilt by male culture. Both beauty and beast—Lulu reflects women's situation in Wedekind's culture.

As historians agree, turn-of-the-century Vienna saw the first attempt to define scientifically the so-called feminine principle.[12] Thinkers such as Scheffler, Georg Simmel, Max Scheler, Ludwig Klages, Sigmund Freud, Otto Weininger, Otto Gross, Karl Kraus, and Lou Andreas-Salomé all attempted to pin down an essence common to all women. Central to this discussion was a notion of human bisexuality. There were many different versions of the theory of bisexuality, to be sure, ranging from Weininger to Wilhelm Fliess, Freud, Andreas-Salomé, Walter Benjamin, and indeed Musil. But they all shared the assumption that "masculinity" and "femininity" are dispositions found in each human individual, male or female: there are feminine men, as well as masculine women.

Many of these theories relied on Johann Jakob Bachofen's influential work *Das Mutterrecht* (1861; "Mother Right"). A Swiss anthropologist and historian of religion, Bachofen argued that humanity had evolved from predominantly matriarchal societies to patriarchal ones, and that later stages of civilization had been shaped by values linked to masculinity. In the same vein, the theories on bisexuality made it possible to analyze individuals, literature, politics, historical epochs, countries, and the zeitgeist itself in terms of their mix of masculine and feminine features.[13] A common assumption was that the principle of femininity was differently disposed toward ethics, creativity, truth, and rationality than was the masculine principle. Whenever a sphere of social and cultural life showed signs of decline, this was typically explained in terms of an inbalance between the masculine principle and the feminine one.

Most of the above-mentioned thinkers ignored the distinction between real women and the fantasms of femininity. It is true that they had little interest in investigating, let alone changing, the social situation of real women.[14] Yet, although they focused mostly on the abstract notion of femininity, their reflections readily mutated into norms for the correct behavior of real female persons. Furthermore, the analysis of femininity and masculinity was often justified as a tool for "social reform." Accordingly, Max Scheler, in an essay called "Zum Sinn der Frauenbewegung" (1915; "The Meaning of the Women's Movement"), argued that philosophers and psychologists should contribute to building a better future by way of identifying the differences between male and female consciousness, thereby determining the appropriate field of activity for each sex.[15] Scheler stipulated that woman is "more earthly, more plantlike, more unitary in all experience, and far more strongly governed by instinct, emotion, and love than the man." [16] Because she acts as a brake on the progress motored by men, women constitute history's conservative element: "With the beautiful and peaceful composure of a tree beside which wild animals make their intricate leaps, she is standing in her innermost being before the restless drama of the history of men—forever intent on holding on to our large and simple foundations." [17] In a similar spirit, Georg Simmel's influential essay "Weibliche Kultur" (1911; "Female Culture") asserted that women are less differentiated and more integrated than men, and that their true accomplishments belong to the realm of reproduction, not to that of creation.[18]

In the sexual ontology elaborated by Scheler, Scheffler, and Simmel, among others, femininity was thus associated with nature, that is, everything except the moral and cognitive *doxa* of bourgeois society.

Often, this doctrine was but a disguise for a biological determinism in accordance with which sexual identity determined the social norms and the distribution of power between men and women. This is what Toril Moi, examining the Anglo-Saxon debate on women and sex in the same period, has called the pervasive picture of sex: "every habit, gesture, and activity is sexualized and categorized as male or female, masculine or feminine." [19] Bovenschen concludes that this ideology always presented woman as something "undifferentiated, molluscous, preindividual, determined by the laws of nature and the species." [20] Scheler even went so far as to deny that men and women have any universal human qualities in common.[21]

Gustav Klimt's paintings offer the strong version of this discourse on femininity. Women are entangled in plants and organisms; they are trees growing in the earth, or mermaids emerging from rivers of desire. They lure the viewer into a realm of nature where reason has no admittance. They promise like the Sirens, and punish like Salome.[22] Obsessed as he was with the female body and sexuality, Klimt painted only women.[23] Yet his work does not only present objects of male desire; it also intends to represent desire as such. Klimt's images are consequently both targets of libidinal energy and representations of its unconscious source, an ambiguity that is analogous of the one at the heart of the myth of femininity. Inhabiting a nowhere between subject and object, "femininity" oscillates between the actual woman and the fantasy of the thinker or artist who invents a primeval life force, which he at the same time contemplates as though it were a territory to be explored.[24]

The discourse on femininity did not amount to sexist ideology only, but was rooted in a paradigm structuring the cultural and political field in its totality, as the work of Andreas-Salomé testifies.[25] In her psychoanalytic theory, femininity is defined as a depository of undifferentiated potentialities that a male must either repress or differentiate in order to actualize the self-identical, unequivocal, and logical mode of being of masculinity. "The properly female expression is just *nature* and not logics," Andreas-Salomé argued.[26] Clearly, even her theory is caught in a logic according to which women cannot ascend to the level of rationality where nature has placed humans with penises. In this paradigm, woman could not be but illogical. Nor could she escape the burden of having to embody an intuitive capacity that eludes masculine categories of reason.

Woman is "a transparency of human shape through which the abundance of the whole, unbroken and unforgotten, is shimmering," Andreas-Salomé stated.[27] Her formulation echoes Nietzsche's definition of "the magic of life": "it puts a gold-embroidered veil of lovely potentialities over itself, promising, resisting, modest, mocking, sympathetic, seductive. Yes, life is a woman!"[28] When Wedekind exposes Lulu in her Pierrot costume, and when Musil's narrator introduces Agathe in the same kind of teasing fabric, they, too, gesture toward a veil that hides a mystery: archetypal woman.

Alpha: *Woman as Anarchist*

In Musil's work, women are often associated with spheres of consciousness that are inaccessible to instrumental reason. Novellas like *Die Vollendung der Liebe* (1911; *The Completion of Love*) and *Die Versuchung der stillen Veronika* (1908/1911; *The Temptation of Quiet Veronica*), as well as the short stories in *Drei Frauen* (1924; *Three Women*) won Musil a reputation as a masterly portrayer of the female psyche. Another example, particularly interesting in our context, is the play *Vinzenz und die Freundin bedeutender Männer* (1923; "Vinzenz and the Mistress of Important Men"). The only farce that Musil ever wrote, it is at once a pastiche and a critique of Wedekind's depiction of femininity in the *Lulu* plays (fig. 6).[29]

Like Lulu, Musil's heroine is encircled by men. Her name is Alpha, which is to say that she is the first or the origin. Being poor in determinations, Alpha is rich in possibilities. She owns a private harem of "important men" and has a girlfriend whose sexual object choices are uncertain. Just as Lulu has her Schigolch, Alpha also has a husband, Halm, who is both her guardian and her jailer. Since Halm does not care much for women, thinking they consist of "too much fat and too many demands," he would not mind a divorce and plans to hand over

Alpha to one of the important men, but not without securing a small profit for himself. Meanwhile, Alpha plays her suitors off against one another: "She says to the scholar that he is not a businessman, and to the musician that he is not a scholar, and to the businessman that he is not a musician, in short, to each and everyone: you are not a human being? And each one suddenly notices that his life is stupid? Because life is stupid" (*GW* 2:420).

Alpha impersonates her roles only to deviate from them. In doing so, however, she only seems to tease the masculine desire all the more. In this, too, her position is akin to that of Lulu, of whom Bovenschen remarks that she on the one hand becomes a myth of everything the men see in her, on the other hand is construed as a figure who destroys all such mythical pictures. Rejecting one image in order to assume a new one, she performs a "dangerous dance toward the heights of ever more dizzying projections." [30]

While for Lulu, this is a dance of death, Alpha is visited by a savior, Vinzenz, who wants to liberate her from the showroom where she is held hostage by husband and suitors. Vinzenz is the love of her youth. Like Ulrich in *The Man Without Qualities,* he is a mathematician. Alpha presents him as a "person who refuses to be tied up," adding, "just like me" (*GW* 2:426). They plan a future together. Vinzenz aims to discover the perfect gambling system that will allow him and Alpha to amass all the wealth on earth and then create the world anew (*GW* 2:431). In this way, Vinzenz's aspirations both prefigure and parody Ulrich's search for the right way to paradise.

Before the publication of *The Man Without Qualities,* many critics associated Musil with expressionism and also linked him to writers like Wedekind. Musil always disavowed this kinship, however.[31] "I detest Wedekind," he wrote in 1929.[32] Still, without the Lulu model introduced by Wedekind's more successful dramas, Musil's *Vinzenz* would be unthinkable. The character system is virtually plagiarized. Wedekind's drama, however, revolves exclusively around Lulu, who already in the prologue is posited as an incarnation of femininity. In Musil's play, this idea of femininity is ridiculed as a patriarchal fantasm. If Wedekind's play condenses the unsettling qualities of femininity into the heroine,

6 A woman with qualities. Lore Busch as Alpha in Robert Musil's *Vinzenz und die Freundin bedeutender Männer,* performed at Deutsche Volkstheater in Vienna, 1924. Leaning over Alpha is Willy Schmieder in the role of Bärli. Bildarchiv, Österreichische Nationalbibliothek Wien.

then Musil's farce dissociates them from her, relocating them to another existential stage, far beyond the frame of expressionism.[33]

Indeed, Musil rejected the expressionistic search for the energizing life forces of nature and femininity. In their stead he established, in *The Man Without Qualities,* that realm of transcendence and possibility which he termed "the other condition." This condition cannot be anchored in any essence but only makes itself felt as a tug of negativity or a call of otherness. Musil thereby disbanded the vertical axis of expressivity that divides life and world into opposites and forces imagination to shuttle infinitely between nature and culture, life and form, interiority and exteriority, essence and appearance, the intérieur and the public sphere, primitivism and civilization, madness and reason, the Dionysiac and the Apollonian, or femininity and masculinity. Still, Musil's realm of possibility remains associated with femininity.[34] This is not mainly because women in Musil's view embody a natural origin. The reason is rather that they, as members of the subordinated sex, must revolt against the dominant system and speak for an alternative order. So we must understand Alpha's rebellion at the end of the drama: "I'm an anarchist. As long as I live. I did not make the world. I would really have made it better, if someone had asked me to; that wouldn't have been difficult. And now you ask me to take this world seriously, a world made by these men. That's what you're asking me, that I should respect the world! Then I would much rather become a suffragette!" (GW 2:442)

Still, Halm and the other men will not let Alpha go. Unless she promises to remarry, Halm refuses to divorce her: "As a woman living on your own you are too vulnerable," one of the men commands (GW 2:443). "You must remarry, Alpha. You need manly protection and order" (GW 2:444). Like Antigone, threatening the order of Creon, Alpha is forced to submit to the law upheld by men.

But Alpha will have a second chance: she is to be reborn in the figure of Agathe. Living the last love story there could ever be, Agathe and her brother Ulrich will destroy the very law that holds society together.

Ideological Fatigue and Historical Trauma

The discourse of femininity that frames Wedekind's Lulu, Klimt's amazons, Andreas-Salomé's psychoanalytic theory, and Musil's Alpha leads in two opposite directions. It invites the male subject to return to the harmony of a unitary identity. Yet it also threatens his status as an independent subject able to master the world. In the writings of Otto Weininger and Daniel Paul Schreber, each of these opposing attitudes reaches an extreme.[35] Weininger is convinced that women pose a threat to all that is valuable. Unless femininity is controlled by masculine qualities of rationality and morality, society regresses to a primitive stage where only sexual instincts prevail. Schreber, for his part, is convinced that he can live a meaningful life—but only if he becomes a woman. Femininity promises to liberate him from the stranger whom he encounters in the shape of his own male identity. Evidently, the myth of femininity either promotes real women because they enable cultural regeneration, as in Schreber's example, or demotes them because they cause degeneration, as in Weininger's case—it all depends on the psychic constitution of the male subject in question. As Jacques Le Rider has suggested, Weininger's fear of woman and Schreber's celebration of the feminine have the same root: a crisis of masculine identity.[36]

Le Rider's conclusion only rephrases the question, however. In presupposing that a less crisis-afflicted masculine identity would entail a more balanced discourse on women, he posits masculine identity as a cultural foundation. Of course, such a foundation does not exist. It is a mistake, as Juliet Mitchell has stressed, to construe masculine identity and feminine identity as two opposing elements that are relationally defined in such a way that "a crisis" of the dominant masculine term would generate a subsequent transformation of femininity.[37] What does exist, however, is an ideology of a foundational *patriarchal* identity. In Mitchell's view, this ideology is as old as culture itself, although its articulations vary with the mode of production and class structure. Like all ideologies, it serves to naturalize the social, to make historically produced identities appear as natural and innate. Identity, in this view, is constituted through the mediation of ideology, and masculine and feminine identities through the mediation of patriarchal ideology.

In a book about Schreber, Eric Santner has examined in detail how this ideological mediation works through processes of what he calls "symbolic investiture." The stability of society as well as the psychological health of its members are correlated to the efficacy of these symbolic processes; it is through them that individuals assume the social essences assigned to them by way of names, titles, degrees, posts, and honors, and by denominations of gender, citizenship, ethnicity, and nationality. Consequently, as long as the "performative magic" of the symbolic investiture works, individuals tend to believe that the names, roles, and positions assigned to them by their cultural and institutional system are natural essences of their innermost being.[38]

In accounting for how ideology is assimilated by the human subject, Santner's notion of symbolic investiture is closely related to what Louis Althusser describes as "ideological interpellation." [39] The processes of symbolic investiture intervene at every stage of the individuation and socialization of the human being, ensuring his or her passage from the naked ipseity of infant subjectivity to the gender-determined and class-conditioned identity of the fully socialized and "ideologized" citizen. According to Althusser, the operative mechanism behind these processes is the "Law of Culture." [40] This law is nowhere codified in abstract form; it is actualized only through representations and symbolic practices, through the repetition and circulation of images, cultural stereotypes, rituals, and narratives, or what can be called *ideologemes*.[41] Often working on an unconscious level, these cultural signifiers imbricate the subject with the social body and condition the identity formation of individuals as well as groups. These ideologemes offer points of identification to our desire, making us recognize our ideal selves in certain imagoes and demanding that we reject others. This process of identification inserts us into the symbolic order and aligns us with ideological norms. Crucially, such ideological mechanisms hold reality together for the subject; without ideology, the individual's identity would disintegrate and the world would fail to make sense.

In choosing to speak of patriarchal ideology, Mitchell wants to reveal the mechanisms that divide all human beings, originally of bisexual disposition, into masculine and feminine identities.[42] On her account, the subject's acquisition of identity first occurs with the resolution of the Oedipal drama. At this point the subject suppresses its desires and resigns before the symbolic law governing family and culture. The subject accepts the identity offered to it by the people around it and, ultimately, by the language enabling it to represent itself as an individual.[43] The approval of this identity is associated with alienation, what Lacan calls the

Spaltung. The subject attains its identity only by alienating its ego from its being. It must project its desire onto a signifier—its ego—which it must substitute for itself. Henceforth, then, the subject is marked by a lack of unity and wholeness; in psychoanalytical terms, the subject's identity is a sign of a symbolic castration.

Crucially, however, the Oedipal drama provides the *male* subject with a way to deny his lack. This denial is made possible by ideologemes that attribute significance to the anatomical difference between the sexes. Although both the male and the female ascend to language and ego-formation only through symbolic castration, they also enter a world already structured by an ideological discourse that defines sexual identities on the basis of the presence or absence of the penis. During the course of the subject's socialization, this discourse transforms the female subject's lack of a penis into an index of a more general lack and incapacity. The male subject, by contrast, comes to identify with the position of power and agency that psychoanalysis names "the phallus." [44] His *masculine* identity thus becomes based on the belief that he has escaped castration. By internalizing images of patriarchal authority as parts of his own ego, and by simultaneously projecting his own lack onto the image of femininity, the male subject will "misrecognize" himself as the source of social power and historical agency. This "misrecognition" is upheld by social processes of investiture that encourages both male and female subjects to regard the male individual as an incarnation of authority.

Now, according to the expressivist paradigm of subjectivity that I discussed in chapter I, the subject's identity is a manifestation of what is taken to be his or her intrinsic nature. As soon as this definition is rephrased in terms of ideology, we begin to see that the notion of inwardness as the source of identity is sustained precisely by ideologemes that allow the male subject to *internalize* the attributes of authority as parts of his own ego. The internalization of the "phallus" allows the male subject to deny the lack and emptiness at the center of his psyche. Through an ideological inversion, he assimilates the symbolic father, the absolute subject, into his own intérieur. Searching for the truth about himself, he looks inward, confident that this truth lies inside his self as a solid foundation for his projects and expressions. The idea of a dominant masculine identity and the expressivist paradigm of subjectivity are thus two aspects of the same patriarchal ideology, which is realized through historical processes of symbolic investiture. As I have suggested in chapter 1, the expressivist paradigm is a response to the male subject's historically induced division between a reified sphere of politics and economy, and a private sphere warding his emotional and noninstrumental qualities. What prevents his world from breaking apart, and what holds the two sides of his split being together, is precisely the expressivist ideology that makes him believe that he has an intrinsic identity, externalized in his words and deeds.

Interestingly, *The Man Without Qualities* contains an analysis that corresponds perfectly to this account of identity and ideology. A person's identity, the novel suggests, is constituted by the subject's *belief* in the truth and necessity of that identity. Similarly, the ideological order is upheld only as long as everyone invests that order with ideological faith. "Although men are not normally aware of it, they must believe that they are something more than they are in order to be capable of being what they are; they need to feel this something more above and around them" (*MWQ* 576 / *MoE* 529). This belief is "something imaginary" (*etwas Imaginäres*), Musil's narrator states. Yet, it is precisely the male subject's identification with such an imaginary surplus of power and authority that accounts for the collective cohesion that "bolster[s] the society's artificial peace of mind" (*MWQ* 575 / *MoE* 527). As long as this identification works, the members of the community will believe that their history and future are expressions of an authoritative identity around which society is structured—a collective soul, *Volksgeist*, or national character—and that some members of society, notably "the Good Emperor in Vienna," are able to maintain and incarnate this position. Due to the medium of ideology, society appears to be an expression of individuals and institutions which embody this normative position. Without the belief in such a center, reality, as we know it, would disintegrate.

What *The Man Without Qualities* shows, however, is that certain historical events or periods may destroy this belief. The result is an ideological fatigue, a crisis of investiture. Social reality is derealized; the world appears to have neither center nor meaning. The male subject recognizes his nonidentity with the site of power, and his impotency in the face of a history whose forces he cannot control and perhaps not even understand. This is the state Kakania has fallen into, according to Musil's narrator. The Kakanians "no longer knew what their smiles, their sighs, their ideas, were for. . . . Their opinions were haphazard, their inclinations an old story, the scheme of things seemed to be hanging in midair, one ran into it as into a net, and there was nothing to do or leave undone with all one's heart, because there was no unifying principle" (*MWQ* 576 / *MoE* 528). What Musil describes is an ideological fatigue; the members of society have lost faith in the imaginary support of their collective identity, realizing instead that their identities are surrogates for something that is missing, prostheses that mask an irreducible lack.

Kaja Silverman has suggested that such historical moments fall under the category of "historical trauma." [45] It designates a situation in which the principle of negativity is activated collectively: the social formation stands without any mechanism for achieving consensus, without any unifying principle. As Julia Hell argues, a traumatic historical moment is typically experienced as a loss of social structures and social identities: "We do not have a society anymore." [46] Such a crisis, in which the social community is no longer directed toward a shared destiny, also implies the absence of a normative narrative that would link the present to a past and a future. Traumatic moments are disconnected from the chain of intelligible history, and cannot be retold as events in a continuously unfolding story.[47] Musil's narrator dramatizes the issue, stating that Kakania crumbled because its members lost faith in their empire.

Indeed, from the turn of the century through the First World War, German and Austrian culture exhibits conspicuous instances of such traumatic discontinuities. It is no coincidence that Freud, in 1920, developed the foundations for a theory of historical trauma, as well as his notion of the death drive, by studying the neuroses afflicting soldiers who had returned from the trenches.[48] Santner locates the causes of this crisis in the processes of modernization that destroy the symbolic rituals and social bonds that once served to secure the belief that certain identities and values were necessary and meaningful. Accordingly, Senatspräsident Schreber's nervous breakdown is caused by his loss of belief in the legitimacy of the values and positions that the judiciary and political order asks him to uphold.[49] In his case, the relation of the male subject to the position of authority with which he used to identify is so profoundly disturbed that it affects the most intimate core of his being. Having lost the sense of a potent masculine ego, he finds himself symbolically relegated to the position of the most marginal figures in his culture, women and Jews.[50]

This, then, explains Schreber's vivid identification with femininity as well as Weininger's violent rejection of the same fantasm. The inflated discourse on femininity in turn-of-the-century Vienna that I have discussed in this chapter may similarly be related to a society undergoing rapid modernization and ideological upheaval. Significantly, this was also the period during which the modern women's movements came into being. Vienna became the center of what Harriet Anderson has called utopian feminism, represented by activists and intellectuals like Rosa Mayreder, Irma von Troll-Borostyáni, and Grete Meisel-Hess.[51] The women's movements demanded a redistribution of human rights and a new division of labor between the sexes. Faced with these demands, numerous writers and philosophers tried to decide what social positions befitted men and women, and in order to do this, they had to establish the "true" differences between the sexes.[52] As a result, feminine identity was either posited as a comforting and supplementing essence, confirming the phallic power of masculine identity, or presented as sheer alterity, a site of lack, onto which the male subject could project his own lack, thereby confirming that he still had access to the phallus. The figures of femininity discussed above are thus to be seen as so many indices of a historical disturbance of the patriarchal ideology that functions to gender the human subject.

At stake was not merely the destabilization of the patriarchal norm that organized the social field, but also the subsequent restructuring of all identities that were construed in relation to this position. The historical pressures affecting Viennese culture between 1900 and 1920 eroded the expressivist paradigm, and it became increasingly difficult to sustain the belief that identities—masculine, feminine, or other—were expressions of essences. Of course, these pressures did not come from the women's movement only, but from all the enormous changes brought about by rapid modernization, the war, and the subsequent breakup of the Austro-Hungarian Empire, which I will discuss in the next chapter. The crisis corroded the idea that identities refer to stable substrata such as biology, sex, sexuality, instinct, tradition, blood, ancestry, culture, territory, nationality, or race. Reactively, however, the crisis also generated fierce attempts to restore belief in a phallic masculinity, which, in turn, caused a series of powerful efforts to reterritorialize not only feminine identity but also identities of class, race, and ethnicity. I have already indicated some symptoms of this ideological shift—Pierrot, Lulu, Alpha, femininity, the sexual ontology of fin-de-siècle Vienna. But there are more.

Joseph Roth: *Castration of the Masculine Subject*

The historian Alfred Pfoser has remarked that World War I created a population of destroyed men and emancipated women.[53] The war has also been designated the greatest sexual catastrophe that has ever befallen civilized man.[54] Franz Werfel exclaimed in one of his novels, "What's at stake in our war is the patriarchal order of the world." [55]

In Joseph Roth's stories, too, masculine identity is everywhere in decay. At the beginning of *Die Kapuzinergruft* (1938; *The Emperor's Tomb*), Roth's narrator Lieutenant Trotta evokes a prewar society in which gender relations are reliable. He muses on how his wife Elizabeth "at that time was lovely, gentle and tender" —a woman conforming perfectly to the myth of the feminine, whose every word echoed the language of creation.[56] As Trotta returns to Vienna after the war, having suffered four years of imprisonment in Siberia, he is shocked to find that his once so submissive Elizabeth now camps with a lesbian woman with short hair and bad manners. As if this were not enough, he also must face that the two women run an arts-and-crafts company manufacturing furniture, lamps, and trinkets after the latest fashion in vogue: African primitivism.[57]

Elizabeth's emancipation is tied to Lieutenant Trotta's decline. Both are symptoms of the social changes that Roth, during the 1920s and 1930s, diagnosed in a series of increasingly reactionary works that testify to the crisis of the expressivist paradigm that supports masculine identity. What propels the crisis is not so much the war as such but a complex of interacting historical processes that enable the female subject to emancipate herself from her pregiven identity, thus letting her escape the ideological order that used to circumscribe the meaning of her being. Exceeding this order, she disrupts the notion of what a woman is. She becomes a being whose nature Roth cannot define as anything but a vicious aberration.

Meanwhile, the male protagonists are thrown off center and unmanned. The narrator in *Hotel Savoy* (1924) is an Austrian soldier, one among many who went to war in 1914 and who in 1918 returned from prison camps, reduced to scavenging beasts.[58] Roth's postwar chaos turns respected citizens and faithful housewives into barbarians. His heroes are symbolically castrated, and all too well aware of it: "We had all lost position, rank and name, home and money and esteem, past, present and future," says Lieutenant Trotta in *The Emperor's Tomb.*[59] What remains in the wake of the collapsed order are figures of madness and abnormality, along with faint reminiscences of a golden age. This scenario is summarized in the epilogue of *Radetzkymarch* (1932; *The Radetzky March*), Roth's major novel. The aged patriarch of the Trottas visits the aristocrat Chojnicki, a key character who has returned from the battlefield in a state of madness and is undergoing treatment at the lunatic asylum Steinhof. As Trotta is waiting in the asylum for Chojnicki to receive him, he watches men with mad and contorted faces pass by, all veterans of the war. But when he speaks with Chojnicki, he notices that the count, despite his madness, has retained a lucid understanding of the political situation and even gained an ability to predict the future.[60] In *The Emperor's Tomb*, the sequel to *The Radetzky March*, the mad Chojnicki returns in a position of unchallenged authority to spell out the final lesson of the fall of the Austro-Hungarian Empire.[61] As the old world is turned upside down, insanity rules. Only a madman is able to understand the world of modernity. Or as Trotta exclaims: "Happy the fathers whose sons are crazy!" [62]

Roth's novels are told from the point of view of someone who once lived securely in the House of Habsburg. He cannot conceive of the future as anything but a fall from grace. In *The Radetzky March,* there is a character who is terrified at the sight of his sleeping children and their rosy faces. There is something monstrous about them, he thinks: "Sometimes I feel it is the cruelty of their time, the future, that overcomes the children in their sleep. I would not care to live that long." [63] In Roth's universe, even one's own children turn against one as dreadful portents of a coming age of darkness. The past can no longer claim the present. The present refuses to take responsibility for the future. The normative power of tradition is exhausted. So it is that the ideological content of Roth's works recalls a paralyzed conservatism for which historical change as such is disastrous.

Roth had good reasons to give the fallen empire a nostalgic tint. Writing from the marginal position of a Galician Jew, he detected the antisemitic tendencies that suppressed the kind of cultural difference that he himself embodied.[64] Compared to the racist nationalism that emerged in the late 1920s and that would exterminate Roth's people, the Dual Monarchy was indeed an empire of tolerance. In his darkest moments, Roth identified the postimperial age with the reign of *Anti-Christ.* Such was the title of a collection of essays, published in 1934, in which he attacked the contemporary world as a whole.[65] Everywhere he detects the works of Anti-Christ—in European high culture, in the workers' republic of the Soviet Union, in the anticolonial movements, and among the imperialists, but above all in the dream factories of Hollywood and Nazi Germany, the juxtaposition of which strangely prefigures Adorno and Horkheimer's proposition that fascist pedagogy and the American culture industry are governed by identical mechanisms of domination. In Roth, "Anti-Christ" functions as a blanket term for a number of political and economic processes that relieve the individual of responsibility in order to subordinate him to the deceptive comfort of the protofascist collective. What is most frightening for Roth is not the ideologies that legitimize totalitarian rule but the uncanny ease with which people adjust to it. The castrated heroes of his novels happily become functionaries of the system. By subjecting themselves to the postimperial chaos, they overcompensate for their lack, using up what little agency they have left and turn it against themselves in a show of masochism. In the late 1920s the stage is set for the entrance of the punishing father. "In my view, the frightening tendency of the present generation to yield to their even more appalling overlords may be understood and certainly forgiven if one bears in mind that it is a part of human nature to prefer a mighty, all-embracing calamity to any particular worry. A monstrous disaster will rapidly swallow a small misfortune—bad luck, so to speak. And so during those years we loved our monstrous wretchedness." [66]

The male individual can no longer identify with the investitures of power. The authoritative ego of the past is folded together as an old uniform. Interestingly, this is also Ulrich's attitude in the opening pages of *The Man Without Qualities.* Just like Roth's hapless heroes, Ulrich associates the modern condition with powerlessness. The very first words he utters—"No matter what you do, . . . within this mare's nest of forces at work, it doesn't make the slightest difference!" (*MWQ* 7 / *MoE* 13)—shows that he is ready to resign before the social and political forces that develop in a totalitarian direction. The rest of the story, however, records his attempts to rid himself of this indifference.

Roth finds another way out of the dilemma. For him the ego-ideal of a bygone historical era stands out as the only possible point of identification. His critique of the present is voiced from the position of a forgotten law and rationality which, in an age as disorderly as the 1920s, can only operate under cover. This is why Roth's novels about the fall of Habsburg give such a privileged role to Chojnicki, the madman. His strategy is similar to the one Hamlet devised when seeing that the world was out of joint. To survive in a society gone mad, reason must be concealed behind a mask of madness.

Moosbrugger: *A Monstrous Alter Ego*

Dramatizing the issue, one might say that Roth and Musil present a choice between madness and fascism. Society attempts to reinvent for itself an identity of race or nationhood that would warrant some stability in the midst of the destabilizing forces of modernization. For Roth and Musil this leads to a derealization of reality. Reality is replaced by what Roth, in *Anti-Christ,* calls "the land of shadows" (*das Land der Schatten*), and what Musil calls "pseudoreality" (*das Seinesgleichen*). These words convey a sense of how the real is experienced as a replica or simulation of hegemonic ideologies. Refusing to model their identities on these political fictions, Roth's and Musil's protagonists lose their foundation and are thrown back upon themselves, forced to conjure up their respective identities from within their own selves. This task is impossible, because identity is by definition produced only through a process of identification with an other. What becomes of the subject, if there is no other to identify with, if the social field offers no possibilities of recognition?

For such a subject the only alternatives are madness or fascism. Either the subject lays down its defense, sacrifices its ego, and solidarizes with the group-ego of the collective. Or the subject shuts itself up in a solitude leading to autism or a schizoid condition. Trying to protect its integrity, it withdraws into the interior. The subject is then frozen in a state of ipseity. R. D. Laing and Louis Sass, respectively, argue that this condition is a preliminary stage of schizophrenia. Interestingly, both these scholars and psychiatrists claim that modern society tends to create "divided selves," split between a society in which every action seems ghostlike and mechanic, and an inwardness becoming ever more petrified and illusory since it is not nourished by any social interaction.[67]

Sass even suggests a direct relation between the experience of schizophrenia and the experience of time and space represented in modernist literature. Using Musil as a major example, he argues that modernist literature demonstrates experiences which otherwise, in less sublimated and self-conscious forms, are manifested in what we call madness.[68]

The schizoid subjects populating Musil's novel would thus be true representatives of cultural modernity. "Having a split personality has long since ceased to be a trick reserved for lunatics," jests Musil's narrator (*MWQ* 424 / *MoE* 391). Ulrich's divided self is a first step toward the psychotic condition from which both Moosbrugger and Clarisse suffer.

On the one hand, then, *The Man Without Qualities* chronicles the increasing eagerness of the elite and the people to celebrate the unity of the nation. As Musil's novel approaches August 1914, the social field of the story is polarized. The atmosphere is thick with yearning and aggression. Things cannot go on, people believe, unless a messiah arrives, and arrives quickly (*MWQ* 567 / *MoE* 520). Longing for a phallic point of identification that would unify the nation, the racialized collective cry for a führer, for armaments, and for the expulsion of Jews and minorities. Society eventually implodes into war and totalitarianism.

On the other hand, there are those who seek ways to preserve an identity that may resist the ideological appeal of nationalism; Ulrich is a case in point. He is attracted to everything that upsets the conformism of his age, and negotiates with a number of asocial and marginal persons, such as Clarisse, the servants Rachel and Soliman, the socialist Schmeisser, and, above all, Moosbrugger. Due to his schizophrenic condition and criminal perversities, Moosbrugger becomes a scapegoat, an imago of evil, which allows normal citizens to repress their own fantasies by releasing them at a point of identification beyond the socius. Musil's narrator examines how the social narratives of Kakania organize the world in dualisms of same and other, which are then translated into oppositions of morality and immorality, sanity and madness, good and evil, hence creating a realm of negative powers that absorbs desires that are potentially disruptive.[69]

Yet Ulrich's self-reflective mode sets him apart from such collective narratives. Playing no part in the stories from which his fellow countrymen draw the meaning of their existence, he "idolize[s] all the villains and monsters of world history" (*MWQ* 309 / *MoE* 286). Ulrich is less liable to identify with any ego-ideal that his society offers than with the image of a murderer. The reason is spelled out in Musil's early sketches: "Aversion against the competent, self-righteous, and enlightened people drives him [Ulrich] toward Moosbrugger" (*MoE* 1951). This affinity is even more striking in Musil's drafts of the novel, where the hero and the murderer suffer from the same disease, syphilis.[70] Indeed, Ulrich is infected with Moosbrugger's madness: "the only thing that still differentiated his life from that of the insane was a consciousness of his situation" (*MWQ* 1563 / *MoE* 1751). We can restate this difference thus: Moosbrugger becomes schizophrenic and criminal because of a foreclosure of the primary order of the symbolic or language, while Ulrich becomes an outcast and borderliner because he rejects the secondary order of *ideology,* or das Seinesgleichen, which determines the individual's identity by compelling him or her to mirror himself or herself in the Absolute Subject of the community. Musil's hero is faced with a simple choice: Either he must run with the pack, or he becomes neurotic.

Tracing the genesis of the Moosbrugger theme, Karl Corino has observed that in the early outlines of the novel, Moosbrugger is more central than he is in the published work of 1930.[71] A comparison between the first and second books of the novel also shows that the sequence of the Moosbrugger chapters, which string the first book together, is cut off in the second. As the novel progresses, the murderer recedes into the background.[72] The interest in him is delegated to Clarisse, whose psychotic breakdown is precipitated by her frequent visits to the lunatic asylum where she, being convinced that Moosbrugger is the messiah, hopes to encounter the madman. The reason why Moosbrugger recedes, I want to suggest, is that he represents the primitive and anarchic stage of the novel's critique of ideology. In order to unmake identities of gender and collectives in a less melodramatic fashion, the narrator needs a more ambiguous and representative symbol of resistance. He needs a different monster, and this monster is Agathe.

Agathe: *A Woman with Qualities*

Agathe is the only major character in *The Man Without Qualities* who has no role to play in the Parallel Campaign. Bonadea, Walter, Meingast,

Clarisse, Diotima, Arnheim, and the other figures, including Moosbrugger, are all wrapped up in the political spectacle of the main plot. Precisely because they are functions of the plot, and thus must surrender to the pressures of the society represented by that plot, none of them can function as a mediator in Ulrich's exploration of subjectivity. This can be done only by someone who is external to the field in which identities are mistaken for realities, the petrified realm of das Seinesgleichen.

This is why Agathe must appear. She is outside, coming from a different city, and will remain outside, occupying the position of the stranger whose arrival turns things upside down. Her presence is necessitated by the needs of the male protagonist, and she does not figure in the story until her encounter with Ulrich at the beginning of part 2 of the novel. Yet as soon as she is established as a character, she is transformed into a subject in her own right. She immediately confesses to her brother that she has decided to leave her husband: "I'll never go back to Hagauer," she informs Ulrich as they are are standing, dressed in Pierrot costumes, in front of their dead father (*MWQ* 736 / *MoE* 677).[73]

Ulrich admits that he never understood how she could stand someone like Hagauer. Agathe replies that the marriage "was their father's idea" (*MWQ* 742 / *MoE* 683). Hagauer's regime is an extension of the order of the Father. A series of remarks on the situation of women in Austria link the order of the Father to the social order in general. As a young girl, Agathe moved from her father to her first husband. When he died she had to return to the house of her father, who soon sent her off to marry Hagauer. As a member of the so-called weaker sex, Agathe is an object of exchange, circulating between men. The novel spells out that this is a patriarchal society in which a woman, in order to get a recognized identity, must have a man, or rather be had by him. Otherwise she is just a negation of the dominant order.

The emerging sympathy between Ulrich and Agathe is based on their shared disgust for this order. Ulrich is delighted by Agathe's resolve to leave her matrimonial prison, and he assists her to expedite her separation. Agathe is of instrumental importance to him. She becomes a living proof that there is a possibility for a life outside the social roles that have been forced upon him throughout his career. The narrative

figure of the "Siamese twins" inaugurates a revolutionary mode of subjectivity that sums up the negativity of Musil's project. "Basically it's
a protest against the world!" Ulrich says, explaining how Agathe and
he now constitute an indivisible force working against society (*MWQ*
1019 / *MoE* 939). The father being dead, the husband abandoned in the
provinces, and society having disappeared, the siblings are left alone
against the rest. At the end of chapter 8, early in the second part of
the novel, the two are well on their way to becoming one. Also, in this
chapter Ulrich starts confessing his experiences of the other condition
to Agathe; later on, he will suggest that they should realize this para-
disiac life together. Yet, the most remarkable feature of this chapter is
the way in which it ends:

> In this fashion and in such a roundabout way they arrived . . . at the dis-
> covery that the two of them constituted a family. And while Ulrich speaks
> of the desire for community . . . Agathe is listening as his words come
> close to her and retreat again, and what he notices, looking at her lying
> quite defenseless in that bright island of light and in her whimsical cos-
> tume, is that for some time now he has been searching for something
> about her that would repel him, as he regrettably tends to do, but he has
> not found anything, and for this he is thankful with a pure and simple
> affection that he otherwise never feels. (*MWQ* 787* / *MoE* 724)

For the first and only time, the narrative turns to the present tense. As
the temporal rhythm shifts, the narrative flow is arrested, and from its
surface emerges a capsule of pure presence in which we see Ulrich and
Agathe gazing at each other in enthrallment. This dramatic shift of the
narrative grammar seals the unity of brother and sister. They now lodge
in a hidden corner of temporality, in a present tense that the narrator
sets aside exclusively for them, far away from the rest of history.

Ulrich and Agathe are indivisible, acting as one: the narrator calls
them "the unseparated." In the same breath, however, he calls them
"the not-united." Having escaped the dominant symbolic order, their
relationship still remains under its spell. The conflict between the children and the regime of the Father is transported, as a seed of inequality
and strife, into the internal order of the siblings. First of all, Agathe

constitutes the audience without which Ulrich (or the narrator) could never develop his ideas. The patient ear of the woman allows the man to become a kind of *Lebensphilosoph*. At the same time, Agathe becomes an incarnation of these ideas. The possibilities lined up by Ulrich are converted into realities by Agathe. This division of labor brings us back to the sexual ontology elaborated by a number of Viennese thinkers in this period. If Ulrich's mind remains a figure of negativity, Agathe is transformed into the very embodiment of this negativity, that is, into a positivity in her own right. If Ulrich is ceaseless becoming, Agathe is being.

Agathe is prepared to give up everything for a life of limitless love that Ulrich has suggested to her. She remembers an old saying: "Cast all thou hast into the fire, even unto thy shoes" (*MWQ* 937 / *MoE* 863). She throws all her old belongings into the fireplace, primary among these a collection of dolls (*MWQ* 978f. / *MoE* 902). Just as Agathe and Ulrich annihilated the order of the Father, she now takes leave of the puppets and idols she used to play with as a child. In a locket on her necklace, she carries a picture of her first husband. She replaces this photography with a capsule of poison. It becomes her "bringer of luck, her talisman" for her "journey to the brink of the possible" (*MWQ* 928 / *MoE* 855). She must reach the other condition or kill herself, but she is afraid that her brother is not equally decided: "Would Ulrich really cast everything into the fire?" (*MWQ* 938 / *MoE* 864).

Meanwhile, Ulrich, now back in Vienna, regrets the bold suggestions he has made to Agathe. The plans of an altogether different existence shrivel up. The promise of a new Millennium that he so daringly proposed boils down to no more than a commitment to be as nice as he can to his sister (*MWQ* 950 / *MoE* 875). Agathe, he thinks, has "very little sense of reality" (*MWQ* 945 / *MoE* 870).

The siblings' different attitudes toward the other condition fall almost too neatly into the categories of masculinity and femininity. Agathe is described as "the most illogical of women"; Ulrich belongs to "one of those mathematicians called logicians, for whom nothing was ever 'correct' " (*MWQ* 931, 939 / *MoE* 858, 865). Whereas Ulrich learns to know the possibility of another existence as a logical hypothesis, Agathe, the woman, learns to know it as a divine reality. "She would have been willing to imagine a God who opens up His world like a hiding place" (*MWQ* 1048 / *MoE* 966). Ulrich is later to conclude that, contrary to a specialized and goal-oriented way of living, the integral and inclusive attitude to the world has in it "something magical and—God help me!— . . . something feminine" (*MWQ* 1306 / *MoE* 1198). He reflects on how all persons hide inside themselves thoughts that may be asocial, monstrous, even criminal. As regards himself, however, he has these thoughts "ausser sich," outside himself, in another person who reveals the secrets of his self (*MWQ* 945 / *MoE* 870). Agathe is this tempting projection of the wild and asocial possibilities of Ulrich's malleable subjectivity. In order to retain his fluidity, he must feed on the dreams and thoughts emanating from that feminine part of himself which materializes in Agathe. "You are my self-love!" he says to her (*MWQ* 975 / *MoE* 899). A case of inverted narcissism, Agathe seems to allow Ulrich to attain an ego—an identity—which he, for the first time, recognizes as his own. But this ego is really an alter ego. It is always decentered in relation to his subjectivity and thus appears as his double.

Yet Ulrich's self-love, which is first inverted into the love of an other who is his self, is then inverted again, so that it now approaches the mystical experience of a love which overflows him from all directions: "Whenever I succeed in shedding all my selfish and egocentric feelings toward Agathe . . . she draws all the qualities out of me the way the Magnetic Mountain draws the nails out of a ship! She leaves me morally dissolved into a primary atomic state, one in which I am neither myself nor her. Could this be bliss?" (*MWQ* 1019f. / *MoE* 940). As the metaphor reveals, Ulrich is a ship while Agathe is a magnetic mountain that takes the vessel of masculinity off course or even sinks it into an ocean of bliss. Femininity must be fixed and constant in order for masculinity to shed its "qualities" and reach a more integrated stage of being. This is what the passage makes clear: a man without qualities presupposes a woman *with* qualities, feminine qualities. The song of the Sirens is eternally the same.

In 1911 Georg Simmel defined masculinity as becoming and femininity as being.[74] Similarly, Andreas-Salomé's theory stated that the man must struggle to become what the woman, by her essence, already is.[75] By the same token, Ulrich tries to become, through thoughts and acts, what Agathe already is. She reproaches him for being overly theoretical: "You carefully dissect according to natural and moral laws the possibility of extending your hand. Why don't you simply reach out?" (*MWQ* 1356 / *MoE* 1278).

Since Ulrich's understanding of identity entails a negation of the dominant idea of expressive individuation, it is no surprise that it implies an affirmation of masculinity's Other, the principle of femininity. Yet, it is surely paradoxical that this affirmation of the feminine also implies that the dominant order of patriarchy remains in place. For although Ulrich and Agathe together negate this order, they end up reproducing in their own internal relationship the same division of labor between the sexes that was instituted by the patriarchal fiction to begin with.

Musil once participated in a debate on *die Frauenfrage,* "the women's issue," by contributing to a book where male intellectuals wrote on the topic "The Woman of Yesterday and Tomorrow — As We Would Like to See Her" (1929). Musil stated that the contemporary woman is tired of being the ideal of man. "She no longer wants to be any ideal at all, but wants to make ideals." The human body cannot in the long run be just a receiver of psychic energies, Musil explained. Sooner or later the body will always begin "to be actor of her own self" (*GW* 2:1198).

The Agathe character is evidently an attempt on Musil's part to envision a woman no longer fixed by masculine ideals of femininity. In contrast to Alpha, Agathe has the power to be the actor of her own self. Yet it is still the male subject, Ulrich, who enjoys and judges her acting. Can Agathe really become the actor of her own self in a society where the identity of women is overdetermined by the fictions of patriarchy? In her discussion of Wedekind's Lulu, Bovenschen asks the same question: "But what is Lulu, when she is no longer playing any role?" [76]

Answering this question, those who still think about identity in terms of an essence hidden in the interiority of the person would continue to look behind the mask, hoping to find "the archetypal woman," "die Urgestalt des Weibes." Bovenschen gives the opposite answer. Apart from

7 A subject without qualities. Robert Musil (left) in the company of Pierrot at a carnival ball in Vienna, circa 1920. The others are, from the left, Ea von Allesch, Martha Musil, and Franz Blei. Collection of Karl Corino.

the tongue that Lulu has learnt from her master, there is only silence; there is no feminine substance—only lack. This insight also dawns on Agathe, having transgressed the identities determining what a woman should be. "Am I the up-to-date woman, active somehow either economically or intellectually? No. Am I a woman in love? No again. Am I the good, nest-building wife and mother who simplifies things and smooths over the rough spots? That least of all. What else is there? Then what in the world am I good for?" (*MWQ* 1035 / *MoE* 954f.).

What am I doing in this world? Agathe's question resonates with a negativity of suicidal dimensions. In this state of despair, Agathe is again visited by Pierrot. Convinced that "her death would be no loss to anyone or anything," she feels that she is surrounded by clowns with sad faces and strange instruments (*MWQ* 936 / *MoE* 863). As the music of the clowns rises toward the ceiling, she imagines herself sitting in tears on a circus floor strewn with sawdust, in total solitude, until she recalls that her brother also was dressed as a clown the first time they met in their Pierrot costumes. Her feelings, the narrator stresses, are marked by senselessness (*Sinnlosigkeit*). Yet he dwells on the scene, the circle of clowns continuing to play around Agathe, and intimates that Agathe's ostensible senselessness has a deeper sense. But much like the music of the clowns, it is a sense that is intelligible only to angels. By evoking this music, the idiom of the sad *Pierrot lunaire,* the Musilian narrator indicates a language of femininity.

"How did Sappho and her women-friends talk among themselves? How did women come to speak?" Walter Benjamin asks in an early essay, reflecting on why women have been assimilated to a figure of otherness, external to reason, culture, and language. "The language of women has remained inchoate. Talking women are possessed by a demented language." [77] Raising the question of what a woman's culture would be, had the dominant patriarchal ideology not existed, Benjamin wonders what we know of woman. As yet, he says, we have no experience of a *woman's culture*.[78]

What could a woman be, beyond the expressivist paradigm that for so long has defined identities of sex, class, generation, and community? As soon as woman transgresses these identities, she starts communicating in a foreign language and with mysterious gestures. In Musil's novel, the onset of Clarisse's madness represents the final stage in the critique of the expressivist paradigm. In her psychotic condition, Clarisse constructs a new language, abandoning grammar and semantics in favor of what she calls "a chemistry of words" (*MoE* 1753). Her signifiers float freely, linked to each other according to that odd logic of rhythm and vocality that Kristeva found to be typical of the semiotic *chora* rather than the linear logic of the symbolic order.[79] As a result, Clarisse's conquest of the semiotic entails an eclipse of her identity and sets her subjectivity adrift in an ocean of signs without common sense.[80]

Indeed, the more Musil's narrator valorizes the feminine, and the more he appeals to female characters as a way of criticizing the dominant order, the further he seems to chase them into the wilderness. What remains, eventually, is the stark opposition between a masculine regime, symbolized by the authoritarian military discipline of General Stumm von Bordwehr, and a feminine counterregime, symbolized by Clarisse's schizophrenia and Agathe's asocial yearning for the Millennium. Again, we run up against the impossible choice between a fascist authoritarianism, on the one hand, and a madness associated with femininity, on the other. Had this been the final implication of Musil's critique, it would merely reinforce what it tried to destroy, that is, the essentialization of feminine and masculine identities.

Monsters in Love

Mortified by her failure to reach a world of love, Agathe breaks open her capsule and pours its deadly contents into a glass of water. She is just about to drink it when Ulrich runs into her room. Agathe explains her decision. "*We are miserable creatures who bear within ourselves the law of another world,* without being able to carry it out. We love what is forbidden and will not defend ourselves." As in a good old melodrama, Ulrich flings himself on the floor and embraces his beloved. "*We will not let ourselves be killed by anything before we have tried it! . . .* The lost paradise!" (*MWQ* 1735 / *MoE* 1651). Agathe's suicide attempt forces

Ulrich to make up his mind. They leave the Parallel Campaign, Vienna, and Austria. They finally leave the world, traveling to the brink of the possible.

The unpublished chapters relating this journey radiate with a beauty bespeaking a profound libidinal investment. The narration has been purged of the highbrow irony that is Musil's hallmark. It switches to a lyrical register, borrowing its qualities from the sunlight and colors of the Mediterranean. The softly breathing rhythm of the narration brings across Ulrich and Agathe's mystical experience, how they are "submerged in this fire that fills up everything; swimming in it as in a sea of desire, and flying in it as in a heaven of rapture" (*MWQ* 1457 / *MoE* 1658). Fire, sea, sky—their desire makes them one with the elements.

Yet what the episode renders is the sexual relationship between brother and sister. Three days and nights in a hotel room furnished, as the narrator underlines, with a *letto matrimoniale:* "charmed by each other again and again. Traversing the scale of the sexual with variations" (*MWQ* 1452 / *MoE* 1653). Give indirect suggestions of repeated coitus, Musil wrote in the margin of these unpublished pages (*MWQ* 1461 / *MoE* 1662).

Remarkably, however, these "indirect suggestions" are couched in a language both inviting and seraphic. Musil reserves the most graceful register of his language for a description of what is considered the most hideous of human crimes.[81] In fact, he is arguably the only writer to have succeeded in inventing a prose capable of raising incest, which conventional morality classifies as bestiality, to the level of the angelic.

Many critics have debated the incestuous relation of Ulrich and Agathe. In particular, there is the issue concerning where in the novel Musil planned to insert their voyage to paradise, and whether he intended to include it at all.[82] Some have also compared Musil's use of the incest motif to its deployment in ancient mythology, fin-de-siècle literature, and later German prose. What has gone unnoticed about Ulrich and Agathe's journey to paradise is that the siblings' incest corresponds to the central principle of negativity from which Musil's whole complex narrative machinery unfolds.[83]

The novel states that the siblings' journey to the brink of the possible led past the dangers of the impossible and the unnatural, even the repugnant, and perhaps not always quite past it (*MWQ* 826 / *MoE* 761). "We have yielded to an impulse against order," Ulrich says (*MWQ* 1471 / *MoE* 1673). His words are certainly true, because the prohibition of incest is what institutes every social order. The constitution of a social community presupposes the possibility of families to unite with one another. This is made possible by incest prohibition, which forces brother and sister to surrender each other to a member of a different family. Exogamy and incest taboo are thus two aspects of the universal law of kinship that founds human culture.[84] Moreover, the incest taboo implies that women, not men, are exchanged between families. If women are the gifts that bind society together, men control the exchange. The circulation of women defines men as the representatives of the social field. This kinship law is thus the rationale of the Oedipal drama and the origin of masculine and feminine identities, as these are then further naturalized by the ideology of patriarchy. The same law is also at the root of the situation of Lulu, Alpha, and Agathe. They are all objects of exchange, circulating among men. The incest prohibition in fact conditions not only gender identities but the construction and distribution of all identities. It determines that each subject must have not just a sexual identity, which decides whether the subject is an object of exchange, but also a group identity, which decides the social limits within which this exchange can take place.

We now begin to grasp the significance of Musil's insertion of the incest theme as a closure to the story about Ulrich and Agathe, and as the final discovery in Ulrich's exploration of subjectivity. We also understand why Musil called this part of the novel "The Criminals." I have argued that the most fundamental principle of *The Man Without Qualities* is the deconstructive mechanism of negativity. Only by identifying negativity as the governing logic of the narrative as a whole can we appreciate the aesthetic, philosophical, and political import of the novel and account for all its apparent peculiarities. The principle of negativity works to erode first the personal identity of Ulrich, then the cultural identity of the social group to which he belongs, and finally the feminine identity of Agathe. Having negated all identities, Musil's story ends in a nothingness that transcends the boundaries of human society. Incest, then, is a logical conclusion of this story, the point that it inexorably approaches.[85] A scandalous realization of pure negativity, the incestuous fulfillment of Ulrich and Agathe's love shatters the novel's narrative, social, and political universe in its entirety. In introducing the incestuous relationship, Musil's novel violates the law on which all identities rely, and without which society as we know it would not come into being. Incest represents the destruction of all ideological appellations of the subject, tearing apart the kinship structure through which groups are formed, and dissolving the fabric of society. It is the last love story there could ever be, the narrator proclaims. But that is an understatement. The story about Ulrich and Agathe is in fact the last story there could be of any kind; the incest takes the novel to the extreme of monstrosity.

Angels at War

Why monstrosity? With this designation I am merely repeating a categorization that throughout a long history has attached itself to deeds of the kind committed by Agathe and Ulrich. Ferdinand Tönnies, for example, asserted that "incest is forbidden according to common law as a monstrosity." [86] In the history of European imagination, monstrosity has a fairly well-defined meaning. A monster is first of all a creature that *demonstrates*—the Latin word *monstrare* means "to show" or "to exhibit" —a disturbance in the order of the world. The monster operates outside the social, and it often demonstrates a vice that threatens the cohesion and reason of the human community.[87] The function of the monster is thus to warn (Latin, *monere*) humanity of the punishment awaiting those who commit such vice.

Discussing Shakespeare's plays, Chris Baldick explains "that it is the vices of ingratitude, rebellion, and disobedience, particularly toward parents, that most commonly attract the appellation 'monstrous': to be a monster is to break the natural bonds of obligation towards friends and especially toward blood-relations." [88] Agathe and Ulrich thus deserve to be brandished as monsters even long before they sleep together.

From the moment they meet at their father's funeral, they join forces against the law of the Father and virtually desecrate his corpse. Later, they violate the very law that ensures the regeneration of society.

It was such vicious disobedience toward parents that Edmund Burke had in mind when he, condemning the French Revolution, extended the usage of the term "monstrous" so that it signified a particular social disorder. In his *Letters on the Proposals for Peace with the Regicide Directory of France* (1796–1797), Burke called France a "monster of state," "the mother of monsters," "a monstrous compound," and a "cannibal republic." [89] What motivated this hysteric terminology was Burke's repugnance of the Republic's violations of the social obligations codified in feudal law. The revolution was monstrous because it demonstrated an unpardonable disobedience of servants toward their masters and of children toward their parents.

When liberal writers defended the revolution against Burke they seized on the theme of monstrosity, stating that it was the monstrous injustice of the feudal system that had caused the rebellion of the French people, whose violence was thus justified. Among those who used this argument were, most famously, Mary Wollstonecraft and William Godwin, the parents of Mary Shelley, who was to write *Frankenstein* (1818).

The debate was the first to pose the problem concerning the legitimacy of social change and its relation to stability and permanence. How do we judge social transformations if we are confined within a discourse of modernity that defines development as a continuous negation of the past? If change for change's own sake becomes modernity's supreme value, this value will also override all other values that might be used to measure the value of change. Thus, in the era of modernity, when the future is no longer seen just as an organic realization of the values of tradition, historical transformation becomes enigmatic, contradictory, and incalculable.

According to Baldick, these topics were all woven into Shelley's *Frankenstein*. The relation between Doctor Frankenstein and his monster, the parent and his fabulous offspring, should be regarded as an allegory of Shelley's attempt to represent the connections between plans made in the present and their uncertain future results. The novel about

Frankenstein's relationship to his monster thus elaborates on the relation of a historical cause to its possible effects. In Frankenstein's case, this causality can only be thought of as an absolute discontinuity, the same kind of discontinuity, that is, as the one pertaining between pre-revolutionary France and the first Republic.[90]

This discontinuity, then, is the sign of a failure to imagine how one society is transformed into another, to conceptualize historical change, and it makes itself felt most sharply in periods of revolution, war, and disaster, that is, during historical traumas. As we have seen, the cultural modernity of Vienna is such a period.[91] A patriarchal ideology inherited from the feudal system was contradicted by an emerging industrial society organized around the nuclear family, in which old laws of kinship lost their meaning. This contradiction interrupted the processes of investiture that used to determine the identities of groups and genders. Cultural life was instead occupied by efforts to restore the old norms, but also by attempts, such as Musil's, to represent the limits of the waning ideology by indicating human possibilities that violated the "law of culture." Hence the preoccupation with incest in this cultural milieu.[92]

Musil's novel teaches us that in Western culture, such contradictory and discontinuous moments breed not only insanity and the specter of femininity, but also monsters. Such creatures emerge when there is no longer any agreement on what the social community is and should be in the future. The monsters are thus the results of our failed attempts to figure out the riddle of history or to understand how one society can be qualitatively different from the preceding one. Monsters emerge as substitutes for historical comprehension. For instance, failing to understand how European society in 1930 could cause the Holocaust, our historical imagination sometimes tends to transform Adolf Hitler the politician into Hitler the monster. Similarly, the cultural imagination in postimperial Austria produced an array of monstrous beings, because it seemed impossible to explain the fall of the empire and the world that replaced it. In such situations, the monster's agency explains, or rather explains away, what seems too difficult to explain.

Victor Hugo was therefore wrong when he wrote that "monsters are the dreams of God." [93] Rather, monsters are the dreams of a humanity struggling to understand history, time, and change. Or, as Ulrich thinks, "If mankind could dream as a whole, that dream would be Moosbrugger" (*MWQ* 77 / *MoE* 76).

A historical trauma effects a symbolic castration of masculine identity. Without any legitimate principle of power and authority, society loses its mechanism for achieving consensus as well as its norms for distinguishing between progress and decline. The monster will then appear as an imaginary substitute, allowing the members of the community to believe that there is agency or rationality at work, if only of a malign and destructive kind, when in fact there may be none. Monsters are therefore most likely to show up in periods when history is most difficult to understand. Pierrot, Lulu, Alpha, Roth's madmen and the Anti-Christ, Moosbrugger, Ulrich, and Agathe are such figures of monstrosity, exterminators of the past and portents of things to come. Eric Santner reaches a similar conclusion in his reading of Kafka's "Metamorphosis." The story represents "a postmythic order" in which the individual can no longer find his place in the texture of fate. He has no idea who he is, or what he is supposed to do. The processes of symbolic investiture have collapsed; the big Other is silent; the transfer of authority from one generation to the next is broken. This interruption of historical continuity, then, explains the uncanny creatures that invade Kafka's story. The disruption of fate, Santner argues, "opens up a space within which monstrosities can appear." [94]

We must finally ask whether the monster only expresses a collective wish for the recovery of patriarchal authority. This would seem to be the case with the collective longing for a führer or a messiah who would again bind the subjects into an expressive community hailing a national or imperial flag. This wish is understandable. Kafka's postmythic universe shows that the modern condition, in which the subject is simply neglected and treated as if it did not exist by some faceless commander, may be far more disturbing than a society in which the subject must subordinate itself, or even sacrifice itself for some higher aim.

Or is the monster really a sign of the destruction of authority, a figure teaching the human subject to affirm the negativity at the heart of its being? This seems to be the case with Musil's monsters. Ulrich identifies first with Moosbrugger, his monstrous alter ego, because the psychotic murderer represents a deviation from the collective identity that he loathes. He then fixes on Agathe, his angelic alter ego, for she allows him to step out of this identity altogether. Posted on a threshold, Ulrich stands between the totalitarian logic of a society mobilizing for war, and the counterlogic of criminality, madness, and femininity. This counterlogic is fully developed in the incestuous relation. From the point of view of society, Ulrich and Agathe are monsters because their love is unlawful. From the perspective of possibility, they are angels warring against a totalitarian reality. They are monsters in love, angels at war.

Musil's incestuous couple thus belong to the monstrous kind that continue their work of negativity, teaching humankind to live with lack. These are the monsters that Benjamin praises in his essay on Karl Kraus (1931), another eccentric of Vienna. Benjamin argues that Kraus was a reactionary, affiliated with the expressionists and celebrating the primeval forces of "the world of the demon" as a remedy against the fallen world of modernity.[95] On more clear-sighted occasions, however, Kraus spoke from the position of what Benjamin calls "der Unmensch," often mistranslated as "the monster." [96] As *Unmensch,* Kraus appeals to a humanity "that proves itself by destruction" (*die sich an der Zerstörung bewährt*).[97] "Destruction" must here be read against the background of Benjamin's philosophy of history. The reference is not the blind powers of destruction unleashed in World War I, but a revolutionary act that liquidates these powers in order to clear the ground for a society in which the productive forces of humanity are liberated from the relations of production that hold capitalist society together. Benjamin writes that Kraus, as Unmensch, delivers the same message as the angel in Paul Klee's painting *Angelus Novus* (1921). It is an angel, Benjamin states, "who preferred to free men by taking from them, rather than making them happy by giving to them." [98]

Realizing a similar logic of emancipation, Musil's novel continually approaches what Christine Buci-Glucksmann has called the angelic spaces of modernity.[99] These spaces are not governed by ideologies that align the subject with the norms of the ethnic or national community. Instead they represent a countermodernity, an other rationality, or a rationality of otherness, which cannot be defined within the limits of the existing ideological paradigm but which keep emerging just outside it, as a corrective and as an escape. This, then, is the role entrusted to Agathe, emancipating humanity by taking from it, robbing society of its ideological belief. Indeed, in 1941 Musil notes that Hitler represents the ultimate bankruptcy of masculinity. After the transformation of patriarchy into fascism, the only acceptable future alternative is a matriarchy, Musil states. He adds that this implies that Agathe must take over the spiritual leadership in *The Man Without Qualities* and bring the story to its end (*T* 1:811).

Agathe is thus a sister of Klee's new angel. Her face is turned toward the past, contemplating the catastrophic scene of a society approaching World War I. Like the angel, Musil's heroine would like to stay and make whole what has been smashed. But a wind has caught her wings and propels her into the future: "She walked, and it was as if each step she took was a step out of life" (*MWQ* 1043* / *MoE* 962). Benjamin calls this storm progress. It is founded upon a notion of instrumental reason that casts Agathe in the role of feminine alterity and bans her from participating in society.

Musil's transgression of the expressivist conceptions of human identity finds a visual parallel in Klee's work, in which the anthropocentric norm is also undone by mathematical precision, monstrous otherness, and angels of possibility, just as the boundaries between interior and exterior space is radically dissolved.[100] This parallel accounts for the close correspondence between Musil's siblings and the creature in Klee's 1930 painting, *The Siblings,* which appears to depict an incestuous couple: what the anthropologists would call their consanguinity is touchingly represented by the fact that Klee's siblings share the same heart (fig. 8). Ulrich and Agathe, the novel states, are like two people who, hand in hand, have stepped out of the circle that used to enclose them, but without being at home in another one (*MWQ* 1519 / *MoE* 1435). Having violated the most universal law of human society, they have

8   Paul Klee, *Die Geschwister* (1930; *The Siblings*). © 1999 Artists Rights
Society (ARS), New York / VG Bild-Kunst, Bonn.

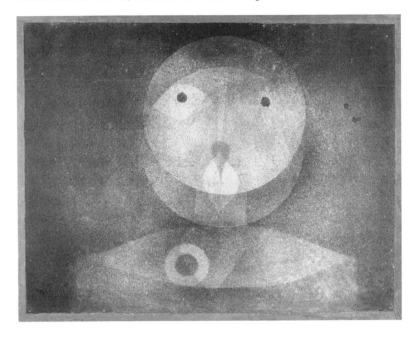

9   Paul Klee, *Pierrot Lunaire* (1925). Honolulu Academy of the Arts, Gift of
Geraldine P. and Henry B. Clark, Jr. at the time of their fortieth wedding
anniversary, 1982.

become unhuman, living in a community of consanguinity and loving
camaraderie that cannot be grasped conceptually. The abundance of
half-human figures and spatial inversions that characterize Klee's work,
however, seems to indicate the different logic that structures this new
world. One of Klee's images shows two superimposed faces that fade
into each other and disappear into the background; it is a truthful portrait of the transient nature of the monstrous or angelic character. The
painting is called *Pierrot Lunaire* (1925; fig. 9). A creature without qualities, Pierrot is pushed away by the madness of modernity to which s/he
has testified, ever further toward the periphery, until his face, her face,
its face, or their face is effaced, fusing with the glowing moon in the
sky over that other utopian planet that must be the true home of Lulu,
Alpha, Moosbrugger, Ulrich, Agathe, and Pierrot.

This is the lesson that *The Man Without Qualities* teaches: the history of modernity is a history about historical traumas that we manage by generating monsters whom we then expel or kill off. Perhaps, then, cultural modernity is best captured by the term that was Wedekind's original subtitle for his *Lulu* plays: *Eine Monstretragödie,* a monster tragedy.

6

The Most Progressive State

Empire, Nation, and Culture

Although there are countless books and articles on *The Man Without Qualities,* the importance of the two most evident traits of the man without qualities himself, Ulrich, has not been sufficiently probed. First, Ulrich is part of a group, the Parallel Campaign, planning to celebrate the emperor. Second, he discovers his sister, Agathe, and becomes so attached to her that he decides to leave the celebration to spend time only with her. These two statements, incidentally, also sum up the plot of the novel.

Thus Ulrich embodies the drama of identity formation on both a personal level, that is, in his relationship to Agathe, *and* on a collective level, through his connections to the Parallel Campaign. In chapter 4, I suggested that the novelistic discourse is motored by a logic of negativity, which results in a new notion of subjectivity and identity. In chapter 5, I demonstrated how this logic of negativity, activated by the historical trauma that Musil's narrator revisits, leads to the rejection of the ideology attributing identities of sexuality, gender, and kinship. We may now begin to sense the overarching concern that structures this multidimensional novel. *The Man Without Qualities,* I want to argue, aims at nothing less than the liquidation of the concept of identity that dominated the political and cultural discourse in Musil's time: the expressivist conception of identity.

In this chapter I will conclude the argument by demonstrating how, in *The Man Without Qualities,* the logic of negativity also intervenes to question ideologies of empire, nation, and culture. Second, I will reverse the argument so as to show that this logic of negativity, which determines the representation of subjectivity and identity in *The Man Without Qualities,* is reactively conditioned by the politics of empire, nation, and culture that Musil experienced during and after World War I.

My primary concerns here are the imperial ideology of the Austro-Hungarian Empire, the nationalist opposition to this ideology, and the racist and fascist movements that emerged in Central Europe in the 1920s, after the destruction of the imperial regimes. As we shall see, Musil's novel responds to these ideologies on several levels. First, the Parallel Campaign simulates the imperial attempt to appease the dissent of various nationalist movements in Austria-Hungary. Second, the novel's achronic, polycentric, and heterologic narrative can be interestingly related to the historical situation in Austria, in which no consensus could be reached either on how to understand the past or on what direction to follow in the future. Third, Musil's novel exhibits an intriguing selection of deviant figures whose actions make sense only as transgressions of the limits and taboos of the cultural community. Fourth, the dichotomous pattern of the novel's conceptual architecture — the antinomies of "possibility" and "order," "pseudoreality" and "the other condition," "man" and "qualities," or "subjectivity" and "identity" — must be considered in the light of the nationality problem in Central Europe.

I will strengthen these arguments by analyzing Musil's essays from the beginning of the 1920s, so as to clarify that the novel's exploration of "the other condition," commonly regarded as an escape into mysticism, is inseparable from Musil's examination of nationalism and collective identities. In my conclusion, finally, I will indicate how Musil's narrator returns to the lost possibility of a *trans*cultural empire precisely at the moments when he attempts to conceptualize the social implications of his antiexpressivist idea of human nature.

On all these levels, Musil's novel places the notion of the human being as a subject of negativity in close proximity with the question of cultural identity. Indeed, once we have identified the Musilian principle of negativity, the seemingly unrelated episodes of *The Man Without Qualities* fall into step and the novel is revealed as a "parallel campaign" in its own right. On the one hand, there is the narrative about incest. The relationship between Ulrich and Agathe destroys gender identities, and above all the specter of femininity. On the other hand, there is the narrative about the Parallel Campaign. In representing the ideological effort to gather the nationalities of the empire under one common idea, Musil's narrator challenges those ideologies which sustain the belief in national, racial, and cultural identities. These, then, are the two ways in which the novel raises a comprehensive critique of the dominant paradigm of identity, and they also expose the true meaning of Ulrich's parallel roles. As a brother in love with his sister, he disputes the psychological and social laws determining identities of gender, kinship, and sexuality. As secretary of the Parallel Campaign, he is perfectly placed to interrogate all aspects of cultural, national, and racial identity.

The Nationality Question in Austria-Hungary

Count Leinsdorf, the founder of the Parallel Campaign, boasts that Vienna is the center of the world. Our Ringstrasse is unique, he asserts, because where else in the world can one see, in the midst of "the finest Western European elegance," a Mohammedan with his red fez, a Slovak in sheepskins, or a bare-legged Tyrolean (*MWQ* 917 / *MoE* 844)?

In 1914 the territories of the Habsburg dynasty stretched from Ukraine in the east to Switzerland in the west, and from the Adriatic Sea in the south to Kraków in today's Poland. The different regions of this superpower were never bound together by nationality or constitutional law.[1] Neither a state, nor a nation, nor a federation, nor a union of states, the Austro-Hungarian Empire was "an unequal union of domains that were historically, culturally, nationally, and legally very differently organized and developed." [2] What united this entity was the fact that all its domains had once sworn allegiance to the House of Habsburg, a constitutional event referred to as the "Pragmatic Sanction." The cohesive force was thus the crown, and to some extent also the Catholic Church, since the Habsburgs successfully carried the banner of Rome in the Counter Reformation. Situated at the crossroads of east and west, of Christianity and Islam, the empire served for many centuries to stabilize the geopolitical relationships among Russia, Turkey, Germany, and France. In 1919 it no longer existed.

Perhaps more than any other historical era and geographical area, this empire—Musil's society—has been draped in historical myths and political fantasies that appear strangely attractive to present-day Europeans, who have seen their continent being dismembered by nationalism, fascism, Stalin's iron curtain, and Milosevic's ethnic cleansings.[3] The historian François Fetjö evokes an imperial past basking in "an atmosphere of nonchalant cosmopolitanism," in which one would take the train to Vienna, Budapest, or Kraków, spend the weekend in Trieste or Fiume, check in at a hotel in Karlsbad to get a share of Western Europe, or go hiking in the Carpathian mountains to look for Dracula's dwelling, without even leaving the country.[4] Styria, Carinthia, Silesia, Galicia, Dalmatia, Bukovina, Gorizia: today the names of Habsburg's crownlands sound like places on a map of some long-forgotten, imaginary Europe, waiting to be activated by unforeseen events, as happened when Bosnia-Herzegovina and Slovenia returned to the international community just some years ago.

Yet the nostalgic idea of the old Habsburg empire is not a recent invention. It emerged almost immediately after the empire's demise. In 1918 Karl Kautsky mourned the extinction of a prewar European geography in which a person traveling by railroad from Hamburg to Bagdad needed to cross only two borders, first to Austria, then to Turkey. After the war the traveler had to do six border crossings—in Czechoslovakia, Austria, Hungary, Yugoslavia, Bulgaria, and Turkey—with all the ensuing complications of immigration and customs controls.[5] Even more nostalgically, Joseph Roth wrote about a chestnut roaster who used to do business all over the empire—in Bohemia, Silesia, Galicia, and all the other crownlands; wherever people ate his chestnuts, they got a taste of the empire and knew themselves to be protected by Franz Joseph.

Then comes 1918: "Now there are no more chestnuts without a visa. What a world!" [6]

The destruction of the Habsburg empire in the fall of 1918 finalized a process that had been going on for at least half a century. In the aftermath of the 1848 revolution in Hungary and consecutive military defeats, the Habsburg dynasty almost lost Hungary and had to agree, in 1867, to a compromise stipulating that Hungary was a sovereign kingdom united with Austria. The Austrian Empire was transformed into a dual monarchy called Austria-Hungary, the king of Hungary being also king *and* emperor of the rest of the Habsburg lands. Apart from the crown, the only joint institutions of Hungary and the rest of the Habsburg territories were the army, the foreign ministry, and a ministry of finance handling common expenses. Hence the nomenclature that Musil ridiculed by inventing the name "Kakania." Institutions shared by both parts of Austria-Hungary were designated as "imperial and royal," *kaiserlich und königlich* or *k.u.k.;* institutions of Austria were "imperial-royal," *kaiserlich-königlich,* or *k.k.;* and Hungarian institutions were "royal-Hungarian," *königlich-ungarisch,* or *k.u.* Another peculiarity is that the Habsburg domain outside Hungary had no proper name. Its official designation was "die im Reichsrate vertretenen Königreiche und Länder," that is, the kingdoms and lands represented in the governing council. Usually, however, these parts were just called Austria, or Austria-Cisleithania, in contradistinction to Hungary, which was then called Austria-Transleithania.

Historians usually break down the population of the Habsburg lands into eleven major and several minor nationalities.[7] The social and economic relationships between these nationalities cannot be described in general terms, for the political, economic, and ethnic boundary lines were not congruent. Robert Kann has stressed three characteristic features of the nationality problem in the Dual Monarchy. First, there was no majority, and hence no minorities either, in the strict sense. In Cisleithania, Germans constituted 35.6 percent of the population in 1910. Among the Transleithanian or Hungarian population, the Magyar part grew from 41 percent in 1880 to 48 percent in 1910, due to aggressive Magyarization.[8]

Second, only five of the eleven major nationalities were entirely confined inside Habsburg territory: Czechs, Slovaks, Croats, Magyars, and Slovenes. The other six shared language and history with their respective conationals living across the border. The Italians tended to identify less with Vienna and more with the newly unified Italian state. The Serb population was drawn to their conationals in Serbia. German Austrians tended to emphasize their connections to the north. Ruthenians identified with the Ukranians in Russia, while Romanians looked toward Romania, and the majority of the conationals of the Habsburg Poles lived in Prussia and Russia.

Third, the nationalities of Austria-Hungary could not be divided along territorial lines. To be sure, all of them were more or less concentrated in some part of the empire, except Germans and Jews. But individuals of most national groups lived in both parts of the Dual Monarchy, the exception being Poles, Czechs, and Italians who were found only in Cisleithania, and the Magyars who populated only Transleithania. Although the constitutions of Austria and Hungary granted equal rights to all nationalities, legal practice differed greatly. Austria was far more tolerant toward non-German nationals than Hungary was toward non-Magyar nationals, despite the fact that Austria and Hungary had the same chief of state. In order to secure the support of the Magyar leaders in economic and political matters, the king and emperor refrained from intervening against Magyar discrimination.

The Magyar leaders, on the other hand, could influence the Austrian government's attitude to its non-German nationals. The compromise of 1867 stipulated that no constitutional changes would be made by either Austria or Hungary without the prior approval of the other part. This meant that the Austrian government could not undertake the constitutional reforms necessary to meet demands for greater independence from its Slav population. The Magyar leaders realized that the establishment of semi-independent Bohemian and Croatian kingdoms within the Habsburg domain would deprive Hungary of its privileged relation to the crown and at the same time generate demands for equality from Slovak, Serb, and Croatian groups in Hungary. They resented such a prospect because it would have meant the end of their dominance of

Hungarian society. Indeed, behind the ethnic dominance of the Magyars in Hungary lay a political one. As late as 1918, the Magyars, roughly half of Hungary's population, controlled 450 seats in Hungary's parliament, while the other half, made up by other nationalities, held 8 seats.[9] Behind this political hegemony stood a system of economic oppression. The right to vote was contingent upon property qualifications, which meant that only 6 percent of Hungary's population could vote. Consequently, the parliament was controlled by a party representing large estates and big business, the so-called Liberal party.[10] Almost half of Hungary's arable land was in fact owned by around three thousand persons.[11] In order to retain this feudal order, Magyar officials had to combat the nationalist movements that constituted the most vital support for democracy and modernization. The Compromise of 1867 provided the Magyar elite with a powerful tool for doing this; as a result, they hindered economic and political progress in Cisleithanian Austria as well. The nationalist movements that gained momentum throughout the nineteenth century in Austria-Hungary are thus indices of an inhibited process of modernization. The demands for national equality were inseparable from demands to end the political and economic dominance of the Magyars in Hungary and the German-Austrians in Cisleithania.

The consequences of the 1867 Compromise were all made manifest by the case of Bosnia-Herzegovina. At the Berlin Congress in 1878, where European powers negotiated a settlement to stabilize the Balkan situation after the war between Russia and Turkey, Austria-Hungary was persuaded to take charge of the Turkish provinces of Bosnia-Herzegovina. The territory was subsequently occupied by *k.u.k.* forces, but its status was to remain uncertain. Hungary did not allow Bosnia-Herzegovina to become part of Cisleithanian Austria, because this would have shifted the balance of power in Vienna's favor. Nor did the Hungarian government want to incorporate Bosnia-Herzegovina into Hungary, because this would have increased its Slav population and hence threatened the Magyar dominance of Hungary. Austria and Hungary agreed on the peculiar compromise that the new territory was to be governed jointly by the finance ministry shared by the two countries, a solution that meant that the Bosnians had no representation in either Vienna or Budapest and were ruled by an appointed governor.[12] In 1908 Bosnia-Herzegovina was formally annexed by Austria, a decision which created new unrest both domestically and internationally.

The occupation of Bosnia Herzegovina in 1870 also disrupted the internal politics of Austria. The liberal party, for a long time the dominant power in Austrian politics, opposed the occupation on the grounds that it would diminish German authority in the empire. The defeat of the liberal party on this issue meant that it was finally deprived of its leading position, and the party was soon to disappear altogether. Its failure underscores the difficulty to found a political position that was independent of the nationality problem. The liberal party opposed the church, encouraged laissez-faire capitalism, supported constitutional monarchy, and turned its back on the nationality problem. Its anticlerical position alienated large sectors of the German middle classes; its implicit German centralism alienated the Slav peoples. When Austria was hit by an economic crisis in 1873, the liberals could not even prove the viability of their economic policies. This failure paved the way for the anticapitalist and antiliberal programs of Karl Lueger's Christian Socialists and Georg von Schönerer's Pan-German movement. Themselves former liberals, Lueger and Schönerer blamed liberalism for the economic crisis. Among the liberal forces they singled out the Jews, whom they identified with the interests of finance capitalism that they blamed for the recession.[13] The failure of liberal centralism thus also put an end to Jewish assimilation into the German population and marked the beginning of Schönerer's violent anti-Semitism. Meanwhile, his Pan-German fantasies had a reactive effect in that it mobilized nationalist sentiment among Czechs, Slovenes, Poles, South Slavs, and Italians—and finally also among the Jews in the form of Theodor Herzl's Zionism.

With the fall of Austrian liberalism, the Austrian parliament split along ethnic lines. It became increasingly difficult to form a majority government, and even more difficult to gather support for governmental propositions. If a specific proposal would favor one nationality more than others, the representatives of other national groups were likely to oppose the proposal, regardless of its overall benefit. For instance, if the economy of Austria as a whole would gain from a new railroad in Bohemia, and if this railroad happened to serve German communities in particular, the government had to propose another railroad, whether necessary or not, in some Czech area of Bohemia.[14] In order to avoid national wrangling (or the extra expenses for an additional railroad), there was also an easier alternative: to leave things as they were. Eduard Taafe, Austrian prime minister from 1879 to 1893, remarked that the secret behind a successful government of Austria was to keep all national groups in a moderate state of dissatisfaction.[15] To describe his political tactics, Taafe coined the word "fortwursteln," that is, the art of "muddling through" without directing policy.[16]

The Man Without Qualities frequently alludes to this political standstill. The narrator at one point makes the seemingly cryptic remark that in Kakania one was suspicious of the principle of "either-or," and instead preferred to follow the principle of "as well as," or, better still, "neither-nor" (*MWQ* 1481 / *MoF* 1445). Musil's novel thereby distills the essence of the politics in a state where the decision to build a railroad *either* in German Bohemia *or* in Czech Bohemia would invite disaster. Should any public works be undertaken, they must benefit one part *as well as* the other, and since this was often too costly or too complicated, the result was that official investments materialized *neither* here *nor* there. As we shall see, the nationality problem is far more than a backdrop in Musil's novel; it is inscribed in the very fiber of its narrative structure.

No national group seriously considered seceding from Habsburg rule. The nationalists normally fought to have their vernaculars recognized in higher education and in administrative use. But such issues could also actualize considerable shifts of power, particularly in areas where two nationalities lived side by side in an unequal economic relationship. When the Austrian government in 1895 decided that the grammar school of Celje in Slovenia should provide instruction in Slovene, German-Austrians in the government resigned to protest against a measure which in their view increased the Slav influence. In 1897 Prime Minister Badeni attempted to appease Czech dissatisfaction by deciding that Czech, in addition to German, was to count as the official language of Bohemia, which meant that officials had to master both German and Czech. Since all Czechs learned German while few Germans knew Czech, Badeni's ordinance effectively provided the Czechs with a monopoly of official positions in Bohemia. His measure led to the worst uprisings since 1848 and gave the German nationalists under Schönerer an opportunity to gather support for the Pan-German cause. Violent demonstrations forced the emperor to dismiss Badeni. After this political drawback, neither the government nor the emperor dared to seek any long-term solution to the nationality question. All reform proposals were instantly neutralized by counterproposals or conditions; decisions were continually postponed.[17]

Even if the Austrian government had launched resolute measures to solve the nationality question, these would certainly have been blocked by the Compromise of 1867. Magyar authorities feared that a reform of the nationality rights in Austria could not be stopped outside the frontier of Hungary; if reform reached Hungary, it would have meant the end of Magyar dominance.[18] The Compromise of 1867 in effect bound Magyar feudalism and German-Austrian centralism together, but back to back, in a struggle against nationalities whose demands for cultural and linguistic equality inevitably actualized demands for political democracy and economic reforms as well.

In 1907, when universal suffrage for men was introduced in Cisleithania, the social democratic party emerged as a potential unifying force, now the only major party not based on ethnicity. The socialist leaders Otto Bauer and Karl Renner suggested far-reaching reforms that would have transformed the empire into a federation and granted each individual the right to declare his or her nationality on the basis of choice rather than on territorial or genealogical origin. The working-class movement was anathema to both emperor and government, however, and the socialists' proposals came to nothing. In 1911 the Czech labor movement formed its own party, thus splitting the socialist forces into "Austrians" and "Slavs." As a consequence, the possibilities for solving the national conflicts were exhausted. Instead of looking for a compromise in Vienna, many Slavs, Poles, Italians, Germans, and even Romanians and Ruthenians oriented themselves toward their conationals outside the borders of Austria-Hungary, a factor that contributed to the outbreak of the war.[19]

The roots of the nationality problem, Robert Kann has argued, reached into the foundation of the empire. The establishment of inter-ethnic solidarity among the peoples of Austria-Hungary would have presupposed reforms that challenged the economic inequality between the upper classes of the privileged national groups and the underprivi-leged nationalities. Such reforms, however, could not have been con-fined to any single national group. For instance, large-scale agricultural reform in Galicia or Slovak parts of Hungary would have encouraged small peasants everywhere to challenge the big estates throughout this semifeudal empire. "Evolutionary reforms . . . would have been fea-sible only in a thoroughly democratic empire. Yet the comprehensive democratization of the Danube monarchy would have alienated those conservative forces which were the strongest pillars of the Habsburg Empire and its feudal tradition." [20]

Posed in this way, the nationality question turns out to be an index of something else. Once again, we confront the difficulty of imagining historical change. The Austrian failure to solve the nationality prob-lem signifies an inability to envision how a semifeudal empire could be transformed into a liberal capitalist society. This problem haunted Aus-trian social thought and politics after the turn of the century.[21] By refus-ing to direct or even acknowledge this transformation, the leaders of the Dual Monarchy contributed to the outbreak of a war that finally liqui-dated the residual structures of feudalism in both Austria and Germany. Hence Otto Bauer's observation that World War I "was the greatest and bloodiest bourgeois revolution in world history." [22]

Only a war or a revolution could break the double bind that blocked political progress in Austria-Hungary: the empire could not solve the nationality problem without questioning its own existence; and, con-versely, it could not secure its existence without solving the nationality problem. Paralyzed by this dilemma, the political and cultural circles of Vienna could not agree on any reforms at all. In fact, it was impossible to agree even on how to interpret the situation. Enter Musil's character General Stumm von Bordwehr. In an effort to drill the current political tendencies into *ordres de bataille,* he establishes a list of "Commanders in Chief of Ideas." But he must finally give in, conceding that the whole situation looks like what any military officer would call one hell of a mess (*MWQ* 405f. / *MoE* 374).

The Nationality Question in *The Man Without Qualities*

The history of the Habsburg empire is dispersed throughout the pages of *The Man Without Qualities*. Historiographical sketches deal with the rise of the Habsburgs in medieval times, the Compromise of 1867, and the emergence of social democracy and Pan-Germanism around 1900. The novel also incorporates most of the events and conflicts that by 1914 had led to a political standstill.

To start, Musil's characters are easily identified as exponents of political and intellectual tendencies in Austria at the beginning of the century. Leinsdorf belongs to the landed nobility of German descent. By placing him at the center, the narrator underscores that the Parallel Campaign is invented by the leading circles of the empire. Also, the narrator uses Leinsdorf as a pretext for dispensing his lectures on Austrian history. Diotima provides the campaign with an intellectual alibi and a cultural superstructure. In describing her aspirations, the narrator charts the intellectual concerns of the era. Diotima devours numberless treatises on aesthetics and philosophy, most of which seek to redeem modern society by appealing to idealist slogans such as soul, art, culture, and *Bildung.*

Leinsdorf and Diotima are encircled by four major players. The Jewish banker Leo Fischel embodies the liberal attitudes that dominated Austria through the 1860s and 1870s and that were destroyed by the economic crisis of 1873 and by the wave of anti-Semitism and nationalism that precludes Fischel's hopes for assimilation. Second, there is General Stumm, whose convictions I have already alluded to.[23] At the first session of the Parallel Campaign, the general takes the opportunity to remind the assembly that the army's need for modern artillery is a worthy cause, should it be difficult to reach an agreement about the guiding idea for the "Austrian Year" scheduled for 1918. Third, there is the Foreign Ministry, represented by the diplomat Tuzzi, Diotima's husband, and "one of the few men who could influence the fate of Europe" (*MWQ* 94 / *MoE* 92). Lobbying for an Austrian alliance with the powers of the Entente rather than with Germany, Tuzzi first steers a moderate course amidst the increasingly fanatic voices in the Parallel Campaign. In the summer of 1914, however, he starts advocating a firm pro-German line. If the narrator focalizes the account of Austrian history through Leinsdorf, he relies on Tuzzi to sketch out the contemporary situation. The fourth major player is Arnheim, who puts colonialism next to Goethe in his global scheme. A representative of Wilhelmine Germany, Arnheim emerges as a proponent of the plans for a so-called Mitteleuropa, where Germany and Austria-Hungary would merge into a giant empire, stretching from the Balkans to the Baltic, infused by Geist and motored by German industriousness.

These characters represent established political tendencies. All of them are centralists, proponents of a strong imperial state. Each of them has his or her own view on which ideology the state should embrace; as regards the candidates for this normative position, Leinsdorf's notion of "Capital and Culture" (*Besitz und Bildung*), Diotima's idea of making Austria into "Europe's true spiritual home" and Fischel's constitutional liberalism are soon overrun by Stumm's military discipline, Tuzzi's secret diplomacy, and Arnheim's imperial capitalism. In their attempts to reintegrate the imperial state, these figures are opposed by subversive elements of the younger generation who embody the empire's centrifugal tendencies: the Pan-German racist Hans Sepp, the young socialist Schmeisser, the pacifist poet Feuermaul, the authoritarian pedagogue Lindner, and the gay philosopher of soldierly virtues Meingast.

By assembling these characters, Musil's novel delineates a geopolitical scenario. The Parallel Campaign, clearly, is a device for mapping the ideological terrain of the era.[24] Musil mobilizes the entire political spectrum: feudalism and capitalism, socialism and imperialism, nationalism and federalism, monarchy and republicanism, militarism and pacifism, racism and cosmopolitanism. Ostensibly, the actors argue about the celebration of the seventieth anniversary of the reign of Franz Joseph;

essentially, however, they struggle over the future of Europe. From the moment Count Leinsdorf unveils his plan, Musil's satire is merciless:

> What has brought us together . . . is the shared conviction that a great testimonial arising from the midst of the people themselves must not be left to chance but needs guidance by an influence that sees far into the future from a place with a broad perspective—in other words, from the top. His Majesty, our beloved Emperor and Sovereign, will in the year 1918 celebrate the almost unique jubilee of the seventieth year since his richly blessed ascent to the throne. . . . We are certain that this occasion will be celebrated by the grateful people of Austria in a manner to show the world not only our deep love for him, but also that the Austro-Hungarian Monarchy stands together, grouped firm as a rock around its Sovereign. (*MWQ* 179f. / *MoE* 169)

The irony is not only that the Parallel Campaign faces the daunting task to organize from above a manifestation that must rise from the grassroots below. The irony is also that the status of Franz Joseph, the object of the celebration, is utterly unclear. Should the people celebrate their emperor and king, or their emperor, or perhaps only their king? And which sectors of the population should line up behind which part of Franz Joseph's multiple identity?

Inch by inch, *The Man Without Qualities* examines the damaged structure of Austrian society. Halfway into the novel, the narrator explains that the inhabitants of the Dual Monarchy confronted a dilemma: "They were supposed to feel like Imperial and Royal Austro-Hungarian patriots, while at the same time being Royal Hungarian or Imperial Royal Austrian patriots." In the face of such difficulties, their understandable motto was *viribus unitis*, or "with joined forces." But the Austrians then had to use "much greater force than the Hungarians," because the Hungarians were first and foremost Hungarians, whereas the Austrians were first and foremost nothing, citizens of a country which did not even have a name (*MWQ* 490* / *MoE* 450f.). The two parts of the Dual Monarchy matched each other like a red-white-and-green jacket with black-and-yellow trousers, the narrator continues. The jacket was a new item; the trousers were the remnant of an old uniform in black and yellow that had been ripped apart in 1867. Ever since then Austria had been searching for its ontological status:

> Austria [was] since then officially referred to as "the kingdoms and lands represented in the Governing Council," meaning nothing at all, of course, because it was only a phrase concocted from various names, for even those kingdoms referred to, such wholly Shakespearean kingdoms as Lodomeria and Illyria, were long gone. . . . So if you asked an Austrian where he was from, of course he wouldn't say: I am a man from one of the kingdoms and lands represented in the governing council which do not exist; so for that reason alone he preferred to say: I am a Pole, a Czech, an Italian, Friulian, Ladino, Slovene, Croat, Serb, Slovak, Ruthenian, or Wallachian—and this was the so-called nationalism. Imagine a squirrel that doesn't know whether it is a squirrel or a chipmunk, a creature with no concept of itself, and you will understand that in some circumstances it could be thrown into fits of terror by catching sight of its own tail. So this was the way Kakanians related to each other, with the panic of limbs which, with joined forces, hindered each other from being anything at all. (*MWQ* 491* / *MoE* 451)

This stunning passage situates the empire at the same level as Ulrich and Moosbrugger, presenting Austria as an entity that has no concept of itself.[25] The Austrian part of the Dual Monarchy is introduced as an empire of negativity, existing only in an endless effort to come to terms with itself, living a history where each part negates the identity of the other parts, yet persisting as a possibility waiting to be realized.

The Parallel Campaign is precisely an attempt to realize the identity of Kakania by investing it with a historical mission. Diotima and Leinsdorf want the campaign to transform the Dual Monarchy into an expressive totality. Leinsdorf visualizes this organism as a patriarchal family, the emperor-father gathering his loyal children around the throne. His goal is "to subordinate the nationalities and ethnic breeds to an all-embracing State" (*MWQ* 492 / *MoE* 452). Diotima sees the campaign as an opportunity to conjure up the true soul of humankind and make it manifest in a solemn event that will send a message of peace and love to the world. The goal of the Parallel Campaign, then, is to restore the

belief in the imperial ideology and to encourage the population to acknowledge Franz Joseph as their leader, much in the same way as the
various kingdoms and countries once pledged allegiance to the dynasty
in the Pragmatic Sanction. In a magnificent show of internal solidarity
and strength, the campaign is also to dwarf the other European powers.
Above all, it wants to surpass the celebration of Wilhelm II of Germany, which is also planned for 1918. The narrator underscores that a
major source of inspiration for Leinsdorf is Fichte's *Addresses to the
German Nation,* which, as I discussed in chapter 1, exemplifies the expressivist ideology according to which every citizen is an expression of
a shared cultural essence. Leinsdorf wants to beat Germany in the discipline where Germany has proved most successful: nation building, the
art of unifying a people into an organic whole.

The satirical force of the novel derives from two equally perplexing
aims of the Parallel Campaign. First, the campaign is to unify an empire
which so far has reacted to such attempts with further fragmentation.
Second, it is to be an authentic popular expression organized by the
elite, which is why Count Leinsdorf emphasizes that "such a forceful,
blunt display of strength must truly come from the midst of the people
and hence be directed from above" (*MWQ* 182 / *MoE* 171, emphasis
added). Leinsdorf and Diotima, convinced that the magic will work, install a huge bureaucracy that is to receive the proposals arriving from
below. On the basis of these proposals, the executive committee will
decide how the popular manifestation is to be directed from above.

This is where Ulrich enters the story. He agrees to become chief secretary in this organization. It falls largely to him to coordinate the in-
coming proposals on how to renovate the ideology of Austria-Hungary.
This means that the Musilian narrator appoints Ulrich to solve the riddle
at the heart of the empire and its future: What is a cultural identity?
Which are the bonds that hold a people together? Since these questions
in fact frame the narrative of *The Man Without Qualities* as a whole, we
fail to understand the philosophical and existential questions raised by
the novel's representation of subjectivity and identity if we do not attend
to its representation of nationalism and cultural identity. In effect, as
secretary of the Parallel Campaign, Ulrich is asked to unravel exactly

the problem that deadlocked Austrian society after the turn of the century and that is once again haunting the world: the nationality question.

Identity Politics in Kakania

Nationalism must be investigated from two directions, Eric Hobsbawm argues. Official ideologies of states are not guides to what is in the mind of the people; nationalism looks different from the peaks of the leaders than it does from the grassroots.[26] Often it is not even possible to know what nationalism meant for a Czech peasant or worker at the beginning of the century. It may be safely assumed, however, that the attitudes of ordinary men and women toward the national or imperial state depended on whether they encountered this state as an oppressor or a benefactor. Homi Bhabha, drawing on Hobsbawm's distinction, argues that the "pedagogics" of nationalism should not be confused with its popular "performance." On the one hand, the people are the object of a nationalist pedagogy coming from above. The people are subjected to confirming a pregiven interpretation of history, which is officially designated as the origin of the people's collective identity. On the other hand the "living principle of the people" is a force through which national life renews itself in a "performance" that transcends the ideology disseminated in schools and other public institutions.[27]

What we encounter in *The Man Without Qualities,* however, is far more complex than a simple antagonism between the nationalist pedagogy imposed from above and the popular performance below. In Musil's novel there is an *imperial* pedagogy, the Parallel Campaign, which is contested by the performance of various nationalist movements. But these nationalisms constitute *national* pedagogies in their own right, and as such they compete with the imperial pedagogy for popular support. As regards the grassroots "performance," there are preciously few ordinary people in Musil's novel, and their performances of the empire are, as we shall see, truly monstrous.

As Musil's narrator makes clear, the struggle between an imperial pedagogy and various nationalist pedagogies accounts for the confusion surrounding the Parallel Campaign. Leinsdorf wants to show that Austria's peoples stand as united around Franz Joseph as the Germans do around their emperor. But although the campaign has an anti-German edge, the non-German nationalities of Austria perceive it as a pro-German initiative. The reason for this is simple. The campaign aims to celebrate Austrian unity, but by 1913 it is predominantly German Austrians, in addition to some Polish nobles in Galicia, who believe that Austrian unity is possible within the existing constitutional framework. The campaign is therefore perceived as their idea, that is, as a German idea, which is to say a pro-German idea, which the ideologists of the other nationalities soon identify as a Pan-German intrigue. Aiming to preempt such conceptions, Leinsdorf appoints a renowned slavophile, the Polish aristocrat Wisnieczky, as the head of the campaign's propaganda committee (*MWQ* 563 / *MoE* 517). But the consequence of this move is that the Parallel Campaign is now attacked in German circles as well, where it counts as a pro-Slav manifestation.

Dividing the groups that it tries to unify, the Parallel Campaign turns into an object lesson about identity politics and multiculturalism. Each group senses a vested interest behind the universalistic claim of the Parallel Campaign. Tuzzi spells out the fatal results: "The Parallel Campaign is arousing international suspicion, . . . and its effects at home, where it's being viewed as both anti-German and anti-Slav, can also be traced in our foreign relations" (*MWQ* 878* / *MoE* 808). The campaign is gradually revealed to be a "false universal" in Austrian society.

As is so often the case with multicultural or interethnic conflicts, however, the ones in Austria-Hungary are an index of more fundamental social conflicts. The Parallel Campaign causes cultural division, to be sure. But the fragmentation, as well as the campaign itself, are caused by Austria-Hungary's uneasy transition from the feudal world embodied by Leinsdorf, to the modern capitalist society represented by Vienna's noisy traffic. Leinsdorf and Diotima are aware of this transition, but they translate it into a fateful choice between "culture" and "civilization." Needless to say, they side with culture. Yet, as Diotima notices that her efforts to revive the hallmarked ideals of culture are in vain, she learns that she belongs not to "an age of culture but merely of civilization." Civilization, the narrator adds, is a frustrating condition, full of radio frequencies, chemical formulas, political economy, and the impossibility of people's living together in harmony. Indeed, civilization "meant everything that [Diotima's] mind could not master" (*MWQ* 105* / *MoE* 103).

Introducing the opposition of "culture" and "civilization," Musil's novel activates a dominant theme in German thought. Civilization, in this context, represents progress, technology, and the disruption of traditional social formations. "Kultur," by contrast, refers to human creations growing like plants in the earth; it includes Bildung, art, religious or philosophical systems, and ideals in which the individuality of a people expresses itself.[28] Like Tönnies's more analytical distinction between *Gemeinschaft* and *Gesellschaft,* the categories of culture and civilization imply opposing notions of subjectivity. "Kultur" connotes an expressive relation between self and world: the person is rooted in a particular cultural ground. Civilization, on the other hand, implies that the individual is cut off and alienated from these roots.

The highest wish of Count Leinsdorf is that everyone would again root themselves, accept "the natural order of things," and find "duty and prosperity" in their allotted places (*MWQ* 91 / *MoE* 90). Leinsdorf also mourns the passing of that order which he calls "Besitz und Bildung," capital and culture (*MWQ* 912–924 / *MoE* 839–851). In late-nineteenth-century Austria, this phrase signified the brief but successful alliance between the hegemonic aristocracy, embodied by Musil's Leinsdorf, and the liberal bourgeoisie, represented by Leo Fischel. It was a transient convergence of interests, allowing capital and culture, as well as industry and art, to merge into a system of values that secured the economic and cultural leadership of the cultivated upper classes.[29] If this was the order of the day in the 1870s, it had been transmuted into disorder by the 1910s. Hence the importance that the ruling classes attribute to the Parallel Campaign. It launches an imperial pedagogics aimed at restoring Kultur, or at least reviving the alliance between culture and capital.

In effect, then, the Parallel Campaign is an ideological effort to resolve the economic and political contradictions blocking Austria's passage from a decaying feudal order to a liberal capitalist system. The narrative rationale of the campaign is to bring this process into focus, and to simultaneously trace the imperial and nationalist responses to it. Musil situates the story at a historical point at which the emerging nationalist movements necessarily clash with the residual values, privileges, and political institutions of the older system.[30] The modernization of Austria-Hungary generates new social groups that seek to be recognized as equal members of the imperial body. People of diverse ethnic origins migrate from the fields and villages in the country to the factories in the city, and they must be educated so as to fit an increasingly diversified labor market. In this process, nationalism and the nation state serve as apparatuses of integration, substituting and compensating for the social bonds that are disbanded along with feudalism.[31]

Yet, the political structure of Austria-Hungary cannot accommodate the demands of these groups, because this would challenge the foundation of the empire, that is, the implicit agreement that Hungarian Magyars and German-speaking Austrians are the normative cultures and the privileged economic groups in their respective parts of the empire. In order to preserve its central and normative position, the dominant culture refuses to integrate its margins, the result being that the marginal groups cease to see themselves as parts of the imperial totality and lose belief in the ability of the center to represent their interests. At this moment, the narrative suggests, German centralism is decentered. The universal disappears; the political and cultural sphere is transformed into an arena of struggling particularisms. The old universal—the emperor who once embodied the binding ideology of the empire—is transformed into a legacy without any cohesive power. The once Absolute Subject, which sanctioned those processes of symbolic investiture that made every subject identify with the imperial center, is relativized, leaving lack and emptiness in its wake.

In a chapter belonging to the unfinished parts of the novel, the narrator sums up the nationality question and its causes. He first renders how Leinsdorf is delayed by nationalist uprisings when he visits the city of B. in Moravia. On one side of the street, the Czechs shout "Down with the Germans!"; on the other side, the Germans scream "Down with

the Czechs!" But as soon as the demonstrators have identified Leinsdorf, both groups start attacking the Parallel Campaign (*MWQ* 1484 /
MoE 1448). The narrator smuggles in the information that all Leinsdorf's estates and farms are situated in the countryside near B. As the
novel proceeds to map the social and economic topography of B., it
becomes clear that Leinsdorf himself incarnates all the causes of the
nationality problem. He is a German-speaking Austrian centralist enjoying the economic privileges derived from his title of nobility, thus
embodying the social stratum that must be removed if the non-German
nationalities are to reach equality.

   Musil's B. alludes to Brünn, today's Brno, where the author himself lived most of his youth. The novel presents it as a microcosm of
Kakania, a place without stable identity, where all the conflicts of the
empire come to the fore. Situated at the outermost tip of the empire's
German-speaking enclave, the city of B. is surrounded by farmland
where Czech villages are squeezed between large feudal estates belonging to nobles like Leinsdorf. B. is also one of the wealthiest cities in
the empire. Its administrative center, dominated by a German-speaking
population, is girdled by a ring of German-owned textile mills, whose
sirens every morning call hordes of Czechs from the villages into the
factories, and in the evening send them back to the countryside. But as
the years went by, Musil's narrator explains, "more and more of these
Czech country people, whose fingers and hands turned dark from the
oily cotton dust of the factories, stayed behind in the city and caused
the Slavic petite bourgeoisie that was already there to grow mightily"
(*MWQ* 1480* / *MoE* 1444). The members of the Czech peasant class,
more or less oppressed by German landowners, are attracted to the
industrial quarters of the city where they soon form a huge industrial
proletariat. Some of them work their way up, contributing to a growing
lower-middle class of Czechs. For them, the status of the Czech language in relation to German becomes an urgent political issue, since the
official recognition of Czech would give them access to higher positions
and professions. The novel goes on to explain how the Czech middle
classes, legitimizing their claims to have the Czech language and culture
officially recognized, begin to reinterpret the history of their region and

oppose an official memory that emphasizes the German legacy of B.; "and in the non-German schools there was no lack of indications that the city was not German and that the Germans were a pack of thieves who steal even other people's pasts" (*MWQ* 1481 / *MoE* 1444).

This, then, is how the narrator in a few pages sketches the social background to the nationality problem. Interestingly, B. is also the hometown of Ulrich and Agathe. This is where they meet each other to attend their father's funeral, both dressed in Pierrot costumes. This is also the city where Ulrich first senses the mystery of "the other condition." Indeed, the cultural conflict in B. is rendered as an explanation of his hatred for national and cultural ideologies. Ulrich's rejection of his father—the race, the bonds, the stream of heredity—is by extension a rejection of the German-speaking bourgeoisie that dominates B. "The true B., of course, is the ring of the factory quarter, the textile and yarn city!" he states (*MWQ* 1480 / *MoE* 1443). Furthermore, the narrator also remarks that B. was the symbolic crucible of the Great War (*MWQ* 1474 / *MoE* 1436).

An Empire Without Narrative

Since it refuses to address the real causes of the nationality problem, the Parallel Campaign only augments the nationalist discontent in B. and elsewhere. To be sure, Leinsdorf and Ulrich are drowned by radical proposals. All kinds of clubs, interest groups, secret societies, and lobbyists deliver their plans on how to put Kakania back on its feet. The propositions are received by clerks working as expediently and impartially as Kafka's functionaries. Each received item is registered, stamped with the word "Ass.," put in a pile, and finally filed in an archive. "Ass." is an abbreviation for "Asserviert," a magic formula meaning "filed for later decision" (*MWQ* 242 / *MoE* 225). Hence, nothing is rejected, nothing is accepted, and no one is offended. Cultivating the art of "muddling through," the campaign solves the nationality issue by postponing the solution.

Ulrich soon comes to realize that all proposals can be divided into two categories. The first he calls "Back to . . . !" It contains letters exhorting the campaign to take mankind back to some happier era in the past. The other category is named "Forward to . . . !" (*MWQ* 251f. / *MoE* 233f.). This is where Ulrich files all suggestions that the contemporary world should be replaced by a new one. All proposals speak of a society that appears as intolerable as it is inescapable. At the first meeting of the campaign, a professor summarizes this political predicament: "He spoke of the path of history. When we look ahead, he said, we see an impenetrable wall. If we look left and right, we see an overwhelming mass of important events without recognizable direction" (*MWQ* 182 / *MoE* 172).

In chapter 3, I argued that the narrative discourse of *The Man Without Qualities* lacks a temporal structure. The chronological frame is constituted only by the information on the first page— "It was a fine day in August 1913" —and the reader's knowledge that the story ends a year later with the outbreak of World War I. As regards the order of the events happening in between, the narrator creates a polycentric and atemporal narrative. Deviating from the pattern of the realist novel, in which events are ordered by the passing of hours, days, seasons, and generations, Musil's narrative effectively negates a continuous view of history. It attempts to render discontinuity: first of all, the unthinkable transition from peace to war, and even more important, the unimaginable step from reality to utopia.

We can now translate this narratological structure onto a historical one. The novel's polycentrism, its disruption of chronological order and its superpositions of differing idioms and discursive registers, bespeaks the experience evoked by the professor above. Ahead, there is the black wall of war; to the right and left, a mess of random events. The materia of everyday social life no longer constitute history, or "Geschichte," but *Seinesgleichen*. Wheels turn in the air. Musil's narrator grasps for a historical moment without intelligible causality; hence the conspicuous lack of narrative development. In chapter 4, I cited the episode where Ulrich realized that modern society has become nonnarrative, no longer following a thread but stretching out in an endless surface. Ulrich is missing the narrative thread that alone could give some constancy to his identity (*MWQ* 709 / *MoE* 650).

The lack of narrative order in Musil's novel helps create a subject that lacks identity. It also orchestrates a historical moment in which development has reached a halt and nobody knows how to move forward. Even more important, the multiplication of narrative lines reflects a social situation in which no normative national and imperial identity exists. In representing a society without organizing temporal and causal framework, Musil's novel stages a world without any sense of imperial or national communality. Indeed, such a communality only exists, as Benedict Anderson has argued, if all the citizens of a nation or an empire synchronize their clocks, as it were. "The idea of a sociological organism moving calendrically through homogeneous, empty time is a precise analogue of the idea of the nation, which also is conceived as a solid community moving steadily down (or up) history." [32] In the imagined community, each individual pins his or her life to the same temporal markers and cultural signifiers that are used by thousands or millions of other individuals. In such a community, there is a spatial and temporal frame, assuring the individual that he or she lives the same story and shares the same past and future as does the collective.

In the imperial community of Kakania, by contrast, only one such point of identification remains, the emperor himself. Yet Franz Joseph's ideological appeal seems to diminish at the same speed as the dissemination of portraits of him increases. Musil's narrator consequently observes that the emperor is like one of those stars that keep shining, and which still provide a point of orientation, although the celestial body itself may have ceased to exist thousands of years ago (*MWQ* 83 / *MoE* 83).

According to Anderson, the clearly defined temporal and spatial universe of the nation corresponds to the temporal and spatial experience rendered by the realist novel. It is no coincidence, he maintains, that this narrative genre emerged in the same period as nationalism. Interestingly, the major components of Anderson's theory were anticipated by Musil's contemporary, Otto Bauer, who defined a nationality as a "community of destiny" (*Schicksalsgemeinschaft*), that is, a collective moving toward a common future.[33] Bauer's notion exposes the significance of the Musilian narrator's statement that Kakania was a country having lost interest in its destiny. Its nationalities no longer agreed on which future they were supposed to share, and many of them foresaw destinies of their own.

Musil's novel removes those structures of causality and chronology which in Anderson's view establish the coherence of both the national community and the realist novel. The disintegration of the empire is thus inscribed in the disintegration of narrative linearity in *The Man Without Qualities*. Musil's novel confirms observations made by Edward Said, Franco Moretti, and Fredric Jameson, who have argued that the emergence of the complex and fragmented narrative of the modernist novel corresponds to a historical period during which the forces that determine the everyday life of the "national" community are no longer found within the nation but outside its boundaries, in a global imperialist power struggle.[34] In Musil's novel, this imperial space is evoked by the figures of Arnheim and Tuzzi. Yet, the position of Kakania does not quite fit this analysis, for this is an empire that is itself destroyed by modernizing forces, which, in Kakanian reality, are represented not by imperial capitalism but by the delayed nationalist movements themselves. As we have seen, Musil's narrator frequently rises above the representation and supplies his own analysis of the events of the story. As a matter of fact, he even offers a theory of the relations of empire, nation, and narration:

> Several times in the course of the Parallel Campaign it could be perceived that world history is made up much as all other stories are — i.e., the authors seldom come up with anything really new and are rather given to copying each other's plots and ideas. But there is also something else involved which has not yet been mentioned, and that is the delight in storytelling itself. . . . Count Leinsdorf had this conviction and this passion, . . . but it had been lost in the farther reaches of Kakania, where the search for a substitute had been under way for the longest time now. There the history of Kakania had been replaced by that of the nation; the

authors were at work on it even now, formulating it in that European taste that finds historical novels and costume dramas edifying. This resulted in a situation not yet perhaps sufficiently appreciated, which was that persons who had to deal with some commonplace problem such as building a school or appointing a stationmaster found themselves discussing this in connection with the year 1600 or 400, arguing about which candidate was preferable in the light of what settlements arose in the Lower Alps during the great Gothic or Slavic migrations, and about battles fought during the Counter-Reformation, and injecting into all this talk the notions of high-mindedness and rascality, homeland, truth, and manliness, and so on. (*MWQ* 560f. / *MoE* 514)

As this passage indicates, Musil's novel is situated at the crossroads between two opposed historiographical paradigms, the national and the imperial. The story of empire competes with the stories of nationalism. Again, the invasion of the margins erodes the dynastic power of the center. People who previously listened to the storyteller in Vienna start to tell their own stories, in their own dialects. There is no longer any universal history powerful enough to integrate these counternarratives in a larger whole. The multiplication of spatial coordinates, the heterogeneous discourse, and the achronic temporality of Musil's narrative: all are consequences of this Kakanian cacophony. It represents a Seinesgleichen with no historical agency or, one could say, with too many agencies.

Mixing Blood, Performing the Empire

When Ulrich and Agathe return from their father's funeral in B., the atmosphere in the Parallel Campaign has changed. Leinsdorf is disappointed by his failure to electrify Austria's *Geist*. He draws the conclusion "that it would be best to give this spirit a push, no matter from what direction" (*MWQ* 882 / *MoE* 812). Diotima agrees: "Our century is thirsting for action. An action." "But what action? What kind of action?" Ulrich asks. "It doesn't matter!" says Diotima (*MWQ* 883 / *MoE*

812). General Stumm, for his part, reports that the executive committee of the campaign has changed its strategy: "The new slogan that's been handed out is 'Action!' " (*MWQ* 841 / *MoE* 774). Everyone realizes that "the times are getting a New Spirit," and the general wonders "if, in the end, that isn't simply the military spirit?" (*MWQ* 845 / *MoE* 778). This yearning for action is subsequently turned into protofascist doctrines by characters like Lindner and Meingast. "Systematically executed cruelty is the only means now available for the European peoples, still stupe-fied by humanitarianism, to find their strength again!" the latter exhorts (*MWQ* 1592 / *MoE* 1520). The period before the Great War was mes-sianic, the narrator submits, and the last session of the Parallel Cam-paign is energized by this excited atmosphere. At last, time to make history. The gathering is more confused than usual, as is the declaration on which everybody finally agrees: "Any man may choose to die for his own ideas, but whoever induces men to die for ideas not their own is a murderer!" (*MWQ* 1124 / *MoE* 1035).

Formulated by the pacifist poet Feuermaul, this declaration osten-sibly asserts the inalienable rights of each individual and each group to choose their own destinies.[35] No one can be forced to fight for a cause that he or she does not believe in. Feuermaul's formula, however, is cheered also by the racist Hans Sepp, a sign that the words may just as well justify a gruesome principle: the war of all against all. Ulrich re-marks that the resolution forebodes "the Millennial War of Religion," adding that the War Ministry can sit back and await the coming mass catastrophe (*MWQ* 1127 / *MoE* 1038). Arnheim and General Stumm take the resolution to be an expression of young people's desire for "sta-bility and leadership" (*MWQ* 1124 / *MoE* 1035). The resolution immedi-ately backfires, igniting empire-wide rebellions. The ruling circles, too, refuse to accept the disruptive ambiguity of Feuermaul's statement, let alone the fact that it is utterly impracticable.

The representatives of civil society, Leinsdorf, Diotima, and, by ex-tension, Ulrich, have thereby forfeited their chance to solve Austria-Hungary's nationality question. The campaign becomes an affair of state, delegated to the Ministries of War and Foreign Affairs. A few chapters later, General Stumm breaks in on Ulrich and Agathe in their

secluded garden, and reveals that the government has decided that the
Parallel Campaign will sponsor a congress for world peace scheduled
for the fall of 1914 (*MWQ* 1212–1221 / *MoE* 1113–1123). Diotima is to
organize a parade on the theme "the clans of Austria and Hungary pay
homage to internal and external peace," which is to be followed by a
procession of the armed forces. In order to ensure that the Peace Congress will not get out of control, the government will push through
an ordinance to rapidly modernize Austria-Hungary's artillery. General
Stumm has his way. Meanwhile, Arnheim hurries to finalize his deals.
His factories will deliver the arms on favorable terms, on condition that
his "World Corporation" obtains access to the oilfields in Galicia near
the heavily fortified Russian border.

The outbreak of World War I is not recorded in the completed parts of
The Man Without Qualities. In the drafts, however, there is an account
of the tumultuous days following Austria-Hungary's declaration of war.
Gerda Fischel, one of Ulrich's admirers, recounts the atmosphere in the
streets: "I've already seen the young men at the mobilization stations.
They're singing. Their wives and fiancées are with them. No one knows
how he is going to come back. But if you walk through the city and look
into people's eyes, including the people who aren't going to the front
yet, it's like a big wedding" (*MWQ* 1676 / *MoE* 1621).

Such is the predictable outcome of the competing pedagogies of
nationality and empire. Only the war can restore the expressive totality
of individuals, nations, and empire, uniting everybody in a community
of destiny. Fascism and madness, discipline and anarchy, reality and
possibility, uniformity and negativity—all are married in a monstrous
celebration. Musil always knew that the novel should end in this way.
In January 1936 he made the following outline:

Concluding portion
Overall problem: war.
Pseudorealities lead to war. The Parallel Campaign leads to war!
War as: How a great event comes about.
All lines lead to the war. Everyone welcomes it in his fashion.

The religious element in the outbreak of the war.

Deed, emotion, and Other Condition join as one.

Someone remarks: that was what the Parallel Campaign had always been looking for. It has found its great idea. (*MWQ* 1755 / *MoE* 1902)

Even if the "grassroots" are almost absent in the novel, that is, even if we see little of the people's performance of nationality, the episodes about two of Musil's most enigmatic characters, Rachel and Soliman, suggest a popular response to the imperialist pedagogics of the campaign. Rachel is Diotima's housemaid, a poor Jewish girl from remote Galicia; Soliman is Arnheim's servant, a young African usually referred to as the Moor. They become lovers, and their story offers a melodramatic parallel to Ulrich and Agathe's love affair. If Ulrich and Agathe violate the incest taboo, Rachel and Soliman disobey a different cultural taboo, the prohibition of miscegenation. Indeed, both couples commit monstrous acts that challenge a fundamental principle of their society. Consider the scenario: while the political and intellectual elites of Austria rally around their tribes, preparing for war and calling for a purification of the race, Rachel and Soliman sneak away to her room near the kitchen to make love. When their erotic affair is disclosed, their masters face a scandalous possibility: the Austrian-African-Jew.

"I don't believe in the distinction between the German and the Negro," Musil states in his 1923 essay "The German as Symptom" (*PS* 160 / *GW* 2:1364). This is how Musil, at a time when "scientific" racism stood at its height, responded to the nationality question. In *The Man Without Qualities,* which Musil had begun working on a couple of years earlier, Rachel and Soliman prove the same point. As we have seen, Musil relies on monstrous and angelic characters to reveal how ideological norms of gender, nationhood, empire, and race restrict human agency and align the subject with hierarchic ideals of the cultural community. Transgressing taboos, "Rachelle" and "the Moor" support Ulrich and Agathe's work of negativity.

Nationality and Negativity

In chapters 2 and 4, I noted how Musil's representation runs up against an absolute limit constitued by antinomies that cannot be solved by the act of thinking. This dilemma typically makes itself felt when the narrator or Ulrich attempts to coordinate "order" and "possibility" within the same system, or subsume the two under one concept; the most apparent instance of this struggle is the passage in which Ulrich ponders "the two trees of life," one growing straight toward unequivocal truth, the other branching out according to "the gliding logic of the soul" (*MWQ* 645–649 / *MoE* 591–594). But the novel's logic of negativity prevents such attempts to resolve the antinomies from succeeding. Without exception, the text renders "order" as petrification and death, and associates it with military regimentation and totalitarian ideologies of race and nationhood. "Possibility," by contrast, implies a subjunctive and utopian imagination. Ulrich and Agathe's incestuous affair belongs here, as do the romantic subplot about Rachel and Soliman and Ulrich's scientific fantasy, which deconstructs existing reality into its constituent parts.

As regards social experience, a similar antinomy is constituted by the categories of *das Seinesgleichen*, the pseudoreal monotony of everyday life, and the other condition, a weightless state of difference blessed by meaning and intensity. On the level of the individual, the corresponding antinomy is set up between the categories "identity" and "subjectivity." We have seen, on the one hand, that pure identity will become a uniform that reduces the subject to a mere reflection of the collective, if it is not motored by the transgressive force of negativity inherent in subjectivity. The negative force of subjectivity, on the other hand, leads to the lunatic asylum, unless it is stabilized by the order of identity. This antinomy then reappears in Musil's key terms, "man" and "qualities." A man *without* qualities equals pure subjectivity, that is, an anarchic madman or a criminal. A man *with* qualities equals pure identity, an individual drilled to become an obedient soldier. The problem arises because Musil, tending toward idealist abstractions, posits the two poles as logical contradictions of each other. This forces him to reject the idea of a compromise. Ulrich cannot enact either alternative without refusing the other, but nor can he realize any of them separately. This double bind accounts for the impossible choice between madness and fascism. Musil evokes this impossibility when he despairs over "the two poles of a Neither-Nor of the age" (*MoE* 1878).

If order and possibility, or identity and subjectivity, are defined as opposites of each other, there is no way to unify them under a common concept. The tension between these antinomies cannot be theoretically sublated, only activated and negotiated through a process of narration that establishes a discursive or social order only to deconstruct it so as to release the category of possibility, and through a process of subjectivity that assumes an identity only to pass beyond it. As there is no unifying concept that mediates between these two sides of social and individual life, the disjunctive character of the novel is irrevocable, as is the schizoid nature of the hero. Interpretations that try to resolve these antinomies by charting the novel's presumed attempt to establish a synthesis between self and world therefore fail to grasp the secret of Musil's enterprise.[36]

This secret is embedded in the historical situation. The antinomies produced by Musil's idealist consciousness are also the point at which his consciousness is most profoundly colored by the political problems of his period. For the antinomies that are immune to the formal procedures of reason derive from the historical dilemma conveyed by the novel, the deadlock between empire and nation. The novel renders the historical experience of a society that is modernized and divided into social subsystems with their own logic of instrumentality. The modern individual must circulate from one function to the other within the social machinery, never being able to grasp the whole, always adapting to the demands of his small tasks. The identity of the Musilian subject is thereby divided and reified, as I discussed in chapter 2. Forced to negotiate among contradictory demands, Ulrich is faced with the choice of being either a man without qualities, a pure subjectivity that refuses interaction, or a bundle of qualities without a man, an obedient functionary without agency or conscience.

In this sense, Musil's antinomies and his redefinition of subjectivity may be explained by the modern logic of rationalization—an observation elaborated by Hartmut Böhme, which is no doubt accurate.[37] Still, a number of specific features in Musil's representation of society and subjectivity remain to be accounted for. This specificity is immediately elucidated, however, if we see the disjunctive structure of the novel as a response to the nationality question. In this view, Musil's narrative represents not only how Austrian society is compartmentalized by the logic of instrumentality, but also by an invasion of intersecting imperial, national, and racial ideologies. As I have already demonstrated, the presence of contradictory and equally persuasive ways of defining and narrating the identity of Kakania and its subjects means that, ultimately, not even the absent emperor is able to assume a neutral stance in relation to the "nationality question." Even the Parallel Campaign becomes the vehicle for nationalist politics. In this situation, then, every act, statement, institution, organization, or political proposal is instantly filtered through the nationality issue and categorized as an *expression of belonging* to one of the rivaling groups. Every aspect of social life turns into a manifestation of a national or cultural essence. Just as every character trait is "sexualized," that is, classified as either masculine or feminine, so is every character "nationalized" and taken as a sign of ethnic membership. This ideological predicament offers two alternatives: either solidarity with a national community, or an existence without identity, that is, a condition of madness. Musil's novel ingeniously highlights the logical, existential, and political conclusions of this dilemma: if every quality is defined in sexual, racial, ethnic, or national terms, a man wanting to resist sexism, racism, ethnocentrism, or nationalism must become a man without qualities.

We may now begin to appreciate the richness of Musil's initial title of the novel, "The Spy" (*Der Spion*). Though Musil later discarded this title, having found a more suggestive alternative, the theme of the spy remained essential to the plot well into the 1930s. In a 1926 interview with Oskar Maurus Fontana, Musil exposed the plan for *The Man Without Qualities* for the first time: "In an act of opposition against an order where the least intelligent one has the greatest chances, my young hero becomes a spy" (*GW* 2:941). Musil also explained that Ulrich will use his sister in his espionage. Ulrich was thus to become a spy, a man with false identity, faking patriotism and cultural affiliation. Musil never reached the point in his novel where this theme was to be activated, but now and then it is announced; at the novel's beginning, for instance, the narrator relates how the young Ulrich refused to pledge allegiance to his Fatherland; and later in the story, Diotima remarks that Ulrich is "such an indispensable bad patriot that all the enemies of the Fatherland . . . must really love [him]" (*MWQ* 1221 / *MoE* 1122).

For a long time, moreover, Musil named his hero not Ulrich but Anders, which means "other" or "different." Except for the psychotic condition of Clarisse and Moosbrugger, the spy and the other would seem to be the only positions available to a person who wants to claim a subjective agency in the face of ideologies that reduce each individual to an expression of the national essence. The double play of the spy also elucidates the play of doubles in Musil's narrative, an issue that I discussed in chapter 2. Seen in the context of the nationality question, the theme of the double emerges as a wish for an alter ego without national affiliation.

The spy, the double, the other, the lunatic, the feminine: Musil's narrative rehearses and revisits these positions of negativity because they are immune to the manipulations by ideologies of empire, nation, and race. In the previous chapter, I designated Moosbrugger, Clarisse, Ulrich, and Agathe as figures of monstrosity; to this group we may now add Rachel and Soliman. They are all monstrous because of their ability to symbolically destroy the ideological order that ascribes identities to persons. Disclosing the borders that institute the imperial and national culture, moving between the inside and the outside of the socius, these characters articulate the arbitrary limits of the imagined community and show that the subject cannot be explained by or reduced to any identity.

Interestingly, the principle of negativity also organizes the portrayal of anti-Semitism and Jewishness in *The Man Without Qualities*. The novel contains several Jewish characters, who occupy social positions stretching from the bottom where we find Rachel, the housemaid from Galicia, to the heights of culture and industry at which Paul Arnheim roams. The Fischel family is situated between these extremes. Leo Fischel is a Jewish banker, married to a woman from a Gentile family, Clementine, who has begun to loathe him on the irrational ground that his ethnic origin prevents him from advancing in a world infested by anti-Semitic prejudice. Gerda Fischel, their daughter, makes her father despair, as she invites Hans Sepp's circle of anti-Semitic activists into their home. Through these characters, and by disclosing the anti-Semitic opinions of Leinsdorf and Stumm von Bordwehr, Musil's narrator exposes the discourse of racism in Austrian culture, cutting through the prejudices with his ironical and analytical edge, and charting the effects of anti-Semitism among its victims and its adherents.

Crucially, the novel makes a point of revealing that these Jewish characters have nothing in common. For instance, Leo Fischel, an assimilated Austrian patriot, is a sworn enemy of Arnheim's cosmopolitan ventures. Moreover, as Gerda Fischel's example illuminates, a person of Jewish descent may readily subscribe to anti-Semitic views, imagining herself to be "blond, free, Germanic, and forceful" (*MWQ* 337 / *MoE* 312). Such is the paradoxical outcome, when the category of negativity is activated in the representation of anti-Semitism and racism. That a Jewish person can espouse anti-Semitism indicates that no Jewish essence exists, and, as a consequence, that the anti-Semitic program, like the expressivist paradigm that supports it, amounts to sheer irrationalism. Embracing the anti-Semitic program that excludes persons like herself, the figure of Gerda Fischel proves that racism is an ideological fantasy, and categories of race and ethnicity wholly imaginary. "The Jew," Musil's novel seem to argue, does not exist.

Thus, to sum up, it is not only the monstrous figures of negativity in *The Man Without Qualities,* but also the novel's representation of Jewish characters, that are conditioned by historical conflicts concerning imperial rule and national belonging. I have already noted how the novel elaborates these historical coordinates in several other ways as well. The most obvious instance is the Parallel Campaign, which incorporates all the aspects of the nationality question in Austria-Hungary. Furthermore, the tensions between nationalism and imperialism are registered by the novel's temporal and spatial structure, where it makes itself felt in the clash between conflicting ways of narrating the history of Kakania. Finally, the political situation in which every identity is interpreted in terms of cultural belonging elucidates the disjunctive structure—the antinomies of order and possibility, or identity and subjectivity—that characterizes the novel as a whole. A view of the postimperial situation in which Musil wrote his book, finally, will help to establish the connections between the nationality question and the representation of subjectivity in *The Man Without Qualities*.

Nationalism and Mysticism

In 1919 the Habsburg empire was replaced by a number of sovereign nation states. These nations came into being because of the fourteen-point agenda formulated by U.S. president Woodrow Wilson, who demanded that the Habsburg empire be disbanded after the war and that, if possible, each nationality should attain its own territorial state. The treaties of St. Germain and Trianon also prohibited the German-speaking part of Austria to unite with Germany, thus precluding the solution sought by most political parties in Germany and Austria alike. So far, this is the only time in history when the nationality principle— one nation, one state—has been applied to redraw the borders on an entire continent. Vienna, once a metropolitan center for fifty million inhabitants, was reduced to a capital governing a small nation state with a population of six million. Whereas many of the nationalities of the former empire had obtained the states they wanted, Austria became "the state that nobody wanted." [38] The subtitle of a 1933 book by Ludwig Bauer sums up the situation: "A State Looking for a People" (*Ein Staat sucht ein Volk*).

What followed the war was thus a total breakdown of the political, administrative, and economic apparatus of the former empire, to the extent that, as one commentator notes, "the whole raison d'être of Austria seemed to have been irrevocably destroyed." [39] The historical and literary documents that I discussed in chapter 5 suggest that the citizens of the remaining truncated state experienced the postwar years as a col-

Kriegsbegeisterung in Wien.

10   "All lines lead to war. Everyone welcomes it in his fashion." The people of
Vienna celebrate Austria's declaration of war against Serbia, August 1914.
Postcard. Private collection.

lective trauma. Large sections of the population did not trust the state as
their legitimate representative and sought to renew their sense of community by affirming their ethnic or racial sense of belonging. Hence the
upsurge of anti-Semitism and racism in the postimperial Austria of the
1920s. Whether they wished to or not, Austrian intellectuals therefore
had to preoccupy themselves with the nationality question throughout
the postwar era, until it was "solved" by Hitler in 1938.

Musil incorporated the historical development of Austria's first republic into his novel. In the chaotic final session of the Parallel Campaign, Hans Sepp asks Ulrich if he has heard of "the great racial theorist
Bremshuber." Shaking his head, Ulrich is enlightened by Gerda Fischel
that "Bremshuber demands the ruthless suppression of all alien races"
(*MWQ* 1105 / *MoE* 1017f.). Josef Strutz has pointed out that Bremshuber
probably alludes to Hitler, arguing that the Nazi successes in German
elections convinced Musil — who lived in Berlin at the beginning of the

11 "It is like a big wedding." Austrian war propaganda in *Österreichs Illustrierte Zeitung*. Painting by R. A. Höger. Direktion der Museen der Stadt Wien.

1930s — that he must strengthen the didactic moment of his novel.[40] The allusion to Hitler in *The Man Without Qualities* is not surprising, given the importance of the nationality question in the novel. Also, Musil kept adding many kinds of postwar material to the prewar world in which the story is set.[41]

Throughout this book I have stressed the many ways in which *The Man Without Qualities* is the result of Musil's experience of the war and its aftermath. The novel's representation of the events in 1913 and 1914 refracts, through an act of backshadowing, the situation in postimperial Austria. With the wisdom of hindsight, Musil revisits the Dual Monarchy in order to sketch a world order that would have rendered the war and its aftermath unnecessary. He revealed this intention in the 1926 interview: "I must contribute to the intellectual mastery of the world." The world needs a new ethics, Musil argues. "My novel is an attempt at a dissolution and a suggestion of a synthesis" (*GW* 2:942). *The Man*

Without Qualities is in this sense an eminently modernist undertaking: an all-encompassing deconstruction followed by a call for global reconstruction.

When the war broke out in August 1914, Musil lived in Berlin. He described the frenzy in his journal—people fighting to get hold of newspapers, the abominable singing in cafés, young men throwing themselves in front of trains because they had not been sent to the front. "Psychotics are in their element, living and acting out" (*T* 1:299). In an article published in the *Die Neue Rundschau* in September 1914, Musil affirmed the nationalist sentiment, conceding that this was not a time for words but for action. Whether one liked it or not, each individual must now follow the elementary instinct to protect the tribe (*GW* 2:1020–1022).

These August days in 1914 left an indelible impression on Musil.[42] He was to return to the experience numerous times, scrutinizing and criticizing the collective fanaticism, yet never denying that it took place.[43] In his essay " 'Nation' as Ideal and as Reality," he defines it as a religious ecstasy: "Contained in this . . . was the intoxicating feeling of having, for the first time, something in common with every German. One suddenly became a tiny particle humbly dissolved in a suprapersonal event and, enclosed by the nation, sensed the nation in an absolutely physical way" (*PS* 103 / *GW* 2:1060).

In the same essay, Musil also coins the expression that the war manifested a "flight from peace," an escape from the complexities of modern society to the comforting simplicity of the community (*PS* 112 / *GW* 2:1071). He dismisses the view that this panic escape was just a historical accident which could now be forgotten. "Are we now to believe that it was nothing when millions of people, who had formerly lived only for their own self-interest and repressed their fear of dying, suddenly, for the sake of the nation, ran with jubilation into the arms of death?" (*PS* 103 / *GW* 2:1060f.). This quasi-religious experience had to be worked through and explained, Musil emphasizes, lest one plant the seeds of a monstrous hysteria in the heart of the nation.

Musil draws two lessons from the war. First, it proved that all ideas about human nature are false. Yet, although the atrocities of the war conclusively refuted the idea that the human being is inherently rational, altruistic, or good, this did not imply, Musil wrote, that it is inherently irrational, egoistic, or evil. The human being is neither good nor bad but a liquid mass shaped by events and institutions. Turning the law-abiding citizen into a murderer and the caring father into a thief, the war was a massive experiment that proved "how easily the human being can move to the most radical extremes and back again without experiencing any basic change. He changes himself—but he does not change his *self*" [44] (*PS* 121* / *GW* 2:1080). In other words, the defining trait of the unchangeable human essence is its limitless capacity to change itself. Expressivist theories of the human subject are therefore wrong: human identity does not rely on any internal and constant disposition.

The second lesson of the war, in Musil's view, was that most persons were unable to bear this insight. In order to be what they are, most individuals must believe that there is a reason for being what they are, that one's identity is, or can become, an expression of a larger value system or unifying narrative. Prewar historical developments in Europe had eroded this belief. Hence what Musil called a "Glaubenssehnsucht," a yearning for belief (*GW* 2:1090, 1367). Almost everybody, he writes, was willing to stake the future on the destiny of the nation. The disappearance of expressivist ideals generated "a tremendous spiritual romanticism that flees from the present into any and every past, looking for the holy grail of a lost security" (*PS* 163 / *GW* 2:1367). This romanticism contributed to the war. The war was a flight from peace, from the present, and from modernity. Writing in the early 1920s, Musil detects a similar yearning everywhere. A residual mental structure continues to generate belief in laws and essences that, while purporting to explain the identities and destinies of peoples as well as persons, in reality prevent them from facing the contingency of their existence.

Although Musil argues that these two lessons were brought to the surface by the war, he derives them from the broader process of modernization, arguing that capitalism has helped destroy old social bonds, notably by reducing the person to a function of his or her social position. Since modern society is so diversified and its causal interconnections are so complex, the identity conferred upon the individual by his or her social position does not "express" society as a whole but only a fragment of it, and the function of this fragment in the social totality remains unknown to the individual. Hence the impression that society is run by an anonymous and self perpetuating machinery that renders the individual superfluous. Connecting the individual to society in an immediate, almost physical way, nationalism and racism are substitutes for those social bonds that capitalist society has dissolved (*PS* 158f. / *GW* 2:1362f.). Musil rejects all such conservative attempts to heal the mechanization and secularization of the modern age.[45] Instead of seeing the present as a fall or a failed solution, it must be seen as a new problem, the solutions of which must be worked out, he claims (*PS* 176 / *GW* 2:1382). His unfinished essay "The German as Symptom" addresses the problem of modernity by developing a social theory. The antiexpressivist view of the human subject, defined in his "Theorem of Shapelessness," emerges as the cornerstone of his theory. As I proposed in chapter 4, this theorem is the seed of the Musilian subject of negativity that we find, fully orchestrated, in *The Man Without Qualities*.

Musil's definition of the subject in "The German as Symptom" is explicitly antiexpressivist. Moreover, the definition is induced by the problem of nationalism, racism, and culturalism. Musil argues that the assumption that the mentality and behavior of a person can be explained by his or her intrinsic disposition is related to the habit of ascribing unchanging essences to historical epochs, peoples, and nations.[46] Hence the title of Musil's essay. It says, first, that "the German" is a symptom of a broader social crisis. Second, it implies that this crisis consists precisely in the common belief, in Germany and elsewhere, that there exists such a thing as "*the* German." A born nominalist, Musil turns this way of thinking upside down, stating that concepts such as "Race and Culture, People and Nation" must be seen not as answers but as questions, not as substrata of phenomena but as complex phenomena in their own right, not as sociological foundations but as results, not as producers but as products (*PS* 162 / *GW* 2:1366). "Frankly speaking, however it has been formulated, 'nation' is a fantasy," Musil writes in his essay on the nation (*PS* 112 / *GW* 2:1071). Why all this talk of "We Germans"? he asks. Such expressions are only ways of faking a community between "manual laborers and professors, gangsters and idealists, poets and film directors." No such community exists: "The true 'we' is: We are nothing to each other" (*PS* 111 / *GW* 2:1070).

The human subject, then, is not determined by any intrinsic disposition, only by the situation. "It appears that the question of the European: What am I? really means: Where am I? It is not a matter of a phase in a process governed by laws, and not a matter of destiny, but simply of a situation" (*PS* 169 / *GW* 2:1375). According to this antiexpressivist theory, then, the subject is "every bit as capable of cannibalism as of *The Critique of Pure Reason*" (*PS* 121 / *GW* 2:1081). The proof, according to Musil, is World War I.

The task, then, is to create social conditions that generate philosophers rather than cannibals, solidarity rather than egoism, and peace rather than war. Musil defines this task as the search for an ideology adequate to modern society. His conception of ideology differs from the Marxist definitions that were dominant in his period, although it has some affinities with Althusser's later redefinition, according to which ideology effects a discursive and institutional interpellation of the subject by which the individual is ascribed a social identity; ideology, for Musil, would also be the "Logos" in which "we live, move and have our being." [47] Musil also anticipates Althusser in thinking that there is no question of going beyond ideology, but only of developing a more or less appropriate one. In his view, ideology is not a symptom or a disguise of social and economic relations. Ideology equals "intellectual ordering of the feelings; an objective connection among them that makes the subjective connection easier. It can be philosophical or religious or a traditional mixture of both" (*PS* 174 / *GW* 2:1379). Ideology shapes and structures emotional life, giving coherence and stability to the "I." Ideology is the mold in which shapeless subjectivity solidifies into identity.

What Musil demonstrates in *The Man Without Qualities* is that all traditional ideologies had been exhausted. "Each ideology, even the pacifist one, leads to war," he writes in his drafts (*MoE* 1890). In exhibiting the disastrous results of the old ideologies, Musil also highlighted the necessity of new ones: if the yearning for belief and identity is a con-

stant desire of the shapeless human subject, this desire must be fulfilled
by other ideologies than racism, nationalism, and imperialism. The vanishing of the expressivist paradigm and the emergence of the shapeless
subject of modernity entailed a risk. The liquid mass of passions and
longing could be activated and manipulated by any interest, and Musil
saw Hitler's successes as an evidence of this (*MoE* 1860–62). "Give me
the newspapers, the radio, the film industry," General von Bordwehr
ominously exclaims, "and within a few years . . . I promise I'll turn
people into cannibals" (*MWQ* 1107 / *MoE* 1020). Yet, the discovery of
human shapelessness also entailed an opportunity, Musil insisted. As
the war had cleared away outdated systems of belief, it was possible
to develop a new ideology on rational principles. Musil envisions an
ideology that creates coherence without inhibiting diversity, for diversity, he states, is the quality of the future. "The challenge is to create an
organization that protects the possibilities. Belief in humanity. Doing
away with half-witted ideologies of state and nation" (*PS* 157 / *GW*
2:1360f.).[48]

Musil was not alone in proclaiming the utopian possibilities liberated
by the end of the war. The same faith in the powers of reason to construct an order that surpassed the constraints of nation and state was
found among Austria's socialists and radical intellectuals.[49] Musil supported socialism in principle but made no contributions of practical or
tactical importance.[50] For this reason, he is similar to his protagonist,
who agrees with the young socialist Schmeisser that sooner or later
humanity will have to be organized according to "some kind of socialist
principles": "For the fact that millions of people are oppressed in the
most brutal way, in order for thousands of others to fail to do anything
worthwhile with the power that derives from this oppression, is not
only unjust and criminal but also stupid, inappropriate, and suicidal!"
(*MWQ* 1491 / *MoE* 1455). You know it, but you don't do anything about
it, Schmeisser rebuts: "you are a social-romantic bourgeois, at best an
individualist anarchist!" (*MWQ* 1491* / *MoE* 1455).

This passage also exposes an affinity between Musil and Austrian socialists like Max Adler, Karl Renner, Otto Bauer, and Otto Neurath.
Like them, Musil's hero emphasizes not only the injustice of capital-

ism but, more strongly, its stupidity and dysfunctionality. Musil shared the rationalist frame of mind, though not the political commitment, of the Austrian socialists.[51] Among the characters in *The Man Without Qualities,* Ulrich is the only one who regards scientific thinking as an advantage. His skepticism dismisses the inflated ideals that contradict the findings of reason. The distinguishing scientist also realizes that the present reality is not a given, but a historical product containing numberless possible futures. On this point, then, Ulrich recognizes his affinity with socialism. Yet, he also suggests that a truly rational organization of society may in fact prove to be rather different than, even superior to, the socialist alternative (*MWQ* 1617 / *MoE* 1575). Indeed, Musil doubted that far-reaching economic and social reforms, such as those taking place in the Soviet Union, would abolish exploitation and injustice. Although he supported economic and social change, he did not think that such reforms would prevent new economic elites and political rulers from emerging. He regarded exploitation as a historical constant (*GW* 2:1382–1399). The most important task, then, was to invent an ideology that would enable people to resist the ideological manipulations by which the ruling elites attempted to augment or justify their power.

The disastrous course of the Parallel Campaign reveals this need for a program of ideological engineering. In a conversation with Agathe during the campaign's last chaotic session, Ulrich tries to make sense of Feuermaul's senseless proclamation and the chain of events leading to war, concluding, finally, "that the emotional life of mankind slops back and forth like water in an unsteady tub" (*MWQ* 1117 / *MoE* 1029). In suggesting that the Parallel Campaign should institute a "World Secretariat for Precision and Soul," Ulrich then proposes a research project that would investigate the unknown laws of human affections and passions. This investigation, in turn, would be the basis of an ideological engineering that could encourage the angelic possibilities of humanity, rather than monstrosity.

This explains why *The Man Without Qualities* almost comes to a halt when Ulrich, in the unpublished chapters of the second half of the novel, embarks upon his attempt to construct a philosophy of emotions (*MWQ*

1239–1311 / *MoE* 1138–1203). Ulrich's probing but tedious discourse
continues the analysis of political passions and ideological fascination
that form the theoretical core of Musil's novel, the difference being that
this analysis is now abstracted from the plot and the social setting. This
section of the novel has commonly been read as an exercise in mysticism. What motivates it, however, is Musil's effort to account for the
unexpected eruption of patriotism in World War I, which again destabilized Europe in the 1930s, when Musil wrote these parts of the novel.
As early as 1914 Musil compared the collective energy released by the
war to the experience reported by mysticists, the exhilarating sense of
being emptied and enveloped by a larger reality. Because such borderline sensations of utopian dimensions would continue to attract people,
it was necessary to examine how this kind of desire and affectation were
produced, and to see if their utopian content could be salvaged and managed in more constructive ways.[52] Hence Ulrich's interest in the seemingly esoteric topics evoked by the titles of these chapters: "A Historical
Synopsis of the Psychology of the Emotions"; "Naïve Description of
How an Emotion Originates"; "Feeling and Behavior: The Precarious-
ness of Emotion"; "Truth and Ecstasy"; "Ulrich and the Two Worlds
of Emotions."

Hence, also, Ulrich's repulsion from the urban masses. As I mentioned in chapter 2, the hero is often situated at windows, observing
and assessing the energies of the crowds, both fascinated and dispar-
aged by their lack of direction. Musil had once participated in the quasi-
religious celebration of a people mobilizing for war, and he had come to
know the results. His interest in political affection and human emotion
was conditioned by this experience. This is also the correct context of
those often quoted lines from Musil's essay "Helpless Europe": "We
do not have too much intellect and too little soul, but too little intellect
in matters of the soul" (*PS* 131 / *GW* 2:1092). As long as the phenomenon of passion and affection remained unknown, there was a risk that it
again would result in a flight from peace into the ecstasies of the tribe.
Of all the elements in Musil's project, this part is perhaps most difficult to grasp: the intrinsic connection between the nationalist passion

released by the war and the mysticist experience of "the other condition": "The religious element in the outbreak of war. Deed, emotion,
and Other Condition fall together" (*MWQ* 1755 / *MoE* 1902). Indeed, it
is difficult to think through these scandalous lines, in which mass violence somehow comes to equal love and collective solidarity: "War is
the same as the other condition" (*MoE* 1932).[53]

Musil's novel should on this point be compared not to Emmanuel
Swedenborg's observations on the lives of the angels, nor to Jacob
Böhme's and Meister Eckhardt's accounts of mysticism, nor even to
Martin Buber's theology, as has been the rule in Musil scholarship. The
novel should instead be situated among a series of other projects of the
same period that sought to explain the political role of affections and the
suggestive power of nationalism and fascism.[54] Elias Canetti's *Crowds
and Power* (1960), Adorno and Horkheimer's chapters on the culture industry and anti-Semitism in *Dialectic of Enlightenment* (1943), as well as
their research project on the authoritarian personality, Wilhelm Reich's
Mass Psychology of Facism (1933), and Sigmund Freud's *Group Psychology and the Analysis of the Ego* (1921)—they all examined the subject's
affective bindings to mass movements, the profound appeal of collective ideologies, and the origins of political passions. After the burn-
ing of the German parliament in 1933, Musil notes that he wants to
write an essay on reason and affection (*Vernunft und Affekt*) in politics
(*T* 1:826).[55] In the same period, he writes the chapters where Ulrich
analyzes the world of emotions.

The most immediate parallel to Musil's ideas on this topic, however,
is Hermann Broch's research project on mass insanity, his *Massenwahntheorie,* which he developed between 1939 and 1948.[56] A virtual realization of Ulrich's proposal for a World Secretariat for Precision and
Soul, Broch's project, supported by the Rockefeller Foundation and
Princeton University, is based on a theory that establishes an intimate
connection between religious ecstasy and nationalist and fascist mass
movements.[57] Mass madness and mysticism, Broch maintained, are two
opposite manifestations of one and the same psychic disposition. His
theory also elucidates Musil's writings on emotionality and affection

throughout the 1920s and 1930s. Musil's aim was to separate the utopian aspects of affective bonding from its destructive aspects; this is
why he wanted to bring more precision into questions of "soul."

Even the mysticist side of Musil's novel is thus mediated by the experience of nationalism and of the political events in 1914 and the early
1930s. As I hope to have shown, the political upheavals and ideological
conflicts that characterized Musil's postimperial predicament entered
directly into the production of *The Man Without Qualities*. All parts of
the novel, including the essays and journals that prepared it, should be
seen as different phases and variations in one immense laboratory experiment. Different strategies of ideological engineering are tried out
and their consequences recorded. Art is a "moral laboratorium," Musil
once asserted (*GW* 2:1351). *The Man Without Qualities* is such a laboratorium, a "vast experimental station for trying out the best ways of
being a human being and discovering new ones," in which Musil
labored all his life. His aim was to construct a human being who is resistant to the appellations of the group-ego of the nation or the race and
yet receptive to future passions of love and solidarity. Such is the ultimate goal of this "attempt to find an other human being." Its result is
the Musilian subject of negativity: a subject without nation.

Epilogue

There is no better place to keep a secret than

in an unfinished novel. —Italo Calvino

As a young schoolboy in Vienna, Ulrich once wrote an essay on the topic "patriotism" (*Vaterlandsliebe*) in which he presented a brilliant idea. Anyone who really loved his Fatherland should never think his Fatherland the best (*MWQ* 13 / *MoE* 18f.). Realizing that the world could have been different, indeed, that he himself could have been someone else, Musil's protagonist had already in his teens gone beyond patriotic ideas. In a society where all children were taught to love the Fatherland, Ulrich's essay was scandalous. His father sent him off to a boarding school in Belgium, where the son extended his disdain for the patriotic ideals of all nations, while learning to follow the principle of "as well as," or "neither-nor," rather than the politics of exclusion obeying the principle of "either-or": if you are not with us, you are against us.

Inserted at the beginning of the novel, this is the only episode that gives any direct information about Ulrich's youth. Musil's narrator obviously prefigures Ulrich's later career as a cultural trangressor, or even a spy. *The Man Without Qualities* explores an idea developed by other Austrian thinkers who defended multinational ideals. In 1907 Otto Bauer wrote about individuals living in border zones inhabited by several nationalities. Bauer first maintains that such persons are influenced by the destinies of two nations and that, if political and economic circumstances allow, they can grow into members of both nations. He then

corrects himself, stating that they become, rather, individuals who belong to neither nation. "For the individual who is affected by the culture
of two or more nations, whose character becomes equally strongly influenced by different cultures, does not simply unite the character traits
of two nations but possesses a wholly new character. [The] mixture of
cultural elements creates a new character." [1]

This is the reason, Bauer adds, why an individual who is the child of
many nations becomes an object of suspicion, and in times of national
struggle even condemned as a traitor and transgressor. Born in the
Czech-German town of B., and fit to become a spy, Ulrich is one of
these transgressors.

Just as Bauer describes how the coexistence of several nationalities
allows an individual to withstand national identities, so does Musil's
narrator evoke a society in which the multiplicity of cultures, histories,
and identities enables the individual to go beyond them. In chapter 8
the narrator stipulates that the inhabitant of a country has at least nine
characters: a professional, a national, a civic, a class, a geographical, a
sexual, a conscious, an unconscious, and perhaps even a private one.
Although each inhabitant combines these identities, they do not add up
to a larger whole. Rather, the narrator suggests, these identities dissolve
the individual, "so that he is really nothing more than a small basin hol-
lowed out by these many streamlets that trickle into it and drain out
of it again, to join other such rills in filling some other basin. Which is
why every inhabitant of the earth also has a tenth character that is nothing else than the passive fantasy of spaces yet unfilled. This permits a
person all but one thing: to take seriously what his at least nine other
characters do and what happens to them" (*MWQ* 30 / *MoE* 34).

In addition to all socially ascribed identities, then, every person has a
surplus identity—the "tenth character"—that cancels the others. In this
land of diversity, no one mistakes identity for subjectivity, and no one
can claim superiority on the grounds of possessing a specific identity. [2]
Since subjectivity surmounts identity, it is impossible to judge anyone
in terms of race, class, gender, or sexuality.

Evidently, the intercultural predicament in Austria at the beginning
of the twentieth century allowed Musil, like Bauer before him, to elabo-

rate a notion of transculturation that anticipates fundamental features of the concepts of hybridity, border culture, and métissage, which have been developed in late-twentieth-century postcolonial theory.[3] *The Man Without Qualities* projects a universal or transcultural society, its driving force being the subject of negativity. In evoking the tenth character that forbids a person to take any of his identities seriously, Musil's narrator speaks of what I have designated as the subject's negativity. Like negativity, Musil's tenth character is an embodiment of a constitutive lack. This lack generates a need that cannot be satisfied by any social identity and that therefore must transgress and negate them all. At the heart of the Musilian subject, there is a power of distantiation and differentiation that prevents the person from investing too much in his or her identities, and which estranges reality, so that the existing social order comes to appear as just one among an infinite number of possible worlds.

What makes *The Man Without Qualities* so remarkable as a philosophical achievement is the novel's conceptualization of human subjectivity in terms of lack, negativity, and multiplicity. The novel introduces a way of understanding subjectivity and identity whose long neglected theoretical and practical consequences I have explored in this book, in an attempt to situate Musil's work as an early instance of the intellectual paradigm that structures present-day discussions of identity and subjectivity. Musil's conceptualization of human subjectivity also approaches a not yet realized universalism, according to which the human individual is constituted not by any intrinsic essence or nature, nor by reason or inalienable rights, but rather by a lack that is always shared by the other. In this view, identity and selfhood are enabled by temporary identifications that compensate and cover the originary lack. If these identifications last, buttressed by ideologies, they will stabilize into qualities and characters, that is, into identities which are mistaken for realities and hence block the release of additional possibilities. Yet the human condition is defined by the urge to supersede every identity, to become more than one is: "das Mehrseinmüssen, als man ist" (*MoE* 1887). Musil's novel thus demonstrates how the human condition precludes the attempt to fix a person to a specific identity. Nomadic, displaced, always in process, the Musilian subject negates ideological appellations and is thus forever deterritorialized.

In the 1930s, however, Musil's notion of subjectivity was likely to become an empty ideal. It was powerless in a world dominated by racialist and nationalist ideologies. In this sense, the negativity of the Musilian subject is not only a promise of limitless possibilities, but also an index of Musil's failure to construe a viable alternative idea of the universal human being. At best, his subject of negativity could find its realization in anarchist actions; at worst in an attitude of self-chosen isolation and misanthropy. As Ulrich states toward the end, "one can't live from a negation alone" (*MWQ* 1472 / *MoE* 1673). Musil's narrator therefore attempts to show how this conception of the human subject can be realized socially and historically, which leads him to conjure up nothing less than a different world. "We have made Italy; now we have to make Italians!" Massimo d'Azeglio proclaimed at the first meeting of the parliament of the newly unified Italian kingdom. The tenor of Musil's *The Man Without Qualities* can be summed up by turning the same statement on its head: "I have made a transcultural human being, now I have to make a transcultural world!" Like his hero, Musil was not satisfied by anything less than a transcultural, even transsexual utopia.

Musil's drafts for the completion of *The Man Without Qualities* testify to a tormenting struggle. Trying to bring closure to his novel, he searched for a complete solution of the scientific, political, psychological, ethical, and aesthetic problems that he spread out in the first thousand pages of his book. Calling for "a systematics of communal life, a psychotechnics for the collective, as a minimum demand," listing "the possibilities for a new order which Ulrich has in mind," or asserting that one must "combine the partial solutions, and summarize the apparently false century and millennium in an all-encompassing solution," Musil remained faithful, up until his death in 1942, to the grand program of 1926, in which he declared that he aimed at an intellectual mastery of the world (*MoE* 1870, 1887, 1881).

But the longer one delves into Musil's notes, the more evident it becomes that the writer doubted his calling. The intellectual mastery of reality? The prospects were bleak when "a fluctuation in the price of cotton, a fall in the price of flour has more influence than an idea" (*MoE* 1886). The author feared that his grand project would shrivel up to an armchair experiment: "What remains then, finally? That there is a sphere of ideals and a sphere of reality? Guidelines, and the like? How profoundly unsatisfactory! Isn't there any better answer?" (*MoE* 1876).

But guidelines (*Richtbilder*) are of course the only contribution that literature can make to humanity, and Musil's novel produces an abundance of them. When the narrator develops these images or models, he returns to the nationality question, as though he were convinced that the Dual Monarchy housed the elements for a new society, which lay hidden in the midst of the intercultural chaos of this multicultural empire. Interestingly, the description of Kakania in chapter 8, which I cited above, belongs to the oldest sediments of the novel. Certain sentences go back to an essay called "Politics in Austria," written as early as 1912:

> There is something uncanny in this obstinate rhythm that has no melody, no words, no feeling. Somewhere in this country a secret must be hidden, an idea, but no one knows where. It is not the idea of the state, not the dynastic principle, not the idea of a cultural symbiosis of different peoples (Austria could be a world experiment): apparently the whole thing is really only motion in the absence of a driving idea, like the weaving of a bicyclist who isn't going forward. (*PS* 19 / *GW* 2:993)

Before the war, then, Musil was critical of the conditions in Austria, lamenting the absence of a driving idea, an ideological direction. What he regarded as a weakness in 1912, however, had become a strength by the early 1920s. In his novel, Musil describes the old empire with affection, even excitement. The narrator does not deny that life in Kakania lacked direction; "one enjoyed a negative freedom there, always with the sense of the insufficient grounds of one's own existence" (*MWQ* 31* / *MoE* 35). But this is no longer a disadvantage. Enjoying the negative freedom of not having to mirror themselves in the ideology of empire, the Kakanians are free to imagine alternative lives. They recognize that the grounds of their existence will always be insufficient, that their identity can never be accounted for by laws, principles, or essences.

By the time Musil discovers this freedom, he has realized that the predominant notions of personal and cultural identities are both false and dangerous. As I have shown, this transformation of Musil's views on human identity, which is best described as a shift from expressivity to negativity, is inseparable from his experience of Austria's transformation from a multicultural empire to a more or less monocultural nation state plagued by anti-Semitism and imbued with fascist yearnings. It is at this time, the early 1920s, that Musil works out his theory of human shapelessness, which then, in *The Man Without Qualities,* becomes the Musilian subject of negativity.

Some commentators have suggested that Musil's commitment to possibility prevented him from completing his novel. True, the novel is motored by a sense of possibility that resists closures and tears open every conceivable ending. To this effect, Anne Longuet Marx has argued that *The Man Without Qualities* realizes a concept of "intrinsic incompleteness." [4] Her reading discloses a feature commonly ignored in Musil scholarship. If the novel's incompletion is not just the result of the author's failure but rather intrinsic to the text, as Longuet Marx submits, this means that *The Man Without Qualities* is founded upon a valorization of lack and heterogeneity, that the novel is rooted, rhizome-like, in a notion according to which personal identities, aesthetic entities, and cultural communities are open-ended processes intersected by multiple determinants. Musil's text knows neither origin nor closure: the disposition that makes it impossible to complete the novel is hence indistinguishable from the impulse that made it possible to write it in the first place. This disposition is what I have called negativity. Explaining why the novel could not be finished, the force of negativity also explains why it was begun. It had to be written because Musil, driven by an impulse to negate the political development of his time, had to explore if and how humanity could resist the ideologies of gender, culture, race, nation, and empire that contributed to World War I and which in the 1920s prepared the ground for yet another war as well as an unimaginable genocide.

Stated differently, the utopian idea that made the novel unfinishable is present in its conception. Herein lies the secret of Musil's novel, what Maurice Blanchot once called "the profundity of its failure." [5] In fact, Musil's failure was more profound than Blanchot imagined, for the ending that is continually postponed, the conclusion that every reader has speculated about, and that even discouraged and eluded the author himself, is situated at the origin. More precisely, it is located in the image of Kakania, for this is the only country in which the Musilian subject can be territorialized, at home in a state that no longer exists and perhaps never existed, but to which the Musilian subject nonetheless strives to return. The impulse that forces Musil to reject expressivity and affirm negativity hence also forces him to reevaluate the lost Danube empire, not as a reality, but as a forfeited possibility. If Kakania is an empire without name or qualities, it is also a land of possibilities, a country where one speaks in a subjunctive mood, coloring every statement with a wish, and where one regards the nation as a fantasy rather than a reality: "Naturally, that would have been the moment when a good Kakanian also could have answered the question of what he was by enthusiastically saying: 'Nothing!', meaning that Something, which is again set free to make of a Kakanian everything that was not yet there" (*MWQ* 577* / *MoE* 529).

Kakania's lack of national identity is affirmed as a negativity which, in its turn, is converted into possibilities. The Kakanian is Nothing, a site of lack which does not even have a name, but this nothingness really means a Something, which can become Everything. In Kakania it is possible to farm in the morning, go fishing in the afternoon, and write poetry in the evening, without having to be either a farmer, a fisherman, or a poet.

The images of Austria-Hungary in *The Man Without Qualities* have typically been seen as products of the author's nostalgia. Had this been the case, the novel could be categorized among the Habsburg myths, along with works by Joseph Roth, Franz Werfel, Stefan Zweig, and others. The radiation reflected by Musil's Kakania, however, does not emanate from the author's nostalgia for a lost reality but from the curiosity of a scientist exploring possibilities. The images of Kakania are not descriptions of the Austro-Hungarian Empire as it once was but were produced by an intellect operating in an experimental mode.

Only in this way can Musil's image of Kakania escape history and retain the actuality of a past opportunity — "Austria could be a world ex-

periment" — which humankind failed to realize. Musil's utopian view
of this opportunity is shared by Giorgio Agamben, who describes "the
coming community" as a coming together of singular subjects, who reject every identity and every condition of belonging, and who are thus
forever antagonistic to the idea of a state, nation, or culture that would
bind them into a community of destiny.[6] Musil's view is also shared
by Robert Kann, the principal historian of the nationality question in
Austria-Hungary, who maintains that the Dual Monarchy was historically unique in its recognition of what he calls "the concept of a supranational union," which recognized neither the notion of a mother country nor that of a master race.[7]

And in a time like ours, when many again gather in the shelter of
crowning ideas and willingly confuse their own lives with an illusory
national and religious identity, using this identity as the foundation of
an ethics calculated to exclude, or to conquer and impose the world
order of the same, it is important to know that there are times when
people may simply hang out in the wings of modernization, unable to
decide which path to take, imagining alternative futures. Progress consequently hesitates; no individual takes her identity so seriously that
she cannot at the same time step back and imagine herself in the place
of the other. These are the great times when history goes on holiday.
Society returns to a prehistoric phase, only just acquiescing in its own
existence. This is what Kakania was like during the intermission preceding the Parallel Campaign, and in this, Musil reminds us, Kakania
was, without the world's knowing it, the most progressive state of all
(*MWQ* 30f. / *MoE* 35).

Notes

Introduction

1 The question of how Musil planned to bring the novel to a closure paralyzed Musil scholarship from the 1950s well into the 1970s. The first alternative, according to which the novel would have continued with Ulrich
and Agathe's utopian project, their effort to realize the millennium, its
eventual failure, and the outbreak of the war, corresponds to the trajectory in Adolf Frisé's 1952 edition of *The Man Without Qualities,* for a long
time the authoritative one. Frisé's edition was challenged by Ernst Kaiser
and Eithne Wilkins, who at that time oversaw the materials in Musil's literary estate and also made the first English translation. They argued that
Musil in the 1930s abandoned the plan to let the novel end in war. Instead he planned to close the story with the platonic ecstasy of the mysticist union between Ulrich and Agathe, depicted in the chapter that Musil
was working on when he died, "Breaths of a summer day" ("Atemzüge
eines Sommertags"). See their *Robert Musil: Eine Einführung in das Werk*
(Stuttgart: Kohlhammer, 1962). This interpretation structures the Italian
edition of *The Man Without Qualities,* which was supervised by Kaiser
and Wilkins. It is difficult to find any support for Kaiser and Wilkins's
view either in Musil's *Tagebücher* or in the drafts, notes, and outlines from
the 1930s that are published in Frisé's 1978 edition, today the authoritative one. I will return to this issue in chapters 4 and 5. The central parts
of the posthumous material are included in the second volume of Frisé's
edition, *Gesammelte Werke* I, vol. 2. All the material is included in the
CD-ROM edition of the posthumous papers: *Der literarische Nachlass,* ed.
Friedbert Aspetsberger, Karl Eibl, and Adolf Frisé (Reinbek bei Hamburg: Rowohlt, 1992).

2 See Musil's essays, " 'Nation' as Ideal and as Reality" (1921; "Die Nation als Ideal und als Wirklichkeit"), "Helpless Europe: A Digressive Journey" (1922; "Das hilflose Europa oder Reise vom Hundertsten ins Tausendste"), "The German as Symptom" (1923; "Der deutsche Mensch als Symptom") (PS, 101-133, 150-192; GW 2:1059-1094, 1353-1400). I will discuss these texts in detail in chapter 6.

3 Jacques Rancière, "Politics, Identification, and Subjectivization," in *The Identity in Question*, ed. John Rajchman (New York: Routledge, 1995), 67. For another concise discussion of these topics, see Ian Hacking, "Making Up People," in *Reconstructing Individualism: Autonomy, Individuality, and the Self in Western Thought*, ed. T. C. Heller, M. Sosna, and D. E. Wellbery (Stanford: Stanford University Press, 1986), 222-240.

4 David Luft offers an exception with his intellectual history of Musil's position in German and Austrian culture. He deals with Musil's response to World War I, but does not discuss the instrinsic links between his postimperial experience and *The Man Without Qualities* (*Robert Musil and the Crisis of European Culture, 1880-1942* [Berkeley: University of California Press, 1980]).

5 The most important contributions to this line of research have been made by Renate von Heydebrand (*Die Reflexionen Ulrichs in Robert Musils Roman "Der Mann ohne Eigenschaften": Ihr Zusammenhang mit dem zeitgenössischen Denken* [Münster: Aschendorff, 1966]) and, above all, Marie-Louise Roth (*Robert Musil—Ethik und Ästhetik: Zum theoretischen Werk des Dichters* [Munich: Paul List, 1972]). On the particular influence of the natural sciences on Musil's novel, see also Laurence Dahan-Gaida, *Musil: Savoir et fiction* (Paris: Presses universitaires de Vincennes, 1994); for an account of Musil's encounter with experimental psychology and Gestalt theory, see Silvia Bonacchi, *Die Gestalt der Dichtung: Der Einfluss der Gestalttheorie auf das Werk Robert Musils*, Musiliana 4 (Bern: Peter Lang, 1998).

6 Frank Maier-Solgk's essay on Musil and Carl Schmitt approaches the topic, but deals mostly with Musil's nonfictional writings on nation and state ("Musil und die problematische Politik: Zum Verhältnis von Literatur und Politik bei Robert Musil, insbesondere zu einer Auseinandersetzung mit Carl Schmitt," *Orbis Literarum* 46 [1991]: 340-363). Joseph Strutz devotes a few pages to the nationality issue in his book on the political dimensions of Musil's novel (*Politik und Literatur in Musils "Mann ohne Eigenschaften": Am Beispiel des Dichters Feuermaul*, Literatur in der Geschichte, Geschichte in der Literatur 6 [Königstein: Anton Hain, 1981],

75–78, 88–99). Strutz does not discuss the significance of the nationality question for the novel as a whole, nor does he connect it to Musil's analysis of subjectivity. Cornelia Blasberg also fails to address the issue of cultural and national identity, despite the promising title of her book (*Krise und Utopie der Intellektuellen: Kulturkritische Aspekte in Robert Musils Roman "Der Mann ohne Eigenschaften"* [Stuttgart: Hans-Dieter Heinz, 1984]). However, she does discuss how the general historical experience conditioned Musil's views on identity (ibid., 308–343). Lothar Georg Seeger's *Die Demaskierung der Lebenslüge: Eine Untersuchung zur Krise der Gesellschaft in Robert Musils "Der Mann ohne Eigenschaften"* (Bern: Francke, 1969) treats Musil's Kakania as a fairy-tale land. Horst Althaus delivers some interesting remarks on the nationality question in *Zwischen Monarchie und Republik: Schnitzler, Hofmannsthal, Kafka, Musil* (Munich: Wilhelm Fink, 1976). I have only been able to survey publications in English, German, French, Spanish, and the Scandinavian languages. Judging from bibliographical overviews, there is not much on this issue in Polish, Russian, or Czech either. See Egon Naganowski, "Von Stefan Zweig zu Robert Musil: Ein Bericht über die Verbreitung der österreichischen Literatur im heutigen Poland," *Musil-Forum,* Wissenschaftliches Beiheft 4 (1990): 5–13; Alexandr W. Belobratow, "Musils Werk in der Sowjetunion," *Musil-Forum,* Wissenschaftliches Beiheft 4 (1990): 15–21; and Ludvík E. Václavek, "Robert Musil in tschechoslowakischer Sicht," *Musil-Forum,* Wissenschaftliches Beiheft 4 (1990): 22–40.

7 But see Strutz, *Politik und Literatur in Musils Mann ohne Eigenschaften;* Friedbert Aspetsberger, *Literarisches Leben im Austrofaschismus: Der Staatspreis* (Königstein: Anton Hain Meisenheim, 1980); Cedric E. Williams, *The Broken Eagle: The Politics of Austrian Literature from Empire to Anschluss* (New York: Barnes and Noble, 1974), 148–186; David R. Midgley, " 'Das hilflose Europa': Eine Aufforderung, die politische Essays von Robert Musil neu zu lesen," *German Quarterly* 67, no. 1 (winter 1994): 16–26; Annette Daigger, "Musils politische Haltung in seinen frühen Essays," in *Robert Musil: Essayismus und Ironie,* ed. Gudrun Brokoph-Mauch, Edition Orpheus 6 (Tübingen: Francke, 1992), 75–90. Discussing Musil's essays, Bernd Hüppauf confronts Musil's ideas of nationality and politics with the program of the Austromarxists Karl Renner, Otto Bauer, and Max Adler ("Von Wien durch den Krieg nach Nirgendwo: Nation und utopisches Denken bei Musil und im Austromarxismus," *Text + Kritik,* 21–22, 3d ed. [November 1983]: 1–28). I will return to this discussion

in chapter 6. After the final revisions of my manuscript, Friedrich Bringazi published *Robert Musil und die Mythen der Nation: Nationalismus
als Ausdruck subjektiver Identitätsdefekte* (Frankfurt am Main: Peter Lang,
1999), which uses Musil's oeuvre to reconstruct a systematic theory of
nationalism. It is unfortunate that Bringazi's book appeared too late to be
considered in the present context.

8 Christian Rogowski, *Distinguished Outsider: Robert Musil and His Critics*
(Columbia, S.C.: Camden House, 1994), 175. This is the best account of
the scholarly reception of Musil's work, and also the most comprehensive
bibliography of the secondary literature.

9 In arguing that Musil's novel is radically "antiexpressivist," I take issue
with most early Musil scholarship, which is largely confined within the
expressivist paradigm. This is particularly true of studies dealing with
Musil's representation of "the self," which tend to construe *The Man
Without Qualities* as an effort to rescue a centered and coherent identity in
the face of an alienating predicament of modernity. For instance, Joseph
Strelka argues that Musil follows Goethe's ideal of an expressive unity of
self and world: "The epic quest and wandering, the search for totality and
knowledge, at last reaches its completion in the reverence of the invulnerable integrity of the living soul of the individual as being also an in-
separably related part of the divine soul of the whole. After all contradictions and obstructions, . . . the subjective and independent search for truth
ends in a final and hard-won conviction which stands in agreement with
the mysticists' *oldest* knowledge as well as with the primeval mythical
traditions and their timeless rightness" (*Auf der Suche nach dem verlorenen Selbst: Zu deutscher Erzählprosa des 20. Jahrhunderts* [Bern: Francke,
1977], 25f., cf. 118–127; see also Strelka, *Kafka, Musil, Broch und die Entwicklung des modernen Romans,* 2d ed. [Vienna: Forum, 1959]). Strelka's
statement is paradigmatic: it regards the subject's quest for truth as a timeless endeavor. The subject-hero is said to confront a society full of conflicts that he attempts to synthesize. The ascent to this synthesis entails
that he reveals the meaning of his existence and realizes his authentic identity. Philip Payne, arguing along similar lines, characterizes Musil's novel
as a drama about self-discovery: "Ulrich, at the outset overwhelmed by
the loss of subjectivity, takes a path which he hopes will ultimately lead
to his intellectual, emotional and moral centre" (*Robert Musil's "The Man
Without Qualities": A Critical Study* [Cambridge: Cambridge University
Press, 1988], 211). Judith Burckhardt also claims that Musil's work is about
autonomous individuation, arguing that Ulrich posits as his life's goal the

cultivation of his personality and the acquisition of qualities (*"Der Mann ohne Eigenschaften" von Robert Musil; oder, Das Wagnis der Selbstverwirklichung* [Bern: Francke, 1973], 11). Strelka, Payne, and Burckhardt presume that the human subject is able to realize his or her intrinsic nature in the form of a harmonious personality. Their conclusions are given in advance: if an expressive individuation is seen as the norm, the subjectivity represented in Musil's novel must be an estrangement from a true state of being. Hence the assertion that Ulrich suffers from a lack of identity and searches for his lost self.

Most commentators of *The Man Without Qualities* construe this lack as an effect of the division between rational and nonrational aspects of reality. Usually, this is displayed in discussions of the grand theme of what Musil himself baptized the *ratioïd* and the non-*ratioïd* in his essay "Sketch of What the Writer Knows" (1918; "Skizze der Erkenntnis des Dichters") (*PS* 61–64 / *GW* 2:1025–1030). Intellect and emotion, thought and feeling, sensation and reflection, mind and sensory perception, understanding and intuition, reason and instinct, science and art, mathematics and mysticism: these conceptual pairs often appear in Musil's works, and they have come to organize the discourse of his interpreters. Karl Dinklage's summary of Musil's work epitomizes this tendency: "a writer, whose literary program lives from the tension between activity and passivity, rationality and mysticism" ("Musils Definition des Mannes ohne Eigenschaften und das Ende seines Romans," in *Robert Musil: Studien zu seinem Werk,* ed. Karl Dinklage [Reinbek bei Hamburg: Rowohlt, 1970], 122). Dinklage's statement is true, in one sense. As Wolfgang Freese has pointed out, however, it is generally Musil's critics, not Musil himself, who arrange these concepts as binary oppositions, thus generating a futile controversy over how Musil presumably attempted to overcome the antinomies in question ("Zur neueren Musil-Forschung: Ausgaben und Gesamtdarstellungen," *Text + Kritik* 21–22, 3d ed. [November 1983]: 118). The result is publications entitled *Ratio und "Mystik," "Mathematik und Mystik," "Wirklichkeit und Mystik," Dichtung und Wissenschaft, Dichtung und Erkenntnis,* or *Studien zur Antinomie von Intellekt und Gefühl* (Elisabeth Albertsen, *Ratio und "Mystik" im Werk Robert Musils* [Munich: Nymphenburger Verlagshandlung, 1968]; Gerolf Jässl, "Mathematik und Mystik in Robert Musils Roman 'Der Mann ohne Eigenschaften,' " [Ph.D. diss., Munich, 1964]; Ingrid Drevermann, "Wirklichkeit und Mystik," in *Ethik und Bewusstheit: Studien zu Robert Musil,* ed. S. Bauer and I. Drevermann [Cologne: Böhlau, 1966], 123–245; Gerd Müller, *Dichtung und Wissenschaft: Studien zu Robert Musils Romanen "Die Verwirrungen des Zöglings Törless" und "Der Mann ohne Eigenschaften"* [Uppsala: Almqvist and Wiksells, 1971]; Stephan Reinhardt, *Studien zur Antinomie von Intellekt und Gefühl in Musils Roman "Der Mann ohne Eigenschaften"* [Bonn: Bouvier, 1969]). Many of the conceptual dualisms of German idealism are present in *The Man Without Qualities,* to be sure. Yet this says little about the specificity of the novel, because, as we shall see in chapter 1, the dualisms in question, between *Geist* and *Leben,* or organic unity and mechanic fragmentation, constitute a discursive formation that tends to frame German and Austrian writing in general from romanticism to expressionism. Moreover, it must be remembered that Musil himself never posited the antitheses of rationality and mysticism as opposites. He tried to penetrate the realm of feeling with the tools of the intellect. In elevating the conflict between rationality and emotions to the principal issue of Musil's work, many scholars enclose themselves inside the expressivist paradigm; what they actually grasp for, I believe, is the historical impossibility for the human subject to let its "inner nature" express itself creatively in the modern world. So even though Peter Pütz is right in stating that many reflections in *The Man Without Qualities* revolve around "the problematic relationship of rationality and irrationality, of diffuse reality and a mysticism of wholeness" ("Robert Musil," in *Deutsche Dichter der Moderne: Ihre Leben und Werk,* ed. Benno von Wiese, 3d ed. [Berlin: Schmidt, 1975], 344), the dualism is not clarified but only mythologized as long as it is seen as a timeless problem, or subsumed under Nietzsche's notions of the Dionysiac and the Apollonian. In some cases the dualisms are even biologized, as when Karl Corino speculates on whether they are caused by neurobiological differences between the halves of the human brain ("Robert Musil," in *Literarische Profile: Deutsche Dichter von Grimmelshausen bis Brecht,* ed. Walter Hinderer [Königstein: Athenäum, 1982], 300–314).

Related to such readings is an eagerness to complete Musil's task and bring a closure to his novel. Many critics, departing from the antinomy between the rational and the nonrational, show how a synthesis may be reached, and how Musil's representation of the so-called other condition (*der andere Zustand*) prefigures such a synthesis. In an investigation of Musil's relationship to Martin Buber, Dietmar Goltschnigg argues that Musil resolves the dualisms by entering a realm of mysticism where the "I" allegedly constitutes itself in expressive harmony with the universe (*Mystische Tradition im Roman Robert Musils: Martin Bubers "Ekstatische Konfessionen" im "Mann ohne Eigenschaften"* [Heidelberg: Lothar Stiehm,

1974], 41, 119–126, 164–168). This is also the interpretation of Ernst Kaiser and Eithne Wilkins (*Robert Musil*), as I discussed above. Peter Nusser reaches a similar conclusion, finding that the ratioïd and the non-ratioïd are tuned together in Musil's ideas on the novel (*Musils Romantheorie* [The Hague: Mouton, 1967], 20, 100–106). Investigating Musil's ideas on psychology, Erhard von Büren applies a related schema. Musil is said to unearth the core of the personality and "the specific character of the centrality of personal cultivation" (*Zur Bedeutung der Psychologie im Werk Robert Musils* [Zürich: Atlantis, 1970], 50). Büren never mentions that Musil rejected the very idea of personal cultivation; and although Büren purports to write about psychology, he fails to define concepts such as "person," "I," "self," or "subject."

Anglo-American commentaries are also frequently structured by the opposition between the rational and the nonrational. In the concluding paragraph of her book, Hannah Hickman sums up Musil's project as a search for a "synthesis between intellect and feeling, exactitude and imagination, action and contemplation, a true synthesis to serve as the foundation of a better life" (*Robert Musil and the Culture of Vienna* [La Salle, Ill.: Open Court Publishing, 1984], 187). David Luft interestingly demonstrates the originality with which Musil struggled "to keep intellect in relation to feeling." But he, too, fails to recognize the historicity of Musil's notion of subjectivity (*Robert Musil and the Crisis of European Culture, 1880–1942,* 297). The division between reason and emotion in Musil is even more accentuated in Luft's introduction to the translation of a selection of Musil's essays (*PS,* xv–xxviii).

Though invaluable on the sources and influences resonating in Musil's work, Marie-Louise Roth's analysis also relies on an expressivist notion of the subject. She maintains that "the mental attitudes that Musil designated as 'ratioïd' and 'non-ratioïd' are the two poles of his creation." In her account these concepts do not form a rigid dualism but branch out in a network of topics springing from a wide variety of sources. Roth presents Musil's work as a virtually Hegelian Geist subsuming all contradictions, and expressing itself in all parts of his oeuvre (*Robert Musil – Ethik und Ästhetik,* 12, 137–149). In a later work, Roth argues that Musil's ideas of subjectivity are transformed after World War I. The relation between subject and situation is foregrounded, and the soul-searching question "Who am I?" is replaced by the situationist "Where am I?" But this important remark is repealed in the conclusion of the same chapter: "despite the transformations . . . a fundamental unity governs the entire work.

The central themes are present from the outset" (*Robert Musil: L'homme au double regard* [Paris: Balland, 1987], 32, 36). Musil and his protagonist remain subjects torn between opposites, searching for their authentic identities.

Elisabeth Albertsen's, Bernd-Rüdiger Hüppauf's, and Gerd Müller's respective investigations have very differing themes and emphases, to be sure, and they all elucidate Musil's work in important ways. Yet they, too, reveal their debts to the expressivist paradigm in their ways of construing Musil as a writer struggling to unify intellect with feeling, and Ulrich as a hero in search for a life that is not stifled by rigid social forms. Hüppauf speaks of the novel's unique attempt to synthesize mysticism and enlightenment (*Von sozialer Utopie zur Mystik: Zu Robert Musils "Der Mann ohne Eigenschaften"* [Munich: Wilhelm Fink, 1971], 164). In Müller's view, Musil continues the literary tradition of German romanticism, which aimed to mediate between literature and science and contain them both in a humanist synthesis (*Dichtung und Wissenschaft,* 13). Albertsen, for her part, argues that Musil's hero tries to attain a "fully integrated personality" by synthesizing the empiricist idea of being able to realize many possible selves with the mysticist idea of having a self with many possibilities. The contradiction between mysticism and science would thus be undone (*Ratio und "Mystik,"* 35f.). Yet, although these three studies tend to read *The Man Without Qualities* as a story of apprenticeship, whose hero desires to realize his identity in an expressive harmony with reality, they have usefully stressed that Ulrich and Agathe's attempted synthesis in a mysticist union is a failure (Hüppauf, *Von sozialer Utopie zur Mystik,* 144–146, 163–165; Albertsen, *Ratio und "Mystik,"* 111–127; Müller, *Dichtung und Wissenschaft,* 237–241).

Again, these works contain many crucial observations. In their effort to disentangle the complex discourse of subjectivity and identity, however, they all come across as more or less ingenious paraphrases of the young Musil's discourse, commenting on the separation between inwardness and external reality, the former associated with emotion, feeling, soul, and selfhood, the latter characterized by reification. Locked in the expressivist paradigm, such readings grasp the Musilian subject, not as a historical problem, but rather as an example of a tragic alienation from an allegedly universal norm of identity. Indeed, what these expressivist readings construe as an *existential* problem represented by Musil is, I claim, the direct opposite; it is a solution to a specific *political* problem facing intellectuals in postimperial Austria and Germany: how to envision a community that does not reduce its subjects to their particular positions in the social hierarchy.

10 This is true also of Annie Reniers-Servranckz, *Robert Musil: Konstanz und Entwicklung von Themen, Motiven und Strukturen in den Dichtungen* (Bonn: Bouvier, 1972), which makes an analytical demonstration of the thematic and philosophical constancy of Musil's work; and Franz Hagmann, *Aspekte der Wirklichkeit im Werke Robert Musils* (Bern: Herbert Lang, 1969), which is informed by a similar argument. Emphasizing the continuity of Musil's enterprise, both ignore Musil's philosophical and political break with the expressivist paradigm.

11 Pierre V. Zima, *L'Ambivalence romanesque: Proust, Kafka, Musil,* rev. ed. (Frankfurt am Main: Peter Lang, 1988); Anne Longuet Marx, *Proust, Musil: Partage d'écritures* (Paris: Presses universitaires de France, 1986); Peter Henninger, *Der Buchstabe und der Geist: Unbewusste Determinierung im Schreiben Robert Musils* (Frankfurt am Main: Peter Lang, 1980); Roger Willemsen, *Robert Musil: Vom intellektuellen Eros* (Munich: Piper, 1985); and *Das Existenzrecht der Dichtung: Zur Rekonstruktion einer systematischen Literaturtheorie im Werk Robert Musils* (Munich: Wilhelm Fink, 1984); Dieter Hcyd, *Musil-Lektüre: Der Text, das Unbewusste: Psychosemiologische Studien zu Robert Musils theoretischem Werk und zum Roman "Der Mann ohne Eigenschaften"* (Frankfurt am Main: Peter Lang, 1980). See also Hartmut Böhme's confrontation of Musil and postmodernism: "Eine Zeit ohne Eigenschaften: Robert Musil und die Posthistoire," in *Natur und Subjekt* (Frankfurt am Main: Suhrkamp, 1988), 308–333.

12 Böhme argues that "1918 is a turning point also in Musil's literary and intellectual development. . . . Against the background of the economic, political, and social upheavals between 1918 and 1923, Musil develops his concept of society, which then becomes the foundation of *The Man Without Qualities*" (*Anomie und Entfremdung: Literatursoziologische Untersuchungen zu den Essays Robert Musils und seinem Roman "Der Mann ohne Eigenschaften"* [Kronberg: Scriptor, 1974], 1). This largely conforms to Peter Henninger's conclusion that 1920 to 1925 was the most productive and decisive period in Musil's career, bringing both social commitment and the beginnings of his great novel ("Die Wende in Robert Musils Schaffen: 1920–1930 oder die Erfindung der Formel," in *Robert Musil: Essayismus und Ironie,* ed. Gudrun Brokoph-Mauch [Tübingen: Francke, 1992], 91–103).

13 Alexander Honold, *Die Stadt und der Krieg: Raum- und Zeitkonstruk-*

tion in Robert Musils Roman "Der Mann ohne Eigenschaften" (Munich: Wilhelm Fink, 1995).

14 Claudio Magris, *Der habsburgische Mythos in der österreichischen Literatur,* trans. M. Pásztory (Salzburg: Otto Müller, 1966), 7–27. More specifically, Magris argues that the Habsburg myth has three major themes, which are affectionately repeated and reinvented in Austrian literature between approximately 1800 and 1930: the multinational nature of the Habsburg empire, its good-natured imperial bureaucracy, and the sensuous hedonism and joie de vivre that characterized its culture.

15 On this point, see Eric Hobsbawm, "The Return of Mitteleuropa," in *Cross Currents: A Yearbook on Central European Culture,* no. 10 (New Haven: Yale University Press, 1991); Jacques Le Rider, *La Mitteleuropa* (Paris: Presses universitaires de France, 1994); and Russell Berman, "Vienna Fascination," in *Modern Culture and Critical Theory: Art, Politics, and the Legacy of the Frankfurt School* (Madison: University of Wisconsin Press, 1989), 204–241.

16 Magris, *Der habsburgische Mythos,* 239–294. On Hofmannsthal's engagement with the Salzburg festival from 1920 onward, which perhaps constitutes the most conspicuous sign of this wish to reconstruct the Austrian nation by drawing on the history of its old imperial culture, see Michael P. Steinberg, *The Meaning of the Salzburg Festival: Austria as Theater and Ideology, 1890–1938* (Ithaca: Cornell University Press, 1990).

17 Hermann Broch, "Nachruf auf Robert Musil," in *Kommentierte Werkausgabe* (Frankfurt am Main: Suhrkamp, 1975), vol. 9, bk. 1, 98f.

18 Manuel Castells provides a comprehensive analysis of how populist movements centered on notions of ethnic or religious identity tend to dissolve political constituencies and collective agreements that are based on class positions, citizenship, certain definitions of rights and values, or future-oriented projects. The same constituencies and agreements are also undermined from abroad and above, by the deterritorializing effects of global capital (*The Information Age: Economy, Society, and Culture,* 3 vols. [Oxford: Blackwell, 1996–98], esp. vol. 1, *The Rise of the Network Society,* 66–150; vol. 2, *The Power of Identity,* 5–67). See also Etienne Balibar, *Masses, Classes, Ideas: Studies on Politics and Philosophy before and after Marx,* trans. James Swenson (New York: Routledge, 1994).

19 Two examples drawn from current discussions on identity will have to suffice here. First, "identity" redefines the concepts that are utilized to interpret and explain cultural and social phenomena. Once we start asking questions of "identity," notions like state, individual, class, history,

man, woman, culture, canon, text, author, and reader lose their apparent neutrality, attain new connotations, and must be supplemented or qualified. On this topic, see Gayatri Chakravorty Spivak, *Outside in the Teaching Machine* (New York: Routledge, 1993); Claude Lévi-Strauss, ed., *L'Identité*, 2d ed. (Paris: Presses universitaires de France, 1987); the special issue of *South Atlantic Quarterly* [*Nations, Identities, Cultures,* ed. V. Y. Mudimbe] 94, no. 4 (fall 1995); and *The Identity in Question*. Further, "identity" also points to a crisis of ethical universalism. It is often argued, and rightly so, that the dominant codification of the shared rights and values of all human beings is modeled upon, and normally interpreted through, a liberal Western understanding of the human condition. An allegedly universal codification thereby turns out to be a manifestation of a particular identity, the result being that there is no longer any consensus regarding what desires, needs, and rights human beings have in common. Two examples of the crisis of ethical universalism are the restructuring of the United Nations system and the reemergence of "civilization" as an explanatory category in international studies. For an example of the latter tendency, see Samuel P. Huntington, *The Clash of Civilizations and the Remaking of World Order* (New York: Simon and Schuster, 1996), where Oswald Spengler's theory of sealed cultural entities returns as farce. For a general overview of the discussion on universalism and human rights, see the following volumes, containing the Oxford Amnesty Lectures: Barbara Johnson, ed., *Freedom and Interpretation* (New York: Basic Books, 1992); Stephen Shute and Susan Hurley, eds., *On Human Rights* (New York: Basic Books, 1993); Olwen Hufton, ed., *Historical Change and Human Rights* (New York: Basic Books, 1995). I have discussed these issues at length in *Andra platser: En essä om kulturell identitet* ["Other places: An essay on cultural identity"] (Stockholm: Norstedts, 1995).

20 This point has been stressed most recently by Slavoj Žižek. Ostensibly, Žižek defends the so-called Cartesian subject against its adversaries among left-wing multiculturalists and right-wing communitarianists alike. Yet this defense of the rational subject as a foundation of knowledge and action is, I take it, just a strategic maneuver that both supports and masks Žižek's true objective, which is not incompatible with the aim of the present book. This objective is to articulate a notion of universalism that is more adequate than the liberal conception of universalism that today legitimizes capitalist expansion throughout the world and that, reactively, generates a host of fundamentalist responses. In the liberal version of universalism, the disembodied individual endowed with certain

inviolable human rights functions as the universal norm in all ethical, epistemological, economic, and political transactions. In Žižek's version, by contrast, universalism is an empty center that organizes the surrounding field of political and cultural struggles. Each agent that seeks to occupy this center of universality inevitably adapts it to its own particular identity and thus betrays the very universalism it wants to embody. Universalism, for Žižek, is therefore incompatible with identity. It signifies a position that can be claimed only in the name of pure political agency. To the extent that the "Cartesian subject" denominates such an agency, it is a subject that we have learned to associate with Lacan rather than Descartes: a subject void of positivity, a subject that assumes the form of pure negativity (*The Ticklish Subject: The Absent Centre of Political Ontology* [London: Verso, 1999], esp. 70–123).

1 Topographies of Inwardness

1 Ludwig Bauer, "Middle Ages," trans. Don Reneau, in *The Weimar Republic Sourcebook,* ed. Anton Kaes, Martin Jay, and Edward Dimendberg (Berkeley: University of California Press, 1994), 385f.; "Mittelalter, 1932," *Das Tagebuch* 13, no. 1 (2 January 1932): 12f.

2 Karl Jaspers, *Man in the Modern Age,* trans. Eden Paul and Cedar Paul (London: George Routledge and Sons, 1933), 241; *Die geistige Situation der Zeit* (Berlin: Walter de Gruyter, 1931), 189.

3 Martin Heidegger, *Nietzsche,* vol. 4, *Nihilism,* trans. Frank A. Capuzzi (San Francisco: Harper and Row, 1982), 28 *; *Nietzsche: Der europäische Nihilismus,* in *Gesamtausgabe* (Frankfurt am Main: Vittorio Klostermann, 1986), 48:52.

4 Heidegger, *Nihilism,* 28; *Nietzsche,* 53.

5 See Domenico Losurdo's analysis of the connection between Heidegger's interpretation of Nietzsche and his reactions to the German victories at the beginning of World War II ("Heidegger and Hitler's War," in *The Heidegger Case: On Philosophy and Politics,* ed. Tom Rockmore and Joseph Margolis [Philadelphia: Temple University Press, 1992], 141–164). See also Hugo Ott, *Martin Heidegger: Unterwegs zur seiner Biographie* (Frankfurt am Main: Campus, 1988); and Victor Farias, *Heidegger and Nazism,* trans. Paul Burrell and Gabriel R. Ricci (Philadelphia: Temple University Press, 1989).

6 For a discussion of this epistemological shift in anthropology, see V. Y.

Mudimbe, *The Invention of Africa: Gnosis, Philosophy, and the Order of Knowledge* (Bloomington: Indiana University Press, 1988), 81ff.

7 Ernst Jünger, "Über die Gefahr," in *Der gefährliche Augenblick: Eine Sammlung von Bildern und Berichten,* ed. Ferdinand Bucholtz (Berlin: Junker und Dünnhaupt, 1931), 13f.

8 Ernst Marcks, *Deutsches Schicksal* (Leipzig, 1921), 14. Quoted in Fritz K. Ringer, *The Decline of the German Mandarins: The German Academic Community, 1890–1933* (Cambridge, Mass.: Harvard University Press, 1969), 225.

9 For an overview of this intellectual history, see Ringer, *The Decline of the German Mandarins;* Christian Graf von Krockow, *Die Entscheidung: Eine Untersuchung über Ernst Jünger, Carl Schmitt, Martin Heidegger* (Stuttgart: Ferdinand Enke Verlag, 1958), esp. 1–43; and Michael Löwy, *Pour une sociologie des intellectuels révolutionaires: L'évolution politique de Lukács* (Paris: Presses universitaires de France, 1976), esp. 25–78.

10 Ferdinand Tönnies, *Community and Society,* trans. Charles P. Loomis (East Lansing: Michigan State University Press, 1957), 33ff.; *Gemeinschaft und Gesellschaft: Grundbegriffe der reinen Soziologie* (Darmstadt: Wissenschaftliche Buchgesellschaft, 1970), 3ff.

11 Tönnies, *Community and Society,* 103; *Gemeinschaft und Gesellschaft,* 87.

12 Tönnies, *Community and Society,* 121ff.; *Gemeinschaft und Gesellschaft,* 108ff.

13 Tönnies, *Community and Society,* 223; *Gemeinschaft und Gesellschaft,* 241.

14 See Krockow, *Die Entscheidung,* 1–43; and Ringer, *The Decline of the German Mandarins,* 253–305, 367–418.

15 See Löwy's discussion of the "romantic anticapitalism" of the period (*Pour une sociologie des intellectuels révolutionaires,* 17–105).

16 Ringer, *The Decline of the German Mandarins,* 188, 254. Cf. 385: "Almost habitually, men continued to lament a loss of soul and of conviction, the growth of relativism and determinism, the isolation of the creative individual. They talked about the tyranny of the natural sciences, about the impoverishment of man's will through a one-sided emphasis upon the intellect, about a general sense of impotence and pessimism. After years of 'spiritual renewal', they still saw their own time as a no-man's-land between decline and revival. They tried to describe the available alternatives in the contrasting images of dryness and vitality, intellect and emotion, powerlessness and creativity. The theme of crisis was was now a ritual and obsession."

17 Ulrich Peters, "Zum Geleit," *Zeitschrift für Deutsche Bildung* 1 (1925):
    1–7; William Stern, *Studien zur Personwissenchaft,* pt. 1, "Personalistik
    als Wissenschaft" (Leipzig: J. A. Barth, 1930), iii–viii; Eduard Spranger,
    *Lebensformen: Geisteswissenschaftliche Psychologie und Ethik der Persön-
    lichkeit,* 6th ed. (Halle: Max Niemeyer Verlag, 1927), 3–10; Aloys Fischer,
    "Das Verhältnis der Jugend zu den sozialen Bewegungen und der Begriff
    der Sozialpädagogik," in *Jugendführer und Jugendprobleme: Festschrift
    zu Georg Kerschensteiners 70. Geburtstag,* ed. A. Fischer and E. Spranger
    (Leipzig: B. G. Teubner, 1924), 223. These examples are all collected from
    Ringer, *The Decline of the German Mandarins,* 252, 373, 380f., 417.

18 In Musil's essays there are indeed several observations concerning the his-
    toricity of subjectivity, but they are never strictly systematized. *The Man
    Without Qualities* is preoccupied by the phenomenology, narratology, and
    pathology of modern life, and in these areas Musil certainly demonstrated
    that the condition of modernity necessitates new modalities of human
    agency and identity; yet he rarely elaborated on the historical determi-
    nants of that need.

19 On the relation between Lukács and Musil, see Karl Corino, *Robert Musil:
    Leben und Werk in Bildern und Texten* (Reinbek bei Hamburg: Rowohlt,
    1988), 267.

20 Georg Lukács, *The Destruction of Reason,* trans. Peter Palmer (London:
    Merlin Press, 1980), esp. 403–664; *Die Zerstörung der Vernunft,* in *Werke*
    (Berlin: Luchterhand, 1962), 9:351–576.

21 Georg Lukács, *History and Class Consciousness: Studies in Marxist Dia-
    lectics,* trans. Rodney Livingstone (Cambridge, Mass.: MIT Press, 1971),
    83–222; *Geschichte und Klassenbewusstsein,* in *Werke* (Darmstadt: Luch-
    terhand, 1977), 2:257–397. I will be following Lukács's argument through
    the first two parts of his seminal essay "Reification and the Consciousness
    of the Proletariat."

22 Horkheimer and Adorno later explained this concisely: "According to
    Kant, philosophic judgment aims at the new; and yet it recognizes nothing
    new, since it always merely recalls what reason has always already de-
    posited in the object" (*Dialectic of Enlightenment,* trans. John Cumming
    [London: Verso, 1979], 26; *Dialektik der Aufklärung: Philosophische Frag-
    mente,* 1944, in *Gesammelte Schriften,* by Max Horkheimer [Frankfurt am
    Main: S. Fischer, 1987], 5:48f.).

23 Cf. Mark C. Taylor, *Altarity* (Chicago: University of Chicago Press, 1987),
    xxii. For a discussion of Lukács's relation to Fichte, see Martin Jay, *Marx-*

ism and Totality: The Adventures of a Concept from Lukács to Habermas (Cambridge: Polity Press, 1984), 104–109.

24 Lukács, *History and Class Consciousness,* 124; *Geschichte und Klassenbewusstsein,* 302.

25 Lukács, *History and Class Consciousness,* 130; *Geschichte und Klassenbewusstsein,* 309.

26 See Löwy, *Pour une sociologie des intellectuels révolutionnaires,* 210.

27 Lukács, *History and Class Consciousness,* 98; *Geschichte und Klassenbewusstsein,* 273.

28 Lukács, *History and Class Consciousness,* 90; *Geschichte und Klassenbewusstsein,* 264f.: "In this environment where time is transformed into abstract, exactly measurable, physical space, an environment at once the cause and effect of the scientifically and mechanically fragmented and specialised production of labour, the subjects of labour must likewise be rationally fragmented. On the one hand, the objectification of their labour-power into something opposed to their total personality (a process already accomplished with the sale of that labour-power as a commodity) is now made into the permanent ineluctable reality of their daily life. Here, too, the personality can do no more than look on helplessly while his own existence is reduced to an isolated particle and fed into an alien system. On the other hand, the mechanical disintegration of the process of production into its components also destroys those bonds that had bound individuals to a community in the days when production was still 'organic'. In this respect, too, mechanisation makes of them isolated abstract atoms whose work no longer brings them together directly and organically; it becomes mediated to an increasing extent exclusively by the abstract laws of the mechanism which imprisons them."

29 Cf. the first chapter, "The Concept of Enlightenment," of Adorno and Horkheimer's *Dialectic of Enlightenment,* 3–42; *Dialektik der Aufklärung,* 25–66.

30 Max Weber, *The Protestant Ethic and the Spirit of Capitalism,* trans. Talcott Parsons (New York: Routledge, 1992); *Die protestantische Ethik und der Geist des Kapitalismus* [1904–1905], in *Gesammelte Aufsätze zur Religionssoziologie* (Tübingen: J. C. B. Mohr, 1920), 1:17–206. See also Charles Taylor, *Sources of the Self: The Making of Modern Identity* (Cambridge, Mass.: Harvard University Press, 1989), 149ff.

31 In one of the few attempts to furnish his analysis of subjectivity with a historical explanation, Taylor clarifies this point: "It is clear for instance

that the forceful imposition of proletarian status on masses of ex-peasants who were chased off the land into the new centers of industrialization preceded and caused the acceptance of atomistic self-consciousness (frequently combated by new formulations of working-class solidarity) by so many of their descendants today" (*Sources of the Self,* 206f.). Taylor's reference is here E. P. Thompson's *The Making of the English Working Classes* (1964).

32 Perhaps needless to say, this did not apply to women, who were now constituted as civil subjects and yet were barred access to concrete political rights. Henceforth the "individual," and the "subject" as well, is a he, if it ever was anything else, and male and female subjectivity develop, as I will discuss shortly, along new yet still distinct historical lines. See Geneviève Fraisse, "A Philosophical History of Sexual Difference," trans. A. Goldhammer; and Nicole Arnaud-Duc, and "The Law's Contradictions," trans. A. Goldhammer, both in *A History of Women in the West,* vol. 4, *Emerging Feminism from Revolution to World War,* ed. Geneviève Fraisse and Michelle Perrot (Cambridge, Mass.: Harvard University Press, 1993), 48–113.

33 "Our fathers," Alexis de Tocqueville states in *L'Ancien Régime et la révolution* (1856), "did not have the word 'individualism', which we have coined for our own use, because in their time there was indeed no individual who did not belong to a group and who could be considered absolutely alone" (quoted in Steven Lukes, *Individualism* [New York: Harper and Row, 1973], 14).

34 Lukes, *Individualism,* 3–42.

35 See Ian Watt, *Myths of Modern Individualism: Faust, Don Quixote, Don Juan, Robinson Crusoe* (Cambridge: Cambridge University Press, 1996). In his analysis of four principal "myths" of modern individualism, Watt demonstrates how Faust, Don Quixote, Don Juan, and Robinson Crusoe all reached a peak of popularity in the romantic period through 1850. In the versions of the myths of Faust and Don Juan that precede this period, the heroes were sent to suffer in hell because of their selfish behavior. In romantic adaptions, however, the heroes no longer have to pay for their violations of social conventions. Had they previously embodied deterrent object lessons of vicious behavior, they now became ideals of virtue. According to Watt, this change demonstrates how Faust, Don Juan, and Don Quixote were reinterpreted through the paradigm of individualism. The admiration that bourgeois society showed for these heroes only makes sense if the autonomous individual had already become a model.

36 Jean-Jacques Rousseau, *Emile; ou, De l'éducation,* in *Oeuvres complètes,* ed. Bernard Gagnebin and Marcel Raymond (Paris: Gallimard, 1969), 4:554ff.

37 Anthony Cascardi, *The Subject of Modernity* (Cambridge: Cambridge University Press, 1992), 182. For Charles Taylor, too, the constitution of inwardness as a consequence of reification and rationalization is the main feature of modern subjectivity: "The new definition of the mastery of reason brings about an internalization of moral sources. When the hegemony of reason comes to be understood as rational control, the power to objectify body, world, and passions, that is, to assume a thoroughly instrumental stance towards them, then the sources of moral strength can no longer be seen as outside us in the traditional mode—certainly not in the way that they were for Plato, and I believe also for the Stoics, where they reside in a world order which embodies a Good we cannot but love and admire" (*Sources of the Self,* 151).

38 Lukács, *History and Class Consciousness,* 135; *Geschichte und Klassenbewusstsein,* 315. This third stage in the process of reification corresponds to the return of nature and mythological providence that Adorno and Horkheimer analyze in *Dialectic of Enlightenment:* "The individual is reduced to the nodal point of the conventional responses and modes of operation expected of him" (28; *Dialektik der Aufklärung,* 51).

39 For a discussion of this ambiguity in the concept of the subject, see Etienne Balibar, "Citizen Subject," in *Who Comes after The Subject?* ed. E. Cadava, P. Connor, and J.-L. Nancy (New York: Routledge, 1991), 33–57.

40 Herbert Marcuse, *Eros and Civilization: A Philosophical Inquiry into Freud,* 2d ed (Boston: Beacon Press, 1966), 57.

41 Lukács, *History and Class Consciousness,* 136; *Geschichte und Klassenbewusstsein,* 316.

42 Denis Diderot, *The Paradox of Acting,* trans. Walter Herries Pollock; published with *Masks or Faces?* by William Archer (New York: Hill and Wang, 1957), 53; "Paradoxe sur le comédien," in *Oeuvres complètes,* ed. Herbert Dieckmann and Jean Varloot (Paris: Hermann, 1995), 20:104.

43 See Herbert Jaumann, ed., *Rousseau in Deutschland: Neue Beiträge zur Erforschung seiner Rezeption* (Berlin: Walter de Gruyter, 1995), and in this volume especially Wilhelm Vosskamp, " 'Un Livre paradoxal': J.-J. Rousseaus 'Émile' in der deutschen Diskussion um 1800," 101–114.

44 Friedrich Schiller, *On the Aesthetic Education of Man, in a Series of Letters,* trans. E. M. Wilkinson and L. A. Willoughby (Oxford: Oxford Univer-

sity Press, 1967), 6th letter; *Über die ästhetische Erziehung des Menschen,* in *Werke und Briefe in Zwölf Bänden,* ed. Otto Dann et al. (Frankfurt am Main: Deutscher Klassiker Verlag, 1992), 8:572f.

45 Expressivist philosophies were not, of course, developed exclusively by German writers. Taylor quotes Samuel Coleridge: "In looking at objects of Nature while I am thinking . . . I seem rather to be seeking, as it were *asking,* a symbolical language for something within me that already and forever exists, than observing anything new"; and William Wordsworth: "I was often unable to think of external things as having external existence, and I communed with all that I saw as something not apart from, but inherent in, my own immaterial nature" (*Sources of the Self,* 301). It must of course be added that Coleridge and Wordsworth attended lectures in Göttingen and were in close contact with intellectual developments in Germany.

46 Johann Gottfried Herder, *Ideen zur Philosophie der Geschichte der Menschheit* [1784–1791], (Darmstadt: Joseph Melzer, 1966), 243 (bk. 9:4).

47 Johann Gottlieb Fichte, *Addresses to the German Nation* [1808], trans. R. F. Jones and G. H. Turnbull (Westport, Conn.: Greenwood Press, 1979), 135f.*; *Reden an die deutsche Nation* (Leipzig: Felix Meiner, 1943), 131. Herder also abhorred "the wild mixture of human races and nations," since this, in his view, was against the law of nature (*Ideen zur Philosophie der Geschichte der Menschheit,* 244).

48 See Musil's *Tagebücher,* 1:958: "The individual can fulfill himself organically only through the natural unity of the people. This thereby gives him the duty to sacrifice himself for the people, when necessary. The popular spirit [*Volksgeist*] of the trueborn people is like that of a beehive state. This is how the nation becomes mythic. Refers to romanticism. Rightly, insofar as it, too, searched to ground thinking upon feeling. Romanticism also sought, in accord with popular ideas, for the myth of the nation. (Novalis, C. D. Friedrich, Schelling, Adam Müller / that's how he saw Individual and Community / Fichte.)"

49 It should be pointed out that Fichte and Herder based their ideas of the people as an expressive totality on opposing assumptions. For Herder, each people is an expression of a natural law: just as each region has different flora and fauna, so each people has a different "Volksgeist." For Fichte, by contrast, each people is a particular expression of a divine law and hence linked to the universal. See Louis Dumont, *Essais sur l'individualisme: Une perspective anthropologique sur l'idéologie moderne* (Paris: Seuil, 1983), 115–132. Hegel's position would seem to bridge this

opposition. See *Vorlesungen über die Philosophie der Geschichte,* in *Werke* (Frankfurt am Main: Suhrkamp, 1986), 12:72.

50   As for the thinkers who elaborated on this expressive relationship, they thus confirmed Novalis's observation that philosophy is another name for homesickness.

51   Taylor, *Sources of the Self,* 376. This view is supported by Norbert Elias's account of the emergence of modern Western society, in which he observes a severance of a private inside from a social outside (*Über den Prozess der Zivilisation* [Frankfurt am Main: Suhrkamp, 1976], 1:251). A similar conclusion may also be drawn from Walter J. Ong's findings about the interiorization of reality occurring with the dissemination of literacy and the written word (*The Presence of the Word: Some Prolegomena for Cultural and Religious History* [Minneapolis: University of Minnesota Press, 1981]). Similarly, Louis A. Sass states that one "of the most fundamental presuppositions of contemporary Western society and thought is that each individual has some kind of inner being or personhood existing apart from or prior to his or her actions or social roles." He adds that this notion is far from universal; it is "absent not only in traditional societies of the non-Westernized world but also in the West prior to the modern age" (*Madness and Modernism: Insanity in the Light of Modern Art, Literature, and Thought* [Cambridge, Mass.: Harvard University Press, 1996], 98). Other principal analyses that support Lukács's account are Cascardi, *The Subject of Modernity;* Adorno and Horkheimer, *Dialectic of Enlightenment;* and Marcuse, *Eros and Civilization.*

52   Taylor, *Sources of the Self,* 111.

53   Eduard Spranger, "Geleitwort," in Fichte, *Reden an die deutsche Nation* (Leipzig: Felix Meiner, 1943), xiv.

54   Silvia Bovenschen, *Die imaginierte Weiblichkeit: Exemplarische Untersuchungen zu kulturgeschichtlichen und literarischen Präsentationsformen des Weiblichen* (Frankfurt am Main: Suhrkamp, 1979), esp. 24–42, 150–164.

55   Jean Bethke Elshtain, *Public Man, Private Woman: Women in Social and Political Thought,* 2d ed. (Princeton: Princeton University Press, 1993), 165. See also Bovenschen's chapter on Rousseau, "Sofie; oder, Über die Erziehung zur Ungleichheit," in *Die imaginierte Weiblichkeit,* 164–181; and Verena Ehrich-Haefli, "Rousseaus Sophie und ihre deutschen Schwestern: Zur Entstehung der bürgerlichen Geschlechterideologie," in *Rousseau in Deutschland,* ed. Jaumann, 115–162.

56 Tönnies, *Community and Society,* 163; *Gemeinschaft und Gesellschaft,* 160.

57 Bovenschen, *Die imaginierte Weiblichkeit,* 180.

58 Johann Wolfgang von Goethe, *Faust: A Tragedy,* ed. and trans. Stuart Atkins, in vol. 2 of *Collected Works* (Boston: Suhrkamp/Insel Publishers, 1984); *Faust: Eine Tragödie,* ed. Albrecht Schöne, in vol. 7:1 of *Sämtliche Werke* (Frankfurt am Main: Deutscher Klassiker Verlag, 1994), 464.

59 Lukács writes that in the late eighteenth and early nineteenth century, aesthetics conferred upon art "a philosophical importance that art was unable to lay claim to in previous ages" (*History and Class Consciousness,* 137; *Geschichte und Klassenbewusstsein,* 317). The construction of the modern notion of aesthetics is in this sense, as Terry Eagleton maintains, "inseparable from the construction of the dominant ideological forms of modern class-society, and indeed from a whole new form of human subjectivity appropriate to that social order" (*The Ideology of the Aesthetic* [Oxford: Blackwell, 1990], 3).

60 M. H. Abrams, *The Mirror and the Lamp: Romantic Theory and the Critical Tradition* (Oxford: Oxford University Press, 1953, 1971), 22. Although Abrams traces this "expressive idea of art" back to Longinus, it did not emerge as a cultural dominant until romanticism.

61 This is reflected in the institutional changes of the aesthetic field concurrent with the bourgeois assumption of cultural hegemony. In this process, aesthetic experience disappears from the village square or the feudal or royal court. It moves inside, locating itself in the seat rows of the theater, or it quietly withdraws to the bourgeois home, retreating into the armchair, occasionally striking up conversations in the salon. Jürgen Habermas has discussed the simultaneous development of bourgeois society and the restructuring of the realm of aesthetic experience, arguing that in feudal society, art enjoyed a representative function in the midst of public life, and that, beginning in the 1750s, it became a concern for the intimate sphere of the closed circle of the bourgeois family and friends, who through literature and music contemplated themselves as representatives of humanity. This sphere thus emerges as a compensatory space, where individuals are relieved of their roles as citizens and can contemplate their "true" nature as human beings. See Habermas, *Strukturwandel der Öffentlichkeit: Untersuchungen zu einer Kategorie der bürgerlichen Gesellschaft* [1962] (Frankfurt am Main: Suhrkamp, 1990), esp. 107–115. In Habermas's view, this is still the predominant function and value of art and the aesthetic. Bourgeois art, he states, has become the refuge for

a satisfaction of needs that have become, as it were, illegal in the social dynamic of bourgeois society. Bourgeois art has no tasks in the economic and political systems and can therefore address residual needs that can find no satisfaction elsewhere (*Legitimationsprobleme im Spätkapitalismus,* 2d ed. [Frankfurt am Main: Suhrkamp, 1973], 109ff.).

62 Horkheimer and Adorno, *Dialectic of Enlightenment,* 34: "The prisoner is present at a concert, an inactive eavesdropper like later concertgoers, and his spirited call for liberation fades like applause. Thus the enjoyment of art and manual labor break apart as the world of prehistory is left behind"; *Dialektik der Aufklärung,* 57.

63 See Musil's reply of December 1935 to a letter from *Frankfurter Zeitung,* which invited him to write an essay on the topic of the bildungsroman (*T* 2:1189); and Lukács, *The Theory of the Novel: A Historico-Philosophical Essay on the Forms of Great Epic Literature,* trans. Anna Bostock (Cambridge, Mass.: MIT Press, 1971), 132–143; *Die Theorie des Romans: Ein geschichtsphilosophischer Versuch über die Formen der grossen Epik,* 2d ed. (Neuwied: Luchterhand, 1963), 135–147.

64 For a discussion of the concept of Bildung, see James Rolleston, *Narratives of Ecstasy: Romantic Temporality in Modern German Poetry* (Detroit: Wayne State University Press, 1987), 11–66.

65 In Schlegel's account, the reader's hermeneutic activity implies, simultaneously, his or her aesthetic education: "Yet he who has an authentic, systematic instinct, a sense for the universe, that primary sensibility which makes Wilhelm so interesting, he feels to an equal extent everywhere the personality and the living individuality of the work, and the deeper he explores, the more inner relationships, affinities, and spiritual correspondances will he discover in it. If there ever was a book with a spirit, this must be the one" ("Über Goethes Meister" [1798], in *Kritische Ausgabe,* vol. 2, *Charakteristiken und Kritiken* I [Munich: Ferdinand Schöningh, 1967], 134).

66 In *Wilhelm Meister,* the representation of the hero's destiny is filtered through holistic ideas which, in Goethe's view, were expressed and confirmed by the structure of nature and of the arts. The great accomplishment of the novel, indeed the founding act of the bildungsroman as such, is due to the successful application of such ideas to the representation of the individual and the social world. Nature, society, individual, art—those are the four realms which in Goethe's hands blend into a harmonious circle of circles. The close relationship between Goethe's research in the natural sciences and his conception of *Wilhelm Meister* is perhaps best illus-

trated by his redefinition of the notion of *Bildungstrieb.* Like an existential kernel, this essence, Bildungstrieb, is present in each individual organic being. Jürgen Scharfschwerdt explains that the Bildungstrieb represents the power that allows all living beings not only to evolve, from their internal kernel, a distinct and individual organism, but simultaneously to grow together with the surrounding world, in order to develop "a harmonious unity between individual and world" (*Thomas Mann und der deutsche Bildungsroman: Eine Untersuchung zu den Problemen einer literarischen Tradition* [Stuttgart: W. Kohlhammer, 1967], 17f.).

67 Lukács, *The Theory of the Novel,* 132; *Die Theorie des Romans,* 135.

68 Franco Moretti, *The Way of the World: The "Bildungsroman" in European Culture* (London: Verso, 1987), 15.

69 Russell Berman, *The Rise of the Modern German Novel: Crisis and Charisma* (Cambridge, Mass.: Harvard University Press, 1986), 74–79.

70 Scharfschwerdt maintains that Goethe had to fall back on the aristocratic values of a precapitalist era in order to realize the harmony between self and world (*Thomas Mann und der deutsche Bildungsroman,* 21). Moretti supports his argument: "The definitive stabilization of the individual, and of his relationship with the world—'maturity' as the story's final stage—is therefore fully possible *only in the precapitalist world*" (*The Way of the World,* 27). The same view is held by Cascardi: "It is enough to see that the reconciliation between the self and the world in *Wilhelm Meister* is made possible only by the introduction of a masonic hierarchy of professions, classes and ranks" (*The Subject of Modernity,* 76). See also Georg Simmel's interesting remarks on Goethe's novel in *Grundfragen der Soziologie (Individuum und Gesellschaft)* [1917], in *Gesamtausgabe,* vol. 16, ed. G. Fitzi and D. Rammstedt (Frankfurt am Main: Suhrkamp, 1999), 144ff.

71 Jean-François Peyret, "Musil; ou, Les contradictions de la modernité," *Critique* 31, nos. 339–340 (August–September 1975): 849. See also Peter Nielsen's discussion on Musil and the novel of apprenticeship in *Mulighedernes Wien: Robert Musils romanaestetik i "Der Mann ohne Eigenschaften"* (Aarhus: Litteraturhistorisk Forlag, 1996), 84–92; and Alexander Honold, *Die Stadt und der Krieg: Raum- und Zeitkonstruktion in Robert Musils Roman "Der Mann ohne Eigenschaften"* (Munich: Wilhelm Fink, 1995), 292–312.

72 For Musil's explicit rejection of the bourgeois concept of *Bildung,* see his 1923 article "Ein wichtiges Buch" (*GW* 2:1622–25).

73 However, the most radicalized form of modernism, the avant-garde, brings this logic of aesthetic autonomization to its end through its attempt

to reintegrate art in society, or even transform society in the image of art. See Peter Bürger, *Theory of the Avant-Garde*, trans. Michael Shaw (Minneapolis: University of Minnesota Press, 1984), 15–34; *Theorie der Avantgarde*, 2d ed. (Frankfurt am Main: Suhrkamp, 1980), 26–44.

74 Friedrich Nietzsche, *History in the Service and Disservice of Life*, in *Unmodern Observations*, trans. Gary Brown, ed. William Arrowsmith (New Haven: Yale University Press, 1990), 104*; *Vom Nutzen und Nachteil der Historie für das Leben* [1874], in *Werke*, ed. Giorgio Colli and Mazzino Montinari (Berlin: Walter de Gruyter, 1967–1972), pt. 3, 1:268f.

75 Nietzsche, *History in the Service and Disservice of Life*, 105*; *Vom Nutzen und Nachteil der Historie*, 270.

76 Nietzsche, *History in the Service and Disservice of Life*, 108; *Vom Nutzen und Nachteil der Historie*, 274.

77 Theodor W. Adorno, *Kierkegaard: Construction of the Aesthetic*, trans. Robert Hullot-Kentor (Minneapolis: University of Minnesota Press, 1989), 27; *Kierkegaard: Konstruktion des Ästhetischen*, in *Gesammelte Schriften* (Frankfurt am Main: Suhrkamp, 1979), 2:45, 42.

78 Adorno, *Kierkegaard*, 44; *Kierkegaard*, 65.

79 Adorno, *Kierkegaard*, 42; *Kierkegaard*, 63.

80 "Paris, die Hauptstadt des XIX. Jahrhunderts" was written in 1935 for the Institut für Sozialforschung, while the French version, "Paris, Capitale du XIXème siècle," was written in 1939. In what follows I quote from both, which appear in Benjamin, *Gesammelte Schriften* (Frankfurt am Main: Suhrkamp, 1972–1989), 5, bk. 1: 45–59; 60–77. The German version is translated into English by Harry Zohn in *Charles Baudelaire: A Lyric Poet In The Era of High Capitalism*, by Walter Benjamin (London: Verso, 1983), 167–169.

81 Benjamin, "Paris, Capitale du XIXème siècle," 68.

82 Siegfried Giedion, in his superior historiography of the intérieur, maintains that this at once architectural and ideological space had been unthinkable without the upholsterer, who set the tone for interior decoration and furniture design during the nineteenth century. "The upholsterer, by embellishment of furniture and artistic hangings, sets up a fairyland to enchant the drabness of the industrial day" (*Mechanization Takes Command: A Contribution to Anonymous History* [Oxford: Oxford University Press, 1948; New York: Norton, 1969], 364).

83 Benjamin, *Charles Baudelaire*, 168f.; "Paris, Capitale du XIXème siècle," 67.

84 Honoré de Balzac, *History of the Thirteen*, trans. William Walton (Phila-

delphia: George Barrie and Son, 1896), 88; *Histoire des treize,* in *La Comédie humaine* (Paris: Gallimard, 1977), 5:838f.

85 "By and large, the house remains the great cultural achievement of women," Simmel states in his essay "Weibliche Kultur" (1911), adding that "to an eminent degree, housekeeping belongs" in the category of "secondary originality" (*Philosophische Kultur: Gesammelte Essais,* 3d ed. [Potsdam: Gustav Kiepenheuer, 1923], 307f).

86 On the "public" and "private" fantasies of the feminine, see Christine Buci-Glucksmann, *Baroque Reason: The Aesthetics of Modernity,* trans. Patrick Camiller (London: Sage, 1994), 91–123; *La Raison baroque: De Baudelaire à Benjamin* (Paris: Galilée, 1984), 113–161. Adorno and Horkheimer reveal the historicity of this constellation as well: "Prostitute and wife are the complements of female self-alienation in the patriarchal world: the wife denotes pleasure in the fixed order of life and property, whereas the prostitute takes what the wife's right of possession leaves free, and—as the wife's secret collaborator—subjects it again to the order of possession: she sells pleasure" (*Dialectic of Enlightenment,* 73f.; *Dialektik der Aufklärung,* 97).

87 Walter Benjamin, "Paris als Göttin: Phantasie über den neuen Roman der Fürstin Bibesco," in *Gesammelte Schriften,* 3:139f. I owe this reference to Marianne Ping Huang; see her "Om metropolernes modernitet och mangeartede rum," *Passage: Tidskrift for litteratur og kritik* (Aarhus), no. 22 (1996): 6.

88 Felix Dörmann, *Sensationen* (Vienna: Leopold Weiss, 1892), 34f. Translated from the German by Zaia Alexander. ("Ein Intérieur von lichter Scharlachseide, / Ein wohldurchwärmtes, traulichenges Heim. / Aus schlankgeformten Ständerlampen quillt, / Von buntgefärbten Abas-jours gedämpft,— / Ein rosig warmer Lichtstrom zitternd nieder. // Auf üppig weichen Eisbärfellen, ruht / Ein schlankes Weib, die Lippen halberbrochen, / Mit leicht-umblauten, müden Schwärmeraugen,— / [. . .] träumt und träumt von seelenheisser Freude, / Von zügellosem Schwelgen, trunknem Rasen, / . . . / Von einem letzten, niegekannten Glück, / Von einer Wonne, die der Wonnen höchste / Und doch nicht Liebe heisst —und träumt und träumt.")

89 Benjamin, *Charles Baudelaire,* 168; "Paris, die Hauptstadt des XIX. Jahrhunderts," 52.

90 Benjamin, *Charles Baudelaire,* 168 *; "Paris, die Haupstadt des XIX. Jahrhunderts," 53.

91 Josef M. Olbrich, "Das Haus der Sezession," *Der Architekt* 5 (January

1899): 5. Quoted in Carl E. Schorske, *Fin-de-Siècle Vienna: Politics and Culture* (New York: Vintage Books, 1981), 217.

92 Schorske, *Fin-de-Siècle Vienna*, 255.

93 Oswald Spengler, *Der Untergang des Abendlandes: Umrisse einer Morphologie der Weltgeschichte* (Munich: C. H. Beck'sche Verlagsbuchhandlung, 1923), 1:251–254. As for Broch, remarks on the ornament are found in many parts of his work, most concisely in "Ornamente (Der Fall Loos)" [1911], in *Kommentierte Werkausgabe* (Frankfurt am Main: Suhrkamp, 1977), 10, bk. 1:32f.: "Yet the ornament was the musical expression of the species and the spirit of *all* art, the quintessence of culture, the symbol of life, more lucid and concentrated than all reason." See also *Die Schlafwandler*, pt. 3, *1918: Hugenau oder die Sachlichkeit* [1931–1932], in *Kommentierte Werkausgabe*, 1:418f., 435ff., 444f.; and *Hofmannsthal und seine Zeit: Eine Studie*, in *Kommentierte Werkausgabe*, 9, bk. 2:111–135, 221–234.

94 See Jacques Le Rider, *Modernity and Crises of Identity: Culture and Society in Fin-de-Siècle Vienna*, trans. Rosemary Morris (New York: Continuum, 1993), 72f.; *Modernité viennoise et crises de l'identité* (Paris: Presses universitaires de France, 1990), 88f.

95 Adolf Loos, "Keramika" [1904], in *Trotzdem, 1900–1930*, 2d ed. (Vienna: Georg Prachner, 1982), 59. Translated from the German by Zaia Alexander.

96 Loos, "Ornament und Verbrechen," in *Trotzdem*, 78–88.

97 According to Benjamin, the historical fate of the expressivist conception of the subject is fulfilled by the hero in Ibsen's drama *Byggmester Solness* (1892; *The Master Builder*). Attempting to express his inner aspirations, love, and vanity in a magnificent house, the Master Builder stretches the capacity of the technical means at his disposal, and as the building comes crashing down, it brings Solness with it. "The attempt of the individual to assert himself, on the grounds of his interiority, against the challenge of technology leads to his downfall," Benjamin concludes (*Charles Baudelaire*, 168*; "Paris, die Hauptstadt des XIX. Jahrhunderts," 53).

98 Arnold Schoenberg and Wassily Kandinsky, *Letters, Pictures and Documents*, ed. Jelena Hahl-Koch, trans. John C. Crawford (London: Faber and Faber, 1984), 23, 25.

99 Thomas Harrison, *1910: The Emancipation of Dissonance* (Berkeley: University of California Press, 1996), 154.

100 Theodor W. Adorno, *Aesthetic Theory*, trans. Robert Hullot-Kentor (Minneapolis: University of Minnesota Press, 1997), 113*; *Ästhetische Theorie*,

in *Gesammelte Schriften,* 7:172. Fredric Jameson discusses this passage in *Late Marxism: Adorno; or, The Persistence of the Dialectic* (London: Verso, 1990), 202–211.

101 Otto Weininger, *Geschlecht und Charakter: Eine prinzipielle Untersuchung* [1903], 22d ed. (Vienna: Wilhelm Braumüller, 1921), 192.

102 Hermann Bahr, "Das unrettbare Ich," in *Dialog vom Tragischen* (Berlin: S. Fischer, 1904), 79–101.

103 Harrison, *1910,* 180.

104 However, this does not justify Harrison's description of *Der Mann ohne Eigenschaften* as a document of a "post-subjective age" (*1910,* 223). Musil's novel does not move beyond the problem of the subject (that would be an impossibility); it poses this problem in new terms.

105 August Strindberg, "Esplanadsystemet," *Dikter på vers och prosa* (Stockholm: Albert Bonniers, 1883).

106 Rainer Maria Rilke, *The Notebooks of Malte Laurids Brigge,* trans. M. D. Herter Norton (New York: Capricorn Books, 1958), 47f.; *Die Aufzeichnungen des Malte Laurids Brigge,* in *Gesammelte Werke* (Leipzig: Insel Verlag, 1927), 5:58.

2 The Architecture of Modern Identity

1 Musil's "Türen und Tore" was first published in *Sport im Bild* (1928), and shortly afterward in *Prager Presse* (1928). A final version is included in *Posthumous Papers of a Living Author,* trans. Peter Wortsman (Hygiene: Eridanos Press, 1987) (1935; *Nachlass zu Lebzeiten*), the last book of fiction by Musil to be published during his lifetime.

2 José Rizal, *Noli me tangere,* trans. León Maria Guerrero (London: Longman, 1986), 2.

3 See Reyner Banham's discussion of Le Corbusier's project, *Theory and Design in the First Machine Age* (London: Architectural Press, 1960), 244.

4 Georg Simmel, "The Metropolis and Mental Life," trans. Edward A. Shils, in Simmel, *On Individuality and Social Forms: Selected Writings,* ed. Donald N. Levine (Chicago: University of Chicago Press, 1971, 324–339; "Die Grossstädte und das Geistesleben," in *Brücke und Tür: Essays des Philosophen zur Geschichte, Religion, Kunst und Gesellschaft,* ed. Michael Landmann, with Margarete Susman (Stuttgart: Koehler, 1957), 227–242. Also Theodor W. Adorno, *Minima Moralia: Reflections from Damaged*

Life, trans. E. F. N. Jephcott (London: Verso, 1978), 38; *Minima Moralia: Reflexionen aus dem beschädigten Leben,* in *Gesammelte Schriften,* 4:42; Martin Heidegger, "Bauen Wohnen Denken," *Vorträge und Aufsätze* (Stuttgart: Neske, 1994), 155f.; Joseph Roth, *Anti-Christ,* trans. Moray Firth (New York: Viking, 1935), 110; *Der Antichrist* [1934], in *Werke* (Cologne: Kiepenhauer and Witsch, 1956), 3:757–59; and Gaston Bachelard, *The Poetics of Space,* trans. Maria Jolas (New York: Orion Press, 1964), 26f.; *La Poétique de l'espace* (Paris: Presses universitaires de France, 1958), 42.

5 For a phenomenological theory of the relation between the human body and space, see Bachelard, *The Poetics of Space.* For an account of the limitations of the phenomenological approach, see Fredric Jameson, "Architecture and the Critique of Ideology," *The Ideologies of Theory: Essays 1971–1986,* vol. 2, *The Syntax of History* (Minneapolis: University of Minnesota Press, 1988), 35ff.

6 Walter Moser has also identified this tendency in Musil's novel, but he sees it as a subversion of a *liberal* notion of the individual. On closer consideration, however, Musil's novel primarily reacts not against a liberal but an expressivist notion of the self that for long dominated German culture and that formed the foundation of various expressivist ideologies of culture, nationality, and race ("R. Musil et la mort de 'l'homme libéral,' " in *Robert Musil,* edited by Jean-Pierre Cometti [Paris: Editions Royaumont, 1986], 172–198).

7 Alexander Honold analyzes the representation of the city in Musil's novel, but without exploring how the novel's account of urban space is intertwined with its representation of human subjectivity (*Die Stadt und der Krieg: Raum- und Zeitkonstruktion in Robert Musils Roman "Der Mann ohne Eigenschaften"* [Munich: Wilhelm Fink, 1995], esp. 25–180).

8 See Eve Blau, *The Architecture of Red Vienna, 1919–1934* (Cambridge, Mass.: MIT Press, 1999).

9 Paul Rabinow, *French Modern: Norms and Forms of the Social Environment* (Cambridge, Mass.: MIT Press, 1989), 12ff.

10 Ibid., 278.

11 Ibid., 343.

12 Klaus R. Scherpe, "The City as Narrator: The Modern Text in Alfred Döblin's *Berlin Alexanderplatz,*" in *Modernity and the Text: Revisions of German Modernism,* ed. Andreas Huyssen and David Bathrick (New York: Columbia University Press, 1989), 165. The only weakness of this

interesting investigation of how modern literature represents urban space is that it neglects the most common reaction to the metropolis: the escape into the intérieur.

13 See William M. Johnston, *The Austrian Mind: An Intellectual and Social History, 1848–1938,* 2d ed. (Berkeley: University of California Press, 1972), 20ff.; and Robert A. Kann, *The Habsburg Empire: A Study in Integration and Disintegration* (New York: Frederick A. Praeger, 1957), 59–66.

14 Scherpe, "The City as Narrator," 166f.

15 A position which Klaus Laermann (*Eigenschaftslosigkeit: Reflexionen zu Musils Roman "Der Mann ohne Eigenschaften"* [Stuttgart: J. B. Metzler, 1970]) and Jochen Schmidt (*Ohne Eigenschaften: Eine Erläuterung zu Musils Grundbegriff* [Tübingen: Max Niemeyer, 1975]) see as the result of Ulrich's peculiar class anxiety.

16 In Eithne Wilkins and Ernst Kaiser's translation of *The Man Without Qualities* (London: Secker and Warburg, 1954), the title of the second part, "Seinesgleichen geschieht," is translated as "The Like of It Now Happens." Sophie Wilkins's solution — "Pseudoreality Prevails" — in the new translation (New York: Knopf, 1995) is more satisfactory. In the main text, however, Sophie Wilkins's translation of "Seinesgleichen" varies with the context.

17 See *The Man Without Qualities,* part 1, chs. 2, 8, 34, and 83.

18 See, for instance, Rainer Roth, ed., *Die letzten Tage der Menschheit: Bilder des Ersten Weltkrieges* (Berlin: Deutsches historisches Museum, 1994).

19 See Mark M. Anderson, *Kafka's Clothes: Ornament and Aestheticism in the Habsburg Fin de Siècle* (New York: Oxford University Press, 1992), 98–122.

20 Gilles Deleuze and Félix Guattari, *Kafka: Toward a Minor Literature,* trans. Dana Polan (Minneapolis: University of Minnesota Press, 1986), 43–71; *Kafka: Pour une littérature mineure* (Paris: Minuit, 1975), 79–130.

21 Alfred Döblin, *Berlin Alexanderplatz: The Story of Franz Biberkopf,* trans. Eugene Jolas (New York: Continuum, 1997), 172–183, 526; *Berlin Alexanderplatz: Die Geschichte vom Franz Biberkopf* (Berlin: S. Fischer, 1929), 151–160, 438.

22 Russell Berman summarizes Jünger's social ideas: "This matrix tolerates nothing but power, and the individual, whose demise is the threshold of all modernisms, is now replaced with the abstract unit of instrumentality. The single person is present only to the extent that he serves the functioning of the machine, and both battlefield and industry are the privileged loci of

the production of that unit" (*The Rise of the Modern German Novel: Crisis and Charisma* [Cambridge, Mass.: Harvard University Press, 1986], 215). See also Jeffrey Herf, *Reactionary Modernism: Technology, Culture, and Politics in Weimar and the Third Reich* (Cambridge: Cambridge University Press, 1984), esp. 70–108; Andrew Hewitt, *Fascist Modernism: Aesthetics, Politics, and the Avant-Garde* (Stanford: Stanford University Press, 1993); and the contributions in Richard J. Golsan, ed., *Fascism, Aesthetics, and Culture* (Hanover, N.H.: University Press of New England), 1992.

23   Johnston is thus mistaken in writing that "Musil yearned for a Gemeinschaft society, where Leibnizian attention to the whole might resume" (*The Austrian Mind*, 393). Equally mistaken is Schmidt in linking Musil's work to the mythology of "Blut und Boden" (*Ohne Eigenschaften*, 27). Although Ulrich Schelling does not administer any political guilt, he wrongly ascribes to Musil a longing for the expressive unity between self and world offered by the countryside (*Identität und Wirklichkeit bei Robert Musil* [Zürich: Atlantis, 1968], 30ff.).

24   Musil, *Beitrag zur Beurteilung der Lehren Machs* (Reinbek bei Hamburg: Rowohlt, 1980). On the relationship of Musil's thought to Mach, see Dieter Kühn's concise summary in *Analogie und Variation: Zur Analyse von Robert Musils Roman "Der Mann ohne Eigenschaften"* (Bonn: Bouvier, 1965), 21–26, 135–137; Renate von Heydebrand, *Die Reflexionen Ulrichs in Robert Musils Roman "Der Mann ohne Eigenschaften": Ihr Zusammenhang mit dem zeitgenössischen Denken* (Münster: Aschendorf, 1966), 48–57; Gerd Müller, *Dichtung und Wissenschaft: Studien zu Robert Musils Romanen "Die Verwirrungen des Zöglings Törless" und "Der Mann ohne Eigenschaften"* (Uppsala: Almqvist and Wiksells, 1971), 64–74; and Henri Arvon, "Robert Musil und der Positivismus," in *Robert Musil: Studien zu seinem Werk*, ed. K. Dinklage (Reinbek bei Hamburg: Rowohlt, 1970), 200–213. Judith Ryan analyzes the influence of early experimental psychology in general on literary modernism, including Musil. Ryan's analysis is not premised on an expressivist definition of the subject and can therefore account for the newness of Musil's conceptualization of subjectivity (*The Vanishing Subject: Early Psychology and Literary Modernism* [Chicago: University of Chicago Press, 1991], 207–223).

25   Otto Weininger, *Geschlecht und Charakter: Eine prinzipielle Untersuchung* [1903], 22d ed. (Vienna: Wilhelm Braumüller, 1921), 192.

26   Franz Hagmann lists passages in *The Man Without Qualities* where houses or interiors are thematized as sociological or existential indicators (*Aspekte der Wirklichkeit im Werke Robert Musils* [Bern: Herbert Lang, 1969],

156). A good analysis is Christoph Asendorf, "Hinter Glas: Wohnformen und Raumerfahrung bei Musil," in *Spiegelungen,* ed. R. Matzker, P. Küchler-Sakellariou, and M. Babias (Frankfurt am Main: Peter Lang, 1991), 185–195. See also Asendorf, " 'Eine sonderbare räumliche Inversion!': Wohnen bei Musil," in *Interieurs: Wiener Künstlerwohnungen, 1830–1930* (Vienna: Historisches Museum der Stadt Wien, 1990), 86–91.

27 This would seem to agree with Paul Smith's view, according to which the Marxist theory of subjectivity and reification works on the presupposition of "complete individuals," of a nonreified state characterized by plenitude and wholeness. This notion is then imposed as a standard against which "real" subjectivity as constituted under capitalism emerges as nothing but an effect of reification and ideology. However, insofar as Smith sees this unfortunate norm of experiential plenitude as a feature of Marxist theories of the subject and of reification *in general,* his critique is misguided. Evidently, it applies only to these theories of subjectivity and reification which depend on a theory of experience, Benjamin's, for instance, but also Lukács's. Smith's critique does not apply to Marx's theory, which is founded on a theory of value, not a theory of experience (*Discerning the Subject* [Minneapolis: University of Minnesota Press, 1988], 3–23).

28 This also accounts for the limited value of reading *The Man Without Qualities* as an object lesson about reification, in the traditional Marxist sense of the term. Three exponents of this tendency, Jochen Schmidt, Klaus Laermann, and Dagmar Herwig, measure Musil's novel against a norm of authentic subjectivity. Schmidt plots Musil against Kafka, arguing that while Kafka's protagonists voice their angst, thus giving expression to life under capitalism, Musil's protagonist withdraws to a mysticist sphere, in a futile attempt to rescue his authenticity (*Ohne Eigenschaften,* 59–62). Klaus Laermann analyzes Ulrich's search for an alternative reality in much the same way as Adorno interprets Kierkegaard's effort to shield himself in the intérieur. The subject's attempt to protect its identity in the face of social constraints does not lead to self-realization, however, but to a degeneration of subjectivity (*Eigenschaftslosigkeit,* ix–xi, 87–105, 131–163). Dagmar Herwig focuses on Musil's attempt to unify "Rationality and Mysticism" in his search for the right way of life, concluding that this project presupposes an unacceptable division between the concrete historical reality of the individual and the speculative mind. Interestingly, Herwig argues that the impossibility of resolving this contradiction pushes Musil's novel into a deadlock in which neither social reform nor

self-realization is thinkable. She points out that this deadlock can only be overcome by abolishing actually existing reality. Consequently, Herwig sees Ulrich as a model for the utopian revolutionary, which is contrary to the views of Schmidt and Laermann, who denounce him as a detached aristocrat (*Der Mensch in der Entfremdung: Studien zur Entfremdungsproblematik anhand des Werkes von Robert Musil* [Munich: Paul List, 1972], 128, 143, cf. 111ff.). In a more elaborate study of the formal aspects of *The Man Without Qualities,* Ulf Schramm registers the repercussions of the widening chasm between subject and world on the level of the narrative discourse, showing that the novel presents the reader with the impossible choice between a world that is real but devoid of meaning—Vienna and the Parallel Campaign—and a world that is meaningful but devoid of reality—the mysticism of what Musil termed "the other condition" (*Fiktion und Reflexion: Überlegungen zu Musil und Beckett* [Frankfurt am Main: Suhrkamp, 1967], 206–229). This marks a return of the dualistic framework that governs Musil criticism in general. In this case, however, the dualisms are posited as historical contradictions confronting Musil. Still, when these critics then thematize the inability of Musil's novel to go beyond these contradictions, their historicizing approach turns normative; Musil's novel fails because it does not construct the mediations that could link the subject to the world as an interrelated part of an expressive social totality. This is also where I disagree with Hartmut Böhme's important work. His argument tends to slide from an analytical course to a normative one. Arguing that the alienation of Musil's protagonist truthfully represents the condition of the individual in capitalist society, Böhme then recriminates Musil for not having shown how the subject could master the historical forces that created him in the first place (*Anomie und Entfremdung: Literatursoziologische Untersuchungen zu den Essays Robert Musils und seinem Roman "Der Mann ohne Eigenschaften"* [Kronberg: Scriptor, 1974], 146–156).

29 Simply stated, Lukács's Marxism, particularly his notions of communism and of the class consciousness of the proletariat, is founded on the ideal of an expressivist totality in which individual and society correspond. The same applies to Lukács's literary theory, in which "critical realism" functions as the norm, while naturalism and modernism are deviations produced by false consciousness. Although I regard Lukács's *History and Class Consciousness* as an exemplary analysis of expressivist subjectivity and its intellectual manifestations, I think his theory is insufficient for ana-

lyzing the advanced stages of commodification and rationalization actualized by Musil's novel. For an analysis of the concept of reification, see Moishe Postone, *Time, Labour, and Social Domination: A Reinterpretation of Marx's Critical Theory* (Cambridge: Cambridge University Press, 1993). See also the chapter on Lukács's concept of totality in Martin Jay, *Marxism and Totality: The Adventures of a Concept from Lukács to Habermas* (Cambridge: Polity Press, 1984).

30 R. D. Laing, *The Divided Self: An Existential Study in Sanity and Madness* [1959] (Harmondsworth, England: Penguin, 1990), 137–159. Similarly, Jacques Lacan argues that the psychotic individual remains in an Imaginary universe that eventually replaces the symbolically mediated experience of the Real. In psychoanalytic theory, psychosis is generally seen as the result of a failed "primal repression." Primal repression is an evolutionary phase during which the child goes through the Oedipal conflict, acquires language, and enters what Lacan calls the "Symbolic order." In the case of the psychotic, entrance into the Symbolic order has never taken place; it has been inhibited by a *foreclosure.* Hence, the psychotic is unable to use language to represent self and world. See Jacques Lacan, "On a Question Preliminary to Any Possible Treatment of Psychosis," *Écrits: A Selection,* trans. Alan Sheridan (London: Tavistock, 1977), 179–225. See also Anika Lemaire, *Jacques Lacan,* trans. David Macey (London: Routledge and Kegan Paul, 1977), 230–246.

31 The classical study of this theme is Otto Rank, *Der Doppelgänger: Eine Psychoanalytische Studie* (Leipzig: Internationaler Psychoanalytischer Verlag, 1925). See also Paul Coates, *The Double and the Other: Identity as Ideology in Post-Romantic Fiction* (New York: St. Martin's Press, 1988).

32 Bertolt Brecht, "Die sieben Todsünden der Kleinbürger," *Gesammelte Werke in 20 Bänden* (Frankfurt am Main: Suhrkamp, 1967), 7:2860.

33 The theme of the double in Musil is treated in, for example, Annie Reniers-Servranckx, *Robert Musil: Konstanz und Entwicklung von Themen, Motiven und Strukturen in den Dichtungen* (Bonn: Bouvier, 1972), 34–46; Pierre V. Zima, *L'Ambivalence romanesque: Proust, Kafka, Musil,* rev. ed. (Frankfurt am Main: Peter Lang, 1988), 201–218; and Andrew Webber, *Sexuality and the Sense of Self in the Works of Georg Trakl and Robert Musil* (London: Modern Humanities Research Association and Institute of Germanic Studies, 1990), 150–181. None of these scholars investigates the historical coordinates of this figure, however.

34 The philosophical and scientific models elaborated and alluded to in this

passage have been interpreted by Asendorf ("Hinter Glas") and Heyde-brand (*Die Reflexionen Ulrichs,* 96–103).

35 Fredric Jameson, *Postmodernism; or, The Cultural Logic of Late Capital-ism* (Durham, N.C.: Duke University Press, 1991), 14.

36 Georg Lukács, *Die Seele und die Formen: Essays* [1911] (Neuwied: Luch-terhand, 1971), 164.

37 See introduction, note 9, which discusses the tendency in Musil scholar-ship to ascribe an ideal of expressive harmony to Musil's novel.

38 This, roughly, is how Musil's mysticism is interpreted by Martina Wagner-Egelhaaf, that is, as an attempt, which eventually must fail, to integrate the experience of mysticism with the experience of modernity (*Mystik der Moderne: Die visionäre Ästhetik der deutschen Literatur im 20. Jahr-hundert* [Stuttgart: Metzler, 1989], 144.

39 This is also the major point of Honold's work, argued convincingly and in detail (*Die Stadt und der Krieg,* 411–485). It might be objected that the model experience of the other condition is what the novel terms "the for-gotten, highly relevant story of the major's wife" (*MWQ* 126–132 / *MoE* 120–126). Yet this experience is never represented as such in the novel, only recalled as a personal memory or myth, in the same way as Ulrich recalls other, collective myths when trying to grasp the vertiginous pos-sibilities of modernity.

40 Charles Baudelaire, *Intimate Journals,* trans. Christopher Isherwood (London: Blackamore Press, 1930), 29; "Journaux intimes: Fusées," *Oeuvres complètes,* ed. F.-F. Gautier and Y.-G. Dantec (Paris: Éditions de la Nouvelle Revue Française, 1937), 6:249.

41 Baudelaire, *Intimate Journals,* 31; "Journaux intimes," 250f. See Buci-Glucksmann's comment on this passage (*Baroque Reason: The Aesthetics of Modernity,* trans. Patrick Camiller [London: Sage, 1994], 169–171; *La Raison baroque: De Baudelaire à Benjamin* [Paris: Galilée, 1984], 239–240).

42 Hermann Bahr, *Dialog vom Tragischen* (Berlin: S. Fischer, 1904), 114.

43 Arnold Hauser, *The Social History of Art,* trans. Stanley Godman and Arnold Hauser (London: Routledge and Kegan Paul, 1951), 871, cf. 907ff.; *Sozialgeschichte der Kunst und Literatur,* 2d ed. (Munich: C. H. Beck, 1967), 929, cf. 969ff. Cf. Claudio Magris, *Der habsburgische Mythos in der österreichischen Literatur,* trans. M. Pásztory (Salzburg: Otto Müller, 1966), 184–190.

3   A Story with Many Ends

1   Catherine Belsey, *Critical Practice* (London: Routledge, 1980), 70.

2   Ibid.

3   Philippe Hamon, "Un Discours contraint," in *Littérature et réalité*, by Roland Barthes et al. (Paris: Seuil, 1982), 159f.

4   This panorama has been mapped by several Musil scholars, for example, Cornelia Blasberg, *Krise und Utopie der Intellektuellen: Kulturkritische Aspekte in Robert Musils Roman "Der Mann ohne Eigenschaften"* (Stuttgart: Hans-Dieter Heinz, 1984); Alexander Honold, *Die Stadt und der Krieg: Raum- und Zeitkonstruktion in Robert Musils Roman "Der Mann ohne Eigenschaften"* (Munich: Wilhelm Fink, 1995), 281ff.; Götz Müller, *Ideologiekritik und Metasprache in Robert Musils Roman "Der Mann ohne Eigenschaften"* (Munich: Wilhelm Fink, 1972); and Karl Corino, *Robert Musil: Leben und Werk in Bildern und Texten* (Reinbek bei Hamburg: Rowohlt, 1988).

5   There are numerous interpretations of chapter 1 of *The Man Without Qualities*. Bernd-Rüdiger Hüppauf focuses on the contrast between the narrative's employment of two incommensurate registers of language and knowledge. In his view, there is a hierarchy of discourses in which the concrete account focalized through the individual is linked to "empirical reality," which is then subordinated to the abstract register, which is said to be metaphorical and conceptual. Hüppauf thus makes an ontological distinction between two realms of the real. By contrast, I want to argue that Musil's differentiation is less concerned with separate domains of reality than with a separation of two epistemological approaches to the same reality. Hence, the novel preserves the tension between these approaches, avoiding positing one of them as more "truthful" than the other (*Von sozialer Utopie zur Mystik: Zu Robert Musils "Der Mann ohne Eigenschaften"* [Munich: Wilhelm Fink, 1971], 90–98). Other useful interpretations are offered by Hartmut Böhme, "Eine Zeit ohne Eigenschaften: Robert Musil und die Posthistoire," *Natur und Subjekt* (Frankfurt am Main: Suhrkamp, 1988), 308–333; Ulf Schramm, *Fiktion und Reflexion: Überlegungen zu Musil und Beckett* (Frankfurt am Main: Suhrkamp, 1967), 13–19; Honold, *Die Stadt und der Krieg,* 25–94. Ulrich Karthaus, *Der andere Zustand: Zeitstrukturen im Werke Robert Musils* (Berlin: E. Schmidt, 1965); Helga Honold, "Die Funktion des Paradoxen bei Robert Musil" (Ph.D. diss., Tübingen, 1963); and Wolfdietrich Rasch, *Über Robert Mu-*

sils Roman "Der Mann ohne Eigenschaften" (Göttingen: Vandenhoeck und Ruprecht, 1967). See also Jochen Schmidt, *Ohne Eigenschaften: Eine Erläuterung zu Musils Grundbegriff* (Tübingen: Max Niemeyer, 1975), 70–78; and Beda Alleman, *"Musil": Ironie und Dichtung* (Pfullingen: Neske, 1956), 177–220. A more questionable interpretation is Günter Graf, *Studien zur Funktion des Ersten Kapitels von Robert Musils Roman "Der Mann ohne Eigenschaften": Ein Beitrag zur Unwahrhaftigkeits-Typik der Gestalten* (Göppingen: Göppingen Arbeiten zur Germanistik, 1969), 14–23, 239–241.

6 Gérard Genette, *Narrative Discourse: An Essay in Method,* trans. Jane E. Lewin (Ithaca: Cornell University Press, 1980), 161; "Discours du récit," in *Figures III* (Paris: Seuil, 1972), 183.

7 For a discussion of the relation between Musil's narrative and early cinematography, see Christian Rogowski, "Ein andres Verhalten zur Welt: Robert Musil und der Film," *Sprachkunst: Beiträge zur Literaturwissenschaft* 23 (1992): 105–118.

8 For an analysis of Musil's satire, see Helmut Arntzen, *Satirischer Stil: Zur Satire Robert Musils im "Mann ohne Eigenschaften,"* 3d ed. (Bonn: Bouvier, 1983).

9 Fredric Jameson's analysis of Alain Robbe-Grillet deals with this tension between surface and subtext in high modernist narratives. See "Modernism and Its Repressed; or, Robbe-Grillet as Anti-Colonialist," *The Ideologies of Theory: Essays 1971–1986* (Minneapolis: University of Minnesota Press, 1988), 1:167–180.

10 Similarly, Schelling, Kühn, and Schramm have demonstrated that the style and organization of Musil's novel continually "derealize" social reality. According to Schelling and Kühn, the narrative works by way of "analogy," inserting unexpected and alogical contrasts and connections through which the "pseudo-real" order of things ("das Seinesgleichen") is undone, so as to disclose a more basic level of reality. Since these critics associate this level with a "true" representation of reality, they ascribe to Musil an expressivist notion of the subject, because they define the subjectivity that Musil, allegedly, is searching for as an expression of this authentic realm of reality. See Ulrich Schelling, "Das analogische Denken bei Robert Musil," in *Robert Musil Studien zu seinem Werk,* ed. Karl Dinklage (Reinbek bei Hamburg: Rowohlt, 1970), 170–199; Dieter Kühn, *Analogie und Variation: Zur Analyse von Robert Musils Roman "Der Mann ohne Eigenschaften"* (Bonn: Bouvier, 1965); and Schramm, *Fiktion und Reflexion.*

11 Pierre V. Zima, *L'Ambivalence romanesque: Proust, Kafka, Musil,* rev. ed. (Frankfurt am Main: Peter Lang, 1988), 291.

12 Cf. Ulrich Schelling: "Musil treats the external course of events which runs through time and space, with its fixed locations, topographical order, and chronological relations, its motivations and causal links, just as carelessly as any narrator of romanticism" ("Das analogische Denken bei Robert Musil," 170). See also Massimo Cacciari: "Time explodes into a myriad of moments that accompany, upon complete disenchantment with any eschatological perspective, maximum attention to the *fact,* the event, the moment" (*Posthumous People: Vienna at the Turning Point,* trans. Rodger Friedman [Stanford: Stanford University Press, 1996], 200f.). And Hüppauf, *Von sozialer Utopie zur Mystik,* 25ff.

13 Dorrit Cohn, *Transparent Minds: Narrative Modes for Presenting Consciousness in Fiction* (Princeton: Princeton University Press, 1978), 14. The categories are defined in this way: (1) psychonarration: the narrator's discourse about a character's consciousness; (2) quoted monologue: a character's mental discourse; (3) narrated monologue: a character's mental discourse in the guise of the narrator's discourse. Quoted monologue would here correspond to Joyce's stream-of-consciousness or "monologue intérieur."

14 Ibid., 43.

15 I am here benefitting from Walter Moser's discussion of Musil's correspondence ("R. Musil et la mort de 'l'homme libéral,' " in *Robert Musil,* ed. Jean-Pierre Cometti [Paris: Editions Royaumont, 1986], 195).

16 Genette, *Narrative Discourse,* 210; "Discours du récit," 223.

17 Ibid.

18 J. P. Stern, " 'Reality' in *Der Mann ohne Eigenschaften,* " in *Musil in Focus: Papers from a Centenary Symposium,* ed. L. Huber and J. J. White (London: Institute of Germanic Studies, University of London, 1982), 77.

19 Musil notes this same idea twice in his journals: "Einen Menschen ganz aus Zitaten zusammensetzen!" (*T* 1:356, 443)

20 Theodor W. Adorno, "The Position of the Narrator in the Contemporary Novel," in *Notes to Literature,* ed. Rolf Tiedemann, trans. Shierry Weber Nicholsen (New York: Columbia University Press, 1992), 1:33; "Standort des Erzählers im zeitgenössischen Roman," in *Noten zur Literatur,* in *Gesammelte Schriften* (Frankfurt am Main: Suhrkamp, 1970–1978), 11:67.

21 The irony is, of course, that Musil constructed Moosbrugger from newspaper reports. Moosbrugger borrows his traits from the murderers and mental patients Christian Voigt, Fritz Haarmann, and Florian Grossru-

batscher, who stirred the imagination of the Viennese public. See Karl Corino's articles "Ein Mörder macht Literaturgeschichte: Florian Grossrubatscher, ein Modell für Musils Moosbrugger," in *Robert Musil und die kulturellen Tendenzen seiner Zeit,* ed. Josef Strutz (Munich: Wilhelm Fink, 1983), 130–147; and "Zerstückt und durchdunkelt: Der Sexualmörder Moosbrugger im 'Mann ohne Eigenschaften' und sein Modell," *Musil-Forum* (Saarbrücken) 10 (1984): 105–119; as well as Corino's remarks in *Robert Musil: Leben und Werk,* 358.

22 Anne Longuet Marx, "La Rhapsodie Musilienne," *Europe* 69, nos. 741–742 (January–February 1991): 16.

23 Genette, *Narrative Discourse,* 113–127; "Discours du récit," 145–156.

24 Zima uses this terminology in *L'Ambivalence romanesque,* 219–308.

25 Jean-François Lyotard, *The Postmodern Condition: A Report on Knowledge,* trans. Geoff Bennington and Brian Massumi (Minneapolis: University of Minnesota Press, 1984), 15; *La Condition postmoderne: Rapport sur le savoir* (Paris: Minuit, 1979), 30f.

26 Cf. Stern, " 'Reality' in *Der Mann ohne Eigenschaften,*" 79.

27 Hermann Broch, *The Death of Virgil,* trans. Jean Starr Untermeyer (New York: Pantheon, 1945), 481; *Der Tod des Vergil,* in *Kommentierte Werkausgabe* (Frankfurt am Main: Suhrkamp, 1976), 4:454.

28 Ernst Fischer, *Von Grillparzer zu Kafka: Sechs Essays* (Vienna: Globus, 1962), 277.

29 Hermann Broch, "Nachruf auf Robert Musil," in *Kommentierte Werkausgabe* (Frankfurt am Main: Suhrkamp, 1975), 9, bk. 1:98f.

30 Burton Pike, *Robert Musil: An Introduction to His Work* (Ithaca: Cornell University Press, 1961), 199.

4   Subjectivity Degree Zero

1 Since Musil scholarship has commonly been framed by an idealist and expressivist paradigm, poststructuralist approaches to Musil's texts have been greatly vitalizing. In some cases, however, new discoveries have been bought at the cost of a certain one-sidedness, perhaps inevitable, as some scholars have treated *The Man Without Qualities* as an illustration of the theory in question; examples are Peter Henninger's Lacanian study, *Der Buchstabe und der Geist: Unbewusste Determinierung im Schreiben Robert Musils* (Frankfurt am Main: Peter Lang, 1980); Dieter Heyd's more general psychoanalytic reading, *Musil-Lektüre: Der Text, das Unbe-*

wusste: Psychosemiologische Studien zu Robert Musils theoretischem Werk und zum Roman "Der Mann ohne Eigenschaften" (Frankfurt am Main: Peter Lang, 1980); and Thomas Pekar's *Die Sprache der Liebe bei Robert Musil* (Munich: Wilhelm Fink, 1989), which borrows many perspectives from Barthes's later writings. Similarly, and as I mentioned in chapter 2, note 28, there are several studies from the 1970s which, inspired by Frankfurt school approaches, reduce Musil's novel to a case study of reification.

2 Paul Ricoeur stresses this point: "It is in telling our own stories that we give ourselves an identity. . . . We recognize ourselves in the stories that we tell about ourselves. It makes very little difference whether these stories are true or false, fiction as well as verifiable history provides us with an identity" ("History as Narrative and Practice," *Philosophy Today* [fall 1985]: 214). In the same vein, Charles Taylor states: "In order to make minimal sense of our lives, in order to have an identity, we need an orientation to the good, . . . [and] this sense of the good has to be woven into my understanding of my life as an unfolding story." A basic condition of making sense of ourselves is thus "that we grasp our lives as *narrative*" (*Sources of the Self: The Making of Modern Identity* [Cambridge, Mass.: Harvard University Press, 1989], 47). Fredric Jameson argues that narrative is one of the prime functions of the human mind: "Much of what passes for conceptual or scientific writing is itself secretly narrative in character. . . . [N]arrative is one of the basic categorial forms . . . under which synchronic and analytic thinking is itself subsumed and put in perspective" ("Symbolic Inference; or, Kenneth Burke and Ideological Analysis," in *The Ideologies of Theory: Essays 1971–1986* [Minneapolis: University of Minnesota Press, 1988], 1:140). Alasdair MacIntyre also argues that experience is always structured like a narrative: "We all live out narratives in our lives and . . . we understand our own lives in terms of the narrative that we live out" (*After Virtue: A Study in Moral Theory* [Notre Dame, Ind.: University of Notre Dame Press, 1984], 212).

3 Walter Benjamin, "The Storyteller: Reflections on the Works of Nikolai Leskov," in *Illuminations,* ed. and intro. Hannah Arendt, trans. Harry Zohn (London: Fontana, 1973), 83–109; "Der Erzähler: Betrachtungen zum Werk Nikolai Lesskows" [1935], in *Gesammelte Schriften,* 2, bk. 2: 438–465.

4 Alain Robbe-Grillet, *Pour un nouveau roman* (Paris: Minuit, 1963), 31.

5 Anthony Paul Kerby, *Narrative and the Self* (Bloomington: Indiana University Press, 1991), 40f.

6 Barbara Hardy, "Towards a Poetics of Fiction: 3. An Approach through Narrative," *Novel* 2, no. 1 (1968): 5.

7 Louis O. Mink, *Historical Understanding*, ed. Brian Fay, Eugene O. Golob, and Richard T. Vann (Ithaca: Cornell University Press, 1987), 60.

8 Michel Foucault, *The Order of Things: An Archaeology of the Human Sciences* (New York: Pantheon Books, 1970), xxi; *Les Mots et les choses: Une archéologie des sciences humaines* (Paris: Gallimard, 1966), 11.

9 Foucault, *The Archaeology of Knowledge*, trans. A. M. Sheridan Smith (New York: Harper and Row, 1972), 27; *L'Archéologie du savoir* (Paris: Gallimard, 1969), 38.

10 Hartmut Böhme, *Anomie und Entfremdung: Literatursoziologische Untersuchungen zu den Essays Robert Musils und seinem Roman "Der Mann ohne Eigenschaften"* (Kronberg: Scriptor, 1974), 102ff.

11 Michael André Bernstein, *Foregone Conclusions: Against Apocalyptic History* (Berkeley: University of California Press, 1994), 1.

12 Alexander Honold is the only critic who has sufficiently emphasized the significance of the First World War for Musil's fiction. He examines how Musil's war experience is stylistically and conceptually reworked into the dominant theme of the other condition, and how this experience then returns in thematic constellations dealing with the experiences of shock, transgression, criminality, mysticism, and other liminal states. Honold's investigation, however, fails to discuss how this experience relates to the structure of subjectivity, and it also does not discuss the paramount issue of cultural and national identity (*Die Stadt und der Krieg: Raum- und Zeitkonstruktion in Robert Musils Roman "Der Mann ohne Eigenschaften"* [Munich: Wilhelm Fink, 1995], 181–274, 471–486).

13 Still, Bernstein's point is well taken, for he mobilizes *The Man Without Qualities* as an example in his critique of certain fatalist tendencies in Zionist ideology, where centuries of European-Jewish diaspora are reduced to a mere foreshadowing of the Holocaust.

14 Cf. Böhme's analysis of the novel's temporal structure: "Theoretische Probleme der Interpretation von Robert Musils Roman 'Der Mann ohne Eigenschaften," in *Robert Musil,* ed. Renate von Heydebrand (Darmstadt: Wissenschaftliche Buchgesellschaft, 1982), 125–131.

15 Albrecht Schöne, "Zum Gebrauch des Konjunktivs bei Robert Musil," in *Robert Musil,* ed. Heydebrand, 19–53.

16 Ibid., 22. According to Schöne, the subjunctive mood is sometimes used by Musil to increase the weight of the real. This is what he calls *conjunc-*

tivus irrealis: first, a situation is described in the indicative mood; second, an action rendered in the subjunctive mood is allowed to transform this situation; third, there is a list of conditions that must apply if this particular action is to be realized; finally, there follows a disclaimer stating that these conditions were not fulfilled, hence the action could not have taken place; and consequently, the status quo still prevails. A certain description of the real is thus not only set in place as real but also notarized as truth by the authorial voice. *Conjunctivus potentialis* takes a divergent route: first, a situation is described in the indicative; second, an action described in the subjunctive is allowed to transform this situation; finally, there follows not a number of limiting conditions but a list of all possible consequences that the action would generate, were it to take place. Or as Schöne puts it: "An experiment is conducted not in order to demonstrate phenomena that are already known, as during a school lesson, but rather in order to establish the as yet unknown result that a certain situation may lead to ('what would happen, if . . .')."

17 Ibid., 25.

18 Ibid., 27.

19 See, for instance, Elisabeth Albertsen: "A novel undertaking to find all possibilities, . . . could have no end, because at each resolution the novelist must say to himself, 'It could just as well be different,' or, alternately, 'it could just as well be phrased differently' " (*Ratio und "Mystik" im Werk Robert Musils* [Munich: Nymphenburger Verlagshandlung, 1968], 20). See also Schöne, "Zum Gebrauch des Konjunktivs"; and Gerd Müller, *Dichtung und Wissenschaft: Studien zu Robert Musils Romanen "Die Verwirrungen des Zöglings Törless" und "Der Mann ohne Eigenschaften"* (Uppsala: Almqvist and Wiksells, 1971), 237–241.

20 See introduction, note 1, which briefly discusses Musil's ideas on the closure of *The Man Without Qualities.*

21 For a thorough investigation of these problems, see Gerd-Theo Tewilt, *Zustand der Dichtung: Interpretationen zur Sprachlichkeit des "anderen Zustands" in Robert Musils "Der Mann ohne Eigenschaften"* (Münster: Aschendorf, 1990).

22 This idea is also suggested by Honold, discussing how Musil's novel portrays the war as at once unavoidable and unnecessary: "Musil thus had to intertwine his *posteventum* historical knowledge into the story about prewar society so that the development of this society toward the war could, at each moment, appear as at once open and yet irreversible" (*Die Stadt und der Krieg,* 260).

23 Fredric Jameson, *The Seeds of Time* (New York: Columbia University Press, 1994), 56. Interestingly, Musil presents this problem of imagining absolute freedom through its symmetrical opposite, by stating the impossibility of imagining absolute repression, or hell: "Hell is not interesting, it is terrifying. If it has not been humanized—as by Dante, who populated it with writers and other prominent figures, thereby distracting attention from the technicalities of punishment—but an attempt has been made to represent it in some original fashion, even the most fertile minds never get beyond childish tortures and unimaginative distortions of physical realities. But it is precisely the bare idea of an unimaginable and therefore inescapable everlasting punishment and agony, the premise of an inexorable change for the worse, impervious to any attempt to reverse it, that has the fascination of an abyss" (*MWQ* 1070 / *MoE* 986).

24 Jameson, *Seeds of Time,* 57.

25 Jean-Paul Sartre, *Being and Nothingness: An Essay on Phenomenological Ontology,* trans. Hazel E. Barnes (New York: Philosophical Library, 1956), 28; *L'Etre et le néant: Essai d'ontologie phénoménologique* (Paris: Gallimard, 1943), 64.

26 Julia Kristeva, *Revolution in Poetic Language,* trans. Margaret Waller (New York: Columbia University Press, 1984), 109; *La Révolution du langage poétique: L'avant-garde à la fin du XIXe siècle—Lautréamont et Mallarmé* (Paris: Seuil, 1974), 101.

27 Slavoj Žižek, *The Sublime Object of Ideology* (London: Verso, 1989), 176ff.

28 Kristeva, *Revolution in Poetic Language,* 111; *La Révolution du langage poétique,* 103. Kristeva quotes Hegel arguing that negativity is "the *innermost* and *most objective* moment of Life and Spirit, by virtue of which a subject, the person, the free, has being."

29 Kristeva, *Revolution in Poetic Language,* 118; *La Révolution du langage poétique,* 109.

30 Kristeva's notion of the semiotic order refers to a modality of subjectivity that precedes symbolization. It is not, however, anterior to the social, since the social is present to the child from the day of its birth through the mediation of family. What takes place in the semiotic order is thus a structuring of psychic energies and a facilitation of certain drives, which together constitute what Kristeva calls the *chora:* "a nonexpressive totality formed by the drives and their stases in a motility that is as full of movement as it is regulated" (*Revolution in Poetic Language,* 25; *Révolution du langage poétique,* 23). The chora does not express anything, but is characterized by a mobility and rhythmicity that, far from being

chaotic or arbitrary, are articulated differently than the symbolic system which enables and restricts the subject's production of meaning and identity (20–30 / 86–89).

31 Cf. Lacan, "The Function and Field of Speech and Language in Psychoanalysis," *Ecrits: A Selection*, trans. Alan Sheridan (London: Tavistock, 1977), 68.

32 I am here following Kaja Silverman's account of the semiotic subject. See her *The Subject of Semiotics* (Oxford: Oxford University Press, 1983), esp. 126–193. See also Kerby, *Narrative and the Self*, 101–108.

33 Hence Žižek's seemingly paradoxical statement that identity and alienation are strictly correlative (*The Sublime Object of Ideology*, 24).

34 Sartre, *Being and Nothingness*, 204–218; *L'Etre et le néant*, 245–261.

35 Kerby, *Narrative and the Self*, 107.

36 Anika Lemaire, *Jacques Lacan*, trans. David Macey (London: Routledge and Kegan Paul, 1977), 40.

37 Kristeva, *Revolution in Poetic Language*, 105f.; *Révolution du langage poétique*, 100.

38 Paul Smith, *Discerning the Subject* (Minneapolis: University of Minnesota Press, 1988), 32.

39 A theoretical clarification of this process of ideologically invested identity construction is provided in Žižek's *The Sublime Object of Ideology*, 11–128. Cf. Kaja Silverman, *Male Subjectivity at the Margins* (New York: Routledge, 1992), 15–51.

40 Musil's novel renders the perfect harmony between sociality and individuality achieved by Ulrich's father thus: "As with many men who achieve distinction, this feeling [the basic feeling of his life] did not at all consist in self-interest but in a deep love of so-called general and impartial interests—in other words, he sincerely venerated the state of affairs that had given him so many advantages, not because it had given him such advantages but because he was in harmony and coexistent with it, and on general principles" (*MWQ* 10* / *MoE* 15).

41 René Girard, *Deceit, Desire, and the Novel: Self and Other in Literary Structure*, trans. Yvonne Freccero (Baltimore: Johns Hopkins University Press, 1965), 83–95; *Mensonge romantique et vérité romanesque* (Paris: Grasset, 1961), 89–100.

42 Kristeva, *Revolution in Poetic Language*, 104; *La Révolution du langage poétique*, 98.

43 Thomas Mann, *The Magic Mountain*, trans. John E. Woods (New York:

Alfred A. Knopf, 1995), 21; *Der Zauberberg* (Frankfurt am Main: Fischer, 1991), 34.

44 Massimo Cacciari, *Posthumous People: Vienna at the Turning Point,* trans. Rodger Friedman (Stanford: Stanford University Press, 1996), 57f.

45 Kerby, *Narrative and the Self,* 40.

46 Kristeva, *Revolution in Poetic Language,* 232ff.; *La Révolution du langage poétique,* 202ff. This is not the place to compare Musil's and Kristeva's respective conceptions of ethics. It should be enough to stress that Kristeva's notion of subjectivity, like Musil's, necessarily posits identity formation as an ethical process, since identity is constituted only in the encounter with the other. Still, these two systems cannot be reduced to each other. They investigate similar problems, but from different sides of the history of modernity and in different codes. I am grateful to Kristen Kramer for critical remarks on this issue.

47 Paul Ricoeur, *Oneself as Another,* trans. Kathleen Blamey (Chicago: University of Chicago Press, 1992), 2; *Soi-même comme un autre* (Paris: Seuil, 1990), 13.

48 Giorgio Agamben, *The Coming Community,* trans. Michael Hardt (Minneapolis: University of Minnesota Press, 1993), 95f.

49 Ibid., 16–19.

50 Ricoeur, *Oneself as Another,* 140–151; *Soi-même comme un autre,* 167–180. See also Ricoeur's *Time and Narrative,* trans. Kathleen McLaughlin and David Pellauer (Chicago: University of Chicago Press, 1984–1988), in which he develops his narrative theory in detail, esp. 3:244–429.

51 Ricoeur, *Oneself as Another,* 149; *Soi-même comme un autre,* 177.

52 Ricoeur, *Oneself as Another,* 166f.; *Soi-même comme un autre,* 196f.

53 Giorgio Agamben, *Language and Death: The Place of Negativity,* trans. Karen E. Pinkus with Michael Hardt (Minneapolis: University of Minnesota Press, 1991), 19–37; Agamben, *The Coming Community,* 27.

54 Agamben, *The Coming Community,* 42.

55 Ibid.

56 For an interesting analysis of the relation of modern German literature and poststructuralist theories of the subject, see Stanley Corngold, *The Fate of the Self: German Writers and French Theory* (New York: Columbia University Press, 1986).

57 Giorgio Agamben, *The Man Without Content,* trans. Georgia Albert (Stanford: Stanford University Press, 1999).

58 Ricoeur emphasizes three such modalities of this altérité: the subject's

body, the otherness of other people, and the subject's conscience (*Oneself as Another*, 317–356; *Soi-même comme un autre*, 367–410). For a more comprehensive discussion of how the body intervenes in the dialectics between self and other, see Maurice Merleau-Ponty, *Phenomenology of Perception*, trans. Colin Smith (1962; London: Routledge, 1995, 67–199; *Phénoménologie de la perception* (Paris: Gallimard, 1945), 81–240.

59 Žižek, *The Sublime Object of Ideology*, 24; R. D. Laing, *The Divided Self: An Existential Study in Sanity and Madness*, 2d ed. (Harmondsworth, England: Penguin, 1990), 139.

60 Georg Simmel, "Die ästhetische Bedeutung des Gesichts," in *Brücke und Tür: Essays des Philosophen zur Geschichte, Religion, Kunst und Gesellschaft*, ed. Michael Landmann with Margarete Susman (Stuttgart: Koehler, 1957), 153.

61 As I discussed in chapter 2, "Modernist Mysticism," and as I will argue further in chapter 5, note 82, Ulrich and Agathe's relationship is generally understood and explained as a variation of a timeless mythological motif of the love between brother and sister. See also my general survey of Musil scholarship in Introduction, note 9.

62 The scene I am discussing exists in several incomplete versions. Apart from the one mentioned above, there is a draft of "Breaths of a Summer Day" where the garden fence is explicitly thematized as a figure for their separation from the world (*MoE* 1316). There is also a draft in which their separation from the strangers in the street is problematized, and which bears the revealing name "Versuche, ein Scheusal zu lieben" (*MoE* 1349–56).

5   Monsters in Love, Angels at War

1 Although the narrator emphasizes the Pierrot motif, the actual description of Ulrich and Agathe's costumes, with their stripes and lozenges, suggests outfits more fitting for Pierrot's companion, Harlequin (*MWQ* 734 / *MoE* 675f.).

2 On the history of Pierrot, see Robert F. Storey, *Pierrot: A Critical History of a Mask* (Princeton: Princeton University Press, 1978); Georges Doutrepont, *L'Evolution du type de Pierrot dans la littérature française* (Brussels: Publications de l'Académie Royal de Langue et de Littérature Françaises, 1925); Thomas Kellein, *Pierrot: Melancholie und Maske* (Munich: Prestel, 1995); Martin Green and John Swan, *The Triumph of Pierrot: The Comme-*

dia dell'Arte and the Modern Imagination (New York: Macmillan, 1986); and Kay Dick, *Pierrot* (London: Hutchinson, 1960).

3 During his long history, Pierrot has impersonated almost every identity and profession. Georges Doutrepont lists 127 of his roles—from "peasant, bus boy, cabaretier, Jupiter, judge, widow, clerc, Juno" all the way to "phantom, prisoner, hermit, magnetizer, murderer"—only to conclude that Pierrot "has been almost everything, even a woman, depending on the occasion" (*L'Evolution du type de Pierrot*, 31f.).

4 Kellein, *Pierrot*, 93.

5 According to Martin Green and John Swan: the "triumph of Pierrot occurred between the years 1890 and 1930" (*The Triumph of Pierrot*, 261).

6 It is possible that one of the unpublished chapters in the *The Man Without Qualities* alludes to Arnold Schoenberg's adaptation of Albert Giraud's poem *Pierrot lunaire* (*MWQ* 1181 / *MoE* 1086f.).

7 Massimo Cacciari, *Posthumous People: Vienna at the Turning Point,* trans. Roger Friedman (Stanford: Stanford University Press, 1996), 42.

8 The eponymous hero of J. H. Liebeskind's fairy tale, *Lulu, oder die Zauberflöte* (1789)—possibly a source for Wedekind's drama, and the most important one for Mozart's opera—is thus male. Another example: the son of Napoleon III was nicknamed Lulu. Wedekind's major source, Félicien Champsaur's *Lulu: Pantomime en un act,* however, features a heroine described as "une clownesse danseuse" carrying "an Italian mask." See Hartmut Vinçon's commentary to his edition of the original 1894 version of Wedekind's play: *Die Büchse der Pandora: Eine Monstretragödie* (Darmstadt: Jürgen Häusser, 1990), 177f., 194f., 200f.

9 For an interpretation of Lulu's costume, see Erhard Weil, "Lulus Pierrot-Kostüm und die Lüftung eines zentralen Kunstgeheimnisses," *Editio: Internationales Jahrbuch für Editionswissenschaft* 2 (1988): 90–110.

10 Silvia Bovenschen, *Die imaginierte Weiblichkeit: Exemplarische Untersuchungen zu kulturgeschichtlichen und literarischen Präsentationsformen des Weiblichen* (Frankfurt am Main: Suhrkamp, 1979), 31, 43–58.

11 Frank Wedekind, *Erdgeist: Tragödie in vier Aufzügen,* in *Ausgewählte Werke* (Munich: Georg Müller, 1924), 2:9f. ("Du hast kein Recht, uns durch Miaun und Fauchen / Die *Urgestalt* des *Weibes* zu verstauchen / Durch Faxenmachen uns und Fratzenschneiden / Des Lasters *Kindereinfalt* zu erleiden! / Du sollst—drum sprech'ich heute sehr ausführlich— / *Natürlich* sprechen und nicht unnatürlich!")

12 See Lisa Appignanesi, *Femininity and the Creative Imagination: A Study of Henry James, Robert Musil, and Marcel Proust* (London: Viking Press,

1973), 5; Jacques Le Rider, *Modernity and Crises of Identity: Culture and Society in Fin-de-Siècle Vienna,* trans. Rosemary Morris (New York: Continuum, 1993), 101–126; *Modernité viennoise et crises de l'identité* (Paris: Presses universitaires de France, 1990), 122–151. See also Christine Buci-Glucksmann, *Baroque Reason: The Aesthetics of Modernity,* trans. Patrick Camiller (London: Sage, 1994), 115–123; *La Raison baroque: De Baudelaire à Benjamin* (Paris: Galilée, 1984), 145–160.

13 For a summary of the discussion on bisexuality and femininity, see Le Rider, *Modernity and Crises of Identity,* 77–126; *Modernité viennoise et crises de l'identité,* 93–151.

14 Bovenschen, *Die imaginierte Weiblichkeit,* 27ff.

15 Max Scheler, "Zum Sinn der Frauenbewegung," in *Vom Umsturz der Werte* (Leipzig: Der neue Geist-Verlag, 1923), 2:224. I am indebted to Bovenschen's discussion of Scheler in *Die imaginierte Weiblichkeit,* 27–35.

16 Scheler, "Zum Sinn der Frauenbewegung," 220.

17 Ibid., 221.

18 Georg Simmel, "Weibliche Kultur," in *Philosophische Kultur: Gesammelte Essais* (Leipzig: Werner Klinkhardt, 1911), 278–319. The key passage is this: "The numerous observations on the differences of the female psyche may be summarized thus: that, for her, the ego and its deed, the center of the personality and its periphery, are more narrowly fused together than in man; that she converts her inner processes into expressions more immediately, so as to account even for the peculiar conjunction which makes mental alterations pass into bodily alterations much more easily in the case of women than in the case of men" (301f.).

19 Toril Moi, *What Is a Woman? And Other Essays* (Oxford: Oxford University Press, 1999), 12.

20 Bovenschen, *Die imaginierte Weiblichkeit,* 31.

21 Max Scheler, "Zur Idee des Menschen," *Vom Umsturz der Werte,* 1:308.

22 See Carl Schorske's analysis in *Fin-de-Siècle Vienna: Politics and Culture* (New York: Vintage Books, 1981), 207–278. In 1894 Klimt was commissioned to do three allegorical paintings for the University of Vienna. His patrons requested a depiction of "the triumph of light over darkness." Klimt did the opposite, however. In his painting *Philosophy* (1900), the institutions of reason are engulfed by an omnipotent nature with female attributes. In *Medicine* (1901), the cycle of life and death is beyond human control. In *Jurisprudence* (1903), finally, the goddesses of Truth, Justice, and Law are shut up in an ornamented tower, high above a human world in

which the Furies have again become the officers of law, a scenario representing the return of the vendetta law and the matriarchal rule that Athena, at the end of Aeschylus' *Oresteia,* once suppressed. The forces of nature that render medicine, justice, and philosophy powerless are all embodied by women.

23 On Klimt's relationship to women, particularly his models, see Susanna Partsch, *Gustav Klimt: Maler der Frauen* (Munich: Prestel, 1994), 96–98.

24 The connections between Musil's early writings and Klimt's paintings have been discussed by Lothar Huber, "Robert Musil und Gustav Klimt: Jugendstil in den frühen Erzählungen," *Musil Forum,* nos. 21–22 (1995–1996): 23–44.

25 Lou Andreas-Salomé's psychoanalytic theory intended to add a distinctly female perspective to Freud's theory of sexuality and the unconscious. For Freud, the sexual drive, the libido, was a quantifiable psychic energy that was cathected and discharged in activity, that is, in relation to external objects of desire. Andreas-Salomé, by contrast, conceived of the libido as a quality and as a condition of passivity. It was a contradictory phenomenon, active or passive depending on the environment, but always striving to receive, integrate, and preserve. According to Andreas-Salomé, the libido is the origin of life, the alpha and omega of existence. This conception of the libido led Andreas-Salomé to dispute Freud's theory of narcissism. Instead of seeing narcissim as a pathological condition, caused by disproportionally large quantities of libidinal energy directed at the ego, she regarded it as a state where psychic energy is not yet separated into ego-libido and object-libido. Narcissism is an originary condition of unconscious harmony. It is not an effect of an exaggerated ego formation but the very source of the process of individuation. This process is not the same for men and women, Andreas-Salomé went on to argue. The male's ego instinct develops into an opposite of his sexual instinct, the former reinforcing his self, the latter engulfing it. In woman, by contrast, the ego instinct will never be fully differentiated from her sexual instinct, because her sexual instincts are not deflected outwardly, as in the man, but oriented toward her body. The result of this confluence of the ego instinct and the sexual instinct is a narcissistic dedifferentiation of her drives. Woman is therefore closer to the narcissistic origin than man. She integrates into her being all the oppositions—activity and passivity, masculine and feminine, ego-libido and object-libido, sensuality and spirituality—that the male, for his part, encounters as a series of external alternatives. While he must repress either his sexual desire or his spiri-

tual, ego-oriented desire, woman can have both ("Narzissmus als Doppelrichtung," in *Das "zweideutige" Lächeln der Erotik: Texte zur Psychoanalyse* [Freiburg: Kore, 1990], 191–222; see also Brigitte Rempp and Inge Weber's introduction).

26 Lou Andreas-Salomé, "Aus dem Tagebuch 1912," in *Das "zweideutige" Lächeln der Erotik,* 51.

27 Lou Andreas-Salomé, "Zum Typus Weib," in *Das "zweideutige" Lächeln der Erotik,* 100.

28 Friedrich Nietzsche, *The Joyful Wisdom (La Gaya Scienza),* trans. Thomas Common, vol. 10 of *The Collected Works of Friedrich Nietzsche,* ed. Oscar Levy (New York: Gordon Press, 1974), 269; *Die fröhliche Wissenschaft* [1882], in *Werke* (Berlin: Walter de Gruyter, 1973), pt. 5, 2:249, para. 339.

29 Wedekind's *Lulu* plays were among the most popular dramas in Germany and Austria at the beginning of the century. From 1902 to 1930, *Earth Spirit* could always be seen on stage in Berlin. In Vienna the success was even greater, partly because censorship was not as severe as in Germany. The peak of success was reached in the early 1920s. In this period, according to theater historian Günter Seehaus, Wedekind's plays, especially *Pandora's Box,* became a fashion unto itself (*Frank Wedekind und das Theater* [Munich: Laokoon, 1964], 37, 216ff.). Between 1921 and 1924 Musil worked in Vienna as a prolific theater and drama critic, mainly for *Prager Presse* and *Deutsche Zeitung Bohemia.* In December 1923 his own farce opened in Berliner Lustspielhaus. Though Musil did not admit it, the allusions to Wedekind's *Lulu* plays were probably carefully calculated and immediately recognized by the critics. See Günther Schneider, *Untersuchungen zum dramatischen Werk Robert Musils* (Frankfurt am Main: Peter Lang, 1973), 182–185, 195–208. In *Berliner Tageblatt,* 5 December 1923, the influential critic Alfred Kerr summarized *Vinzenz* as "a parody not only of expressionism but of our times," and as a "Wedekindian dance around woman." See reprint in Karl Corino, *Robert Musil: Leben und Werk in Bildern und Texten* (Reinbek bei Hamburg: Rowohlt, 1988), 312f.

30 Bovenschen, *Die imaginierte Weiblichkeit,* 48.

31 See Fabrizio Cambi, "Musil und der Expressionismus," in *Robert Musil und die kulturellen Tendenzen seiner Zeit,* ed. Josef Sturtz (Munich: Wilhelm Fink, 1983), 59–73.

32 Letter of 8 December 1923 to Alfred Kerr. Musil discusses the reviews of *Vinzenz* that pointed out its similarities to Wedekind's plays (*Briefe,* 325–328). Musil returned to the topic in 1929, on the occasion of the staging of his other play, *Die Schwärmer* (The enthusiasts); see "Der Schwärmer-

skandal," *Das Tagebuch,* 20 April 1929 (*GW* 2:1190). Discussing a possible preface for the published play, Musil situates it in a tradition of socially biting comedy leading from the early Morgenstern, over Dada, to Brecht and Bronnen (*T* 1:631).

33 The most extensive interpretation of *Vinzenz,* Christian Rogowski's *Implied Dramaturgy: Robert Musil and the Crisis of Modern Drama* (Riverside, Calif.: Ariadne Press, 1993), 185–275, appears to confirm this conclusion. Rogowski's comparison of Musil's farce and August Strindberg's *Miss Julie* seems far-fetched, however.

34 See, *MWQ* 747f., 819, 982f. / *MoE* 688f., 754, 905f.

35 In 1903 Otto Weininger and Daniel Paul Schreber each published a tormented account of the crisis of masculine identity: *Geschlecht und Charakter: Eine prinzipielle Untersuchung,* 22d ed. (Vienna: Wilhelm Braumüller, 1923) and *Denkwürdigkeiten eines Nervenkranken,* reprint, ed. Peter Heiligenthal and Reinhard Volk (Frankfurt am Main: Syndikat, 1985).

36 Le Rider, *Modernity and Crises of Identity,* 145; *Modernité viennoise et crises de l'identité,* 175.

37 Juliet Mitchell, *Psychoanalysis and Feminism* (New York: Pantheon Books, 1974), 401–406.

38 Eric L. Santner, *My Own Private Germany: Daniel Paul Schreber's Secret History of Modernity* (Princeton: Princeton University Press, 1996), xi–xiii.

39 Louis Althusser, "Ideology and Ideological State Apparatuses (Notes towards an Investigation)," in *Lenin and Philosophy and Other Essays,* trans. Ben Brewster (New York: Monthly Review Press, 1971), 127–186, esp. 170–177; "Idéologie et appareils idéologiques d'état (Notes pour une recherche)" [1970], in *Positions (1964–1975)* (Paris: Editions sociales, 1976), 67–125, 110–116.

40 Althusser, "Freud and Lacan," in *Lenin and Philosophy,* 209ff.; "Freud et Lacan" [1964–1965], in *Positions,* 23ff. Jacques Rancière and Kaja Silverman have further theorized "the Law of Culture" as the "dominant fiction." See Silverman, *Male Subjectivity at the Margins* (New York: Routledge, 1992), 15–65. According to Jacques Rancière, the dominant fiction is "the privileged mode of representation by which the image of the social consensus is offered to the members of a social formation and within which they are asked to identify themselves" ("Interview: The Image of Brotherhood," trans. Kari Hanet, *Edinburgh Magazine,* no. 2 [1977]: 28; quoted in Silverman, *Male Subjectivity at the Margins,* 30). In Sla-

voj Žižek's elaborations of Lacan's notion of "the big Other" we find yet another description of the same phenomena (*The Sublime Object of Ideology*, [London: Verso, 1989], 87–129).

41 See Fredric Jameson, *The Political Unconscious: Narrative as a Socially Symbolic Act* (Ithaca: Cornell University Press, 1981), 76, 87f.

42 Mitchell, *Psychoanalysis and Feminism*, 378–398.

43 Lacan, "The Function and Field of Speech and Language in Psychoanalysis," in *Écrits: A Selection*, trans. Alan Sheridan (London: Tavistock, 1977), 68.

44 Silverman maintains that the "dominant fiction calls upon the male subject to see himself, and the female subject to recognize and desire him, only through the images of an unimpaired masculinity" (*Male Subjectivity at the Margins*, 42).

45 Silverman defines historical trauma as an instance of "the purest negativity" (ibid., 401). She also states that it is "any historical event, whether socially engineered or of natural occurrence, which brings a large group of male subjects into such an intimate relation of lack that they are . . . unable to sustain an imaginary relation with the phallus" (ibid., 55). Her major example is World War II.

46 Julia Hell, *Post-Fascist Fantasies: Psychoanalysis, History, and the Literature of East Germany* (Durham, N.C.: Duke University Press, 1997), 253.

47 See Cathy Caruth, *Unclaimed Experience: Trauma, Narrative, and History* (Baltimore: Johns Hopkins University Press, 1996), 1–24, 57–72; and Michael S. Roth, "Trauma, Representation, and Historical Consciousness," *Common Knowledge* 7, no. 2 (fall 1998): 99–111.

48 Sigmund Freud, *Beyond the Pleasure Principle*, trans. James Strachey, in *The Standard Edition of the Complete Psychological Works* (London: Hogarth Press, 1955), 18:12–14, 29–33.

49 Santner, *My Own Private Germany*, 32.

50 Ibid., 115.

51 Harriet Anderson, *Utopian Feminism: Women's Movements in Fin-de-Siècle Vienna* (New Haven: Yale University Press, 1992).

52 Bovenschen, *Die imaginierte Weiblichkeit*, 27f.

53 Alfred Poser, "Verstörte Männer und emanzipierte Frauen," in *Aufbruch und Untergang: Österreichische Kultur zwischen 1918 und 1938*, ed. Franz Kadrnoska (Vienna: Europa Verlag, 1981), 205–222.

54 Magnus Hirschfeld, *Sittengeschichte des Weltkrieges* (Leipzig, 1930), 437. Quoted in Le Rider, *Modernity and Crises of Identity*, 121; *Modernité viennoise et crises de l'identité*, 145.

55 Franz Werfel, *Nicht der Mörder, der Ermordete ist schuldig* [1920] (Frankfurt am Main: Suhrkamp, 1982), 46.

56 Joseph Roth, *The Emperor's Tomb,* trans. John Hoare (Woodstock, N.Y.: Overlook Press, 1984), 20*; *Die Kapuzinergruft,* in *Werke* (Cologne: Kiepenheuer und Witsch, 1956), 1:323f.

57 Ibid., 97–112 / 379–394.

58 Joseph Roth, *Hotel Savoy,* in *Werke,* 1:852.

59 Roth, *The Emperor's Tomb,* 118f.; *Die Kapuzinergruft,* 401.

60 Joseph Roth, *The Radetzky March,* trans. Joachim Neugroschel (Woodstock, N.Y.: Overlook Press, 1995), 324–331; *Radetzkymarsch,* in *Werke,* 1:304–311.

61 Roth, *The Emperor's Tomb,* 143–150; *Die Kapuzinergruft,* 420–425.

62 Roth, *The Radetzky March,* 325; *Radetzkymarsch,* 305.

63 Roth, *The Radetzky March,* 243; *Radetzkymarsch,* 229.

64 See Roth's *Juden auf Wanderschaft* (Berlin: Die Schmiede, 1927).

65 Joseph Roth, *Antichrist,* trans. Moray Firth (New York: Viking Press, 1935); *Der Anti-Christ,* in vol. 3 of *Werke* (Cologne: Kiepenhauer und Witsch, 1956).

66 Roth, *The Emperor's Tomb,* 119; *Die Kapuzinergruft,* 401f.

67 R. D. Laing, *The Divided Self: An Existential Study in Sanity and Madness,* 2d ed. (Harmondsworth, England: Penguin, 1990), 65–93; Louis A. Sass, *Madness and Modernism: Insanity in the Light of Modern Art, Literature, and Thought* (Cambridge, Mass.: Harvard University Press, 1996), esp. 75–115.

68 Sass, *Madness and Modernism,* 119–209.

69 As Vladimir Propp demonstrated in his analysis of the Russian folktale, this is a major social function of collective narratives. On the latent level of the narrative, Propp deciphered a struggle between "donors" and "villains," the former being agents who help the hero, while the villains attempt to block him from reaching the happy ending of the tale. In this sense, the villains mark the externality of the borders that a society draws around itself by way of collective narratives and ideological projections (*Morphology of the Folktale,* trans. Laurence Scott [Bloomington: Indiana University Press, 1958], passim).

70 Corino, "Ein Mörder macht Literaturgeschichte: Florian Grossrubatscher, ein Modell für Musils Moosbrugger," in *Robert Musil und die kulturellen Tendenzen seiner Zeit,* ed. Josef Strutz (Munich: Wilhelm Fink, 1983), 145. In a later article, Corino argues that a more important model for Moosbrugger was a murderer of young women called Christian Voigt,

who did indeed suffer from a sexually transmitted disease ("Zerstückt und durchdunkelt: Der Sexualmörder Moosbrugger im 'Mann ohne Eigenschaften' und sein Modell," *Musil-Forum,* no. 10 [1984]: 105–119). There are also early sketches in which the hero attempts to rescue Moosbrugger from the asylum and witnesses his execution (*MoE* 1727ff.).

71 Corino, "Ein Mörder macht Literaturgeschichte," 144ff.

72 In Corino's view, the diminishing importance of Moosbrugger indicates that Musil's experiences of the 1920s changed his ways of responding to society. As the social order itself became murderous, a murderer like Moosbrugger no longer served as an example of dissent (ibid.).

73 The narrator emphasizes that Agathe expresses her decision to leave her husband so loudly that it seems as if she wanted "that the dead man should hear it too" (*MWQ* 736 / *MoE* 677).

74 Simmel, "Weibliche Kultur," 280ff.

75 Andreas-Salomé, "Zum Typus Weib," 102.

76 Bovenschen, *Die imaginierte Weiblichkeit,* 51.

77 Walter Benjamin, "The Metaphysics of Youth," trans. Rodney Livingstone, in *Selected Writings,* ed. Marcus Bullock and Michael W. Jennings (Cambridge, Mass.: Harvard University Press, 1996), 1:9; "Metaphysik der Jugend," in *Gesammelte Schriften,* 2, bk. 1:95.

78 Walter Benjamin, *Briefe* (Frankfurt am Main: Suhrkamp, 1978), 1:65.

79 Julia Kristeva, *Revolution in Poetic Language,* trans. Margaret Waller (New York: Columbia University Press, 1984), 25–38; *La Révolution du langage poétique: L'avant-garde à la fin du XIXe siècle — Lautréamont et Mallarmé* (Paris: Seuil, 1974), 22–37.

80 Clarisse's and Agathe's positions in Musil's novel are further clarified by Sigrid Weigel's use of Kristeva's theory in her analysis of linguistic practice and feminine subjectivity in the modernist period; see *Topographien der Geschlechter: Kulturgeschichtlichen Studien zur Literatur* (Reinbek bei Hamburg: Rowohlt, 1990), 18–35.

81 This strategy is similar to Mary Shelley's decision in *Frankenstein* to let the monster be the most eloquent figure in the novel. See Peter Brooks, "What Is a Monster? According to *Frankenstein,*" in *Body Work: Objects of Desire in Modern Narrative* (Cambridge, Mass.: Harvard University Press, 1993), 101f.

82 On the alternative ways of organizing the last, incomplete parts of *The Man Without Qualities,* see introduction, note 1.

83 Thomas Pekar is the only critic who has stressed that the incest theme

in Musil's novel "must be regarded as a sociostructural problem." Pekar
fails to develop this point, however (*Die Sprache der Liebe bei Robert
Musil* [Munich: Wilhelm Fink, 1989], 274f.). Appignanesi also mentions
the social implications of the incest, but then moves on to a psychological interpretation (*Femininity and the Creative Imagination*, 145ff.).
Anja Elisabeth Schoene discusses the theme of incest in a wide variety
of literary works from the turn of the century. Her argument conforms
to mine in the sense that she regards the sheer frequency of incestuous
relationships in the literature of the era as a sign of a transformation of
"contemporary theories of the subject." When explaining this transformation, however, she treats it almost exclusively as an epistemological
issue, "a crisis of knowledge and perception" caused by scientific and
technological advances. The strength of Schoene's study is, rather, its rich
intertextual analysis of the ways in which Musil conforms to, and differs
from, other writers' representations of incest in the same period (*"Ach,
wäre fern, was ich liebe!": Studien zur Inzestthematik in der Literatur der
Jahrhundertwende (von Ibsen bis Musil)* [Würzburg: Königshausen und
Neumann, 1997], 9–15, 158–171, 246–249). Other critics have interpreted
the incest theme either by clarifying its mythological resonances, or in
psychological terms, or by comparing Musil's treatment of the theme to
other writers, especially Ingeborg Bachmann. See Achim Auernhammer,
"L'Androgynie dans 'L'Homme sans qualités,' " *L'Arc*, 74 (1978): 35–40;
Ortrud Gutjahr, " '. . . Den Eingang ins Paradies finden': Inzest als Motiv und Struktur im Roman Robert Musils und Ingeborg Bachmanns,"
in *Genauigkeit und Seele: Zur österreichischen Literatur seit dem Fin de
Siècle*, ed. Josef Strutz and Endre Kiss (Munich: Wilhelm Fink, 1990),
139–157; Irena Omelaniuk, "Androgyny and the Fate of the Feminine:
Robert Musil and Ingeborg Bachmann," *AUMLA* 58 (November 1982):
146–163; Götz Müller, "Isis und Osiris: Die Mythen in Robert Musils
Roman der Mann ohne Eigenschaften," *Zeitschrift für deutsche Philologie* 102 (1983): 583–604; Agata Schwartz, "Geschwisterliebe und Androgynie in Robert Musils 'Die Schwärmer' und 'Der Mann ohne Eigenschaften,' " in *Proceedings and Commentary: German Graduate Students
Association Conference at New York University*, ed. Patricia Doykos Duquette, Matthew Griffin, and Imke Lode (New York University, 1993).
Andrew Webber's study of Musil and Georg Trakl claims to inventory the
sexual scenes in *The Man Without Qualities*, yet it fails to even discuss the
passages about Ulrich's and Agathe's sexual encounters (*Sexuality and the*

Sense of Self in the Works of Georg Trakl and Robert Musil [London: Modern Humanities Research Association and Institute of Germanic Studies, University of London, 1990], 150–181).

84 According to Claude Lévi-Strauss, the incest taboo "expresses the passage from the natural fact of consanguinity to the cultural fact of alliance"; furthermore, "the prohibition of incest constitutes the fundamental departure, thanks to which, through which, and, above all, in which the passage from nature to culture is accomplished" (*Structures élémentaires de la parenté* [Paris: Presses universitaires de France, 1949], 36, 30). For a discussion of Lévi-Strauss's argument, see Mitchell, *Psychoanalysis and Feminism,* 364–376; and Silverman, *Male Subjectivity at the Margins,* 34ff.

85 There is a poem by Musil called "Isis and Osiris" about the incestuous siblings in early Egyptian mythology. Written in 1923, the same year as *Vinzenz,* Musil's poem relates how the sister first eats her brother's sexual organ, and how they then devour each others' hearts (*GW* 2:465). In 1931, Musil stated that the poem "contains the novel in nucleus" (*T* 1:847). Musil, in other words, was aware that the negativity invested in the incest motif is a basic principle of the work. The novel's representation of incest is politically and socially overdetermined, however; hence it cannot be accounted for by clarifying its mythological allusions only, nor by treating it, as is frequently done in psychoanalytic readings, as an aesthetic release of repressed wishes. Jacques Perronnet has presented a detailed analysis of Musil's poem, without, however, investigating its sociohistorical resonances in Musil's work ("Isis und Osiris," in *Beiträge zur Musil-Kritik,* ed. Gudrun Brokoph-Mauch [Bern: Peter Lang, 1983], 273–288).

86 Ferdinand Tönnies, *Community and Society,* trans. Charles P. Loomis (East Lansing: Michigan State University Press, 1957), 201; *Gemeinschaft und Gesellschaft: Grundbegriffe der reinen Soziologie* (Darmstadt: Wissenschaftliche Buchgesellschaft, 1970), 210.

87 See Lorraine Daston and Katharine Park, *Wonders and the Order of Nature, 1150–1750* (New York: Zone Books, 1998), 173–214, 329–363; Rosamond Purcell, *Natural Anomalies and Historical Monsters* (San Francisco: Chronicle Books, 1997), 15–20.

88 Chris Baldick, "The Politics of Monstrosity," in *Frankenstein: Mary Shelley,* ed. Fred Botting (New York: St. Martin's Press, 1995), 50f. Baldick defines the monster as a "moral advertisement."

89 Quoted in ibid., 56.

90 This analysis would also conform to Gayatri Spivak's reading of *Frankenstein.* In addition, Spivak explains how this discontinuity or difference gets

coded in terms of femininity and masculinity (*A Critique of Postcolonial Reason: Toward a History of the Vanishing Present* [Cambridge, Mass.: Harvard University Press, 1999], 112–148).

91 Indeed, this is the conclusion reached by most works dealing with Viennese culture at the beginning of the twentieth century. The title of Kadrnoska's influential anthology speaks for itself, *Aufbruch und Untergang.* See also Schorske, *Fin-de-Siècle Vienna;* Le Rider, *Modernity and Crises of Identity;* Alland Janik and Stephen Toulmin, *Wittgenstein's Vienna* (New York: Simon and Schuster, 1973). Thus Christine Buci-Glucksmann exaggerates only slightly when stating that in this society "discontinuity . . . breaks out in the form of the most radical and dangerous otherness—woman—and arouses the limitless fear stemming from self-hatred in which madness, the double and nothingness combine their evil powers" (*Baroque Reason,* 115; *La Raison baroque,* 145).

92 On this aspect of Viennese modernity, see Mitchell, *Psychoanalysis and Feminism,* 407–435. In early-twentieth-century Vienna, Freud develops his psychoanalytical theory, largely based on the postulation of the child's incestuous desire for the mother and/or father. In a classical analysis of 1912, Otto Rank then expands Freud's theory of incest into a theory about artistic creation in general, treating all artistic creations, and particularly those that represent incest, as aesthetic sublimations of wishes that are repressed by the incest taboo (*Das Inzest-Motiv in Dichtung und Sage: Grundzüge einer Psychologie des dichterischen Schaffens,* 2d ed. [Leipzig: Franz Deuticke, 1926]). Meanwhile, Musil uses the theme of incest to explore new definitions of human subjectivity as well as new ways of describing the formation of personal and collective identities. Musil's relationship to psychoanalysis is a contested matter. He dismissed Freud and psychoanalysis, just as he dismissed most contemporary writers and thinkers. In an interesting study, however, Johannes Cremerius suggests that Musil closely followed Freud's theory. In fact, he might even have tried to outdo it, in his novel and his essays, by building his own theory of human subjectivity and emotions on the basis of experimental psychology ("Robert Musil: Das Dilemma eines Schriftstellers vom Typus *poeta ductus* nach Freud," *Psyche* 33, no. 8 [1979]: 733–772). Apparently, Freud and Musil shared a historical situation that forced them to construe new antiexpressivist theories of human subjectivity and identity.

93 Quoted in Léon Cellier, "Les Rêves de Dieu," *Circé: Cahiers de recherche sur l'imaginaire,* no. 4 (1975): 83–86.

94 Santner, *My Own Private Germany,* 133.

95 Walter Benjamin, "Karl Kraus," in *One-Way Street and Other Writings,* trans. Edmund Jephcott and Kingsley Shorter (London: New Left Review, 1979), 268–277; "Karl Kraus" [1931], in *Gesammelte Schriften,* 2, bk. 1:354–367. Incidentally, this nostalgia for origins explains why Kraus was a keen admirer of Wedekind's *Lulu* plays, which he introduced to the Viennese public in 1905, at the occasion of the staging of *Pandora's Box.* See Kraus's article "Die Büchse der Pandora," *Die Fackel,* no. 182 (9 June 1905), 1–14.

96 See Jephcott and Shorter's translation: Benjamin, *One-Way Street,* 277–290.

97 Benjamin, "Karl Kraus," 289; "Karl Kraus" [1931], 367.

98 Benjamin, "Karl Kraus," 289; "Karl Kraus" [1931], 367.

99 Buci Glucksmann defines angelic spaces thus: "Magical spheres of all the correspondences and metamorphoses, all the metaphorical displacements of desire. They are the spaces of Klee's 'intermediate world', of 'all those worlds which are not visible to everyone and can really only be seen by children, mad people and primitives' " (*Baroque Reason,* 58; *La Raison baroque,* 47).

100 Like Musil, Klee dissolves the anthropocentric idea of "man" as the center of agency, practiced in literature in the form of the realist novel and in art, since the Renaissance, in the form of iconographic and formal conventions based on a human control of both the perspective and the subject matter of painting. Against this paradigm, Klee, like Musil, affirms a postexpressivist or posthumanist idea of the world and the human subject, reconstituting both within a forcefield of energy where they interact and interconnect in ever new compounds. When this idea is put into practice with a view to represent the human condition of the 1920s, the result, in both cases, is a materialization of monstrous and angelic beings. There are thus interesting and unexplored parallels between Musil's figures of monstrosity and the hundreds of angels, clowns, masks, monsters, and odd puppets that Klee's created in his workshop during the same traumatic period of the 1920s. See Margaret Plant, *Paul Klee: Figures and Faces* (London: Thames and Hudson, 1978); and Paul Klee, *Puppen, Plastiken, Reliefs, Masken, Theater* (Neuchâtel: Editions Galerie Suisse de Paris, 1979). The similarities between the aesthetic practices of Klee and Musil are briefly touched upon by Mark Roskill in *Klee, Kandinsky, and the Thought of Their Time: A Critical Perspective* (Urbana: University of Illinois Press, 1992), 164–177.

6 The Most Progressive State

1 My account of the nationality problem in Austria-Hungary relies mainly on the following works by Robert Kann: "Zur Problematik der Nationalitätenfrage in der Habsburgermonarchie, 1848–1918," in *Die Habsburgermonarchie 1848–1918*, ed. Adam Wandruszka and Peter Urbanitsch, vol. 3, *Die Völker des Reiches* (Vienna: Verlag der Österreichische Akademie der Wissenschaften, 1980), 1304–1338; *The Multinational Empire: Nationalism and National Reform in the Habsburg Monarchy, 1848–1918*, 2 vols. (New York: Columbia University Press, 1950); *The Habsburg Empire: A Study in Integration and Disintegration* (New York: Frederick A. Praeger, 1957). I have also consulted A. J. P. Taylor, *The Habsburg Monarchy, 1809–1918: A History of the Austrian Empire and Austria-Hungary*, 2d ed. (New York: Harper and Row, 1965); Gerald Stourz, "Die Gleichberechtigung der Volksstämme als Verfassungsprinzip, 1848–1918," in *Die Habsburgermonarchie, 1848–1918*, 3:975–1206; François Fetjö, *Requiem pour un empire défunt: Histoire de la destruction de l'Autriche-Hongrie*, 2d ed. (Paris: Seuil, 1993); and Barbara Jelavich, *History of the Balkans*, vol. 2, *Twentieth Century* (Cambridge: Cambridge University Press, 1983).

2 Kann, *The Multinational Empire*, 2:288.

3 See Claudio Magris, *Der habsburgische Mythos in der österreichischen Literatur*, trans. M. Pásztory (Salzburg: Otto Müller, 1966). See also introduction above, 13–14.

4 Fetjö, *Requiem pour un empire défunt*, 375.

5 Karl Kautsky, *Habsburgs Glück und Ende* (Berlin: Paul Cassirer, 1918), 79.

6 Joseph Roth, *The Emperor's Tomb*, trans. John Hoare (Woodstock, N.Y.: Overlook Press, 1984), 140; *Die Kapuzinergruft*, in *Werke* (Cologne: Kiepenheuer und Witsch, 1956), 1:418.

7 The standard reference on this subject is *Die Habsburgermonarchie, 1848–1918*, vol. 3, *Die Völker des Reiches*. The eleven major peoples are German, Magyar, Czech, Pole, Ruthene, Slovak, Slovene, Serb, Croat, Italian, Romanian. The statistics also include Jews, Ladinos, Romani, Bulgars, Bosnians or Muslims, Illyrians, Dalmatians, Hispanics, in addition to "Krassowaner, Schokatzen, und Bunjewatzen."

8 Kann, *The Multinational Empire*, 2:302f.

9 Kann, *The Habsburg Empire*, 69f.

10 Alan Sked, *The Decline and Fall of the Habsburg Empire, 1815–1918* (London: Longman, 1989), 209.
11 Kann, *The Habsburg Empire*, 65.
12 Barbara Jelavich, *History of the Balkans*, 2:59–63.
13 For an account of Schönerer and Lueger's careers, see Carl Schorske, *Fin-de-Siècle Vienna: Politics and Culture* (New York: Vintage Books, 1981), ch. 3.
14 Kann, *The Habsburg Empire*, 100.
15 Ibid., 100f.
16 William M. Johnston, *The Austrian Mind: An Intellectual and Social History, 1848–1938*, 2d ed. (Berkeley: University of California Press, 1972, 1983), 45–50.
17 Kann sums up the situation: "Reforms pertaining to any one national group or to a combination of groups, be it the Poles, the Czechs, or the Southern Slavs, would have brought the claims of all the others stormily to the fore and might have led to revolt. This served precisely as a tragic though understandable reason for not undertaking any reform at all" (*The Habsburg Empire*, 58). Hence, the bureaucracy governed the country over extended periods. An Austrian parliamentarian of the period remarked that in Austria the "most permanent state of affairs is the provisional" (Kann, *The Multinational Empire*, 2:15).
18 Kann, *The Habsburg Empire*, 81.
19 For a discussion of how the nationality problem contributed to World War I and the destruction of Austria-Hungary, see Alan Sked, "Historians, the Nationality Question, and the Downfall of the Habsburg Empire," *Transactions of the Royal Historical Society*, 5th series, 31 (1981): 175–193; as well as Kann, *The Habsburg Empire*.
20 Kann, *The Multinational Empire*, 2:339.
21 Johnston, *The Austrian Mind*, 76.
22 Otto Bauer, *Die Österreichische Revolution* (Vienna: Wiener Volksbuchhandlung, 1923), 110.
23 For an analysis of the worldview of the Royal and Imperial officer corps, see István Deák, *Beyond Nationalism: A Social and Political History of the Habsburg Officer Corps, 1848–1918* (Oxford: Oxford University Press, 1992).
24 Almost all the characters are, to a greater or lesser extent, modeled on real persons. Karl Corino's biography establishes the following relations: Leinsdorf—Aloys Prinz Liechtenstein and Franz Graf Harrach, conservative politicians of the nobility; Diotima—Agnes Harder, Margarete

Sussmann, and Ellen Key, writers and social reformers; Section Chief (Sektionsrat) Tuzzi—Hermann Schwarzwald, senior official in the Ministries of Trade and Finance; Arnheim—Walther Rathenau, industrialist and writer; Leo Fischel—Wolfgang Reichle Pate, Sektionsrat; General Stumm—Max von Becher, military colleague of Musil's; Feuermaul—Franz Werfel and Anton Wildgans, famous poets; Meingast—Ludwig Klages, famous philosopher; Lindner—Friedrich Wilhelm Foerster, professor of pedagogy. Diotima's salon is modeled on the salon of Eugenie Schwarzwald, frequented in the postwar years by several of Vienna's most notable artists, writers, and thinkers (*Robert Musil: Leben und Werk in Bildern und Texten* [Reinbek bei Hamburg: Rowohlt, 1988], 363–399).

25 Hartmut Böhme rightly observes that "the existential pattern of the Man without qualities is valid for Kakania as a whole" (*Anomie und Entfremdung: Literatursoziologische Untersuchungen zu den Essays Robert Musils und seinem Roman "Der Mann ohne Eigenschaften"* [Kronberg: Scriptor, 1974], 329).

26 Eric J. Hobsbawm, *Nations and Nationalism since 1780: Programme, Myth, Reality,* 2d ed. (Cambridge: Cambridge University Press, 1992), 11. Hobsbawm consequently divides his analysis into two parts, one dealing with "popular proto-nationalism," the other with "the government perspective."

27 Homi K. Bhabha, "DissemiNation: Time, Narrative, and the Margins of the Modern Nation," in *Nation and Narration,* ed. Homi K. Bhabha (London: Routledge, 1990), 297.

28 Norbert Elias, "Zur Soziogenese der Begriffe 'Zivilisation' und 'Kultur,'" in *Über den Prozess der Zivilisation* (Frankfurt am Main: Suhrkamp, 1976), 1:1–64.

29 Schorske, *Fin-de-Siècle Vienna,* 297. Fritz Ringer analyzes the sociological conditions of the alliance between culture and capital in *The Decline of the German Mandarins: The German Academic Community, 1890–1933* (Cambridge, Mass.: Harvard University Press, 1969), 14–80.

30 The sheer weight and pace of change in this period would be enough to explain why friction between groups multiplied, Eric Hobsbawm states with particular reference to Austria-Hungary: "All that was required for the entry of nationalism into politics was that groups of men and women who saw themselves, in whatever manner, as Ruritanians, or were so seen by others, should become ready to listen to the argument that their discontents were in some way caused by the inferior treatment (often undeniable) of Ruritanians, by, or compared with, other nationalities, or by

a non-Ruritanian state or ruling class" (*Nations and Nationalism since 1780*, 109).

31 On the relationship of nationalism to modernization, see Ernest Gellner, *Nations and Nationalism* (Oxford: Blackwell, 1983). See also his "Nationalism and Politics in Eastern Europe," *New Left Review* 189 (1991): 128.

32 Benedict Anderson, *Imagined Communities: Reflections on the Origin and Spread of Nationalism* (London: Verso, 1983), 31.

33 Otto Bauer, *Die Nationalitätenfrage und die Sozialdemokratie*, rev. ed. (1924; Glashütten im Taunus: Detlev Auvermann, 1971), 112. The first chapter is translated as "The Nation," in *Mapping the Nation*, ed. Gopal Balakrishnan (London: Verso, 1996), 39–77.

34 Edward Said, *Culture and Imperialism* (New York: Knopf, 1993), 18; Franco Moretti, "Modern European Literature: A Geographical Sketch," *New Left Review*, no. 206 (July–August 1994): 86–109; Fredric Jameson, "Cognitive Mapping," in *Marxism and the Interpretation of Culture*, ed. C. Nelson and L. Grossberg (Urbana: University of Illinois Press, 1988), 347–360.

35 Feuermaul's phrase is excerpted from a book by the pacifist thinker Josef Popper, *Das Recht zu leben und die Pflicht zu sterben: Socialphilosophische Betrachtungen* (1878). Feuermaul is largely modeled on the author Franz Werfel, whom Musil despised because of what he perceived as Werfel's inconsequential idealism and eagerness to please public opinion with slogans that were co-opted by less noble interests. See Josef Strutz, *Politik und Literatur in Musils "Mann ohne Eigenschaften": Am Beispiel des Dichters Feuermaul* (Königstein: Anton Hain, 1981), 21–52.

36 As I argued in the introduction, above, this kind of interpretation has dominated Musil scholarship.

37 Böhme, *Anomie und Entfremdung*, 57.

38 *Der Staat, den keiner wollte* is the title of the third volume of Helmut Andic's *Österreich, 1804–1975: Österreichische Geschichte von der Gründung des Kaiserstaates bis zur Gegenwart in vier Bänden* (Vienna: Molden-Taschenbuch-Verlag, 1968).

39 Frank Field, *The Last Days of Mankind: Karl Kraus and His Vienna* (New York: St. Martin's Press, 1967), 139. For useful accounts of the political instability of postimperial Austria, see Andics, *Österreich 1804–1975*, vol. 3, *Der Staat, den keiner wollte;* Gerhard Botz, *Gewalt in der Politik: Attentate, Zusammenstösse, Putschversuche, Unruhen in Österreich 1918 bis 1938* (Munich: Wilhelm Fink, 1983); and Ernst Hanisch, *Der lange*

Schatten des Staates: Österreichische Gesellschaftsgeschichte im 20. Jahrhundert, 1890–1990 (Vienna: Überreuter, 1998).

40 Strutz, *Politik und Literatur in Musils "Mann ohne Eigenschaften,"* 25–29. In January 1932, while preparing the final manuscript for the publication of the first thirty-eight chapters of book 2 of *The Man Without Qualities* (printed in December 1932), Musil composed an outline for book 2 in its entirety where he refers to the rise of National Socialism and the significance of these events for the representation of Hans Sepp. Musil concludes that "the didactic moment of the book is to be strengthened, a practical formula to be presented" (*MoE* 1856). He notes that the idea of letting Ulrich become a spy would be a way of achieving this.

41 Examples of this are found in some passages I have discussed in previous chapters. The futuristic cityscape evoked in chapter 8 of the novel is derived from cinematic imagery of the 1920s, possibly Fritz Lang's *Metropolis*. Many characters are modeled on persons that Musil came to know only after the war. The traffic accident evoked in chapter 1 of the novel was not likely to happen in 1913. Automobiles were rare at that time. For more examples of such anachronisms, see Bernd-Rüdiger Hüppauf, *Von sozialer Utopie zur Mystik: Zu Robert Musils "Der Mann ohne Eigenschaften"* (Munich: Wilhelm Fink, 1971), 21f.

42 For an account of the war enthusiasm in 1914 Berlin, see Modris Eksteins's *Rites of Spring: The Great War and the Birth of the Modern Age* (Boston: Houghton Mifflin, 1989), 55–94.

43 See the following essays, articles, and unpublished texts: "Das Ende des Krieges" (1918), "Buridan's Austrian" (1919), "*Anschluss* with Germany" (1919), "Und Nationalismus. Internationalismus" (1919/1920), " 'Nation' as Ideal and as Reality" (1921), "Helpless Europe, a Digressive Journey" (1921), "The German as Symptom" (1923). All texts are reprinted in *GW* 2, the ones referred to by English titles also appear in translation in *PS;* I refer to them by inserting page references in the main text.

44 See also Musil's "Und Nationalismus. Internationalismus," which he never published during his life (*GW* 2:1347–1348).

45 "Except for socialism, the remedy is nearly always sought regressively in turning away from the present. For the liberated man the old bonds are recommended: faith, prescientific thinking, simplicity, humanity, altruism, national solidarity, subordination of the citizen to the state. . . . People believe there is a degeneration they must cure" (*PS* 176 / *GW* 2:1382).

46 In an extensive critique of Oswald Spengler's *Der Untergang des Abend-*

landes (1918), Musil objects to the philosophical and historiographic paradigm that is based on this expressivist assumption, which was predominant in the period. See "Mind and Experience: Notes for Readers Who Have Eluded the Decline of the West" (1921, "Geist und Erfahrung: Anmerkungen für Leser, welche dem Untergang des Abendlandes entronnen sind") (*PS* 134–149 / *GW* 2:1042–1059).

47 Louis Althusser, "Ideology and Ideological State Apparatuses (Notes towards an Investigation)," in *Lenin and Philosophy and Other Essays,* trans. Ben Brewster (New York: Monthly Review Press, 1971), 171; "Idéologie et appareils idéologiques d'état (Notes pour une recherche)," in *Positions (1964–1975)* (Paris: Editions sociales, 1976), 111.

48 Hence, Musil's theory of subjectivity does not support Böhme's conclusion: "The hollowness of the human being, shifting between cannibalism and pure reason, can always only be refilled 'decisionistically,' through the gratuitous act" (*Anomie und Entfremdung,* 111).

49 See, for instance, Max Adler's proposals for educational reforms in the first Austrian republic: *Neue Menschen: Gedanken über sozialistische Erziehung* (Berlin: E. Laub'sche Verlagsbuchhandlung, 1924). In the last chapter of the book, Johann Gottlieb Fichte's *Reden an die deutsche Nation* reappears, now adapted by Adler for internationalist purposes (182–201).

50 Musil's journals and essays suggest that he may be classified as leftist and internationalist. He shared the utopian hope of many socialists after the war and continued to be loyal to socialism, although, by 1930, he appears to have resigned his political hope. His most straightforward political statements are found in an interview for *Wiener Allgemeine Zeitung,* published on 1 January 1928 (*GW* 2:1719f.). In 1918 he signed the program of Kurt Hiller's Political Council of Intellectual Workers, which demanded, among other things, socialization of landed property, confiscation of fortunes exceeding a specific level, transformation of capitalist enterprises into collectively managed units, educational reforms, and gender equality. It also proposed to institute a "council of intellectuals" that would participate in the government. Musil doubted the value of collective political action, however, and he defended the reflective ability of the artist and intellectual—what he called *Geist*—as superior to politics. This position is brought out in a 1921 article on Henri Barbusse, the socialist writer who founded the international organization for intellectuals called Clarté ("Der Dichter am Apparat"; *GW* 2:1514–1516). Needless to say, the effort to remain above politics was difficult to defend as World War II approached. See Musil's speech at the Writers' Congress for the Defense

of Culture in Paris 1935 (*PS* 264–67 / *GW* 2:1259–1269). Hüppauf's analysis, "Musil in Paris," demonstrates that Musil saw himself as an outsider among outsiders; insisting on his independence and therefore refusing to unite with those predominantly communist writers who argued that all leftist intellectuals should join in the political struggle against fascism. The cultural elitism expressed in the Paris speech has led some commentators to blame Musil for lack of democratic conviction, if not playing into the hands of the right. For a refutation of this view, see Adolf Frisé, "Missdeutungen und Fehlschlüsse: Wie Robert Musil bisweilen von der Kritik gesehen wird," *Musil-Forum,* Wissenschaftliches Beiheft 5 (1991): iv–xvii. According to Hüppauf, Musil might be designated as belonging to a Nietzschean Left that agreed with Marxism's rejection of capitalism and bourgeois democracy but not with its belief in progress, and which also did not support the Soviet model. This made Musil's position in relation to the political left a marginal one, comparable, in this sense, to the positions of Adorno, Benjamin, Marcuse, Landauer, and Viktor Adler, according to Hüppauf ("Musil in Paris: Robert Musils Rede auf dem Kongress zur Verteidigung der Kultur [1935] im Zusammenhang seines Werkes," *Zeitschrift für Germanistik* [new series] 1, no. 1 [1991]: 61). On Musil's political views, see further Jürgen C. Thöming, "Der optimistische Pessimismus eines passiven Aktivisten," in *Robert Musil: Studien zu seinem Werk,* ed. Karl Dinklage (Reinbek bei Hamburg: Rowohlt, 1970), 214–235. Another useful overview is Josef Strutz, *Politik und Literatur in Musils "Mann ohne Eigenschaften."* See also C. E. Williams, *The Broken Eagle: The Politics of Austrian Literature from Empire to Anschluss* (New York: Barnes and Noble, 1974), 148–186; Friedbert Aspetsberger, *Literarisches Leben im Austrofaschismus: Der Staatspreis* (Königstein: Anton Hain, 1980), 13–114; Frank Maier-Solgk, "Musil und die problematische Politik: Zum Verhältnis von Literatur und Politik bei Robert Musil, insbesondere zu einer Auseinandersetzung mit Carl Schmitt," *Orbis Literarum* 46 (1991): 340–363; Josef Strutz, "Robert Musil und die Politik: 'Der Mann ohne Eigenschaften' als 'Morallaboratorium', in *Robert Musil und die kulturellen Tendenzen seiner Zeit,* ed. Josef Strutz (Munich: Wilhelm Fink, 1983), 160–171; Böhme, *Anomie und Entfremdung,* 400ff.; Marie-Louise Roth, *Robert Musil — Ethik und Ästhetik: Zum theoretischen Werk des Dichters* (Munich: Paul List, 1972), 112ff.; David R. Midgley, " 'Das hilflose Europa': Eine Aufforderung, die politischen Essays von Robert Musil neu zu lesen," *German Quarterly* 67, no. 1 (winter 1994): 16–26; Annette Daigger, "Réflexions politiques de Robert Musil dans les années 1920," *Europe* 69, nos. 741–742 (January–February 1991): 50–53; and Primus-Heinz Kucher, "Literarische Reflexionen auf die politische Wirklichkeit in Österreich in den 20er Jahren des 20. Jahrhunderts," in *Robert Musil und die kulturellen Tendenzen seiner Zeit,* ed. Josef Strutz (Munich: Wilhelm Fink, 1983), 74–92. On the relation between Musil's writings and Nietzschean anarchism, see Cay Hehner, *Erkenntnis und Freiheit: Der "Mann ohne Eigenschaften" als "Übergangswesen"* (Munich: Wilhelm Fink, 1994).

51 For a comparison of Musil and Austromarxism, see Bernd Hüppauf, "Von Wien durch den Krieg nach Nirgendwo: Nation und utopisches Denken bei Musil und im Austromarxismus," *Text + Kritik,* nos. 21–22, 3d. ed. (November 1983): 1–28. Hüppauf deals exclusively with Musil's essays, not *The Man Without Qualities.*

52 See Luft's interesting discussion (*Robert Musil and the Crisis of European Culture, 1880–1942* [Berkeley: University of California Press, 1980], 122f.).

53 Alexander Honold is the only Musil scholar so far who has observed the intrinsic relation between the experience of the other condition and the experience of war and analyzed how it structures Musil's project (*Die Stadt und der Krieg: Raum- und Zeitkonstruktion in Robert Musils Roman "Der Mann ohne Eigenschaften"* [Munich: Wilhelm Fink, 1995], 443f.). Honold is mistaken, however, when stating that Musil might have been uncomfortable with his own suggestion concerning the parallel between mysticism and war and that this would explain why he did not attempt to describe, "not even in the experimental form of a draft," the collective reactions on the outbreak of war (ibid., 448). I would argue that Musil did precisely this in the episode where Gerda Fischel reports about the mobilization, and also, though symbolically, in the episode about Hans Sepp's suicide (*MWQ* 1674–1680 / *MoE* 1611–1615, 1621–1623).

54 See Stefan Jonsson, "Masses Mind Matter: Political Passions and Collective Violence in Postimperial Austria," in *Representing the Passions,* ed. Richard Meyer (Los Angeles: Getty Research Institute, forthcoming).

55 See Frisé's discussion, "Missdeutungen und Fehlschlüsse," xi.

56 In the spring of 1939, Broch completed a detailed proposal for the foundation of a research institute for the study of political psychology and manifestations of collective madness. The proposal was submitted to Albert Einstein at the Institute for Advanced Study at Princeton, and to Alvin Johnson at the New School for Social Research. Neither of them supported the idea of founding a separate institute but encouraged Broch

to continue his research. Einstein also helped Broch to get funding for his project by the Office of Public Opinion Research at Princeton. The project was never completed. Various fragments of the project, as well as a detailed outline of its contents, are published as *Massenwahntheorie: Beiträge zu einer Psychologie der Politik,* in *Kommentierte Werkausgabe,* vol. 12 (Frankfurt am Main: Suhrkamp, 1979).

57 Ibid., 26ff.

Epilogue

1 Otto Bauer, "The Nation," in *Mapping the Nation,* ed. Gopal Balakrish-nan (London: Verso, 1996), 54f.*; *Die Nationalitätenfrage und die Sozial-demokratie,* rev. ed. (1924; Glashütten im Taunus: Detlev Auvermann, 1971), 117.

2 In 1926, Musil sketches the multinational history of Vienna in similar, though more playful terms, jesting that this history generates a subject influenced by so many identities that it transcends them all: "For this city has been besieged by the Turks and bravely defended by the Poles; in the eighteenth century it was the biggest Italian city; it is proud of its pastries, which stem from Bohemia and Hungary; and throughout the centuries it has proven that it is possible to accomplish beautiful, even profound things, if one has no character" ("Interview mit Alfred Polgar," *GW* 2: 1156).

3 See, for example, Homi K. Bhabha, *The Location of Culture* (London: Routledge, 1994); D. Emily Hicks, *Border Writing: The Multidimensional Text* (Minneapolis: University of Minnesota Press, 1991); and Trinh T. Minh-ha, *Woman, Native, Other: Writing Postcoloniality and Feminism* (Bloomington: Indiana University Press, 1989), 94: "Not One, not two either," writes Trinh Minh-ha, " 'I' is, therefore, not a unified subject, a fixed identity, or that solid mass covered with layers of superficialities one has gradually to peel off before one can see its true face. 'I' is, itself, *infinite layers.*"

4 Anne Longuet Marx, *Proust, Musil: Partage d'écritures* (Paris: Presses universitaires de France, 1986).

5 Maurice Blanchot, "Musil," in *Le Livre à venir* (Paris: Gallimard, 1959), 184.

6 Giorgio Agamben, *The Coming Community,* trans. Michael Hardt (Min-neapolis: University of Minnesota Press, 1993), 84–86.

7 Robert A. Kann, *The Multinational Empire: Nationalism and National Reform in the Habsburg Monarchy, 1848–1918* (New York: Columbia University Press, 1950), 2:293. "The idea which guided the multinational empire consciously and, even more so, unconsciously, was . . . the concept of the supranational union. . . . There is nothing mystical in this idea. It simply means that a complex political body like Austria, composed of so many diverse elements, might have proved that the political organization of mankind can be established on higher principles than the national idea, with its determinist dogma of subordination under one exclusive principle alone. The national state, superior in the dynamics of its political ideology, though not necessarily morally superior, to the supranational empire, cannot offer this proof, since it is not built on the premise of national diversity. Neither can the great empire type, stretching, with its overseas possessions, over several continents. Though it may comprise many races, its foundations are based on the supremacy of a mother country with a longer tradition, greater resources, and greater power than the other domains. The supranational state organization of Austria did not recognize the notion of a mother country and a master race. When Renner and Bauer conceived strong supranational ties between the Austrian nationalities in the establishment of an equal social order, they had such an idea in mind."

Bibliography

1. Works by Robert Musil; 2. Primary and secondary literature on Austrian and German history and culture; philosophy, theory, varia; 3. Secondary literature on the works of Robert Musil

1 Works by Robert Musil

Robert Musil's work was interrupted at the time of his death in 1942, and many of his writings have been edited and published posthumously. The authoritative edition is Robert Musil, *Gesammelte Werke,* edited by Adolf Frisé (Reinbek bei Hamburg: Rowohlt, 1978), to which I am referring throughout this book.

Frisé's edition consists of two volumes. Volume 1, *Der Mann ohne Eigenschaften,* is divided into two parts. The first contains the sections of the novel that Musil published in 1930 and 1933; the second comprises a broad selection of unpublished chapters and early drafts for the novel, as well as sketches and commentaries drawn from Musil's notebooks, which are today kept in the manuscript collection of the Österreichische Nationalbibliothek in Vienna. Volume 2, *Prosa und Stücke; Kleine Prosa, Aphorismen; Autobiographisches; Essays und Reden; Kritik,* contains other published works by Musil, in addition to a multitude of unpublished and/or unfinished pieces. With the exception of *The Man Without Qualities,* all Musil's major works are included in this volume: his first novel, *Die Verwirrungen des Zöglings Törless* (1906), the two novellas in *Vereinigungen* (1911), his two plays, *Die Schwärmer* (1924) and *Vinzenz und die Freundin bedeutender Männer* (1924), the three short stories published as *Drei Frauen* (1924), the prose work *Nachlass zu Lebzeiten* (1936), and his essays and articles on politics, ethics, literature, and aesthetics.

The greater part of Musil's important notebooks has been published by Adolf Frisé in a carefully annotated two-volume edition entitled *Tagebücher*

(Reinbek bei Hamburg: Rowohlt, 1976). The title is somewhat misleading, however, because what is called "Diaries" (*Tagebücher*) actually amounts to an intellectual laboratory in which Musil summarized books that he read, related personal experiences, compiled philosophical aphorisms, expressed political views, and drafted literary works and essays.

A comprehensive edition of posthumous papers related to *The Man Without Qualities* is available in CD-ROM form: *Der literarische Nachlass,* edited by Friedbert Aspetsberger, Karl Eibl, and Adolf Frisé (Reinbek bei Hamburg: Rowohlt, 1992). Musil's doctoral dissertation (1908) is reprinted as *Beitrag zur Beurteilung der Lehren Machs* (Reinbek bei Hamburg: Rowohlt, 1980). His correspondence has been edited and annotated by Adolf Frisé and published in two volumes under the title *Briefe, 1901–1942* (Reinbek bei Hamburg: Rowohlt, 1981), with index and commentary in volume 2.

As regards English translations of *Der Mann ohne Eigenschaften,* I have used the most recent one: Robert Musil, *The Man Without Qualities,* 2 vols., translated by Sophie Wilkins and Burton Pike, editorial consultation by Burton Pike (New York: Knopf, 1995), the second volume contains a selection of unfinished material included in Frisé's German edition. A selection of Musil's essays is to be found in Robert Musil, *Precision and Soul: Essays and Addresses,* edited and translated by Burton Pike and David S. Luft (Chicago: University of Chicago Press, 1990). Translations of texts from *Nachlass zu Lebzeiten* are taken from the edition that has appeared under the title *Posthumous Papers of a Living Author,* translated by Peter Wortsman (Hygiene, Colo.: Eridanos Press, 1987). Musil's doctoral dissertation has been published in English under the title *On Mach's Theories,* translated by Kevin Mulligan (Washington, D.C.: Catholic University of America Press; Munich: Philosophia, 1982). Finally, a truncated and abbreviated version of Adolf Frisé's edition of Musil's *Tagebücher* has recently appeared in English: Robert Musil, *Diaries: 1899–1942,* selected and translated by Philip Payne, edited and introduced by Mark Mirsky (New York: Basic Books, 1999). Since this translation appeared after the completion of my manuscript, I have not been able to refer to it.

2 Primary and Secondary Literature on Austrian and German History and Culture; Philosophy, Theory, Varia

Abrams, M. H. *The Mirror and the Lamp: Romantic Theory and the Critical Tradition.* 1953. Oxford: Oxford University Press, 1971.

Adler, Max. *Neue Menschen: Gedanken über sozialistische Erziehung.* Berlin: E. Laub'sche Verlagsbuchhandlung, 1924.

Adorno, Theodor W. *Aesthetic Theory.* Translated and edited by Robert Hullot-Kentor. Minneapolis: University of Minnesota Press, 1997. Originally published under the title *Ästhetische Theorie* [1970], in vol. 7 of *Gesammelte Schriften.*

———. *Gesammelte Schriften.* 22 vols. Edited by Rolf Tiedemann. Frankfurt am Main: Suhrkamp, 1970–1978.

———. *Kierkegaard: Construction of the Aesthetic.* Translated by Robert Hullot-Kentor. Minneapolis: University of Minnesota Press, 1989. Originally published under the title *Kierkegaard: Konstruktion des Ästhetischen* [1933], vol. 2 of *Gesammelte Schriften.*

———. *Minima Moralia: Reflections from Damaged Life.* Translated by E. F. N. Jephcott. London: Verso, 1978. Originally published under the title *Minima moralia: Reflexionen aus dem beschädigten Leben* [1951], in vol. 4 of *Gesammelte Schriften.*

———. *Notes to Literature.* Edited by Rolf Tiedemann. Translated by Shierry Weber Nicholsen. 2 vols. New York: Columbia University Press, 1991–1992. Originally published under the title *Noten zur Literatur* [1958–1974], in vol. 11 of *Gesammelte Schriften.*

Agamben, Giorgio. *The Coming Community.* Translated by Michael Hardt. Minneapolis: University of Minnesota Press, 1993. Originally published under the title *La Communità che viene* (Turin: Einaudi, 1990).

———. *The Man Without Content.* Translated by Georgia Albert. Stanford: Stanford University Press, 1999. Originally published under the title *L'Uomo senza contenuto* (Milan: Rizzoli, 1970).

———. *Language and Death: The Place of Negativity.* Translated by Karen E. Pinkus with Michael Hardt. Minneapolis: University of Minnesota Press, 1991. Originally published under the title *Il linguaggio e la morte: Un Seminario sul luogo della negatività* (Turin: Einaudi, 1982).

Althaus, Horst. *Zwischen Monarchie und Republik: Schnitzler, Hofmannsthal, Kafka, Musil.* Munich: Wilhelm Fink, 1976.

Althusser, Louis. *Lenin and Philosophy and Other Essays.* Translated by Ben Brewster. New York: Monthly Review Press, 1971. Originally published under the title *Positions (1964–1975)* (Paris: Editions sociales, 1976).

Anderson, Benedict. *Imagined Communities: Reflections on the Origin and Spread of Nationalism.* 2d ed. London: Verso, 1983.

Anderson, Harriet. *Utopian Feminism: Women's Movements in Fin-de-Siècle Vienna.* New Haven: Yale University Press, 1992.

Anderson, Mark M. *Kafka's Clothes: Ornament and Aestheticism in the Habsburg Fin de Siècle.* Oxford: Oxford University Press, 1992.

Andics, Helmut. *Österreich 1804–1975, vol. 3, Der Staat, den keiner wollte: Österreich von der Gründung der Republik bis zur Moskauer Deklaration.* 1968. Vienna: Molden-Taschenbuch-Verlag, 1976.

Andreas-Salomé, Lou. *Das "zweideutige" Lächeln der Erotik: Texte zur Psychoanalyse.* Edited and introduced by Brigitte Rempp and Inge Weber. Freiburg: Kore, 1990.

Arnaud-Duc, Nicole. "The Law's Contradictions." Translated by A. Goldhammer. In *A History of Women in the West,* vol. 4, *Emerging Feminism from Revolution to World War,* edited by Geneviève Fraisse and Michelle Perrot. Cambridge, Mass.: Harvard University Press, 1993.

Aspetsberger, Friedbert. *Literarisches Leben im Austrofaschismus: Der Staatspreis.* Königstein: Anton Hain, 1980.

Bachelard, Gaston. *The Poetics of Space.* Translated by Maria Jolas. New York: Orion Press, 1964. Originally published under the title *La Poétique de l'espace* (Paris: Presses universitaires de France, 1958).

Bahr, Hermann. *Dialog vom Tragischen.* Berlin: S. Fischer, 1904.

Baldick, Chris. "The Politics of Monstrosity." In *Frankenstein: Mary Shelley,* edited by Fred Botting. New York: St. Martin's Press, 1995.

Balibar, Etienne. "Citizen Subject." In *Who Comes after the Subject?* edited by E. Cadava, P. Connor, and J.-L. Nancy. New York: Routledge, 1991.

——. *Masses, Classes, Ideas: Studies on Politics and Philosophy before and after Marx.* Translated by James Swenson. New York: Routledge, 1994.

Balzac, Honoré de. *History of the Thirteen.* Translated by William Walton. Philadelphia: George Barrie and Son, 1896. Originally published under the title *Histoire des treize* [1831–1835], in vol. 5 of *La Comédie humaine* (Paris: Gallimard, 1977).

Banham, Reyner. *Theory and Design in the First Machine Age.* London: Architectural Press, 1960.

Baudelaire, Charles. *Intimate Journals.* Translated by Christopher Isherwood. London: Blackamore Press, 1930. Originally published under the title "Journaux intimes: Fusées," in vol. 6 of *Oeuvres complètes,* edited by F.-F. Gautier and Y.-G. Dantec (Paris: Editions de la Nouvelle Revue Française, 1937).

Bauer, Ludwig. "The Middle Ages." Translated by Don Reneau. In *The

Weimar Republic Sourcebook, edited by Anton Kaes, Martin Jay, and Edward Dimendberg. Berkeley: University of California Press, 1994. Originally published under the title "Mittelalter, 1932," *Das Tagebuch* 13, no. 1 (2 January 1932).

Bauer, Otto. "The Nation." In *Mapping the Nation,* edited by Gopal Balakrishnan. London: Verso, 1996.

———. *Die Nationalitätenfrage und die Sozialdemokratie.* 1907. Rev. ed. 1924. Reprint, Glashütten in Taunus: Detlev Auvermann, 1971.

———. *Die österreichische Revolution.* Vienna: Wiener Volksbuchhandlung, 1923.

Belsey, Catherine. *Critical Practice.* London: Routledge, 1980.

Benjamin, Walter. *Briefe.* 2 vols. Edited and annotated by Gershom Scholem and Theodor W. Adorno. Frankfurt am Main: Suhrkamp, 1966.

———. *Charles Baudelaire: A Lyric Poet in the Era of High Capitalism.* Translated by Harry Zohn. London: Verso, 1983.

———. *Gesammelte Schriften.* 7 vols. Edited by Rolf Tiedemann and Hermann Schweppenhäuser. Frankfurt am Main: Suhrkamp, 1972–1989.

———. *Illuminations.* Edited and introduced by Hannah Arendt. Translated by Harry Zohn. London: Fontana, 1973.

———. *One-Way Street and Other Writings.* Translated by Edmund Jephcott and Kingsley Shorter. London: New Left Review, 1979.

———. *Selected Writings.* Vol. 1, *1913–1926.* Edited by Marcus Bullock and Michael W. Jennings. Cambridge, Mass.: Harvard University Press, 1996.

Berman, Russell A. *Modern Culture and Critical Theory: Art, Politics, and the Legacy of the Frankfurt School.* Madison: University of Wisconsin Press, 1989.

———. *The Rise of the Modern German Novel: Crisis and Charisma.* Cambridge, Mass.: Harvard University Press, 1986.

Bernstein, Michael André. *Foregone Conclusions: Against Apocalyptic History.* Berkeley: University of California Press, 1994.

Bhabha, Homi K. *The Location of Culture.* London: Routledge, 1994.

———, ed. *Nation and Narration.* London: Routledge, 1990.

Blau, Eve. *The Architecture of Red Vienna, 1919–1934.* Cambridge, Mass.: MIT Press, 1999.

Botz, Gerhard. *Gewalt in der Politik: Attentate, Zusammenstösse, Putschversuche, Unruhen in Österreich 1918 bis 1938.* Munich: Wilhelm Fink, 1983.

Bovenschen, Silvia. *Die imaginierte Weiblichkeit: Exemplarische*

Untersuchungen zu kulturgeschichtlichen und literarischen Präsentationsformen des Weiblichen. Frankfurt am Main: Suhrkamp, 1979.

Brecht, Bertolt. *Gesammelte Werke in 20 Bänden.* Frankfurt am Main: Suhrkamp, 1967.

Broch, Hermann. *The Death of Virgil.* Translated by Jean Starr Untermeyer. New York: Pantheon, 1945. Originally published under the title *Der Tod des Vergil,* in vol. 4 of *Kommentierte Werkausgabe.*

——. *Kommentierte Werkausgabe.* 13 vols. Edited by Paul Michael Lützeler. Frankfurt am Main: Suhrkamp, 1974–1979.

Brooks, Peter. "What Is a Monster? According to Frankenstein." In *Body Work: Objects of Desire in Modern Narrative.* Cambridge, Mass.: Harvard University Press, 1993.

Buci-Glucksmann, Christine. *Baroque Reason: The Aesthetics of Modernity.* Translated by Patrick Camiller. London: Sage, 1994. Originally published under the title *La Raison baroque: De Baudelaire à Benjamin* (Paris: Galilée, 1984).

Bürger, Peter. *Theory of the Avant-Garde.* Translated by Michael Shaw. Minneapolis: University of Minnesota Press, 1984. Originally published under the title *Theorie der Avantgarde,* 2d ed. (Frankfurt am Main: Suhrkamp, 1980).

Cacciari, Massimo. *Posthumous People: Vienna at the Turning Point.* Translated by Rodger Friedman. Stanford: Stanford University Press, 1996. Originally published under the title *Dallo Steinhof: Prospettive viennesi del primo Novecento* (Milan: Adelphi, 1980).

Cadava, Eduardo, Peter Connor, and Jean-Luc Nancy, eds. *Who Comes after the Subject?* London: Routledge, 1991.

Caruth, Cathy. *Unclaimed Experience: Trauma, Narrative, and History.* Baltimore: Johns Hopkins University Press, 1996.

Cascardi, Anthony. *The Subject of Modernity.* Cambridge: Cambridge University Press, 1992.

Castells, Manuel. *The Information Age: Economy, Society, and Culture.* 3 vols. Vol. 1, *The Rise of the Network Society;* vol. 2, *The Power of Identity;* vol. 3, *End of Millennium.* Oxford: Blackwell, 1996–1998.

Cellier, Léon. "Les Rêves de Dieu." *Circé: Cahiers de recherche sur l'imaginaire,* no. 4 (1975): 83–86.

Coates, Paul. *The Double and the Other: Identity as Ideology in Post-Romantic Fiction.* New York: St. Martin's Press, 1988.

Cohn, Dorrit. *Transparent Minds: Narrative Modes for Presenting Consciousness in Fiction.* Princeton: Princeton University Press, 1978.

Corngold, Stanley. *The Fate of the Self: German Writers and French Theory.* New York: Columbia University Press, 1986.

Daston, Lorraine, and Katharine Park. *Wonders and the Order of Nature, 1150–1750.* New York: Zone Books, 1998.

Deák, István. *Beyond Nationalism: A Social and Political History of the Habsburg Officer Corps, 1848–1918.* Oxford: Oxford University Press, 1992.

Deleuze, Gilles, and Félix Guattari. *Kafka: Toward a Minor Literature.* Translated by Dana Polan. Minneapolis: University of Minnesota Press, 1986. Originally published under the title *Kafka: Pour une littérature mineure* (Paris: Minuit, 1975).

Dick, Kay. *Pierrot.* London: Hutchinson, 1960.

Diderot, Denis. *The Paradox of Acting.* Translated by Walter Herries Pollock. Published together with *Masks or Faces?* by William Archer. New York: Hill and Wang, 1957. Originally published under the title "Paradoxe sur le comédien" [1773], in vol. 20 of *Oeuvres complètes,* edited by Herbert Dieckmann and Jean Varloot (Paris: Hermann, 1995).

Döblin, Alfred. *Berlin Alexanderplatz: The Story of Franz Biberkopf.* Translated by Eugene Jolas. New York: Continuum, 1997. Originally published under the title *Berlin Alexanderplatz: Die Geschichte vom Franz Biberkopf* (Berlin: S. Fischer, 1929).

Dörmann, Felix. *Sensationen.* Vienna: Leopold Weiss, 1892.

Doutrepont, Georges. *L'Evolution du type de Pierrot dans la littérature française.* Brussels: Publications de l'Académie Royal de Langue et de Littérature Françaises, 1925.

Dumont, Louis. *Essais sur l'individualisme: Une perspective anthropologique sur l'idéologie moderne.* Paris: Seuil, 1983.

Eagleton, Terry. *The Ideology of the Aesthetic.* Oxford: Blackwell, 1990.

Eksteins, Modris. *Rites of Spring: The Great War and the Birth of the Modern Age.* Boston: Houghton Mifflin, 1989.

Elias, Norbert. *Über den Prozess der Zivilisation.* Vol. 1, *Wandlungen des Verhaltens in den weltlichen Oberschichten des Abendlandes.* Frankfurt am Main: Suhrkamp, 1976.

Elshtain, Jean Bethke. *Public Man, Private Woman: Women in Social and Political Thought.* 2d ed. Princeton: Princeton University Press, 1993.

Farias, Victor. *Heidegger and Nazism.* Translated by Paul Burrell and Gabriel R. Ricci. Philadelphia: Temple University Press, 1989.

Fetjö, François. *Requiem pour un empire défunt: Histoire de la destruction de l'Autriche-Hongrie.* 2d ed. Paris: Seuil, 1993.

Fichte, Johann Gottlieb. *Addresses to the German Nation.* Translated by R. F. Jones and G. H. Turnbull. 1922. Reprint, Westport, Conn.: Greenwood Press, 1979. Originally published under the title *Reden an die deutsche Nation* [1808], Der Philosophische Bibliothek, vol. 24 (Leipzig: Felix Meiner, 1943).

Field, Frank. *The Last Days of Mankind: Karl Kraus and his Vienna.* New York: St. Martin's Press, 1967.

Foucault, Michel. *The Archaeology of Knowledge.* Translated by A. M. Sheridan Smith. New York: Harper and Row, 1972. Originally published under the title *L'Archéologie du savoir* (Paris: Gallimard, 1969).

———. *The Order of Things: An Archaeology of the Human Sciences.* New York: Pantheon Books, 1970. Originally published under the title *Les Mots et les choses: Une archéologie des sciences humaines* (Paris: Gallimard, 1966).

Fraisse, Geneviève. "A Philosophical History of Sexual Difference." Translated by A. Goldhammer. In *A History of Women in the West,* vol. 4, *Emerging Feminism from Revolution to World War,* edited by Geneviève Fraisse and Michelle Perrot. Cambridge, Mass.: Harvard University Press, 1993.

Freud, Sigmund. *Beyond the Pleasure Principle.* Translated by James Strachey. In vol. 18 of *The Standard Edition of the Complete Psychological Works.* London: Hogarth Press, 1955.

Gellner, Ernest. "Nationalism and Politics in Eastern Europe." *New Left Review,* no. 189 (1991): 127–134.

———. *Nations and Nationalism.* Oxford: Blackwell, 1983.

Genette, Gérard. *Narrative Discourse: An Essay in Method.* Translated by Jane E. Lewin. Ithaca: Cornell University Press, 1980. Originally published under the title "Discours du récit: Essai de méthode," in *Figures III* (Paris: Seuil, 1972).

Giedion, Siegfried. *Mechanization Takes Command: A Contribution to Anonymous History.* Oxford: Oxford University Press, 1948; New York: Norton, 1969.

Girard, René. *Deceit, Desire, and the Novel: Self and Other in Literary Structure.* Translated by Yvonne Freccero. Baltimore: Johns Hopkins University Press, 1965. Originally published under the title *Mensonge romantique et vérité romanesque* (Paris: Grasset, 1961).

Goethe, Johann Wolfgang von. *Faust: A Tragedy.* Edited and translated by

Stuart Atkins. In vol. 2 of *Collected Works.* Boston: Suhrkamp/Insel
   Publishers, 1984. Originally published under the title *Faust: Eine
   Tragödie* [1832], edited by Albrecht Schöne, in vol. 7:1 of *Sämtliche
   Werke* (Frankfurt am Main: Deutscher Klassiker Verlag, 1994).
———. *Wilhelm Meister's Apprenticeship.* Edited and translated by Eric A.
   Blackall. In vol. 9 of *Collected Works.* New York: Suhrkamp Publishers,
   1989. Originally published under the title *Wilhelm Meisters Lehrjahre*
   [1795–1796], edited by Wilhelm Vosskamp and Herbert Jaumann, in
   vol. 9 of *Sämtliche Werke* (Frankfurt am Main: Deutscher Klassiker
   Verlag, 1992).
Golsan, Richard J., ed. *Fascism, Aesthetics, and Culture.* Hanover, N.H.:
   University Press of New England, 1992.
Green, Martin, and John Swan. *The Triumph of Pierrot: The Commedia
   dell'Arte and the Modern Imagination.* New York: Macmillan, 1986.
Habermas, Jürgen. *Legitimationsprobleme im Spätkapitalismus.* 2d ed.
   Frankfurt am Main: Suhrkamp, 1973.
———. *Strukturwandel der Öffentlichkeit: Untersuchungen zu einer
   Kategorie der bürgerlichen Gesellschaft.* 1962. Frankfurt am Main:
   Suhrkamp, 1990.
Hacking, Ian. "Making Up People." In *Reconstructing Individualism:
   Autonomy, Individuality, and the Self in Western Thought,* edited by T. C.
   Heller, M. Sosna, and D. E. Wellbery. Stanford: Stanford University
   Press, 1986.
Hamon, Philippe. "Un Discours contraint." In *Littérature et réalité,* by
   Roland Barthes et al. Paris: Seuil, 1982.
Hanisch, Ernst. *Der lange Schatten des Staates: Österreichische
   Gesellschaftsgeschichte im 20. Jahrhundert, 1890–1990.* Vienna:
   Überreuter, 1998.
Hardy, Barbara. "Towards a Poetics of Fiction: 3. An Approach through
   Narrative." *Novel* 2, no. 1 (Fall 1968): 5–14.
Harrison, Thomas. *1910: The Emancipation of Dissonance.* Berkeley:
   University of California Press, 1996.
Hauser, Arnold. *The Social History of Art.* Translated in collaboration with
   the author by Stanley Godman. London: Routledge and Kegan Paul,
   1951. Originally published under the title *Sozialgeschichte der Kunst und
   Literatur,* 2d ed. (Munich: C. H. Beck, 1967).
Hegel, G. W. F. *Vorlesungen über die Philosophie der Geschichte.* 1840. In
   vol. 12 of *Werke,* edited by E. Moldenhauer and K. M. Michel. Frankfurt
   am Main: Suhrkamp-Taschenbuch, 1986.

Heidegger, Martin. "Bauen Wohnen Denken." 1952. In *Vorträge und Aufsätze.* Stuttgart: Neske, 1994.

———. *Nietzsche.* vol. 4, *Nihilism.* Translated by Frank A. Capuzzi. San Francisco: Harper and Row, 1982. Originally published under the title *Nietzsche: Der europäische Nihilismus* [1940], vol. 48 of *Gesamtausgabe* (Frankfurt am Main: Vittorio Klostermann, 1986).

Hell, Julia. *Post-Fascist Fantasies: Psychoanalysis, History, and the Literature of East Germany.* Durham, N.C.: Duke University Press, 1997.

Heller, Thomas C., Morton Sosna, and David E. Wellbery, eds. *Reconstructing Individualism: Autonomy, Individuality, and the Self in Western Thought.* Stanford: Stanford University Press, 1986.

Herder, Johann Gottfried. *Ideen zur Philosophie der Geschichte der Menschheit.* 1784–1791. Text edition, Darmstadt: Joseph Melzer, 1966.

Herf, Jeffrey. *Reactionary Modernism: Technology, Culture, and Politics in Weimar and the Third Reich.* Cambridge: Cambridge University Press, 1984.

Hewitt, Andrew. *Fascist Modernism: Aesthetics, Politics, and the Avant-Garde.* Stanford: Stanford University Press, 1993.

Hicks, D. Emily. *Border Writing: The Multidimensional Text.* Minneapolis: University of Minnesota Press, 1991.

Hobsbawm, Eric. J. *Nations and Nationalism since 1780: Programme, Myth, Reality.* 2d ed. Cambridge: Cambridge University Press, 1992.

———. "The Return of Mitteleuropa." In *Cross Currents: A Yearbook on Central European Culture,* no. 10. New Haven: Yale University Press, 1991.

Horkheimer, Max, and Theodor W. Adorno. *Dialectic of Enlightenment.* Translated by John Cumming. London: Verso, 1979. Originally published under the title *Dialektik der Aufklärung: Philosophische Fragmente* [1944], vol. 5 of *Gesammelte Schriften,* by Max Horkheimer, edited by Gunzelin Schmid Noerr (Frankfurt am Main: S. Fischer, 1987).

Huang, Marianne Ping. "Om metropolernes modernitet och mangeartede rum." *Passage: Tidskrift for litteratur og kritik* (Aarhus), no. 22 (1996): 3–6.

Hufton, Olwen, ed. *Historical Change and Human Rights.* Oxford Amnesty Lectures. New York: Basic Books, 1995.

Huntington, Samuel P. *The Clash of Civilizations and the Remaking of World Order.* New York: Simon and Schuster, 1996.

Huyssen, Andreas, and David Bathrick, eds. *Modernity and the Text:*

Revisions of German Modernism. New York: Columbia University Press, 1989.

Jameson, Fredric. "Cognitive Mapping." In *Marxism and the Interpretation of Culture,* edited by C. Nelson and L. Grossberg. Urbana: University of Illinois Press, 1988.

―――. *The Ideologies of Theory: Essays 1971–1986.* 2 vols. Vol. 1, *Situations of Theory;* vol. 2, *The Syntax of History.* Minneapolis: University of Minnesota Press, 1988.

―――. *Late Marxism: Adorno; or, The Persistence of the Dialectic.* London: Verso, 1990.

―――. *The Political Unconscious: Narrative as a Socially Symbolic Act.* Ithaca: Cornell University Press, 1981.

―――. *Postmodernism; or, The Cultural Logic of Late Capitalism.* Durham, N.C.: Duke University Press, 1991.

―――. *The Seeds of Time.* New York: Columbia University Press, 1994.

Janik, Allan, and Stephen Toulmin. *Wittgenstein's Vienna.* New York: Simon and Schuster, 1973.

Jaspers, Karl. *Man in the Modern Age.* Translated by Eden Paul and Cedar Paul. London: George Routledge and Sons, 1933. Originally published under the title *Die geistige Situation der Zeit* (Berlin: Walter de Gruyter, 1931).

Jaumann, Herbert, ed. *Rousseau in Deutschland: Neue Beiträge zur Erforschung seiner Rezeption.* Berlin: Walter de Gruyter, 1995.

Jay, Martin. *Marxism and Totality: The Adventures of a Concept from Lukács to Habermas.* Cambridge: Polity Press, 1984.

Jelavich, Barbara. *History of the Balkans.* Vol. 2, *Twentieth Century.* Cambridge: Cambridge University Press, 1983.

Johnson, Barbara, ed. *Freedom and Interpretation.* Oxford Amnesty Lectures. New York: Basic Books, 1992.

Johnston, William M. *The Austrian Mind: An Intellectual and Social History, 1848–1938.* Berkeley and Los Angeles. University of California Press, 1972, 1983.

Jonsson, Stefan. *Andra platser: En essä om kulturell identitet.* Stockholm: Norstedts, 1995.

―――. "Masses Mind Matter: Political Passions and Collective Violence in Postimperial Austria." In *Representing the Passions,* edited by Richard Meyer. Los Angeles: Getty Research Institute, forthcoming.

Jünger, Ernst. "Über die Gefahr." In *Der gefährliche Augenblick: Eine*

Sammlung von Bildern und Berichten, edited by Ferdinand Bucholtz. Berlin: Junker und Dünnhaupt, 1931.

Kadrnoska, Franz, ed. *Aufbruch und Untergang: Österreichische Kultur zwischen 1918 und 1938.* Vienna: Europa Verlag, 1981.

Kann, Robert A. *The Habsburg Empire; A Study in Integration and Disintegration.* New York: Frederick A. Praeger, 1957.

————. *The Multinational Empire: Nationalism and National Reform in the Habsburg Monarchy, 1848–1918.* 2 vols. Vol. 1, *Empire and Nationalities;* vol. 2, *Empire Reform.* New York: Columbia University Press, 1950.

————. "Zur Problematik der Nationalitätenfrage in der Habsburgermonarchie, 1848–1918." In vol. 3 of *Die Habsburgermonarchie 1848–1918,* ed. Adam Wandruszka and Peter Urbanitsch.

Kautsky, Karl. *Habsburgs Glück und Ende.* Berlin: Paul Cassirer, 1918.

Kellein, Thomas. *Pierrot: Melancholie und Maske.* Munich: Prestel, 1995.

Kerby, Anthony Paul. *Narrative and the Self.* Bloomington: Indiana University Press, 1991.

Klee, Paul. *Puppen, Plastiken, Reliefs, Masken, Theater.* Neuchâtel: Galerie Suisse de Paris, 1979.

Kristeva, Julia. *Revolution in Poetic Language.* Translated by Margaret Waller. New York: Columbia University Press, 1984. Originally published under the title *La Révolution du langage poétique: L'avant-garde à la fin du XIXe siècle—Lautréamont et Mallarmé* (Paris: Seuil, 1974).

Krockow, Christian Graf von. *Die Entscheidung: Eine Untersuchung über Ernst Jünger, Carl Schmitt, Martin Heidegger.* Stuttgart: Ferdinand Enke, 1958.

Lacan, Jacques. *Écrits: A Selection.* Translated by Alan Sheridan. London: Tavistock, 1977.

Laing, R. D. *The Divided Self: An Existential Study in Sanity and Madness.* 2d ed. Harmondsworth, England: Penguin, 1990.

Lemaire, Anika. *Jacques Lacan.* Translated by David Macey. London: Routledge and Kegan Paul, 1977.

Le Rider, Jacques. *La Mitteleuropa.* Paris: Presses universitaires de France, 1994.

————. *Modernity and Crises of Identity: Culture and Society in Fin-de-Siècle Vienna.* Translated by Rosemary Morris. New York: Continuum, 1993. Originally published under the title *Modernité viennoise et crises de l'identité* (Paris: Presses universitaires de France, 1990).

Lévi-Strauss, Claude, ed. *L'Identité.* 2d ed. Paris: Presses universitaires de France, 1987.

———. *Structures élémentaires de la parenté.* Paris: Presses universitaires de France, 1949.

Loos, Adolf. *Trotzdem 1900–1930.* 1931. 2d ed. Vienna: Georg Prachner, 1982.

Losurdo, Domenico. "Heidegger and Hitler's War." In *The Heidegger Case: On Philosophy and Politics,* edited by Tom Rockmore and Joseph Margolis. Philadelphia: Temple University Press, 1992.

Löwy, Michael. *Pour une sociologie des intellectuels révolutionnaires: L'évolution politique de Lukács.* Paris: Presses universitaires de France, 1976.

Lukács, Georg. *The Destruction of Reason.* Translated by Peter Palmer. London: Merlin Press, 1980. Originally published under the title *Die Zerstörung der Vernunft* [1953], vol. 9 of *Werke* (Neuwied: Luchterhand, 1962).

———. *History and Class Consciousness: Studies in Marxist Dialectics.* Translated by Rodney Livingstone. Cambridge, Mass.: MIT Press, 1971. Originally published under the title *Geschichte und Klassenbewusstsein* [1923], vol. 2 of *Werke* (Neuwied: Luchterhand, 1977).

———. *Die Seele und die Formen: Essays.* 1911. Neuwied: Luchterhand, 1971.

———. *The Theory of the Novel: A Historico-Philosophical Essay on the Forms of Great Epic Literature.* Translated by Anna Bostock. Cambridge, Mass.: MIT Press, 1971. Originally published under the title *Die Theorie des Romans: Ein geschichtsphilosophischer Versuch über die Formen der grossen Epik* [1916], 2d ed. (Neuwied: Luchterhand, 1963).

———. *Werke.* 15 vols. Neuwied: Luchterhand, 1962–.

Lukes, Steven. *Individualism.* New York: Harper and Row, 1973.

Lyotard, Jean François. *The Postmodern Condition: A Report on Knowledge.* Translated by Geoff Bennington and Brian Massumi. Minneapolis: University of Minnesota Press, 1984. Originally published under the title *La Condition postmoderne: Rapport sur le savoir* (Paris: Minuit, 1979).

MacIntyre, Alasdair. *After Virtue: A Study in Moral Theory.* Notre Dame, Ind.: University of Notre Dame Press, 1984.

Magris, Claudio. *Der habsburgische Mythos in der österreichischen Literatur.* Translated by M. Pásztory. Salzburg: Otto Müller, 1966.

Mann, Thomas. *The Magic Mountain.* Translated by John E. Woods. New

York: Alfred A. Knop, 1995. Originally published under the title *Der Zauberberg* [1924]. (Frankfurt am Main: Fischer, 1991).

Marcuse, Herbert. *Eros and Civilization: A Philosophical Inquiry into Freud.* 1955. 2d ed. Boston: Beacon Press, 1966.

Merleau-Ponty, Maurice. *Phenomenology of Perception.* Translated by Colin Smith. 1962. London: Routledge, 1995. Originally published under the title *Phénoménologie de la perception* (Paris: Gallimard, 1945).

Minh-ha, Trinh T. *Woman, Native, Other: Writing Postcoloniality and Feminism.* Bloomington: Indiana University Press, 1989.

Mink, Louis O. *Historical Understanding.* Edited by Brian Fay, Eugene O. Golob, and Richard T. Vann. Ithaca: Cornell University Press, 1987.

Mitchell, Juliet. *Psychoanalysis and Feminism.* New York: Pantheon Books, 1974.

Moi, Toril. *What Is a Woman? And Other Essays.* Oxford: Oxford University Press, 1999.

Moretti, Franco. "Modern European Literature: A Geographical Sketch." *New Left Review,* no. 206 (July–August 1994): 86–109.

———. *The Way of the World: The "Bildungsroman" in European Culture.* London: Verso, 1987.

Mudimbe, V. Y. *The Invention of Africa: Gnosis, Philosophy, and the Order of Knowledge.* Bloomington: Indiana University Press, 1988.

———, ed. *Nations, Identities, Cultures.* Special issue of *South Atlantic Quarterly* 94, no. 4 (fall 1995).

Nietzsche, Friedrich. *History in the Service and Disservice of Life.* In *Unmodern Observations,* translated by Gary Brown, edited by William Arrowsmith. New Haven: Yale University Press, 1990. Originally published under the title *Vom Nutzen und Nachteil der Historie für das Leben,* in *Unzeitgemässe Betrachtungen* [1874]. In pt. 3, vol. 1 of *Werke.*

———. *The Joyful Wisdom ("La Gaya Scienza").* Translated by Thomas Common. In vol. 10 of *The Complete Works of Friedrich Nietzsche,* edited by Oscar Levy. New York: Gordon Press, 1974. Originally published under the title *Die fröhliche Wissenschaft* [1882], in pt. 5, vol. 2 of *Werke.*

———. *Werke: Kritische Gesamtausgabe.* Edited by Giorgio Colli and Mazzino Montinari. Berlin: Walter de Gruyter, 1967–1972.

Ong, Walter J. *The Presence of the Word: Some Prolegomena for Cultural and Religious History.* Minneapolis: University of Minnesota Press, 1981.

Ott, Hugo. *Martin Heidegger: Unterwegs zur seiner Biographie.* Frankfurt am Main: Campus, 1988.

Partsch, Susanna. *Gustav Klimt: Maler der Frauen.* Munich: Prestel, 1994.

Pfoser, Alfred. "Verstörte Männer and emanzipierte Frauen." In *Aufbruch und Untergang: Österreichische Kultur zwischen 1918 und 1938,* edited by Franz Kadrnoska. Vienna: Europa Verlag, 1981.

Plant, Margaret. *Paul Klee: Figures and Faces.* London: Thames and Hudson, 1978.

Postone, Moishe. *Time, Labour, and Social Domination: A Reinterpretation of Marx's Critical Theory.* Cambridge: Cambridge University Press, 1993.

Propp, Vladimir. *Morphology of the Folktale.* 1928. Translated by Laurence Scott. Publications of the Indiana University Research Center in Anthropology, Folklore and Linguistics, vol. 10. Bloomington, 1958.

Purcell, Rosamond. *Natural Anomalies and Historical Monsters.* San Francisco: Chronicle Books, 1997.

Rabinbach, Anson. *The Crisis of Austrian Socialism: From Red Vienna to Civil War 1927–1934.* Chicago: University of Chicago Press, 1983.

Rabinow, Paul. *French Modern: Norms and Forms of the Social Environment.* Cambridge, Mass.: MIT Press, 1989.

Rajchman, John, ed. *The Identity in Question.* New York: Routledge, 1995.

Rancière, Jacques. "Politics, Identification, and Subjectivization." In *The Identity in Question,* edited by John Rajchman. New York: Routledge, 1995.

Rank, Otto. *Der Doppelgänger: Eine Psychoanalytische Studie.* Leipzig: Internationaler Psychoanalytischer Verlag, 1925.

———. *Das Inzest-Motiv in Dichtung und Sage: Grundzüge einer Psychologie des dichterischen Schaffens.* 1912. 2d ed. Leipzig: Franz Deuticke, 1926.

Ricoeur, Paul. "History as Narrative and Practice." *Philosophy Today* (fall 1985): 213–222.

———. *Oneself as Another.* Translated by Kathleen Blamey. Chicago: University of Chicago Press, 1992. Originally published under the title *Soi-même comme un autre* (Paris: Seuil, 1990).

———. *Time and Narrative.* Translated by Kathleen McLaughlin and David Pellauer. 3 vols. Chicago: University of Chicago Press, 1984–1988. Originally published under the title *Temps et récit* (Paris: Seuil, 1983–1985).

Rilke, Rainer Maria. *The Notebooks of Malte Laurids Brigge.* Translated by M. D. Herter Norton. New York: Capricorn Books, 1958. Originally published under the title *Die Aufzeichnungen des Malte Laurids Brigge* [1910], in vol. 5 of *Gesammelte Werke,* (Leipzig: Insel, 1927).

Ringer, Fritz K. *The Decline of the German Mandarins: The German*

Academic Community, 1890–1933. Cambridge, Mass.: Harvard University Press, 1969.

Rizal, José. *Noli me tangere.* 1886. Translated by León Maria Guerrero. London: Longman, 1986.

Robbe-Grillet, Alain. *Pour un nouveau roman.* Paris: Minuit, 1963.

Rolleston, James. *Narratives of Ecstasy: Romantic Temporality in Modern German Poetry.* Detroit: Wayne State University Press, 1987.

Roskill, Mark. *Klee, Kandinsky, and the Thought of Their Time: A Critical Perspective.* Urbana: University of Illinois Press, 1992.

Roth, Joseph. *Antichrist.* Translated by Moray Firth. New York: Viking Press, 1935. Originally published under the title *Der Anti-Christ* [1934], in vol. 3 of *Werke.*

———. *The Emperor's Tomb.* Translated by John Hoare. Woodstock, N.Y.: Overlook Press, 1984. Originally published under the title *Die Kapuzinergruft* [1938], in vol. 1 of *Werke.*

———. *The Radetzky March.* Translated by Joachim Neugroschel. Woodstock, N.Y.: Overlook Press, 1995. Originally published under the title *Radetzkymarsch* [1932], in vol. 1 of *Werke.*

———. *Werke.* 3 vols. Cologne: Kiepenhauer und Witsch, 1956.

Roth, Michael S. "Trauma, Representation, and Historical Consciousness." *Common Knowledge* 7, no. 2 (fall 1998): 99–111.

Roth, Rainer, ed. *Die letzten Tage der Menschheit: Bilder des Ersten Weltkrieges.* Berlin: Deutsches historisches Museum, 1994.

Rousseau, Jean-Jacques. *Emile; ou, De l'éducation.* 1762. In vol. 4 of *Oeuvres complètes,* edited by Bernard Gagnebin and Marcel Raymond. Paris: Gallimard, Bibliothèque de la Pléiade, 1969.

Ryan, Judith. *The Vanishing Subject: Early Psychology and Literary Modernism.* Chicago: University of Chicago Press, 1991.

Said, Edward. *Culture and Imperialism.* New York: Knopf, 1993.

Santner, Eric L. *My Own Private Germany: Daniel Paul Schreber's Secret History of Modernity.* Princeton: Princeton University Press, 1996.

Sartre, Jean-Paul. *Being and Nothingness: An Essay on Phenomenological Ontology.* Translated and introduced by Hazel E. Barnes. New York: Philosophical Library, 1956. Originally published under the title *L'Etre et le néant: Essai d'ontologie phénoménologique* (Paris: Gallimard, 1943).

Sass, Louis A. *Madness and Modernism: Insanity in the Light of Modern Art, Literature, and Thought.* Cambridge, Mass.: Harvard University Press, 1996.

Scharfschwerdt, Jürgen. *Thomas Mann und der deutsche Bildungsroman:*

Eine Untersuchung zu den Problemen einer literarischen Tradition.
Stuttgart: W. Kohlhammer, 1967.

Scheler, Max. *Vom Umsturz der Werte.* 2 vols. Leipzig: Der neue Geist, 1923.

Scherpe, Klaus R. "The City as Narrator: The Modern Text in Alfred Döblin's *Berlin Alexanderplatz.*" In *Modernity and the Text: Revisions of German Modernism,* edited by Andreas Huyssen and David Bathrick. New York: Columbia University Press, 1989.

Schiller, Friedrich. *On the Aesthetic Education of Man, in a Series of Letters.* Translated by E. M. Wilkinson and L. A. Willoughby. Oxford: Oxford University Press, 1967. Originally published under the title *Über die ästhetische Erziehung des Menschen* [1795], in vol. 8 of *Werke und Briefe in zwölf Bänden,* edited by Otto Dann et al. (Frankfurt am Main: Deutscher Klassiker Verlag, 1992).

Schlegel, Friedrich. "Über Goethes Meister." 1798. In vol. 2 of *Kritische Ausgabe,* edited by Hans Eichner. Munich: Ferdinand Schöningh, 1967.

Schoenberg, Arnold, and Wassily Kandinsky. *Letters, Pictures and Documents.* Edited by Jelena Hahl-Koch. Translated by John C. Crawford. London: Faber and Faber, 1984.

Schoene, Anja Elisabeth. *"Ach, wäre fern, was ich liebe!" Studien zur Inzestthematik in der Literatur der Jahrhundertwende (von Ibsen bis Musil).* Würzburg: Königshausen und Neumann, 1997.

Schorske, Carl E. *Fin-de-Siècle Vienna: Politics and Culture.* New York: Vintage Books, 1981.

Schreber, Daniel Paul. *Denkwürdigkeiten eines Nervenkranken.* 1903. Edited by Peter Heiligenthal and Reinhard Volk. Frankfurt am Main: Syndikat, 1985.

Seehaus, Günter. *Frank Wedekind und das Theater.* Munich: Laokoon, 1964.

Shute, Stephen, and Susan Hurley, eds. *On Human Rights.* Oxford Amnesty Lectures. New York: Basic Books. 1993.

Silverman, Kaja. *Male Subjectivity at the Margins.* New York: Routledge, 1992.

——. *The Subject of Semiotics.* Oxford: Oxford University Press, 1983.

Simmel, Georg. *Brücke und Tür: Essays des Philosophen zur Geschichte, Religion, Kunst und Gesellschaft.* Edited by Michael Landmann with Margarete Susman. Stuttgart: Koehler, 1957.

——. *Grundfragen der Soziologie (Individuum und Gesellschaft).* 1917. In vol. 16 of *Gesamtausgabe,* edited by G. Fitzi and G. Rammstedt. Frankfurt am Main: Suhrkamp, 1999.

————. *On Individuality and Social Forms: Selected Writings.* Edited and introduced by Donald A. Levine. Chicago: Chicago University Press, 1971.

————. *Philosophische Kultur: Gesammelte Essais.* Leipzig: Werner Klinkhardt, 1911.

Sked, Alan. *The Decline and Fall of the Habsburg Empire, 1815–1918.* London: Longman, 1989.

————. "Historians, the Nationality Question, and the Downfall of the Habsburg Empire." *Transactions of the Royal Historical Society,* 5th series, 31 (1981): 175–193.

Smith, Paul. *Discerning the Subject.* Minneapolis: University of Minnesota Press, 1988.

Spengler, Oswald. *Der Untergang des Abendlandes: Umrisse einer Morphologie der Weltgeschichte.* vol. 1, *Gestalt und Wirklichkeit.* Munich: C. H. Beck'sche Verlagsbuchhandlung, 1923.

Spivak, Gayatri Chakravorty. *A Critique of Postcolonial Reason: Toward a History of the Vanishing Present.* Cambridge, Mass.: Harvard University Press, 1999.

————. *Outside in the Teaching Machine.* New York: Routledge, 1993.

Steinberg, Michael P. *The Meaning of the Salzburg Festival: Austria as Theater and Ideology, 1890–1938.* Ithaca: Cornell University Press, 1990.

Storey, Robert F. *Pierrot: A Critical History of a Mask.* Princeton: Princeton University Press, 1978.

Stourz, Gerald. "Die Gleichberechtigung der Volksstämme als Verfassungsprinzip, 1848–1918." In vol. 3 of *Die Habsburgermonarchie, 1848–1918,* edited by Adam Wandruszka and Peter Urbanitsch.

Strindberg, August. *Dikter på vers och prosa.* Stockholm: Albert Bonniers, 1883.

Taylor, A. J. P. *The Habsburg Monarchy, 1809–1918: A History of the Austrian Empire and Austria-Hungary.* 2d ed. New York: Harper and Row, 1965.

Taylor, Charles. *Sources of the Self: The Making of Modern Identity.* Cambridge, Mass.: Harvard University Press, 1989.

Taylor, Mark C. *Altarity.* Chicago: University of Chicago Press, 1987.

Tönnies, Ferdinand. *Community and Society.* Translated by Charles P. Loomis. East Lansing: Michigan State University Press, 1957. Originally published under the title *Gemeinschaft und Gesellschaft: Grundbegriffe der reinen Soziologie* [1887], (Darmstadt: Wissenschaftliche Buchgesellschaft, 1970).

Walcott, Derek. *The Antilles: Fragments of Epic Memory.* Nobel Lecture.
New York: Farrar, Straus, Giroux, 1992.
Wandruszka, Adam, and Peter Urbanitsch, eds. *Die Habsburgermonarchie,
1848–1918.* vol. 3, *Die Völker des Reiches.* Vienna: Verlag der
Österreichische Akademie der Wissenschaften, 1980.
Watt, Ian. *Myths of Modern Individualism: Faust, Don Quixote, Don Juan,
Robinson Crusoe.* Cambridge: Cambridge University Press, 1996.
Weber, Max. *The Protestant Ethic and the Spirit of Capitalism.* Translated
by Talcott Parsons. New York: Routledge, 1992. Originally published
under the title *Die protestantische Ethik und der Geist des Kapitalismus*
[1904–1905], in vol. 1 of *Gesammelte Aufsätze zur Religionssoziologie*
(Tübingen: J. C. B. Mohr, 1920).
Wedekind, Frank. *Die Büchse der Pandora: Eine Monstretragödie.*
Historical-critical edition of the original version of 1894. Edited and
introduced by Hartmut Vinçon. Darmstadt: Jürgen Häusser, 1990.
———. *Erdgeist: Tragödie in vier Aufzügen.* 1895. In vol. 2 of *Ausgewählte
Werke.* Munich: Georg Müller, 1924.
Weigel, Sigrid. *Topographien der Geschlechter: Kulturgeschichtlichen
Studien zur Literatur.* Reinbek bei Hamburg: Rowohlt, 1990.
Weil, Erhard. "Lulus Pierrot-Kostüm und die Lüftung eines zentralen
Kunstgeheimnisses." *Editio: Internationales Jahrbuch für
Editionswissenschaft* 2 (1988): 90–110.
Weininger, Otto. *Geschlecht und Charakter: Eine prinzipielle Untersuchung.*
1903. 22d ed. Vienna: Wilhelm Braumüller, 1921.
Werfel, Franz. *Nicht der Mörder, der Ermordete ist schuldig.* 1920. Frankfurt
am Main: Suhrkamp, 1982.
Williams, Cedric E. *The Broken Eagle: The Politics of Austrian Literature
from Empire to Anschluss.* New York: Barnes and Noble, 1974.
Žižek, Slavoj. *The Sublime Object of Ideology.* London: Verso, 1989.
———. *The Ticklish Subject: The Absent Centre of Political Ontology.*
London: Verso, 1999.

3 Secondary Literature on the Works of Robert Musil

Albertsen, Elisabeth. *Ratio und "Mystik" im Werk Robert Musils.* Munich:
Nymphenburger Verlagshandlung, 1968.
Alleman, Beda. *"Musil": Ironie und Dichtung.* Pfullingen: Neske, 1956.
Appignanesi, Lisa. *Femininity and the Creative Imagination: A Study of*

Henry James, Robert Musil and Marcel Proust. London: Vision Press, 1973.

Arntzen, Helmut. *Satirischer Stil: Zur Satire Robert Musils im "Mann ohne Eigenschaften."* 3d ed. Bonn: Bouvier, 1983.

Asendorf, Christoph. "Hinter Glas: Wohnformen und Raumerfahrung bei Musil." In *Spiegelungen,* Festschrift für Hans Schumacher zum 60. Geburtstag, edited by R. Matzker, P. Küchler-Sakellariou, and M. Babias. Frankfurt am Main: Peter Lang, 1991.

―――. " 'Eine sonderbare räumliche Inversion!': Wohnen bei Musil." In *Interieurs: Wiener Künstlerwohnungen, 1830–1930.* Vienna: Historisches Museum der Stadt Wien, 1990.

Auernhammer, Achim. "L'Androgynie dans 'L'Homme sans qualités.' " *L'Arc* 74 (1978): 35–40.

Bauer, Sibylle, and Ingrid Drevermann. *Studien zu Robert Musil.* Cologne: Böhlau, 1966.

Belobratow, Alexandr W. "Musils Werk in der Sowjetunion." *Musil-Forum* (Saarbrücken), Wissenschaftliches Beiheft 4 (1990): 15–21.

Blanchot, Maurice. "Musil." In *Le Livre à venir.* Paris: Gallimard, 1959.

Blasberg, Cornelia. *Krise und Utopie der Intellektuellen: Kulturkritische Aspekte in Robert Musils Roman "Der Mann ohne Eigenschaften."* Stuttgart: Hans-Dieter Heinz, 1984.

Böhme, Hartmut. *Anomie und Entfremdung: Literatursoziologische Untersuchungen zu den Essays Robert Musils und seinem Roman "Der Mann ohne Eigenschaften."* Kronberg: Scriptor, 1974.

―――. "Theoretische Probleme der Interpretation von Robert Musils Roman 'Der Mann ohne Eigenschaften.' " In *Robert Musil,* edited by Renate von Heydebrand. Darmstadt: Wissenschaftliche Buchgesellschaft, 1982.

―――. "Eine Zeit ohne Eigenschaften: Robert Musil und die Posthistoire." In *Natur und Subjekt.* Frankfurt am Main: Suhrkamp, 1988.

Bonacchi, Silvia. *Die Gestalt der Dichtung: Der Einfluss der Gestalttheorie auf das Werk Robert Musils.* Musiliana 4. Bern: Peter Lang, 1998.

Bringazi, Friedrich. *Robert Musil und die Mythen der Nation: Nationalismus als Ausdruck subjektiver Identitätsdefekte.* Frankfurt am Main: Peter Lang, 1999.

Brokoph-Mauch, Gudrun, ed. *Robert Musil: Essayismus und Ironie.* Edition Orpheus 6. Tübingen: Francke, 1992.

Burckhardt, Judith. *"Der Mann ohne Eigenschaften" von Robert Musil; oder,*

Das Wagnis der Selbstverwirklichung. Basler Studien zur deutschen Sprache und Literatur 48. Bern: Francke, 1973.

Büren, Erhard von. *Zur Bedeutung der Psychologie im Werk Robert Musils.* Zürcher Beiträge zur deutschen Literatur- und Geistesgeschichte 37. Zürich: Atlantis, 1970.

Cambi, Fabrizio. "Musil und der Expressionismus." In *Robert Musil und die kulturellen Tendenzen seiner Zeit,* edited by Josef Sturtz. Musil-Studien, vol. 11. Munich: Wilhelm Fink, 1983.

Cometti, Jean-Pierre. *Robert Musil; ou, L'alternative romanesque.* Paris: Presses universitaires de France, 1985.

Corino, Karl. "Ein Mörder macht Literaturgeschichte: Florian Grossrubatscher, ein Modell für Musils Moosbrugger." In *Robert Musil und die kulturellen Tendenzen seiner Zeit,* edited by Josef Strutz. Musil-Studien, vol. 11. Munich: Wilhelm Fink, 1983.

———. *Robert Musil: Leben und Werk in Bildern und Texten.* Reinbek bei Hamburg: Rowohlt, 1988.

———. "Robert Musil." In *Literarische Profile: Deutsche Dichter von Grimmelshausen bis Brecht,* edited by Walter Hinderer. Königstein: Athenäum, 1982.

———. "Zerstückt und durchdunkelt: Der Sexualmörder Moosbrugger im 'Mann ohne Eigenschaften' und sein Modell." *Musil-Forum* (Saarbrücken), no. 10 (1984): 105–119.

Cremerius, Johannes. "Robert Musil: Das Dilemma eines Schriftstellers vom Typus *poeta ductus* nach Freud." *Psyche* 33, no. 8 (1979): 733–772.

Dahan-Gaida, Laurence. *Musil: Savoir et fiction.* Paris: Presses universitaires de Vincennes, 1994.

Daigger, Annette. "Musils politische Haltung in seinen frühen Essays." In *Robert Musil: Essayismus und Ironie,* edited by Gudrun Brokaph-Mauch. Edition Orpheus 6. (Tübingen: Francke, 1992).

———. "Réflexions politiques de Robert Musil dans les années 1920." *Europe* 69, nos. 741–742 (January–February 1991): 50–53.

Dinklage, Karl. "Musils Definition des Mannes ohne Eigenschaften und das Ende seines Romans." In *Robert Musil: Studien zu seinem Werk,* edited by Karl Dinklage. Reinbek bei Hamburg: Rowohlt, 1970.

Drevermann, Ingrid. "Wirklichkeit und Mystik." In *Ethik und Bewusstheit: Studien zu Robert Musil,* edited by S. Bauer and I. Drevermann. Cologne: Böhlau, 1966.

Fischer, Ernst. *Von Grillparzer zu Kafka: Sechs Essays.* Vienna: Globus, 1962.

Freese, Wolfgang. "Verinnerte Wirklichkeit: Zur epischen Funktion der
Liebe im 'Mann ohne Eigenschaften.' " In *Robert Musil: Studien zu
seinem Werk,* edited by Karl Dinklage. Reinbek bei Hamburg: Rowohlt,
1970.

———. "Zur neueren Musil-Forschung: Ausgaben und
Gesamtdarstellungen." *Text + Kritik: Zeitschrift für Literatur,* nos. 21–21,
3d ed. (November 1983): 86–148.

Frisé, Adolf. "Missdeutungen und Fehlschlüsse: Wie Robert Musil
bisweilen von der Kritik gesehen wird." *Musil-Forum* (Saarbrücken),
Wissenschaftliches Beiheft 5 (1991): iv–xvii.

———. *Plädoyer für Robert Musil: Hinweise und Essays 1931 bis 1980.*
Reinbek bei Hamburg: Rowohlt, 1980.

Goltschnigg, Dietmar. *Mystische Tradition im Roman Robert Musils: Martin
Bubers "Ekstatische Konfessionen" im "Mann ohne Eigenschaften."*
Heidelberg: Lothar Stiehm, 1974.

Graf, Günter. *Studien zur Funktion des Ersten Kapitels von Robert Musils
Roman "Der Mann ohne Eigenschaften": Ein Beitrag zur
Unwahrhaftigkeits-Typik der Gestalten.* Göppingen: Göppingen Arbeiten
zur Germanistik, 1969.

Gutjahr, Ortrud. " '. . . Den Eingang ins Paradies finden:' Inzest als Motiv
und Struktur im Roman Robert Musils und Ingeborg Bachmanns." In
*Genauigkeit und Seele: Zur österreichischen Literatur seit dem Fin de
Siècle,* edited by Josef Strutz and Endre Kiss. Musil-Studien, vol. 18.
Munich: Wilhelm Fink, 1990.

Hagmann, Franz. *Aspekte der Wirklichkeit im Werke Robert Musils.* Bern:
Herbert Lang, 1969.

Hehner, Cay. *Erkenntnis und Freiheit: Der "Mann ohne Eigenschaften" als
"Übergangswesen."* Musil-Studien, vol. 24. Munich: Wilhelm Fink, 1994.

Henninger, Peter. *Der Buchstabe und der Geist: Unbewusste Determinierung
im Schreiben Robert Musils.* Frankfurt am Main: Peter Lang, 1980.

———. "Die Wende in Robert Musils Schaffen: 1920–1930, oder die
Erfindung der Formel." In *Robert Musil: Essayismus und Ironie,* edited by
Gudrun Brokoph-Mauch. Tübingen: Francke, 1992.

Herwig, Dagmar. *Der Mensch in der Entfremdung: Studien zur
Entfremdungsproblematik anhand des Werkes von Robert Musil.* Munich:
Paul List, 1972.

Heyd, Dieter. *Musil-Lektüre: Der Text, das Unbewusste:
Psychosemiologische Studien zu Robert Musils theoretischem Werk und*

zum Roman "Der Mann ohne Eigenschaften." Frankfurt am Main: Peter Lang, 1980.

Heydebrand, Renate von. *Die Reflexionen Ulrichs in Robert Musils Roman "Der Mann ohne Eigenschaften": Ihr Zusammenhang mit dem zeitgenössischen Denken.* Münster: Aschendorff, 1966.

————, ed. *Robert Musil.* Wege der Forschung, no. 588. Darmstadt: Wissenschaftliche Buchgesellschaft, 1982.

Hickman, Hannah. *Robert Musil and the Culture of Vienna.* La Salle, Ill.: Open Court Publishing, 1984.

Honold, Alexander. *Die Stadt und der Krieg: Raum- und Zeitkonstruktion in Robert Musils Roman "Der Mann ohne Eigenschaften."* Musil-Studien, vol. 25. Munich: Wilhelm Fink, 1995.

Honold, Helga. "Die Funktion des Paradoxen bei Robert Musil, dargestellt am 'Mann ohne Eigenschaften.'" Ph.D. diss., Tübingen, 1963.

Huber, Lothar. "Robert Musil und Gustav Klimt: Jugendstil in den frühen Erzählungen." *Musil Forum* (Saarbrücken), nos. 21–22 (1995–1996), 23–44.

Huber, Lothar, and John J. White, eds. *Musil in Focus: Papers from a Centenary Symposium.* Institute of Germanic Studies, University of London, 1982.

Hüppauf, Bernd. "Musil in Paris: Robert Musils Rede auf dem Kongress zur Verteidigung der Kultur (1935) im Zusammenhang seines Werkes." *Zeitschrift für Germanistik* (new series) 1, no. 1 (1991): 55–69.

————. "Von Wien durch den Krieg nach Nirgendwo: Nation und utopisches Denken bei Musil und im Austromarxismus." *Text + Kritik: Zeitschrift für Literatur,* nos. 21–21, 3d ed. (November 1983): 1–28.

Hüppauf, Bernd-Rüdiger. *Von sozialer Utopie zur Mystik: Zu Robert Musils "Der Mann ohne Eigenschaften."* Musil-Studien, vol. 1. Munich: Wilhelm Fink, 1971.

Jässl, Gerolf. "Mathematik und Mystik in Robert Musils Roman 'Der Mann ohne Eigenschaften.'" Ph.D. diss., Munich, 1964.

Kaiser, Ernst, and Eithne Wilkins. *Robert Musil: Eine Einführung in das Werk.* Stuttgart: Kohlhammer, 1962.

Karthaus, Ulrich. *Der andere Zustand: Zeitstrukturen im Werke Robert Musils.* Philologische Studien und Quellen, vol. 25. Berlin: E. Schmidt, 1965.

Kucher, Primus-Heinz. "Literarische Reflexionen auf die politische Wirklichkeit in Österreich in den 20er Jahren des 20. Jahrhunderts." In

Robert Musil und die kulturellen Tendenzen seiner Zeit, edited by Josef Strutz. Musil-Studien, vol. 11. Munich: Wilhelm Fink, 1983.

Kühn, Dieter. *Analogie und Variation: Zur Analyse von Robert Musils Roman "Der Mann ohne Eigenschaften."* Bonn: Bouvier, 1965.

Kühne, Jörg. *Das Gleichnis. Studien zur inneren Form von Robert Musils Roman "Der Mann ohne Eigenschaften."* Tübingen: Max Niemeyer, 1968.

Laermann, Klaus. *Eigenschaftslosigkeit: Reflexionen zu Musils Roman "Der Mann ohne Eigenschaften."* Stuttgart: J. B. Metzler, 1970.

Longuet Marx, Anne. *Proust, Musil: Partage d'écritures.* Paris: Presses universitaires de France, 1986.

———. "La Rhapsodie Musilienne." *Europe* 69, nos. 741–742 (January–February 1991): 11–18.

Luft, David S. Introduction to *Precision and Soul: Essays and Addresses,* by Robert Musil. Edited and translated by Burton Pike and David S. Luft. Chicago: University of Chicago Press, 1990.

———. *Robert Musil and the Crisis of European Culture, 1880–1942.* Berkeley: University of California Press, 1980.

Maier-Solgk, Frank. "Musil und die problematische Politik: Zum Verhältnis von Literatur und Politik bei Robert Musil, insbesondere zu einer Auseinandersetzung mit Carl Schmitt." *Orbis Literarum* 46 (1991): 340–363.

Midgley, David R. " 'Das hilflose Europa': Eine Aufforderung, die politische Essays von Robert Musil neu zu lesen." *German Quarterly* 67, no. 1 (winter 1994): 16–26.

Moser, Walter. "R. Musil et la mort de 'l'homme libéral.' " In *Robert Musil,* edited by Jean-Pierre Cometti. Colloque de Royaumont. Paris: Editions Royaumont, 1986.

Müller, Gerd. *Dichtung und Wissenschaft: Studien zu Robert Musils Romanen "Die Verwirrungen des Zöglings Törless" und "Der Mann ohne Eigenschaften."* Uppsala: Almqvist and Wiksells, 1971.

Müller, Götz. *Ideologiekritik und Metasprache in Robert Musils Roman "Der Mann ohne Eigenschaften."* Musil-Studien, vol. 2. Munich: Wilhelm Fink, 1972.

———. "Isis und Osiris: Die Mythen in Robert Musils Roman 'Der Mann ohne Eigenschaften.' " *Zeitschrift für deutsche Philologie* 102 (1983): 583–604.

Naganowski, Egon. "Von Stefan Zweig zu Robert Musil: Ein Bericht über die Verbreitung der österreichischen Literatur im heutigen Poland." *Musil-Forum* (Saarbrücken), Wissenschaftliches Beiheft 4 (1990): 5–13.

Nielsen, Peter. *Mulighedernes Wien: Robert Musils romanaestetik i "Der Mann ohne Eigenschaften."* Aarhus: Litteraturhistorisk Forlag, 1996.

Nusser, Peter. *Musils Romantheorie.* The Hague: Mouton, 1967.

Omelaniuk, Irena. "Androgyny and the Fate of the Feminine: Robert Musil and Ingeborg Bachmann." *AUMLA: Journal of the Australasian Universities Language and Literature Association* 58 (November 1982): 146–163.

Payne, Philip. *Robert Musil's "The Man Without Qualities": A Critical Study.* Cambridge: Cambridge University Press, 1988.

Pekar, Thomas. *Die Sprache der Liebe bei Robert Musil.* Musil-Studien, vol. 19. Munich: Wilhelm Fink, 1989.

Perronnet, Jacques. "Isis und Osiris." In *Beiträge zur Musil-Kritik,* edited by Gudrun Brokoph-Mauch. New Yorker Studien zur Neueren Deutschen Literaturgeschichte, vol. 2. Bern: Peter Lang, 1983.

Peyret, Jean-François. "Musil; ou, Les contradictions de la modernité." *Critique* 31, nos. 339–340 (August–September 1975): 846–863.

Pike, Burton. *Robert Musil: An Introduction to His Work.* Ithaca: Cornell University Press, 1961.

Pütz, Peter. "Robert Musil." In *Deutsche Dichter der Moderne: Ihre Leben und Werk,* edited by Benno von Wiese. 3d ed. Berlin: Schmidt, 1975.

Rasch, Wolfdietrich. *Über Robert Musils Roman "Der Mann ohne Eigenschaften."* Göttingen: Vandenhoeck und Ruprecht, 1967.

Reinhardt, Stephan. *Studien zur Antinomie von Intellekt und Gefühl in Musils Roman "Der Mann ohne Eigenschaften."* Bonn: Bouvier, 1969.

Reniers-Servranckz, Annie. *Robert Musil: Konstanz und Entwicklung von Themen, Motiven und Strukturen in den Dichtungen.* Bonn: Bouvier, 1972.

Rogowski, Christian. " 'Ein andres Verhalten zur Welt': Robert Musil und der Film." *Sprachkunst: Beiträge zur Literaturwissenschaft* 23 (1992): 105–118.

———. *Distinguished Outsider: Robert Musil and His Critics.* Columbia, S.C.: Camden House, 1994.

———. *Implied Dramaturgy: Robert Musil and the Crisis of Modern Drama.* Riverside, Calif.: Ariadne Press, 1993.

Roth, Marie-Louise. *Gedanken und Dichtung: Essays zu Robert Musil.* Saarbrücken: Saarbrücker Druckerei und Verlag, 1987.

———. *Robert Musil — Ethik und Ästhetik: Zum theoretischen Werk des Dichters.* Munich: Paul List, 1972.

———. *Robert Musil: L'homme au double regard.* Paris: Balland, 1987.

Schelling, Ulrich. "Das analogische Denken bei Robert Musil." In *Robert*

Musil: Studien zu seinem Werk, edited by Karl Dinklage. Reinbek bei Hamburg: Rowohlt, 1970.

———. *Identität und Wirklichkeit bei Robert Musil.* Zürcher Beiträge zur deutschen Literatur- und Geistesgeschichte 30. Zürich: Atlantis, 1968.

Schmidt, Jochen. *Ohne Eigenschaften. Eine Erläuterung zu Musils Grundbegriff.* Tübingen: Max Niemeyer, 1975.

Schneider, Günther. *Untersuchungen zum dramatischen Werk Robert Musils.* Frankfurt am Main: Peter Lang, 1973.

Schöne, Albrecht. "Zum Gebrauch des Konjunktivs bei Robert Musil." 1961. In *Robert Musil,* edited by Renate von Heydebrand. Darmstadt: Wissenschaftliche Buchgesellschaft, 1982.

Schramm, Ulf. *Fiktion und Reflexion: Überlegungen zu Musil und Beckett.* Frankfurt am Main: Suhrkamp, 1967.

Schwartz, Agata. "Geschwisterliebe und Androgynie in Robert Musils 'Die Schwärmer' und 'Der Mann ohne Eigenschaften.' " In *Proceedings and Commentary: German Graduate Students Association Conference at New York University,* edited by P. Doykos Duquette, M. Griffin, and I. Lode. New York University, 1993.

Seeger, Lothar Georg. *Die Demaskierung der Lebenslüge: Eine Untersuchung zur Krise der Gesellschaft in Robert Musils "Der Mann ohne Eigenschaften."* Bern: Francke, 1969.

Stern, J. P. " 'Reality' in *Der Mann ohne Eigenschaften.*" In *Musil in Focus: Papers from a Centenary Symposium,* edited by L. Huber and J. J. White. Institute of Germanic Studies, University of London, 1982.

Strelka, Joseph. *Auf der Suche nach dem verlorenen Selbst: Zu deutscher Erzählprosa des 20. Jahrhunderts.* Bern: Francke, 1977.

———. *Kafka, Musil, Broch und die Entwicklung des modernen Romans.* 2d ed. Vienna: Forum, 1959.

Strutz, Josef. *Politik und Literatur in Musils "Mann ohne Eigenschaften": Am Beispiel des Dichters Feuermaul.* Literatur in der Geschichte, Geschichte in der Literatur 6. Königstein: Anton Hain, 1981.

———. "Robert Musil und die Politik: 'Der Mann ohne Eigenschaften' als 'Morallaboratorium.' " In *Robert Musil und die kulturellen Tendenzen seiner Zeit,* edited by Josef Strutz. Musil-Studien, vol. 11. Munich: Wilhelm Fink, 1983.

———, ed. *Robert Musil und die kulturellen Tendenzen seiner Zeit.* Internationales Robert-Musil-Sommerseminar 1982. Musil-Studien, vol. 11. Munich: Wilhelm Fink, 1983.

———, ed. *Robert Musils 'Kakanien'—Subjekt und Geschichte.* Festschrift für Karl Dinklage zum 80. Geburtstag. Musil-Studien, vol. 15. Munich: Wilhelm Fink, 1987.

Strutz, Josef, and Endre Kiss, eds. *Genauigkeit und Seele: Zur österreichischen Literatur seit dem Fin de siècle.* Musil-Studien, vol. 18. Munich: Wilhelm Fink, 1990.

Tewilt, Gerd-Theo. *Zustand der Dichtung: Interpretationen zur Sprachlichkeit des "anderen Zustands" in Robert Musils "Der Mann ohne Eigenschaften."* Literatur als Sprache 7. Münster: Aschendorf, 1990.

Thöming, Jürgen C. "Der optimistische Pessimismus eines passiven Aktivisten." In *Robert Musil: Studien zu seinem Werk,* edited by Karl Dinklage. Reinbek bei Hamburg: Rowohlt, 1970.

Václavek, Ludvík E. "Robert Musil in tschechoslowakischer Sicht." *Musil-Forum* (Saarbrücken), Wissenschaftliches Beiheft 4 (1990): 22–40.

Wagner-Egelhaaf, Martina. *Mystik der Moderne: Die visionäre Ästhetik der deutschen Literatur im 20. Jahrhundert.* Stuttgart: Metzler, 1989.

Webber, Andrew. *Sexuality and the Sense of Self in the Works of Georg Trakl and Robert Musil.* London: Modern Humanities Research Association and Institute of Germanic Studies, University of London, 1990.

Willemsen, Roger. *Das Existenzrecht der Dichtung: Zur Rekonstruktion einer systematischen Literaturtheorie im Werk Robert Musils.* Munich: Wilhelm Fink, 1984.

———. *Robert Musil: Vom Intellektuellen Eros.* Munich: Piper, 1985.

Zima, Pierre V. *L'Ambivalence romanesque: Proust, Kafka, Musil.* Rev. ed. Frankfurt am Main: Peter Lang, 1988.

Index

Abrams, M. H., 40
Achronic time, 113–116, 124–125
Adler, Max, 258, 273n. 7, 331n. 49
Adorno, Theodor, W., 41, 193, 261; on dwelling, 62–63; on Kierkegaard, 47–49; on modernist novel, 121–126; on subjectivity, 57–58
Aesthetic education, 34–35, 40–45
Aesthetics, 40–45, 290n. 59, 290–291n. 61; in Kierkegaard, 47–48
Agamben, Giorgio, 9, 270; on identity, 164–170
Albertsen, Elisabeth, 278
Alienation: in modern metropolis, 62–78; modernist literature and, 167–168; Musil's depiction of, 2–3. See also Modernity; Reification
Altenberg, Peter, 95
Althaus, Horst, 273
Althusser, Louis, 186, 257
Andersen, Hans Christian, 86
Anderson, Benedict, 240–241
Anderson, Harriet, 190
Andreas-Salomé, Lou, 178, 180–181, 184, 201, 317–318n. 25
Angels: cultural meaning of, 176, 212–216, 326n. 99
Animals: as figures of subjectivity, 76
Anti-Semitism, 224, 249–250, 261, 268
Apollinaire, Guillaume, 177
Appignanesi, Lisa, 323n. 83

Archipenko, Alexander Porfirievich, 177
Architecture, 48–56, 59–72; interior decoration and, 78–83. See also Intérieur; Urban planning
Art nouveau. See Jugendstil
Austria: Habsburg myth and, 14; as postimperial society, x–xiii, 4, 7–9, 255–260; reconstruction of after World War I, 7, 251–252. See also Austro-Hungarian Empire; Vienna
Austro-Hungarian Empire: collapse of after World War I, x, 7, 191, 251; cultural diversity of, x, 218–221, 263–264, 267–270; geography, politics, and history of, 219–228; modernization of, 23–24, 68–70; nationality question and, 221–228, 263–264; as supranational union, 336n. 7; as utopian empire of negativity, 231, 267–270. See also Austria

Bachelard, Gaston, 63
Bachmann, Ingeborg, 323n. 83
Bachofen, Johann Jakob, 178–179
Bahr, Hermann, 58, 95
Baldick, Chris, 208–209
Balzac, Honoré de, 32, 50–53
Barbusse, Henri, 332n. 50
Barthes, Roland, 43
Baudelaire, Charles, 51, 94, 177
Bauer, Ludwig, 21–22, 251

Stefan Jonsson is an independent scholar and writer. Between 1998 and 2000 he was a fellow at the Getty Research Institute in Los Angeles. He is the author of *De andra: Amerikanska kulturkrig och europeisk rasism* ("The Others: American Culture Wars and European Racism," 1993) and *Andra platser: En essä om kulturell identitet* ("Other Places: An Essay on Cultural Identity," 1995).

Library of Congress Cataloging-in-Publication Data

Jonsson, Stefan
Subject without nation : Robert Musil and the history of modern identity / Stefan Jonsson.
p. cm. — (Post-contemporary interventions)
Includes bibliographical references and index.
ISBN 0-8223-2551-9 (alk. paper) — ISBN 0-8223-2570-5 (pbk. : alk. paper)
1. Musil, Robert, 1880–1942. Mann ohne Eigenschaften.   2. Identity (Psychology) in literature.   I. Title.   II. Series.
PT2625.U8 M3792 2000
833'.912—dc21   00-027746